The Psychology of Interrogations, Confessions and Testimony

Wiley Series in
Psychology of Crime, Policing and Law

Series Editor

Professor Graham Davies
University of Leicester, UK

The Psychology of Interrogations,
Confessions and Testimony
Gisli Gudjonsson

Children as Witnesses
Edited by Helen Dent and Rhona Flin

The Psychology of Interrogations, Confessions and Testimony

Gisli H. Gudjonsson
Institute of Psychiatry, London

JOHN WILEY & SONS

Chichester · New York · Brisbane · Toronto · Singapore

Copyright © 1992 by John Wiley & Sons Ltd,
Baffins Lane, Chichester,
West Sussex PO19 1UD, England

Reprinted March 1993

Other Wiley Editorial Offices

John Wiley & Sons, Inc., 605 Third Avenue,
New York, NY 10158-0012, USA

Jacaranda Wiley Ltd, G.P.O. Box 859, Brisbane,
Queensland 4001, Australia

John Wiley & Sons (Canada) Ltd, 22 Worcester Road,
Rexdale, Ontario M9W 1L1, Canada

John Wiley & Sons (SEA) Pte Ltd, 37 Jalan Pemimpin #05-04,
Block B, Union Industrial Building, Singapore 2057

Library of Congress Cataloging-in-Publication Data:

Gudjonsson, Gisli H.
    The psychology of interrogations, confessions and testimony /
Gisli H. Gudjonsson.
        p.   cm.
    Includes bibliographical references and index.
    ISBN 0-471-92663-9 (ppc)
    1. Police questioning—Psychological aspects. 2. Confession
(Law)—Psychological aspects. 3. Confession (Law)—Great Britain.
I. Title.
HV8073.G889 1992
363.2'54—dc20   91-41516
                                                                    CIP

British Library Cataloguing in Publication Data:

A catalogue record for this book is
available from the British Library.

ISBN 0-471-92663-9

Typeset in 10/12pt Century Schoolbook by Dobbie Typesetting Limited, Tavistock, Devon
Printed and bound in Great Britain by Bookcraft (Bath) Ltd

24796258
1-6 95
P 7

Contents

Series Preface

The Wiley Series in Psychology of Crime, Policing and Law will publish concise and integrative reviews in this important emerging area of contemporary research. The purpose of the series is not merely to present research findings in a clear and readable form, but also to bring out their implications for both practice and policy. In this way it is hoped that the series will be useful to psychologists, but also to all those concerned with crime detection and prevention, policing and the judicial process.

Given these aims, it is appropriate that the first volume of the new series should be devoted to the topic of interrogation and confessions. Recent years have seen a succession of apparent miscarriages of justice, from the Guildford and Birmingham Bomb cases to the murder of PC Blakelock, in which innocent suspects have been released by the Court of Appeal only after serving long prison sentences. Their incarceration has in large part been caused by incriminating statements apparently made by the accused themselves while in police custody. It is clearly in the interests of justice that the psychological vulnerabilities of suspects be recognized and identified and that the fruits of research on interviewing be made available for police training.

The Psychology of Interrogations, Confessions and Testimony is unique in bringing together knowledge of the vulnerabilities of witnesses and integrating this with research on interviewing skills and practice in a way which is both academically innovative and practically useful. It provides a clear and detailed treatment of the issue of suggestibility together with its measurement and role in the production of false confessions all of which is illustrated by much graphic case material. Researchers and practitioners alike will welcome the full treatment of suggestibility under interviewing— particularly of the young and those with learning difficulties, whose special problems have been highlighted by recent court cases.

There are few persons better placed to write this book than Dr Gudjonsson. He has pioneered the empirical measurement of suggestibility which he has applied to devastating and impartial effect in a number of landmark cases. In many of these trials he has appeared as an expert witness in court, a role in which he has few rivals among psychologists. His description of his work, with Dr MacKeith, in cases such as those of the Guildford Four and the Birmingham Six, sheds new light on the original trials as well as providing lessons on how interviewing procedures could be amended and refined so as to avoid major judicial errors in the future. I am sure that *The Psychology of Interrogations, Confessions and Testimony*, with its comprehensive and practical approach, will be of great value to all those charged with the difficult task of identifying the guilty person while protecting the psychologically vulnerable, but innocent, suspect.

GRAHAM DAVIES
University of Leicester

Preface

My interest in interrogations and confessions dates back to my career, almost 20 years ago, as a detective with the Reykjavik Criminal Investigation Department (currently known as the State Criminal Investigation Police) in Iceland. It subsequently stimulated my interest in forensic psychology and provided me with many valuable lessons that I have been able to put to practical use in my current profession as a clinical psychologist.

One of the most significant lessons I learned when I served as a police officer was the importance of corroborating confessions obtained during interrogations. When someone confessed to a crime, we were required by Icelandic law to investigate thoroughly the validity of the confession given. The criteria of corroboration required were stringent and often a great deal of time was taken up with investigating the validity of a confession. For example, in one major enquiry we spent 2 days sifting through the refuse at the Reykjavik Corporation Rubbish Dump looking for a murder weapon in order to corroborate the confession of a suspect, and we eventually found it!

I had originally interviewed the murder suspect in a routine enquiry concerning people who knew the occupants of the house where the murder took place. After his alibi had been carefully checked out, and important omissions in his statement noticed, he became a suspect in the case. We spent days gathering evidence which positively placed him in the vicinity of the victim's home on the night of the murder. After several interviews comprising repeated denials, the evidence against him grew and he became ready to confess, but was reluctant to do so in his native language, Icelandic, and to an Icelandic police officer. Instead, he offered to confess in German to a German Ex-police Commissioner who was assisting the Icelandic police on another murder case. Only afterwards did he confess fully in Icelandic! Who says that confessing to murder is easy?

The other important lesson I learned as a police officer was that false confessions can occur, even in the absence of any obvious interrogative pressure. The first false confession I ever came across I actually unwittingly elicited myself from a suspect who had a history of memory blackouts. All that was necessary, because of his psychological vulnerability and complete trust in the victim's allegation, was to confront him with the allegation against him. He immediately accepted that he must have committed the crime, even though he had no recollection of having done so.

Unknown to both of us, at the time, was the fact that no crime had actually been committed!

During the past 10 years I have been privileged to investigate, as a clinician, the psychological aspects of many of the most notorious cases brought before the British courts, including those of the Guildford Four and the Birmingham Six. There have also been numerous other cases, not so famous perhaps, but of unique interest and contribution to forensic psychology. I have been able to collect research data from over 200 criminal suspects who allege that they made a false confession during interrogation, and to develop psychological assessment techniques so badly needed in this area. As a result of the extensive research that I have carried out into the theory and measurement of "interrogative suggestibility" and their forensic applications, clinical psychologists, both in Britain and abroad, are increasingly being asked to prepare court reports on cases where self-incriminating admissions or confessions have been retracted. However, clinical psychologists are still ill-prepared for the often complex assessment of such cases. Consequently, there is an urgent need for a comprehensive volume that offers them theoretical, empirical and practical information and advice. This was the main impetus for writing this book, although I must emphasize that it was not written exclusively for clinical psychologists. As the book considers in depth police interrogation methods and the processes by which confessions, true or otherwise, are elicited, it will hopefully also be of interest and value to police officers, legal advocates, researchers and psychiatrists.

The basic approach taken in this book is one that relates to clinical assessment and individual differences. This does not mean that the social psychology of the interrogation process is ignored or underplayed. Interrogation comprises an important dynamic and social process and I am fully aware of its importance. Indeed, I have attempted to cover the social psychological aspects of investigative interviewing and confessions as far as I thought was appropriate. However, my training is in clinical psychology, accompanied by extensive forensic experience and previous work as a police detective. My expertise in social psychology is limited, but I hope this has not affected the overall value of the book to more socially orientated readers.

Acknowledgements

I am particularly grateful to my wife, Julia, and to Professor Graham Davies, the Series Editor, for their continued encouragement and support throughout my writing this book. They have both read through the entire manuscript and offered useful suggestions for improvements. Other persons who provided helpful comments on one or more of the individual draft chapters are: Professor Lionel Haward, Professor Udo Undeutsch, Jenny McEwan, Alastair Logan, Dr James MacKeith, Professor Richard Ofshe and Isabel Clare. Professor Lionel Haward provided me with material from two of his cases which was important in exploring the role of mental illness in producing "voluntary" false confessions. I am grateful to the Birmingham Six, Carol Richardson of the Guildford Four, and Engin Raghip, for allowing me to present in the book "confidential" psychological data from my assessment of them. Lastly, I am indebted to John Wiley & Sons for allowing me to produce a manuscript which was substantially longer than originally contracted for, so that detailed case illustrations could be provided to highlight important points and issues.

To my wife Julia

CHAPTER 1

Introduction

On a Saturday morning in the early part of 1987 a 17-year-old youth was arrested and taken to a police station for questioning. A few hours later he had confessed in great detail as to how he had sexually molested and then murdered two elderly women before leaving their house. The following day the youth confessed again to the murders, in the presence of a solicitor. In spite of the lack of forensic evidence to link the youth to the murders, the case against the youth was potentially strong because: (a) eyewitnesses who knew the youth by sight had placed him near the scene; and (b) during interrogation the youth had apparently given the police detailed and specific information about the crime, which the police believed could only have been known by the murderer. On the strength of the available evidence the youth's case was referred to the Crown Court, during which time he was remanded in custody. The case had all the hallmarks of a successful crime detection, which would result in a conviction for two murders and sexual molestation.

Whilst on remand in prison the youth consistently told his solicitor and his family that he was innocent of the crimes he had been charged with. He claimed that his self-incriminating confession was due to persuasive police questioning. Matters had been made worse for the youth because during early detention in prison he had confessed to the murders to prison officers and to a fellow inmate. The youth clearly had been interviewed quite extensively and persuasively by the police officers, but he was a young man of reasonable education and without any obvious mental illness or handicap. On the face of it, the youth had confessed due to skilful interrogation carried out by experienced police officers who had reason to believe that he had committed the crimes. The murder inquiry was thus successfully conducted except for one important fact: the youth was innocent of the crimes with which he had been charged. While the youth was in prison on remand, the real murderer committed another very serious offence before being apprehended.

This brief case history, which will be discussed in more detail in Chapter 11, is one of many that are used in this book to illustrate some of the processes and mechanisms involved in producing erroneous testimony, including a false confession.

The terms "interview" and "interrogation", as applied to the police investigative process, imply some form of questioning, whether of a witness to a crime, a victim, a complainant or a suspect. Both are essentially a way of gathering information for use in further enquiries and perhaps judicial purposes. The term "interrogation" is more commonly used in the literature, and in police practice, to refer to the questioning of criminal suspects, whereas witnesses and victims are "interviewed". Such a distinction is, however, quite an arbitrary one and the term "investigative interviewing" has recently been proposed to cover the interviewing of both witnesses and suspects (Moston, 1991).

The purpose of the book is to examine in detail the various aspects of investigative interviewing and to highlight the factors that influence the *accuracy* and *completeness* of the information collected. The emphasis is on the application of psychological knowledge and principles to investigative interviewing. The major issue addressed is to what extent psychological knowledge and principles can assist the police, psychologists, social workers, probation officers and the legal profession in the gathering and evaluation of human testimony.

The main theme of the book is that there have recently been major advances in psychological theory and research relevant to interrogations and confessions. These advances, and their implications, are discussed in detail in this book.

Chapter 2 will cover the basic principles and theory of interviewing within the broader framework of the investigative process, as it applies to victims, witnesses, complainants and suspects. These are extended in *Chapter 3* to the tactics and techniques available to the police when interviewing suspects. Here the emphasis is on the practical aspects of interviewing, integrating theory and practice whenever possible.

Chapter 4 deals with the psychological aspects of confession. In particular, the Chapter provides a review of five theories that attempt to explain what motivates suspects to confess to crimes which they have committed, in spite of the personal consequences that typically follow. This is followed by a discussion of recent research that has empirically investigated some of the hypotheses generated by the models.

Chapter 5 covers the basic psychological processes of memory within which the reliability of interviewees' testimony needs to be evaluated. There are separate sections in the Chapter on child witnesses and psychogenic amnesia.

In *Chapter 6* "interrogative suggestibility" is defined and described. After a brief historical review of the concepts of suggestion and suggestibility, a theoretical model is presented of the special type of "interrogative suggestibility". It provides a comprehensive framework for understanding the process involved in producing erroneous testimony. The practical implications of the model for police interviewing are discussed. This is followed in *Chapter 7* by a detailed review of relevant research findings and the objective measurement of "interrogative suggestibility".

Chapter 8 gives a detailed description of three major procedures currently available for *enhancing* memory retrieval. These are "investigative hypnosis", "drug-aided interviews" and the "cognitive interview". This is complemented in *Chapter 9* by a review of three different techniques which can be used to *evaluate* the truthfulness or reliability of testimony. These are the psychophysiological detection of deception (i.e. the "polygraph"), "stylometry", which comprises procedures for identifying the authorship of documents as derived from literary studies, and "Statement Reality Analysis", which is a semi-objective technique for assessing the truthfulness of witnesses' statements.

In *Chapter 10* the literature and review studies into false confession are discussed within the broader framework of the miscarriage of justice. Theoretical approaches to false confession are reviewed in detail and the implications of the different types of false confession are discussed. The psychological mechanisms and processes that are thought to facilitate false confession are highlighted. Detailed case examples of the different psychological types of false confession are given in *Chapter 11*. Ten separate case illustrations are provided.

In *Chapter 12* the cases of the Guildford Four and the Birmingham Six are discussed in detail. The Chapter is prepared jointly with my psychiatrist colleague, Dr James MacKeith. We were both involved in the two cases and present some of our medical and psychological findings.

Chapter 13 illustrates the basic legal issues that are relevant to the psychological and psychiatric assessment of disputed confessions in England and the United States of America. Case illustrations are provided in order to give the reader an insight into how cases are dealt with judicially.

Chapter 14 provides the reader with a comprehensive psychological framework for the assessment of disputed confession cases. Specific assessment techniques are highlighted by case examples, involving both major English and American cases.

In the *final Chapter* I draw together the main findings from the previous Chapters and provide a conceptual framework for future work on police interviewing and confessions.

This book is aimed primarily at practitioners involved with different aspects of investigative interviewing. This includes clinical psychologists who have been asked by legal advocates to assist with the evaluation of the likely validity of a statement made by a witness, victim or suspect. Detailed assessment techniques will be provided for this purpose, including the assessment of specific and idiosyncratic psychological states and traits. Techniques available for the assessment of documents and statements will be described in detail and their forensic application highlighted.

Police officers will find parts of the book directly applicable to their investigative work. The book is not a training manual for police officers on how to interview, but it does provide police officers with a further understanding of the processes involved in producing erroneous and misleading testimony. In addition, it identifies the circumstances under which information can be collected most effectively. At a policy level, the book has major implications for police training which are highlighted in the final Chapter.

Social workers and probation officers will find several of the Chapters useful as they commonly have to interview and assess groups of individuals who need special care, such as persons with a mental handicap, the mentally ill, children and the sexually abused. The increased role of social workers as "appropriate adults" during custodial interrogation in England, and the recent criticism they have received about their interviewing techniques with allegedly sexually abused children, means that this book is going to be particularly timely for them.

The legal profession will learn from the book what kind of contributions clinical psychologists can offer to judicial proceedings. Anecdotal case histories will be used to illustrate specific points throughout the book and these provide an important insight into how the judicial system deals with the problems created by human testimony. Many of the findings highlighted in the book provide an important insight into safeguards against false confession.

The book is not primarily written for academics. However, the combination of theoretical ideas, empirical findings and anecdotal case histories brings together knowledge which may appeal to academics as well as practitioners. Hopefully, it will highlight the immense scope for research, both theoretical and practical, in a field that has been largely neglected by academics.

CHAPTER 2

Interviewing: Basic Principles and Theory

In this Chapter the basic principles and theory of interviewing are discussed in relation to the broader aspects of the investigative process. It is emphasized that interviewing is only one of the fact-finding methods the police have at their disposal when investigating crime. In many cases it is the most important method. The Chapter functions in many respects as the basic theoretical and practical foundation for the rest of the book, where the nature and function of interviewing are discussed in some detail.

There are several different theoretical approaches to interviewing and no single theory can satisfactorily cover all the facets of interviewing. Gorden (1975) views interviewing as a "practical art to which many types of theory apply" (p.104). This is the position I take, and I shall attempt to integrate the different theoretical approaches. The emphasis in this Chapter is on *psychological approaches*, drawing upon experimental studies and theoretical concepts and extending these to the *practice of interviewing*. Whereas the theory of interviewing assists the interviewer in planning and carrying out the interview, certain practical skills are required for anticipating and dealing with factors that can *inhibit* and *facilitate* the flow of communication (Gorden, 1975).

Different types of deception during interviewing are discussed in some detail as these can significantly affect the validity of the information obtained.

THE INVESTIGATIVE PROCESS

A police investigation consists of a number of stages and may involve several different methods of information gathering. Commonly, the first stage involves the reporting of the crime to the police or the police observing a crime being committed. The police then have to decide whether the alleged crime is to be investigated, and if it is, to whom the case will be designated. In serious crimes "an incident room" may be set up and a team of officers is selected, bringing to the investigation their individual and collective skills.

In a murder inquiry a forensic pathologist conducts a post-mortem examination on the body and in most instances discovers the cause of death and other important information. Meanwhile, police photographers, fingerprint experts, scene-of-crime officers and scientists from a forensic science laboratory carefully examine the scene of the crime for evidence. A team of police officers may carry out door-to-door enquiries and look for witnesses to the crime. Eventually a suspect may be apprehended and brought to the police station for questioning. A statement is taken, which may or may not contain self-incriminating admissions. The police then have to decide whether or not to charge the suspect with the alleged offence. Once the investigation is completed the case is sent to the Public Prosecutor for decisions regarding the prosecution of the suspect.

Broadly speaking, most crimes are solved by the use of one or more of the following sources of information:

1. There may be witnesses to the crime and they need to be interviewed and possibly give evidence in court in due course. Victims and police officers are also potential witnesses. An identification parade may be set up if the police have a potential suspect.
2. Information may be supplied by informants, whose motivation to talk may include financial considerations, revenge, or moral considerations.
3. Criminal suspects may give information to the police during interviewing, including self-incriminating admissions or confessions.
4. Forensic science techniques may provide the police with tangible evidence. This includes the work of the pathologist, the fingerprint expert, the forensic scientist, and the scene-of-crime officer.

The relative importance of the different sources of information mentioned above will depend on the individual case. In some cases the forensic evidence is paramount and no other evidence is needed for successful conviction. In other cases information obtained by interviewing, e.g. confessions, can be sufficient on its own. In England, for example, defendants can be convicted on the basis of their uncorroborated confession. As I will discuss later in this book, many people are convicted on the basis of their confession alone, even when it is disputed at the trial.

Undoubtedly, the most important practical development in forensic sciences this century was the discovery in 1984 by Dr Alec Jeffreys at Leicester University of "DNA profiling". The technique involves looking closely at the structure of the DNA molecules that determine heredity (Jeffreys, Wilson, and Thein, 1985a, 1985b; Gill, Jeffreys, and Werrett, 1985; Gill et al., 1987). DNA is the genetic material found in all human cells. Visualization of the specific parts of the DNA varies immensely in size from one individual to another. The specific combination of these parts or fragments in a particular individual, referred to as "genetic markers", gives an excellent indication of whether a specific tissue (e.g. blood, semen, hairs) found at the scene of a crime belongs to the suspect. The advantage of DNA profiling is that not only can it determine with extremely high probability who the assailant is; it can with equal certainty exonerate an innocent suspect—as indeed it did in a recent murder case in Leicester (Gill and Warrett, 1987; Wambaugh, 1989).

However, in a majority of criminal cases powerful forensic evidence is lacking and information collected from interviews becomes the most important evidence. Furthermore, a certain type of evidence by its nature can generally only be obtained from interviews, such as that related to issues about intent, thoughts and feelings. In view of the above, it is true to conclude that interviewing is often the most important fact-finding method available to the police.

THE INTERVIEW PROCESS

In its broadest sense, an interviewer is any person who utilizes conversation in order to obtain information from another person (Gorden, 1975). The police typically interview four groups of subjects:

1. *Victims* are the people who have been offended against. This may involve damage to or theft of their property, a break-in at their home, or violent or sexual assaults upon them. A victim is also commonly a potential witness to the facts of the case.
2. *Witnesses* are the people who are potentially able to provide the police with information about the alleged offence or the offender. This could include an eyewitness to the alleged offence, an alibi witness or an informant.
3. *Complainants* are the people who report a particular crime to the police. They are commonly also the victims, and in some instances witnesses.
4. *Suspects* are the people who the police have a reason to believe may have been involved in the commission of the alleged offence. As will become evident later in this book, victims, witnesses and suspects differ in certain respects as far as police interviewing is concerned.

Interviews differ greatly in their purpose, scope and subject matter, although they share the common overall objective of information gathering or fact-finding. The nature of the information sought by the police varies widely, depending on the nature of the case being investigated and who is being interviewed. In its simplest form, the interview consists of a straightforward description of events, as, for example, in the case of a witness or a victim who is required to give a narrative account of what he or she observed happening. The information sought, whether it is from a victim, witness or suspect, may involve a description of events, behaviour, feelings, thoughts or intentions. Considering the potential evidential value of interview statements, it is important that the information obtained by the police is *accurate* as well as *complete*. The word "accurate" is used here to mean that the information obtained can be relied upon as an accurate record of what happened. In English law this means that the piece of information elicited, which is legally referred to as "evidence" or "testimony", is "reliable".

In the area of psychological theory and testing, known as "psychometrics", reliability always means *consistency* and should not be confused with the legal use of the term. People can be consistent over time in the information they give or in their performance on psychological tests, but this does not mean that the information or pieces of data obtained are necessarily *valid* (i.e. data conforming to the facts, or tests measuring what they are meant to measure). Put simply, psychologists use the term "valid" to mean what lawyers refer to as "reliable".

The Basic Phases of Interviewing

Lawyer–Client Interviews

Sherr (1986), in his book *Client Interviewing for Lawyers*, argues that most interviews with clients can be divided into three phases according to the type of activity engaged in by the participants during different parts of the interview. During the "listening" phase (Phase 1) the client tells the lawyer or the mental health professional what he or she wishes to have help with. During the "questioning" phase (Phase 2) the interviewer takes a more active part in the interview and asks specific questions in order to obtain a clearer and more complete account of the various points that emerged during the listening phase. In Phase 3, "advising", the client is given general or specific advice concerning his or her concerns. The effect of not going systematically and carefully through each phase in turn is that the area of inquiry may be narrowed down too quickly (i.e. Phase 1 has been neglected), the necessary follow-up questions have been omitted (i.e. Phase 2 has been neglected), and inappropriate or incomplete advice is given (i.e. Phase 3 has been neglected).

Standard Police Interviews

Table 2.1. The four phases of the police interview

Phase 1, "orientation"
(a) Purpose of interview stated
(b) Introducing participants
(c) Legal requirements fulfilled

Phase 2, "listening"
(a) Subject gives free recall account

Phase 3, "questions and answers"
(a) Subject asked specific questions

Phase 4, "advice"
(a) Reading through statement
(b) Signing statement
(c) Subject informed of further actions
(d) Interview session terminated

Table 2.1 shows the four phases commonly seen in a standard police interview. These differ in some respects from those illustrated above in a client-lawyer interview. In Phase 1, "orientation", three basic tasks have to be completed. First the purpose of the interview has to be made explicit to the person being interviewed. In the case of a suspect a general outline of the allegations may be sufficient, such as, "I am investigating allegations of sexual assault made by your daughter Lucy Smith and I want to ask you some questions about it." In the case of victims and witnesses the police state in general terms why they wish to take a statement. The second task is to introduce formally all the people present during the interview. These may include one or more police officers and a suspect's solicitor. The introductions may take place in some instances before the purpose of the interview is made explicit to the subject. The third task is to fulfil certain legal requirements. In the case of a suspect, his or her rights must be explained, including the right of silence. Victims and witnesses are told that they have to tell the truth to the best of their knowledge and that a false statement may result in a prosecution. It is necessary in law that the person knows whether he or she is being interviewed as a witness or a suspect. A person may first be interviewed as a witness and then subsequently become a suspect, in which case they are entitled to consult a solicitor and must have their rights explained to them. Not informing the subject about whether he or she is being interviewed as a witness or a suspect may cause confusion, resulting in potentially unreliable testimony (Gudjonsson and Lebegue, 1989).

In Phase 2, "listening", the person gives a general description of "what happened". Most of the talking is done by the subject, with the police listening and recording what is being said. The main purpose of the listening phase is to open up the area of the interview and give the police a general idea of the sequence of events that brought the subject to the police station. The police then use the information obtained during the free recall to formulate the specific questions to be asked.

During Phase 3, "questions and answers", the police ask specific questions in order to:

1. Reduce ambiguities and uncertainties;
2. Have the most relevant points expanded or discussed in more detail;
3. Fill in gaps in the person's free narrative account;
4. Obtain specific information, self-incriminating or otherwise, which the interviewing officer believes is needed for evidential purposes;
5. Allow the police officer to have greater control over the interview.

Phase 4, "advising", involves the person reading through the statement, making any necessary alterations, and then signing it. Where the interview has been tape-recorded the tape has to be sealed and signed by the police and the subject. The police then inform the person of what further action is to be taken (e.g. that the person has to be interviewed further or attend an identification parade, or that he or she is going to be charged). The interview is then terminated.

In practice, police officers may on occasions confuse the phases, particularly Phases 2 and 3, because they do not allow witnesses to give their own complete account. This commonly results in specific questions being asked before the subject has been allowed to give a detailed and coherent description of events. Conversely, since the subject generally does not know precisely what information the interviewer is seeking, too much emphasis on Phase 2 may cause irrelevant information to be collected.

QUESTIONING

Open and Closed Questions

The police interview is basically a *non-standardized* and an *individualized* interview. That is, the interviewer does not generally know in advance all the pieces of information that need to be sought and questions may need to be developed as the interview progresses. Each question asked, regardless of its subject matter, will give the subject an indication of the length and type of response required. An *open question*, e.g. "Tell me what happened?", requires a descriptive account in more than a few words and is likely to be used at the beginning of an interview (during Phase 2). Open questions are particularly important in the case of victims and witnesses because the interviewer often lacks the background information necessary to formulate the relevant specific and closed questions. As "closed questions" are more restrictive then open questions, valuable new information may be lost if the interviewer starts the interview with a closed question.

Richardson, Dohrenwend and Klein (1965) define a *closed question* as "a question which can be answered adequately in a few words". These types of question are very important in the police interview because they allow the interviewer to narrow down the focus of the inquiry to the most relevant issues. Closed and direct questions are particularly important when interviewing subjects about sensitive matters such as sex, where evasiveness is common, as indeed Kinsey, Pomeroy and Martin (1948) found in their classic work into human sexual behaviour. Their work highlighted many of the difficulties involved in interviewing people about sexual matters and the authors offered guidelines for interviewing which are as essential today as they were 40 years ago. Kinsey and his colleagues (1948, pp. 47–59) recommended 23 "technical devices in interviewing", which included "putting the subject at ease", "assuring privacy", "establishing rapport", "recognizing the subject's mental status", "systematic coverage" of the material sought, avoiding bias and leading questions, cross-checking information for accuracy, and "placing the burden of denial on the subject". Table 2.2 shows that closed questions are of three main types, referred to as "identification", "selection" and "yes--no" types, respectively. An example of each type of question is provided.

Table 2.2. The characteristics of open and closed questions*

Type of question	Definition	Example
Open question:	A question requiring several words for an adequate response	"What happened to you this morning?"
Closed question:	A question that can be answered adequately in a few words	
Identification type	A question requiring the identification of person, place, group, time, etc.	"What time did you see Mr. Allen yesterday?"
Selection type	A closed-alternative question, where the subject has to select one from the two or more possible responses suggested by the interviewer	"Was the assailant armed with a knife or a a gun?"
Yes-no type	A question that can be answered satisfactorily "Yes" or "No"	"Did you take the missing money?"

*Adapted from Richardson, Dohrenwend and Klein (1965)

The *identification* type calls for an identification of some kind by asking questions relating to "who", "where", "when", "how many" or "which". This includes witnesses being required to identify a suspect from a police line-up ("identification parade") or indicating how many persons they had seen committing the crime. The *selection* type comprises questions where the interviewer indicates to the subject that he or she has to select one alternative from two or more possible responses provided. As will become evident later in this Chapter, this type of question can be very misleading when it is based on an "uninformed premise". A *yes-no* type of a question is commonly used during police interviews and may be particularly useful when interviewing people who have problems with articulating their answers. However, the validity of closed yes-no questions may be undermined when individuals have a strong tendency towards acquiescence (i.e. they answer questions in the affirmative irrespective of content). Furthermore, questions requiring yes-no type of answers have an affirmative response bias, in that when in doubt many subjects will answer questions affirmatively (Sigelman et al., 1981; Gudjonsson, 1986).

Antecedents of the Question

Most questions asked by the police during an interview have certain antecedents, i.e. the interviewer has a particular reason for asking the question because of his prior knowledge of the subject or the case.

There are at least two main antecedents to a question:

1. The interviewer has been informed or otherwise knows that a particular person has information about an alleged crime. It may be a victim or a witness and the interviewer may have a general idea of what happened prior to interviewing the subject.
2. The interviewer may be following up a previous response given by the subject, or a previous question asked.

According to Richardson, Dohrenwend and Klein (1965), questions that are based on salient antecedents give the interviewer greater control over the interview, and increase the likelihood of his asking relevant questions and achieving adequate coverage of the subject matter under investigation.

Leading Questions

A *leading question* is the type of question that indicates the wanted answer. Richardson, Dohrenwend and Klein (1965) have shown that questions are leading because they contain certain "premises" and "expectations". A question contains a premise when it is based on prior information or assumption. For example, the question "Do you still beat your wife?" is based on the interviewer's assumption or knowledge that the subject is married and has a history of beating his wife. The interviewer's premise may or may not be correct. The potential for distorting the subject's response depends on whether the premise is "informed" or "uninformed". An *informed premise* is where the interviewer is knowledgeable (i.e. well informed) about the subject's background and the matters being discussed. An *uninformed premise*, on the other hand, indicates that the interviewer is poorly informed and is asking questions that may be erroneously agreed with by the subject. That is, the interviewer introduces an incorrect premise, with which the subject either unwittingly or knowingly agrees.

In general, the more closed the question the greater the likelihood that the subject will agree with an incorrect premise. "Closed alternative" questions, where only some of all possible answers are presented, are particularly prone to distortion. For example, in one study (Gudjonsson, 1984a) I found that an incorrect premise in closed false alternative questions, such as "Were the assailants tall or short?", "Did the woman have one or two children?", "Were the assailants black or white?", were particularly likely to be accepted during interviewing. It seemed that most of the subjects assumed that the closed alternative question was based on an informed and correct premise and were not able to detect that they were being misled.

An *expectation* comprises that part of a question where an interviewer indicates the response he or she wants. For example, the question "Are you married?" does not indicate the expected answer, but the question "You are married, aren't you?" clearly does so. An expectation is most easily identified by the syntax and logic of the question but, as Richardson, Dohrenwend and

Klein (1965) suggest, an expectation may also be communicated by the interviewer's intonation and non-verbal behaviour. Intonation means that the interviewer emphasizes a particular word in a sentence and thereby suggests to the subject how he expects the question to be answered.

Richardson, Dohrenwend and Klein (1965) argue that expectations can be subdivided into two categories according to their suggestive potential. A *weak expectation* indicates to the subject that the interviewer is not sure or confident about its correctness. For example, the question "Am I correct in assuming that you do not want us to press charges?" has weak expectation and could easily be overridden by the subject giving an unexpected response. A *strong indication* communicates a strong degree of certainty; for example, "You certainly do not wish us to press charges, do you?" makes it difficult for the subject to give a reply that contradicts the expectation.

According to Richardson, Dohrenwend and Klein, questions are most likely to distort responses when they are based on an *uninformed premise* and *uninformed strong expectation*. Distortions are least likely to occur when there is an *informed premise* and either no expectation or a *well informed expectation* contained in the question.

It is important to note that questions can be leading because of the *context* in which they appear (Gorden, 1975; Moston, 1990a). This means that the same question may be answered differently depending on the context. This can be illustrated by the following hypothetical questions which could in some cases bias the response.

Context 1: "We have arrested the person who attacked you last Tuesday. Do you recognize any of the people in the identification parade as the assailant?"

Context 2: "We have strong reason to believe that we have caught the person who attacked you last Tuesday. Do you recognize any of the people in the identification parade as the assailant?"

Context 3: "We have arrested somebody who may or may not be the person who attacked you last Tuesday. Do you recognize any of the people in the identification parade as the assailant?"

Context 1 is most leading and Context 3 the least. Police officers commonly use leading contexts prior to questioning, for example, when they inform criminal suspects before they interview them that they have carried out extensive enquiries and that they know about their involvement in the crime.

The Effects of Leading Questions

A number of psychological experiments have shown that leading questions produce distorted responses during interviewing (Stern, 1938; Loftus, 1979a).

Even if the questions do not contain strong expectations they can nevertheless markedly distort responses (Gudjonsson, 1984a). Loftus and Palmer (1974) showed subjects films of car accidents and afterwards asked them questions about events in the films. It was found that the subjects' responses could be markedly altered by changing the verb in a sentence. For example, when the subjects were asked to estimate the speed of the cars that collided, the speed estimated was consistently highest when the verb "smashed" was used instead of "collided", "hit", "bumped" or "contacted". Furthermore, at 1 week follow-up it transpired that the subjects who had been given the sentence with the verb "smashed" in it ("About how fast were the cars going when they smashed into each other?") were more likely to answer affirmatively the question "Did you see any broken glass?", even though there was no mention of broken glass in the film. The effects of leading questions on memory recall and the importance of "suggestibility" in the process and outcome of police interviewing will be discussed in detail in Chapters 6 and 7.

Interrogation Bias

Trankell (1972) argues that there is a powerful fundamental difference between police interviewing and ordinary conversation, depending upon the extent to which there is "a *mutual* exchange of information" (p. 24). Whereas in the ordinary conversation there is generally a mutual exchange of information, in the police interview this is not so. Here the flow of information is mainly one-way (i.e. the police officer asks the questions and the interviewee answers them).

Police officers have control over the immediate situation and enter the interview with certain assumptions, expectations and hypotheses about the event they are investigating. This affects the direction and nature of the interview. The stronger the interviewer's prior assumptions and beliefs, the greater the interrogation bias. As I shall discuss in Chapter 5, perception is *selective* and interrogation bias may result in police officers being particularly vigilant and receptive to information that is consistent with their prior assumptions and beliefs, whilst ignoring, minimizing or distorting information that contradicts their assumptions. Information that does not support the interviewer's hypotheses may be erroneously interpreted as lies, misunderstanding, evasiveness or defensiveness. The end result is that items of information confirming the interviewer's hypotheses are likely to be reinforced, whereas those to the contrary may "produce frustration, disappointment, and are likely to trigger cognitive dissonance reduction" (Underwager et al., 1988, p. 31).

Underwager et al. (1988) argue that cognitive dissonance may affect police interviewers' behaviour in the sense that

"[information] dissonant with prior convictions is ignored, demeaned, or the source of the information is attacked to reduce the anxiety level caused by the dissonance" (Festinger, 1957).

The main premise of Festinger's (1957) theory of cognitive dissonance is that when people hold two cognitions or thoughts that are inconsistent or contrary, they will experience an aversive motivational state, called "cognitive dissonance". This aversive state will motivate people to remove or alter one of the "dissonant" cognitions which they experience. There is evidence from experimental manipulation studies that dissonance is indeed arousing, whether measured subjectively, behaviourally or physiologically (Kiesler and Pallak, 1976).

Trankell (1972) makes the important point that because of the nature and function of police interviewing, even skilled interviewers may to a certain extent be prone to bias. This bias can influence the process and outcome of the interview as illustrated below:

"Summarizing, we get the following picture of the interrogation situation. On the one hand the interrogator who unintentionally directs the interrogation in accordance with his hypotheses concerning what has happened. On the other hand the witness who, because of his feelings of inferiority and uncertainty, is extra keen to please the interrogator and filled with the desire to give an impression of reliability. In every question the interrogated listens for the interrogator's aims, and with each answer he favours these aims by slipping past the details in his observations which are not wanted. In building up his theory about what has occurred the examiner chooses those details which fit his preliminary hypotheses whilst he ignores those parts which contradict them. When he formulates his questions he bases them on the distorted results of his own listening. In this manner the witness's original perception gradually grows into a distorted picture which is more likely to gratify the interrogator's desire to prove his own theory than elucidate the interrogated's memory" (Trankell, 1972, p. 27).

The above discussion implies that an interrogation bias is always undesirable. This is clearly not so. Certain assumptions, expectations and hypotheses, when based on well informed premises, may facilitate the interview process by making it more appropriately focused. On occasions this may save a great deal of time and reduce the amount of irrelevant and peripheral information collected. It is also worth noting that biased questions, even when based on an unfounded premise and strong unfounded expectations, may not necessarily give completely invalid results. This is because the bias may only invalidate one part of the person's answer. For example, the question "You broke into Mr Jones's flat and beat him to death, didn't you?" (answer, "Yes, I did") may only partly result in bias. The respondent may be replying correctly to that part of the question which refers to the break-in, and he may have had nothing to do with the beating or Mr Jones's death. In addition, the interviewer may be working on the erroneous assumption that the beating was associated with Mr Jones's death, which may or may not be the case. This assumption may be communicated to a suspect who is misled to believe that his beating of Mr Jones resulted in his death.

SOME FACTORS DETERMINING
THE SUCCESS OF THE INTERVIEW

The objectives of a "good" police interviewer are to obtain efficiently accurate, relevant and complete accounts from victims, witnesses, complainants and suspects, without causing undue stress and inconvenience to the person being interviewed. The information obtained must be relevant to the particular inquiry or investigation. It must also be complete and accurate and have evidential value. A police interviewer may obtain relevant, accurate and complete accounts from people, but unless the information is obtained in accordance with the existing Codes of Practice for the police it may have no evidential value. This is, of course, particularly true in cases of criminal suspects and detainees (Home Office, 1985b, 1991). It is perhaps for this reason that English police forces concentrate more on courses in the law and relevant procedures rather than in the training of appropriate interviewing skills (Shepherd, 1991a).

Since many people interviewed by the police are experiencing a certain amount of stress at the time, interviewers should be sensitive to their needs and be fully aware of how their questioning is affecting the subject. Shepherd (1991b) argues for "ethical" police interviewing as a way of minimizing distress and maximizing outcome effectiveness. An "ethical" interview involves the police communicating respect for the person being interviewed and talking to him or her as an "equal". "Unethical" interviews are seen as interfering with the interviewee's ability to make sound judgements and free choices.

Whether or not a police interview is successful in achieving its objectives may depend on a number of factors, including the circumstances and nature of the interview, the personality and attitudes of the interviewer and the subject, the relationship between the interviewer and the subject, and the experience, skills and training of the interviewer. What makes a "good" police interviewer is not easy to identify and there clearly are a diversity of skills required, depending on who is being interviewed and the nature and circumstances of the case. The skills required for interviewing a young child or a rape victim are undoubtedly different to those required when interviewing a hardened criminal. Similarly, people who are mentally ill or handicapped may require an interviewer with special knowledge and skills.

Gorden (1975) makes the important point that a successful interviewer must be able to use a number of different interviewing methods, depending on the situation. He or she must be able to adapt flexibly to the purpose of the interview and the specific requirements of the situation.

Shepherd and Kite (1988) argue that interviews are inherently complex because, unlike ordinary conversations, they have to be "*consciously managed*". Within an investigative context the interviewer has to manage himself, the interviewee, third parties (e.g. solicitors, parents, social workers) and, most recently, audio- or video-recording technology.

Types of Inhibitors and Facilitators

Gorden (1975) argues that an important objective during interviewing is to minimize the inhibitors and maximize the facilitators of communication. *Inhibitors* are seen as barriers to communication and need to be avoided or removed. *Facilitators* are "a positive force motivating the respondent to communicate" (p. 104). A good interviewer needs to possess certain knowledge and skills so that inhibitors can be satisfactorily minimized and facilitators maximized. According to Gorden, the knowledge and skills required for effective interviewing can be learned. This is not to say that certain personal qualities, such as intelligence, empathy, observation and listening skills, are not important. They certainly are, and to a certain extent can be developed further by training. Furthermore, new concepts, strategies and techniques can be learned quite quickly and this is where the dividends of training can pay off fruitfully in the short term.

Gorden (1975) presents an *inhibitor–facilitator model of communication* that views the interview situation as a field of social-psychological forces. These forces arise from "the relationships between the information sought, the respondent, the interviewer, the interview situation and the larger social context" (p. 123). In view of the potential importance of these inhibitors and facilitators for effective communication, they will be described in detail.

Gorden lists eight potential inhibitors to effective communication. Four of these are associated with the *unwillingness* of the subject to give relevant and valid information and four relate to the *inability* to do so.

The factors associated with *unwillingness* relate to perceived time demands and threat to self-esteem or privacy. An important inhibitor to the flow of relevant and valid communication within the police interview, which is not mentioned in detail by Gorden (1975), is deliberate deception. This type of inhibitor will be discussed in some detail in view of its significance.

The four inhibitory factors associated with the *inability* to communicate satisfactorily relate to the interviewee's mental state or disabilities (e.g. memory problems, mental confusion).

Gorden (1975) makes the point that these inhibitors are not always easily recognized by interviewers, "because the unwilling respondent may fill the air with irrelevancies, ambiguities, or pure fabrication to make a smokescreen concealing his lack of cooperation" (p. 120). However, not all "smokescreens" are deliberate lies; they may be confabulation due to disorder of memory or emotional problems.

The main functions of the *facilitators* of communication are to maximize the flow of relevant information and to maintain optimal interpersonal relations. Gorden emphasizes that facilitators do not merely imply an absence of inhibitors; rather, they are "a positive force motivating the respondent to communicate" (p. 104).

The most important facilitators which need to be maximized are:

1. "Fulfilling expectations" (the interviewer communicates verbally or non-verbally what is expected or required from the subject);
2. "Recognition" (the subject's need for recognition and approval are acknowledged in order to enhance his or her self-esteem);
3. "Altruistic appeals" (the interviewer appeals to the subject's altruistic needs for information; for example, a police officer tells a witness or a victim how important it is to obtain a good description of the assailant so that he is caught before he commits a further offence);
4. "Sympathetic understanding" (most people have a desire to be understood and accepted);
5. "New experience" (people can be motivated by the interviewer stressing the novelty of the experience);
6. "Catharsis" (subjects may obtain relief from an unpleasant experience by talking about their feelings or unpleasant experiences);
7. "The need for meaning" (people often have the need to make sense of the situation or what has happened);
8. "Extrinsic rewards" (the interviewer may utilize a number of extrinsic rewards in order to enhance the subject's cooperation).

Motivational Factors

A number of motivational factors may make it difficult for the interviewer to obtain an accurate and complete account of the information sought. These motivational factors fall into two groups, which will be referred to as "self-deception" and "other-deception", respectively. *Self-deception* means that subjects lie to themselves and therefore give an account of their feelings and behaviour which is incomplete or distorted. *Other-deception* means that subjects deliberately lie to others in order to either conceal or falsify information (Ekman, 1985). *Concealing* means that they intentionally withhold information from the interviewer. *Falsifying* occurs when subjects intentionally give the interviewer false information which they claim is true. Other-deception may range from "impression management" (e.g. subjects trying to present themselves in a socially favourable light) to deliberate lying aimed to escape punishment. Both self-deception and other-deception are relevant to police interviewing. Their primary functions are: (a) to protect and maintain the person's self-esteem, including the avoidance of embarrassment and negative social evaluation; and (b) to avoid specific consequences such as external punishment.

At the most basic level subjects may be reluctant to discuss specific issues or topics because they cause embarrassment to them. For example, many people find it difficult to talk about sexual matters and commonly require especially sensitive and careful interviewing. Related to this is the tendency among people to deny or suppress unpleasant thoughts, intentions and emotional experiences. Self-deception is particularly important here and seems to have important adaptive value, in that it helps to regulate people's mood and self-esteem (Sackeim, 1983). I have found (Gudjonsson, 1990b) that among offenders other-deception is more situation-bound than self-deception. That is, whereas other-deception is markedly affected by the context in which it occurs, self-deception is not. This is evident from the work of Paulhus (1983) and Gudjonsson (1990b). My paper is particularly relevant to investigative interviewing because it was carried out on different groups of offenders.

I administered the self-deception (SDQ) and other-deception (ODQ) questionnaires of Sackeim and Gur (1979) to 109 subjects undergoing forensic assessment before or after trial. The two 20-item questionnaires were factor analysed and rotated using a Varimax procedure. For each scale three factors and the total scores were compared according to type of offence. Violent offenders (mainly homicide cases) and sex offenders had the highest ODQ scores for all offender groups, but no difference was found for the SDQ scores. The most striking difference in the ODQ scores for violent and sex offenders was on factor 2. This factor seemed to reflect claims of respect and consideration for others, and it is tempting to speculate that these two groups (who had committed either violent or sexual assault on others) had elevated scores because they were trying hard to give the impression that they were basically considerate to others, in spite of what their offence indicated!

What was interesting about self-deception was that the factor scores did not differentiate between violent and sex offenders on subscales relating to the denial of aggressive and sexual feelings respectively. That is, sex offenders were no more likely to deny generalized feelings related to sex than they were hostile and angry feelings. The same pattern emerged for violent offenders.

Looking at the frequencies with which subjects denied the individual items or themes on the SDQ reveals an important finding. People generally find it very difficult to admit to themselves that they have ever had any wish or desire to murder or rape anybody, even when they have committed these offences with clear intent! Such denials undoubtedly serve to protect the person's self-esteem and highlight the importance of cognitive distortions in regulating mood (Roth and Ingram, 1985).

Generally speaking, the more reprehensible the offence committed, the more offenders are likely to operate denial mechanisms when being interviewed, although there clearly are very marked individual differences in this respect. There may be a number of different reasons for the denial, including not wanting to be "branded" as an offender, not wanting others to know what one has done or what one's intentions were, not wanting to acknowledge fully to oneself what one has done, and not wanting to face up to the consequences of one's actions. In one case I had seen a man in his mid-20s who over several years vehemently denied having committed the offence he had been convicted of. The offence involved the murder of a young child for no apparent reason. Eventually the man admitted that he had lost his temper with the child and murdered it as he passed by where the child was playing. The man explained his reason for the continual denial, "I did on no account want to be branded a child-killer". Perhaps with time he learned to accept that he was after all a child-killer.

Salter (1988) makes the valuable point in relation to sex offenders that denial is a complex multifaceted phenomenon. It comprises several different components, which include denial of the acts themselves, denial of fantasy and planning, denial of responsibility for the acts (e.g. claiming he only did it because he was drunk at the time), and denial of the seriousness of the behaviour. Perhaps the most important point she makes is that many offenders, and particularly sex offenders, typically only reveal a fraction of their deviant thoughts and behaviours initially. The fact that an offender has admitted to certain things (e.g. having had sexual intercourse with his daughter) does not mean that he has revealed the entire truth. Offenders commonly only admit to part of their offending behaviour and seem to make idiosyncratic distinctions between what they are prepared to reveal or conceal, and these may appear incomprehensible to an outsider. Salter quotes as an example fathers who admit to having had full sexual intercourse with their daughters but for some reason lie about another aspect, such as the length of time during which the sexual abuse had taken place or the number of occasions on which it happened.

Recent research into "cognitive distortions" among rapists, paedophiles and incest offenders (Abel et al., 1984) has illustrated how these types of offenders have a strong tendency to justify, minimize and rationalize their criminal acts. In short, they have persuaded themselves that their behaviour is not harmful or that the victims only got what they deserved. Statements along the following lines are commonly seen among sex offenders: "Having sex with children is a good way of teaching them about sex", "Most children want to have sex", "I show my love for children by having sex with them", and "Women who are out on their own late at night deserve to be raped". Salter (1988) argues that rapists are particularly likely to justify their criminal behaviour and minimize the extent of their deviant thoughts and behaviour.

The above discussion indicates that offenders are often motivated to deny, minimize or justify their criminal acts. What they say should therefore not be taken at face value. Their accounts should be checked and corroborated as far as possible, especially when there are discrepancies between their accounts and those of the victims or witnesses.

The concealment of information is undoubtedly the most important form of deception among offenders. Some offenders are very skilled at deceiving the interviewer, no matter how experienced and well-informed the interviewer is. As will become evident later in this book, the detection of deception is no simple matter and the discovery of deception may only come about once a further offence has been committed.

So far I have been discussing deception among offenders. The interviewer should always be aware that there are also instances when victims, witnesses and complainants are motivated to deceive, either deliberately or unwittingly.

For example, witnesses and victims may be over-zealous to assist the police and unwittingly misidentify suspects. On occasions people may deliberately lie and implicate others because of revenge, spite, or for some instrumental gain. For example, in one recent case involving the murder of two sisters, the assailant tried to throw suspicion on somebody else by giving the police a description of a person whom he claimed to have seen running away from the murder scene at the material time. In other instances people may be motivated to conceal their mistakes, deficiencies or past experiences, as shown by the following example.

In one murder case referred to me by the police, the girlfriend of the prime suspect had lied to the police about the time when her boyfriend had arrived home one night. The lie made the police suspicious that the girlfriend was trying to cover up for her boyfriend by providing him with an alibi for the murder. The truth, as it transpired, turned out to be more basic than that. The woman had initially made a mistake about the time her boyfriend arrived home and tried to cover up by telling lies, including a statement that she had spent 2 hours having sex with her boyfriend when he came home at 2.30 a.m. What she had overlooked was the fact that her boyfriend was so drunk at the time that there was no way he was capable of having sexual intercourse with her at all! The woman told me that she was totally unable to tell the police the truth, even though it meant that she and her boyfriend had spent several unnecessary hours in police custody, because of the embarrassment of having to admit to them that she had not only made a mistake but also tried to cover it up subsequently by telling the police numerous lies.

The case illustrates Ekman's (1985) important point that there are two kinds of punishment at stake in deceit. First, the punishment that occurs if the lie fails, and secondly, the punishment for being caught deceiving. What may make some people determined to persist with covering up their mistakes and deficiencies is the fact that the perceived punishment for being caught deceiving about them may be considered to be much worse than the punishment the lie was designed to avoid in the first place!

Although this chapter is primarily concerned with deception among suspects, witnesses, victims and complainants, there are instances when the interviewer may be deceptive. This may include "information bluffs" (e.g. the interviewer pretending to a suspect that he or she has information to implicate the suspect in the crime); promises that the interviewer cannot or does not intend to keep (e.g. telling a suspect that after confessing he will be allowed to go home when this is not the case); and the interviewer pretending to be sympathetic to a suspect in order to gain his or her confidence and trust. Such manipulations are undoubtedly widespread and may influence the outcome of the police interview.

Under the law of the United States of America such manipulations, and indeed deliberate lying by interrogators in order to obtain confessions from suspects, are permitted. In England and Wales, deliberate lying to suspects is likely to be against the spirit of the Police and Criminal Evidence Act 1984 (Home Office, 1985b) and its Codes of Practice (Home Office, 1985a, 1991).

More serious deception occurs when police interviewers make up "verbals" (self-incriminating statements) and attribute them to suspects. "Verballing" occurs when the police claim that a suspect admitted to an offence which is denied in a subsequent statement. There are reported instances of this happening and of a suspect finding it difficult to substantiate his claim when the case goes to court (Kirby and Coulson, 1989). In one case a prisoner was able surreptitiously to tape-record a conversation with a police officer in order to show fabrication of verbal evidence. Such proof is obviously very rarely available to substantiate fabrication of police evidence when it does occur.

Symptoms of Resistance

Probably the two most common types of resistance by interviewees during police interviewing involve denial of knowledge ("I don't know anything about that") and denial of memory ("I don't remember"). Of course, sometimes these types of denials may be statements of fact rather than attempts to avoid the interviewer's questions. Gorden (1975) points out that inexperienced interviewers may respond to symptoms of resistance by making the person even more cautious, increasing confrontation (e.g. "I can't". "Yes you can"), and also failing to facilitate the person's memory processes. He suggests that the best tactic is to give the person ample time to answer the question, since the immediate reaction of subjects is often to underestimate their own knowledge and memory. Encouragement and prompting may be required, but under no circumstance should the interviewer show disappointment and hostility towards the subject, as it is likely to increase the subject's resistance even further.

Moston (1991) points out that there are many different types of denial strategies that suspects can utilize during interrogation. Not all of these are indicative of guilt and deception, although interrogators almost invariably interpret denials as "lie signs". According to Moston, denials may result from memory problems and particular types of interrogation techniques, rather than deliberate deception.

Shepherd (1991a) argues that resistance can be overcome by skilful interviewing and without the need for persuasive questioning. He provides some guidance about how to minimize the likelihood that resistance will occur during interviewing, through the use of careful preparation and planning.

CONCLUSIONS

Interviewing is one of several fact-finding methods that the police have at their disposal when investigating crime. Its importance as evidence varies considerably from case to case. In some cases interview data derived from victims, witnesses and suspects may be the only evidence against a defendant.

Even in criminal cases where there is ample forensic evidence available to convict a suspect, careful interview data may be essential for establishing the mental state of the person at the material time and the motive behind the crime. In England, suspects can be convicted on the basis of their self-incriminating admissions alone, even when these are subsequently retracted.

The single most important function of the police interview is to maximize *relevant* and *valid* pieces of information. In order to achieve this the interviewer has to maintain *optimal* rapport and interpersonal relations with the subject being interviewed. A number of factors may *inhibit* the flow of relevant and valid information during interviewing. These may relate to people being either *unwilling* or *unable* to provide the interviewer with the information sought. Communication can be maximized by utilizing a range of *facilitators*, which are ways of motivating subjects to cooperate optimally with the interview.

A police interview generally comprises four phases: "orientation", "listening", "questions and answers", and "advising". Within this conceptual framework, which is consistent with general theories of interviewing, most valid information is obtained when subjects, especially victims and witnesses, are asked to provide a free narrative account of "what happened" before specific questions are asked. In practice police officers may confuse the phases, particularly the "listening" and "questions and answers" phases, where they do not pay sufficient attention to the former. Conversely, too much emphasis on the "listening" phase may cause irrelevant information to be collected since the subject may not know precisely what information the interviewer is seeking.

There is a certain bias inherent in most police interviews in that police officers enter the interview with certain assumptions, expectations and hypotheses about the event they are investigating. This bias may not cause problems when the police officers' premises are well founded, and indeed may facilitate the interview process by making it more focused on the essential issues. Problems may arise when police officers approach the interview situation with unfounded or erroneous premises. Interviewers should try to minimize bias as far as they can; they should be aware of the possible misleading effects of bias and take the appropriate steps to verify the information they obtain.

CHAPTER 3

Interrogation Tactics and Techniques

The purpose of this Chapter is to discuss in detail the tactics and techniques advocated by practical interrogation manuals and the context in which interrogations occur. Nearly all published interrogation manuals originate in the United States of America. One exception is Walkley's (1987) *Handbook for Investigators*, which is the first manual written for British police officers. These manuals are based on the extensive experience of interrogators and can be highly effective techniques for breaking down suspects' resistance. The authors of these manuals argue that most criminal suspects are reluctant to confess because of the shame associated with what they have done and the fear of the legal consequences. In their view, a certain amount of pressure, deception, persuasion and manipulation are required in order for the "truth" to be revealed. Furthermore, they view persuasive interrogation techniques as essential to police work and feel justified in using them. There is a general reluctance among the authors of these manuals to accept the possibility that their recommended techniques could, in certain instances, make a suspect confess to a crime that he or she had not committed.

Zimbardo (1967) argues that the techniques recommended in police manuals are psychologically sophisticated and "coercive". He goes so far as to suggest that they are an infringement of the suspect's dignity and fundamental rights, and may result in a false confession.

The opposing views of Zimbardo and the authors of police interrogation manuals are the result of looking at police interrogation from different perspectives. Police interrogation manuals base their techniques on instincts and extensive experience, whilst psychologists like Zimbardo view the recommended techniques within the framework of what is known in the literature about the psychology of attitudes, compliance and obedience. The fundamental problem is the lack of scientific research into the police interrogation process and the techniques utilized. Some recent research in Britain into police interrogation techniques has significantly advanced our knowledge in this very important area.

THE CONTEXT OF THE INTERROGATION

The context in which the interrogation takes place and the conditions of detention can vary immensely. In some cases suspects are detained in custody, even incommunicado, for days. They may be physically exhausted, emotionally distraught and mentally confused when interrogated. With improved legal provisions in England and Wales (Home Office, 1985a) the police are obliged to follow certain stringent guidelines and procedures with regard to detention and interrogation (Home Office, 1985b, 1991). This restricts the length of time during which suspects can be detained without being formally charged to 24 hours, except in suspected terrorist cases, where there are special provisions for the police to hold suspects for considerably longer (Mitchell and Richardson, 1985). Whilst in custody, suspects must be given sufficient rest between interviews and their physical and mental well-being is the responsibility of the duty "Custody Officer".

Even with markedly improved legal provisions for detainees, it is difficult to think of any custodial interrogation that is not potentially "coercive". Indeed, it is recognized by the United States Supreme Court that all custodial interrogations are to a certain extent "inherently coercive" (for reviews see Driver, 1968; Ayling, 1984; Inbau, Reid and Buckley, 1986). This is because the interrogator is part of a system that gives him or her certain powers and controls (e.g. powers of arrest and detention, the power to charge the suspect, the power to ask questions, and being in charge of the suspect's freedom of movement and access to the outside world). Therefore, it is inevitable that there are certain "coercive" aspects to any police interrogation. Not only is the inevitable "coerciveness" associated with the nature and circumstances of the interrogation and confinement, but the characteristics of the detainee affect the extent to which his free will is likely to be overborne (e.g. *Schneckloth v. Bustamonte*, 412 U.S. 218).

Anxiety and Fear During Interrogation

Inbau, Reid and Buckley (1986) point out that signs of nervousness may be evident during interrogation among both innocent and guilty subjects. They list three reasons why innocent suspects may be nervous when interrogated:

1. They may be worried that they are erroneously assumed to be guilty;
2. They may be worried about what is going to happen to them whilst in custody and during interrogation;
3. They may be concerned that the police may discover some previous transgressions.

Inbau, Reid and Buckley speculate that the main difference between the anxiety (they use the word "nervousness") of innocent and guilty suspects is one of degree. That is, both innocent and guilty suspects may experience and exhibit signs of anxiety when interrogated, but the latter will experience a greater degree of anxiety, because they have committed an offence and really have something to worry about. Another alleged difference between innocent and guilty suspects is that the anxiety of innocent suspects, unlike that of guilty suspects, diminishes as the interrogation progresses.

Irving and Hilgendorf (1980) discuss in considerable detail the types of factor that may cause stress or anxiety in suspects during interrogation, irrespective of whether they are innocent or guilty of the alleged offence. Their work is particularly important because it relates experimental and laboratory findings to stressors that pertain to a police station.

Irving and Hilgendorf describe three general classes of stressors that are relevant to police interrogation situations:

1. Stress caused by the physical environment at the police station;
2. Stress caused by confinement and isolation from peers;
3. Stress caused by the suspect's submission to authority.

Each of these classes of stressors can cause sufficient anxiety, fear and physiological arousal in the suspect to markedly impair his performance during interrogation.

The physical characteristics of the interrogation environment may cause anxiety and fear in some suspects. This is particularly true if the suspect has never been in a police station before, so that the environment is unfamiliar to him. The more often a suspect has been in a police station on previous occasions, the greater the opportunity he has had for learning the rules of conduct of the setting. In addition, the more likely he is to know his legal rights. Therefore, a familiar police environment is likely to be less stress-provoking than an unfamiliar one.

Having been at a police station before is not always a stress-reducing factor, but this possibility is not discussed by Irving and Hilgendorf. Indeed, a stressful experience at a police station may result in psychiatric disability and could easily exacerbate the suspect's anxieties and fears when interrogated on a subsequent occasion (Gudjonsson and MacKeith, 1982). This happens when suspects have been so traumatized by the previous interrogative experience that their ability to learn constructively from it is adversely affected (Shallice, 1974). Further types of stressors associated with the physical environment at the police station are *uncertainty* and *lack of control* over the environment. Suspects have little or no control over what is happening. If arrested, they cannot leave the police station until they are told that they are free to go. They cannot move freely within the police station, they are not free to obtain refreshments, make telephone calls, receive visits, or use toilet facilities without permission. They have limited opportunity for privacy, and indeed, interrogators may cause stress by positioning themselves very close to the suspect during the interrogation. Such invasion of the suspect's personal space can cause agitation and increased physiological arousal (Sommer, 1969).

As suspects have little or no control over the physical environment at the police station, they are inevitably faced with a number of uncertainties, which include uncertainties about the fulfilment of their basic needs, and not knowing how long they are going to be detained at the police station or what is going to happen to them. The timing and duration of the interrogation, confinement, and social isolation from others, are very important factors which are discussed by Irving and Hilgendorf.

Irving and Hilgendorf argue that the inevitable subordination of suspects to police officers' authority, when detained at a police station, can cause considerable stress for the suspect. Irving and Hilgendorf point out an important parallel between experimental findings of obedience to authority (Milgram, 1974) and what may happen to suspects who are interrogated by the police:

> ". . .the parallel lies in the way both Milgram's subjects, and suspects in interrogation, are prone to obey instructions which they would ordinarily dismiss. Under certain conditions, the subject will, against his principles, inflict pain. Likewise, we would argue under similar conditions of obedience to authority, suspects will provide information or even confess, even though normally they would not do so because of the obvious negative consequences" (p. 39).

Projects researching the effects of the historic decision in *Miranda v. Arizona* (383 U.S. 436, 1966) indicate that interrogations may be so stressful to most suspects that it impairs their ability to exercise their powers of judgement and legal rights (Wald et al., 1967; Griffiths and Ayres, 1967; Leiken, 1970). Stress was assumed to be mainly caused by the fact that there was a great deal at stake for the suspects. Furthermore, all three studies showed that police interrogation techniques following *Miranda* are very subtle and persuasive and greatly influence the decision of suspects to incriminate themselves. Griffiths and Ayres (1967) give an example of the subtlety of the police questioning:

> "Often the pressure consisted of little more than reiteration by a detective of the same question several times alternated with small talk and appropriate urging" (p. 313).

Anger During Interrogation

Interrogation manuals generally acknowledge that anger, whether experienced by the suspect or the interrogator, is an undesirable emotion during interrogation as it inhibits constructive communication between the suspect and the interrogator. Rapport, trust and cooperation are considered to be essential components for the process of successful interrogation, and feelings of anger and suspiciousness interfere with this process.

An expression of anger among suspects during interrogation is often difficult to interpret, but an important difference is assumed to exist between guilty and innocent subjects. Inbau, Reid and Buckley (1967) point out that innocent suspects may be genuinely angry, and on occasions outraged, about being accused or suspected of a crime of which they are innocent. However, guilty suspects may on occasions pretend to be angry and their feigned anger may be difficult to differentiate from the genuine anger of innocent suspects. These authors argue that an important difference between the behavioural symptoms of anger among innocent and guilty suspects relates to the persistence and duration of the expressed emotion. Innocent suspects are assumed to persist with their anger over time, whereas guilty suspects will find it difficult to maintain the emotion over long periods of time. In other words, Inbau, Reid and Buckley speculate that the feigned anger among guilty suspects will subside more quickly than the genuine anger among innocent suspects. I am not aware of any published scientific study which provides empirical support for such differentiation between innocent and guilty suspects in their anger responses, but Inbau, Reid and Buckley derived their interpretation from extensive experience of real-life interrogations.

Inbau, Reid and Buckley argue that impatience and anger among interrogators interferes with sound judgement and reasoning, which could result in unprofessional behaviour, such as the use of threats and violence. An arrogant attitude of the suspect is a psychological characteristic which is considered to be highly undesirable during interrogation (Royal and Schutt, 1976). The reason is that like anger and suspiciousness, it reduces the suspect's cooperation with the interrogation and makes him less receptive to the suggestions offered by the interrogator.

Emotional vs. Non-emotional Offenders

When advising interrogators about the tactics and techniques to use when interrogating suspects who are considered guilty, Inbau, Reid and Buckley make a distinction between emotional and non-emotional offenders. This distinction determines to a certain extent the tactics and techniques that the interrogator utilizes in a particular case. Emotional offenders are those who experience remorse for what they have done and they "can be identified behaviorally during an interrogation in that they tend to be emotionally moved by the interrogator's words and actions" (p. 78). These offenders' "troubled conscience" about the offence they have committed is considered to be an important internal driving force that facilitates a confession. Therefore, the best approach that the interrogator can use with this kind of an offender is sympathy and compassion. An apparent understanding by the interrogator of the suspect's circumstances, predicament and feelings, will greatly expedite a confession.

A non-emotional offender, according to Inbau, Reid and Buckley is not normally troubled by conscience for his wrongdoing. He or she can be identified by resistance to becoming emotionally involved with the interrogation. The most effective interrogation approach with a non-emotional offender is a *"factual analysis approach"*. This approach uses commonsense explanations and arguments rather than focusing on the suspect's emotions. The suspect is confronted with reasons why it is futile to deny the offence. This may involve the interrogator informing the suspect about all the "evidence" the police have which implicates him or her in the crime, or the police may exaggerate the strength of the evidence they have against the person. Inbau, Reid and Buckley point out that the two approaches—the sympathetic and the factual—should normally both be used during interrogation, but the emphasis of their use in a particular case will depend on the personality of the suspect.

Later in this Chapter it will be shown how precisely individual differences related to personality can influence the type of "themes" or "scenarios" interrogators offer to suspects in an attempt to obtain confessions.

Desirable Attributes of the Interrogator

Inbau, Reid and Buckley list a number of indispensable attributes that make a good interrogator. In terms of personal qualities, the following are most important in their view:

1. Good intelligence.
2. Good understanding of human nature.
3. The ability to get on well with others.
4. Patience and persistence.

In addition, the interrogator should be interested in police interrogation and needs to study the range of tactics and techniques. He or she should be familiar with new developments in the art of interrogation and be aware of the laws and regulations that govern interrogation procedures. An understanding of the psychological principles and theories of interrogation and confessions is considered very important. In particular, a good understanding and insight into signs of deception, including non-verbal cues, is essential. This is because the effectiveness of interrogation tactics and techniques is largely based on the ability of interrogators to detect defensiveness, evasiveness and various forms of deception, and turn it to their advantage in breaking down resistance.

Inbau, Reid and Buckley make the interesting and valuable point that interrogation is a highly specialized area of police work and that the qualities that make a good interrogator may not necessarily be the same qualities as those that make a good investigator. They quote, as an example, that impatience may be an advantage for investigators in completing certain assignments, but it is a handicap when interrogating people. These authors argue that interrogation should be a specialism within police departments, implying that investigators, as a rule, should not interrogate suspects. They argue that increased specialism is likely to increase the number of confessions obtained from criminal suspects, that confessions are more likely to meet the necessary legal requirements, and that innocent suspects would be more expeditiously and reliably identified.

The Physical Environment of the Interrogation

There are a number of physical features associated with the police interrogation and confinement environment that can have major effects on the way suspects react to police interrogation. Inbau, Reid and Buckley (1986) describe various ways in which the physical environment can be deliberately arranged to maximize the likelihood that the suspect will confess. These include isolating the suspect from outside influences, making sure that there are no objects in the interrogation room that can distract the suspect's attention, sitting close to the suspect, and having colleagues surreptitiously observing the interview behind a one-way mirror for suspects' signs of vulnerabilities.

An excellent experimental illustration of the powerful emotional reactions of normal and healthy individuals to custodial confinement is seen in the classic study of Haney, Banks and Zimbardo (1973). Twenty-one Stanford University students were assigned to either a "guard" or a "prisoner" condition in a simulated prison environment. The purpose of the study was closely to analyse the behaviour and reactions of the two experimental groups to the respective roles over a 2-week period. The study had to be terminated after 6 days because of the severe distress and emotional disturbance of about half of the "prisoners". This was in spite of the fact that all the subjects had been carefully selected for the study because of their emotional stability. The typical reactions of the "prisoners" comprised "passivity, dependency, depression, helplessness and self-deprecation" (p. 89). The relevant processes that brought about these reactions were described by the authors as:

1. "Loss of personal identity" (i.e. loss of recognition of one's individuality and privacy);
2. "Arbitrary control" (i.e. the arbitrary and often unpredictable exercise of power and control by the "guards");
3. "Dependency and emasculation" (i.e. being dependent on the "guards" for exercising basic human activities).

The limitation of this study relates to the fact that the "guards" were role-playing what they construed as typical prison officers' behaviour, rather than exhibiting behaviour which happens in a real-life "prison". Nevertheless, what is interesting was the apparent ease with which even stable individuals become immensely distressed by "prison" confinement.

Irving (1980), in an observation study, emphasized the importance of the physical environment in influencing the decision-making of suspects. The facts he considered important included unfamiliarity with the physical environment of the police station, the effect of confinement on "under-arousal", and the absence of control that the suspect has over the physical environment.

The ways in which the physical environment can affect the physiological state of suspects whilst they are in police custody have been discussed in detail by Hinkle (1961) and Shallice (1974). Social isolation, sensory deprivation, fatigue, hunger, the lack of sleep, physical and emotional pain and threats are all factors that can powerfully influence the decision-making of suspects and the reliability of their statements. According to Hinkle (1961), these factors commonly result in impaired judgement, mental confusion and disorientation, and increased suggestibility. He concludes by stating:

> "Most people who are exposed to coercive procedures will talk and usually reveal some information that they might not have revealed otherwise" (p. 44).

However,

> ". . .the personality of a man and his attitude towards the experience that he is undergoing affect his ability to withstand it" (p. 33).

In my own experience of assessing defendants for a pretrial examination, many complain of having had insufficient sleep prior to the interrogation. They often claim that this seriously impaired their ability to cope with the demands of interrogation. There is considerable evidence that lack of sleep impairs mental functioning, especially if it continues for 2 or 3 days (Hinkle, 1961; Mikulincer et al., 1989). Loss of sleep is associated with increased circadian oscillations (e.g. heart rate irregularity), lack of motivation to initiate and perform tasks, attentional problems, cognitive confusion and slowness of thought (Mikulincer et al., 1989). The peak hours for reported problems occur between 4 and 8 a.m.

INTERROGATION TECHNIQUES

Although many police interrogation manuals have been produced (see Walkley, 1987 for a detailed bibliography), undoubtedly the most authoritative and influential manual is the one written by Inbau, Reid and Buckley (1986). The original book was published by Inbau and Reid (1962) 30 years before. There was a second edition of the book published in 1967 and the third edition, published in 1986 by Inbau, Reid and Buckley, gives the up-to-date state of the art of interrogation. Since the work of these authors is highly sophisticated and detailed, and is commonly used by police and military interrogators, I shall review it in some detail.

The "Steps" for Effective Interrogation

Inbau, Reid and Buckley suggest nine steps to effective interrogation of allegedly guilty suspects. These are the types of case where the interrogator feels reasonably certain that the suspect is guilty of the alleged offence.

The nine steps of interrogation were developed over many years of careful observation of successful interrogations and by interviewing suspects after they had confessed. The advantage of interviewing suspects after they have confessed is that the interrogator can learn more about the processes and mechanisms that elicit successful confessions. The nine steps of interrogation are briefly discussed below, whereas the theory behind the development of the nine steps, and why they are effective in eliciting a confession, is discussed in Chapter 4.

Prior to proceeding through the nine steps the interrogator should be thoroughly familiar with all the available facts about the case and the suspect. In other words, he must be well prepared before conducting the interrogation. An ill-prepared interrogator will be at a serious disadvantage when trying to elicit a confession from an allegedly guilty suspect, because the tactics and techniques of effective interrogation are dependent upon the interrogator coming across as confident and fully knowledgable about the case. Another advantage of good preparation, which is implicit in the use of interrogative "theme development" (see below), is that the more the interrogator knows about the suspect and his background the more he can identify the suspect's weaknesses and use them to his advantage when attempting to break down resistance.

STEP 1: "Direct Positive Confrontation"

This step consists of the suspect being told firmly that he is considered to have committed the alleged offence. The interrogator states confidently that the results of extensive enquiries by the police indicate that the suspect committed the offence. Even if the interrogator has no tangible evidence against the suspect, he should not give any indication of this to the suspect and if necessary he must pretend that there is evidence. After the initial confrontation there is a brief pause, during which the suspect's behavioural reactions are closely observed. The suspect is then confronted with the accusations the second time. Passive reaction to the accusation is considered to be evidence of deception. Indeed, according to Inbau, Reid and Buckley (1986) ". . .the easiest confessions are obtained from suspects who fail to make a denial after the positive confrontation" (p. 87). The interrogator then proceeds to Step 2.

STEP 2: "Theme Development"

Here it is important that the interrogator displays an understanding and sympathetic attitude in order to gain the suspect's trust. The interrogator suggests various "themes" to the suspect which are aimed to either minimize the moral implications of the alleged crime or give the suspect the opportunity of accepting "moral excuses" for the commission of the crime. In this way the suspect can accept physical responsibility for the crime while at the same time minimizing either the seriousness of it or the internal blame for it. Inbau, Reid and Buckley point out that this kind of theme development is most effective with emotional offenders, because they have the greatest amount of emotional guilt. Giving them the opportunity of relieving their guilt by accepting moral excuses for what they have done acts as a powerful confession-inducing factor.

With regard to theme development, Inbau, Reid and Buckley emphasize:

> "Throughout the theme presentation process, the interrogator should not lose sight of the fact that the normal or psychological excuses offered to the suspect do not even have to approximate the true motivation underlying the offence. All that is required is the creation of a perception on the part of the suspect that he is a less reprehensible person, morally speaking, than the bare facts of the case would indicate" (p. 97).

Themes for Emotional Suspects It is recommended that the type of themes utilized by interrogators should take into account the personality of the suspect. The following themes are recommended for the emotional type of suspects:

(a) *Tell the suspect that anyone else being faced with the same situation or circumstance might have committed the same type of offence.* This has the effect of normalizing the criminal behaviour of the suspect and, combined with the comfort from the interrogator's apparent sympathy with the suspect, makes it easier for the latter to confess. Inbau, Reid and Buckley appear to take theme development far beyond ethical and professional limits when they recommend that:

> "In sex cases, it is particularly helpful to indicate to the suspect that the interrogator has indulged, or has been tempted to indulge, in the same kind of conduct as involved in the case under investigation" (p. 98).

(b) *Attempt to reduce the suspect's feelings of guilt for the offence by minimizing its moral seriousness.* This can be achieved, for example, by the interrogator commenting that many other people have committed more shameful acts than that done by the suspect. This has the effect of reducing the suspect's embarrassment over talking about the offence. Inbau, Reid and Buckley suggest that this theme is particularly effective when suspects are questioned about sex crimes, although it is also effective with many other types of crime.

(c) *Suggest to the suspect a morally acceptable reason for the offence.* This includes such ploys as telling the suspect that he probably only committed the offence because he was intoxicated or on drugs at the time. Another ploy, in certain types of offence, is to suggest that the suspect never really meant to do any harm, or attributing the offence to some kind of an accident. The purpose is to "ease" the suspect into some kind of self-incriminating admission, no matter how small, which makes him more amenable to making a full and detailed confession at a later stage of the interrogation. Being able to provide the suspect with some face-saving explanations for the crime greatly increases the likelihood of a confession being forthcoming.

(d) *Condemnation of others as a way of sympathizing with the suspect.* The rationale for this theme is that it will make it much easier for the suspect to confess if some responsibility for the offence can be attributed to the victim, an accomplice or somebody else. The interrogator can use this ploy to his advantage by exploiting the readiness of many suspects to attribute partial blame for what they have done to others. Inbau, Reid and Buckley suggest that this type of a theme can be particularly effective in certain sex crimes, for example, where children and women are victims.

(e) *Using praise and flattery as a way of manipulating the suspect.* The argument here is that most people enjoy the approval of others, and the appropriate use of praise and flattery facilitates rapport between the suspect and the interrogator. This ploy is considered particularly effective with people who are uneducated and dependent upon the approval of others.

(f) *Point out that perhaps the suspect's involvement in the crime has been exaggerated.* The emphasis here is that the interrogator makes the suspect believe that perhaps the victim has exaggerated his involvement in the offence. Pointing out the possibility of exaggeration may make some offenders more willing to make partial admission, which can subsequently be built upon.

(g) *Make the suspect believe that it is not in his interest to continue with criminal activities.* This theme is considered particularly effective with first-time offenders. It is pointed out to them that it is in their own interest to own up to what they have done in order to prevent serious trouble later in life. In other words, the suspect is told that by confessing he can learn from his mistakes and escape more serious difficulties.

Themes for Non-emotional Suspects Inbau, Reid and Buckley suggest the following themes for non-emotional suspects:

(a) *Try to catch the suspect telling some incidental lie.* Once a suspect has been caught telling a lie regarding the case under investigation, no matter how small the lie is, he will be at psychological disadvantage; in fact, from then onwards he has to make serious attempts to convince the interrogator that everything he is saying is now the truth.

Inbau, Reid and Buckley make an important point regarding the use of this technique:

> ". . . the interrogator should bear in mind that there are times and circumstances when a person may lie about some incidental aspect of the offense without being guilty of its commission" (p. 128).

The lesson to be learned for interrogators is that innocent suspects as well as guilty ones may lie during interrogation about some incidental aspect of the offence, such as giving a false alibi because they do not want to reveal where they really were at the time.

(b) *Try to get the suspect to somehow associate himself with the crime.*
     This ploy may form part of some other theme, but it can be used as an effective theme in its own right. This consists of, for example, trying to get the suspect to agree to having been at or near the scene of the crime, or somehow having incidental links with the crime. This should be done early on during the interrogation so that the suspect does not fully realize at the time the implications of agreeing to his presence at the scene of the crime.

(c) *Try to convince the suspect that there is no point in denying his involvement.* Here the interrogator points out to the suspect that all the evidence points to his guilt and that it is futile to attempt to resist telling the truth. The effectiveness of this theme depends upon the ability of the interrogator to persuade the suspect that there is sufficient evidence to convict him, regardless of any forthcoming confession. The suspect is told that the interrogator is only concerned about the suspect being able to tell his side of the story, in case there were any mitigating circumstances.

(d) *Play one co-offender against the other.* When there is more than one person suspected of having committed the offence, then each one will be very concerned about the possibility that the other(s) will confess in an attempt to obtain special consideration when the case goes to court. This fear of mutual distrust can be used to "play one against the other". The main ploy is to inform one, usually the assumed leader, that his co-offender has confessed and that there is no point in his continuing to deny his involvement in the commission of the offence.

STEP 3: "Handling Denials"

It is recognized that most offenders are reluctant to give a confession, even after direct confrontation, and their denials need to be handled with great care and expertise. Repeated denials by the suspect are seen as being very undesirable because they give the suspect a psychological advantage.

Therefore, they must be stopped by the interrogator. This means that the interrogator does not allow the suspect to persist with the denials. The suspect's attempts at denial are persistently interrupted by the interrogator, who keeps telling the suspect to listen to what he has got to say.

Inbau, Reid and Buckley argue that there are noticeable qualitative differences between the denials of innocent and guilty suspects, and these can be detected from various verbal and non-verbal signs. For example, innocent suspects' denials are said to be spontaneous, forceful and direct, whereas the denials of guilty suspects are more evasive, qualified and hesitant. Similarly, innocent suspects more commonly look the interrogator in the eye, and lean forward in the chair in a rather rigid and an aggressive posture. In addition, the "intensity and frequency of denials from the innocent will increase as the interrogation continues"(p. 148).

Inbau, Reid and Buckley recommend the use of the "friendly-unfriendly" technique (when the various attempts at sympathy and understanding have failed). The "friendly-unfriendly" technique also known as the "Mutt and Jeff" technique (Irving and Hilgendorf, 1980), can be applied in various ways. This commonly involves two interrogators working together, one of whom is friendly and sympathetic and the other unfriendly and critical. A variant of this technique is for the same interrogator to play both roles at different times during the interrogation.

The purpose of the "friendly-unfriendly" technique, according to Inbau, Reid and Buckley, is to highlight the difference between a friendly and unfriendly approach, which in the end makes the suspect more responsive to the sympathetic approach. This technique is said to be particularly effective with the quiet and unresponsive suspect.

STEP 4: "Overcoming Objections"

This consists of the interrogator overcoming various objections that the suspect may give as an explanation or reasoning for his innocence. Innocent suspects are said to more commonly continue with plain denials, whereas the guilty suspect will move from plain denials to objections. There are various ways of overcoming these objections, which are said to be an attempt, particularly by guilty suspects, to gain control over the conversation as their denials begin to weaken. Once the suspect feels that the objections are not getting him anywhere he becomes quiet and begins to show signs of withdrawal from active participation in the interrogation. He is now at his lowest point and the interrogator needs to act quickly in order not to lose the psychological advantage he has gained.

STEP 5: "Procurement and Retention of Suspect's Attention"

Once the interrogator notices the suspect's passive signs of withdrawal, he tries to reduce the psychological distance between himself and the suspect and to regain the suspect's full attention. He achieves this, Inbau et al. argue, by moving physically closer to the suspect, leaning forward towards the suspect, touching the suspect gently, mentioning the suspect's first name, and maintaining good eye contact with the suspect. The suspect will look defeated and depressed. As a result of this ploy, a guilty suspect becomes more attentive to the interrogator's suggestions.

STEP 6: "Handling Suspect's Passive Mood"

This step is a direct continuation of Step 5. As the suspect appears attentive to the interrogator and displays indications that he is about to give up, the interrogator should focus the suspect's mind on a specific and central theme concerning the reason for the offence. The interrogator exhibits signs of understanding and sympathy and urges the suspect to tell the truth. Attempts are then made to place the suspect in a more remorseful mood by having him become aware of the stress he is placing upon the victim by not confessing. The interrogator appeals to the suspect's sense of decency and honour, and religion if appropriate.

The main emphasis seems to be to play upon the suspect's potential weaknesses in order to break down his residual resistance. Some suspects cry at this stage and this is reinforced and used to the interrogator's advantage. Suspects who do not break down and cry commonly

> ". . .indicate defeat by a blank stare and complete silence. They are no longer resistant to the interrogator's appeal for the truth. This blank stare and complete silence is an indication that the suspect is ready for the alternatives in Step 7" (p. 165).

STEP 7: "Presenting an Alternative Question"

Here the suspect is presented with two possible alternatives for the commission of the crime. Both alternatives are incriminating, but they are worded in such a way that one alternative acts as a face-saving device whilst the other implies some repulsive or callous motivation.

The psychological reasoning behind the alternative question ploy, is that

> "It is much easier to admit a mistake or any kind of wrongdoing if, at the time of the admission, a person is permitted to explain *why* it was done" (p. 168).

In other words, the suspect is given the opportunity to provide an explanation or an excuse for the crime, which makes self-incriminating admission much easier to achieve. The timing of presenting the alternative question is critical. If presented at the right time it will catch the suspect by surprise and make him more likely to confess.

Inbau, Reid and Buckley point out that occasionally suspects will persist with their face-saving excuses, but the interrogator will usually have no problem in obtaining a more incriminating explanation for the crime by pointing out flaws in the excuses given.

STEP 8: "Having Suspect Orally Relate Various Details of the Offence"

This relates to the suspect having accepted one of the alternatives given to him in Step 7 and consequently providing a first self-incriminating admission. In Step 8 the initial admission is developed into a full-blown confession which provides details of the circumstances, motive and nature of the criminal act.

Inbau, Reid and Buckley emphasize that it is important at this point in the interview that the interrogator is alone with the suspect, because the presence of another person may discourage the suspect from talking openly about the offence. Once a full confession has been obtained the interrogator asks somebody to witness the confession. This is done in case the suspect refuses to sign a written statement.

STEP 9: "Converting an Oral Confession into a Written Confession"

This step is very important because a signed confession is much stronger legally than an oral one. Furthermore, as a large number of suspects subsequently retract or withdraw their self-incriminating confession, it is considered advisable to convert the oral confession into a written statement as soon as practicable. Suspects can easily deny that they ever made an oral confession, whereas it is much more difficult to challenge a written confession that has the suspect's signature on it.

It is important to point out that throughout their book, Inbau, Reid and Buckley make it clear that interrogators should under no circumstances minimize the legal responsibility for the offence, although they can in various ways manipulate suspects and play on their weaknesses in order to obtain a confession from them.

Kassin and McNall (1991) argue that the interrogation techniques incorporated into the above nine steps consist of two main approaches, which they refer to as "maximization" and "minimization", respectively. The former approach, which Inbau, Reid and Buckley recommend for non-emotional suspects, involves the interrogator frightening the suspect into a confession by exaggerating the strength of evidence against him or her and the seriousness of the offence. The "minimization" approach, in contrast, is recommended for remorseful suspects. Here the interrogator tricks the suspect into a confession by offering sympathy, providing face-saving excuses, partly blaming the victim or circumstances for the alleged offence, and minimizing the seriousness of the charges. Kassin and McNall (1991) provide convincing experimental evidence to show some of the inherent dangers of these so-called "subtle" interrogation approaches on the perceptions of potential judges and jurors. That is, these interrogation approaches contain implicit ("hidden") messages which have important conviction and sentencing implications, generally against the interest of the defendant.

THE FORMAT AND RECORDING OF THE CONFESSION

Inbau, Reid and Buckley argue that confession statements can be prepared in two different ways. First, the interrogator can obtain a narrative account from the suspect, which gives all the necessary details of the offence itself and its circumstances. Secondly, a written confession can be prepared in the form of "questions and answers"; that is, the interrogator asks the specific questions and the suspect provides his answers to the questions asked. Probably the best approach is to combine the two formats as appropriate, according to the nature of the case and the ability of the suspect to give a detailed narrative account. Inbau, Reid and Buckley point out that the main legal advantage of a question-and-answer format is that parts of the statement can more easily be deleted if considered inadmissible by the trial judge.

Inbau, Reid and Buckley recommend that the suspect be initially interrogated without the entire content being formally recorded. Once the confession has been obtained, the interrogator then draws up a concise summary, using the suspect's own words as far as possible. These authors argue strongly against the use of tape- and video-recording of interrogation, maintaining that it results in a number of practical problems and would dramatically reduce the number of confessions given by suspects. Similar concerns have been raised by some British police officers who were initially resistant to the introduction of tape-recorded interrogations (McConville and Morrell, 1983).

My own experience is that when confessions are disputed it then becomes very difficult to evaluate the merit of the confession, unless there is a complete record of the entire police interrogation. According to McConville and Morrell, (1983):

> "The main impetus behind the pressure to monitor police interrogations has been a concern to ensure that suspects are fairly treated and that evidence of alleged confessions is based on something more than the bare word of the interrogators" (p. 162).

With the implementation of the Police and Criminal Evidence Act 1984 (Home Office, 1985a) and its Codes of Practice (Home Office, 1985b, 1991), police interviews in England and Wales are contemporaneously recorded and there is a "Custody Record" that details all significant events whilst the suspect is detained in custody. The early work of Barnes and Webster (1980) showed that a routine system of tape-recording could provide an important means of "strengthening police interrogation evidence whilst helping to ensure that the rights of suspects are safeguarded" (pp. 47–48). More recently, experience with tape-recordings has shown that it does not interfere unduly with standard interrogation practices (Willis, Macleod and Naish, 1988). Tape-recording is now common practice in England and became standard police practice in 1991 (Home Office, 1988).

At present video-recording is being tried on an experimental basis in the West Midlands (Baldwin, 1990) and it is likely that in the near future most police interrogations in England will be video-recorded. A recent experimental project in Canada with the video-recording of police interrogations produced favourable results (Grant, 1987). Most importantly perhaps, video-recording did not appear to inhibit suspects from making self-incriminating admissions and confessions, and it provided the court with important information for assessing the reliability of the confession. However, in spite of the advantages of video-recording police interviews, it is not without certain dangers, such as undue reliance being placed by jurors on non-verbal signs and the fact that even the position of the camera can influence perceptions of coercion (Lassiter and Irvine, 1986).

Heaton-Armstrong (1987) draws attention to deficiencies in the Codes of Practice concerning alleged self-incriminating statements that are made outside the police interrogation room. Indeed, it is not uncommon to find "verbals" which are not followed up by a written or tape-recorded statement. Heaton-Armstrong recommends that

> "...the Code of Practice urgently requires amendment so that, in future, suspects are given the earliest possible opportunity to endorse or indicate disagreement with all records of oral statements claimed to have been made by them to the police about an alleged offence" (p. 472).

BRITISH WORK ON INTERROGATION

There have been four major pieces of work on the interrogation tactics and techniques used by British police officers. First, Softley (1980) carried out an observational study in four English police stations. Secondly, Irving (1980) looked closely at the current practice of interrogation at one police station on the South Coast of England. The original study has been replicated twice by Irving and McKenzie (1989). Thirdly, Walsh (1982) carried out a very limited study into police interrogation practices with suspected terrorists in Northern Ireland. Finally, a researcher at the University of Kent (Moston, 1990b) has analysed tape-recordings of real-life police interviews.

In addition to the above studies, Walkley (1987) has produced the first British police interrogation manual. This manual is in many respects similar to the one by Inbau, Reid and Buckley (1986), with certain notable exceptions.

First, Walkley's manual is placed within the framework of the Police and Criminal Evidence Act 1984 (PACE), although some of the persuasive and manipulative tactics recommended for influencing the decision-making of the suspect might prove a breach of the Codes of Practice. Furthermore, some of its contents may go against the general trend in England to place police interviewing training within the context of a social skills model rather than manipulative procedures (Shepherd, 1984, 1991a, 1991b).

Secondly, Walkley's manual is heavily influenced by his own extensive experience of interrogations and the academic research which he has done in the field. The findings of his own research into police interrogation techniques among British police officers are of some interest to psychologists.

Thirdly, unlike Inbau, Reid and Buckley (1986), Walkley acknowledges that interrogation techniques can result in a false confession being elicited. He states:

"Perhaps even more powerfully, if an interviewer wrongly assesses the truth-teller as a lie-teller he may subject that suspect to questioning of a type which induces a false confession" (p. 5).

The Softley Study

In 1979, a team from the Home Office Research Unit conducted an observational study into police questioning of suspects at four police stations in England (Softley, 1980). The study was modelled on that previously conducted in the United States of America by Wald et al. (1967).

Softley and his colleagues observed the interviews of 218 criminal suspects, of which 187 were interviewed at a police station. The police stations were situated in different regions in England. Forty-eight per cent of the suspects interviewed at a police station made a confession, and a further 13% made a damaging admission that fell short of a full-blown confession. Two suspects subsequently retracted their confession, but they were nevertheless convicted. Only 12% of the 187 suspects exercised their right to silence.

The observers noted persuasive interviewing tactics in about 60% of the initial interviews. The most common tactic, reported in 22% of the interviews, involved the police officer pointing to a contradiction or an inconsistency in the suspect's statement. In 13% of cases, the police told suspects firmly about the overwhelming evidence against them. In a further 15% of cases the police appeared to "bluff or hint that other evidence would be forthcoming" (p. 79). In about 6% of the initial interviews the police minimized the seriousness of the offence or the suspect's part in it. This tactic was commonly used in cases where suspects were unduly ashamed of what they had done, or where they appeared to have exaggerated views about the severity of the likely sentence they would receive. In about 7% of the initial interviews the police hinted that, unless the subjects cooperated, they would be detained for a longer period at the police station.

Irving's Observational Study

Irving (1980) observed the interviews of suspects by detectives at Brighton Police Station. The study was commissioned by the Royal Commission on Criminal Procedure. Its purpose was to look at the police interview process at English police stations, with particular emphasis on the tactics and techniques used by interrogators. Irving also carefully monitored the mental state of the suspects prior to and during the police interviews. Over a 6-month period interviews involving 60 suspects were observed. Although interviews in only one police station were observed, the study gave important information about various aspects of the police interview process.

Thirty-three suspects (55%) were interviewed within 3 hours of arriving at the police station and 48 (80%) within 8 hours. Long delays were typically caused by the unfitness of the suspect to be interviewed (e.g. severe intoxication, a psychotic episode). Forty-three (81%) of the suspects were interviewed only once or twice. The average interview lasted 76 minutes (range 5–382 minutes) and the average length in police custody was 12 hours (range 50 minutes to over 26 hours).

According to Irving, the main purpose of the interrogation was to obtain a confession, either as the main evidence in the case or as subsidiary evidence. It was considered in the majority of cases to be central to the police investigation. Even when there was forensic, documentary or witness statement evidence against the suspect, a confession helped to secure a conviction and often provided evidence about other crimes which could be "cleared up". Of the 60 suspects, 35 (58%) made self-incriminating admissions during the interviews observed. A further four suspects confessed after the interviews were terminated.

Below are the main findings from Irving's observations concerning the impact of custody, the interrogation itself and the suspects' mental state whilst being interrogated.

1. *The effects of custody.* Many suspects showed distress and seemed to be in an abnormal mental state before their interrogation. Part of the distress was, according to Irving, caused by unfamiliarity with the police cells, being confined against their will, being isolated from social contact, and being under the physical control of the police.

    The individual reaction of the suspects varied considerably. Those with claustrophobia reacted violently when being locked up. Irving believed that for most suspects, confinement prior to interrogation causes significant *under-arousal*, which suspects find uncomfortable and motivates them to talk to the police. A particular danger involves the interviewing of suspects who are claustrophobic, because terminating an interview means that they will be placed back in their cells, which is terrifying for them.

    Irving noticed that it was the first-time offenders, and particularly those suspected of sexual crimes, that showed the greatest amount of fear reactions during the interrogation. A confession commonly resulted in almost immediate relief of behaviourally-related stress symptoms, which Irving interpreted as being due to reduced uncertainty about the suspects' immediate predicament.

2. *Suspects' mental state.* Immediately prior to the interrogation, 16 suspects (26%) were observed by Irving as being either intoxicated (18%) or mentally ill (8%). A number of other suspects were considered to be in an abnormal mental state due to the fear and anxiety of the interrogation itself. Thus, taken together, about half of the suspects were in some way mentally disordered during their interrogation.

3. *Interrogation tactics used.* In about two-thirds of cases the police were observed to use persuasive and manipulative interrogation tactics in order to obtain information and admissions. Each tactic was sometimes used more than once with each suspect and more than one type of tactic was commonly used. Irving noted that each detective seemed to have a repertoire of approaches that he tended to use, which were "not particularly finely tuned to the suspect" (Irving, 1980, p. 148).

Irving classified the tactics used into five different groups according to their type. The most frequently used types involved:

(a) *Telling suspects that it was futile to deny their involvement* in the crime and they might as well own up to it. This included the use of "information bluffs" (i.e. the police pretending they had more information to link the suspect with the crime than they had). A variant of this tactic was used with about half of the suspects;

(b) *Influencing the suspects' perception of the consequences of confession* was used with 28 suspects (47%). This included minimizing the seriousness of the offence and manipulating the suspects' self-esteem so as to make it easier for them to confess;

(c) *Advising suspects that it was in their best interest to confess* was used in one-third of all cases. Here the police implied or suggested to suspects that it was in the suspects' best interest to provide the wanted information, e.g. by pointing out the advantages of confessing and disadvantages of persistent denial;

(d) *Using custodial conditions, such as confinement and asserting authority.* In this way the police officer may influence the decision-making of the suspect. This tactic was used with 24 suspects (40%);

(e) *The offer of promises relating to police discretion,* such as hinting that accomplices would never find out who informed on them and suggesting that unless the suspect cooperated friends and acquaintances would be interviewed. This type of tactic was used with 14 suspects (23%).

Irving (1980) concluded that the police commonly used manipulative and persuasive interrogation techniques, which were in many respects similar to those recommended in American police interrogation manuals. However, the English detectives did not appear to have had any formal training in these tactics and used a personal repertoire of approaches. These were not always related to the suspect's characteristics and vulnerabilities, but were nevertheless, in Irving's view, highly effective in securing admissions.

Irving's Subsequent Research

Irving's original research at Brighton Police Station has been replicated twice with his colleague Dr Ian McKenzie (Irving and McKenzie, 1989). In 1986, 6 months after the implementation of the Police and Criminal Evidence Act 1984 (PACE) (Home Office, 1985a), which has had radical effects on police interrogation procedures, Irving and McKenzie replicated Irving's original study. The interviews of 68 criminal subjects were observed by McKenzie at Brighton Police Station. As certain noticeable changes had been detected with the implementation of PACE, Irving and McKenzie decided to replicate the second study in 1987, again observing the interviews of 68 suspects. The main methodological difference between the 1986 and 1987 studies was that more serious cases were observed in the latter study (Irving and McKenzie, 1989). One of the main purposes of the two replication studies was to look at the effect that the new legislation might have had on police interviewing behaviour.

The 1986 study indicated that there had been a dramatic fall in the number of manipulative and persuasive tactics used by detectives at Brighton Police Station (Irving and McKenzie, 1989). In the 1979 sample of 60 suspects, a total of 165 tactics had been used. In 1986 the number of tactics used had fallen to 42 in 68 cases. This fall in the number of manipulative tactics used by the police was almost certainly due to the implementation of PACE, which is the first Act in England that attempted to provide a comprehensive code of police powers and practices for the investigation of crime (Bevan and Lidstone, 1985).

Between 1986 and 1987 the number of tactics used at the Brighton Police Station rose from 42 to 88, which may have been due to the diminishing of initial rigidity in applying the new rules. However, the number of tactics observed was still below that observed in 1979. In the 1986 and 1987 samples, the most persuasive tactics were used in the more serious cases. Nevertheless, the rate of admissions for the most serious crimes fell in 1986 and 1987. This left Irving and McKenzie with confusing findings. They concluded:

> "Either some of the essential power of the tactics used was destroyed by the cumbersome note-taking procedure, or by the general reduction in the potential of custody conditions to produce compliance, or by a combination of both. The advent of tape-recording will partly resolve these issues because skilled interrogators in serious cases will be able to get back to their previous standard of performance" (Irving and McKenzie, 1989, p. 182).

The main conclusion is that the new Act appears to have markedly reduced the number of manipulative and persuasive tactics that police officers use when interrogating suspects, except perhaps in the most serious cases. The overall effect on the confession rate of suspects needs further research in the future.

The Walsh Study

Walsh (1982) examined the arrest and interrogation practices under the emergency legislation in Northern Ireland. The Royal Ulster Constabulary (RUC) had refused Walsh access to the records of interrogation, so instead he interviewed 60 people who had been subjected to custodial interrogation by the RUC between September 1980 and June 1981, in connection with suspected terrorist activities. Thirty subjects (50%) claimed to have requested access to a solicitor, and of these only seven (23%) were allowed access to one, but only after having been in custody for more than 48 hours. This means that none of the subjects was allowed access to a solicitor within 48 hours of arrest. All the subjects were released by the RUC without being charged. Of the total sample, 35% claimed to have been pressured to provide in the future information about the activities of others. Almost half (48%) of the sample alleged that they had been subjected to verbal abuse by the police during their interrogation. Two subjects claimed to have been physically beaten.

   In his paper, Walsh quotes some official statistics which indicate that the great majority of suspects (89%) who were interrogated in 1980 in connection with suspects' terrorist activities were released without being charged. According to Walsh, the corresponding figure for England and Wales, for all offences, was between 10 and 20%. Walsh's main conclusion was that the RUC had failed to implement many of the recommendations of the Bennett Committee in June 1979, including the absolute right of suspects to have access to a solicitor after having spent 48 hours in custody. The Bennett Committee had been set up to carry out an extensive official inquiry into police interrogation in Northern Ireland, following allegations that suspects were being beaten and tortured whilst in police custody. The allegations resulted in international publicity and condemnation.

   There is a fundamental weakness in Walsh's study, in that the information of the subjects about their arrest, interrogation and detention could not be verified by either the official record or an independent source. Furthermore, the sample selected was very small and may not have been representative of all those arrested. However, it remains a matter of public record that in the early 1970s the RUC were using interrogation techniques which amounted to torture (Shallice, 1974). Shallice argues that the techniques used in Ulster, which included isolation, sensory deprivation, "hooding" and other forms of torture, were aimed at completely breaking the suspects' resistance. As a result many suspects suffered long-term mental effects (Wade, 1972; Shallice, 1974).

The Research at the University of Kent

Researchers at the University of Kent have carried out a number of valuable projects into police interrogation (Williamson, 1990; Moston, 1990b; Moston, Stephenson and Williamson, 1990).

   The work of Williamson (1990) is particularly important in showing the growth of professionalism in the questioning of suspects following the implementation of the Police and Criminal Evidence Act (PACE) 1984, making it inherently less coercive. Consistent with the post-PACE studies of Irving and McKenzie (1989) and Brown (1989), fewer suspects are now being interrogated at night, there are fewer repeated interrogations, more suspects consult a solicitor prior to interrogation, and there is better recording of what is said during interrogation. However, it is evident from Williamson's (1990) study that: (a) the "appropriate adult" is extremely infrequently used (i.e. in only five out of 1627 cases); and (b) English police officers are generally reluctant to accept that suspects can and do sometimes make false confessions and they often appear to fail to appreciate the potentially deleterious effects of psychological vulnerabilities (e.g. mental handicap and mental illness) on the reliability of evidence. Furthermore, many police officers do not appear to know the difference between mental illness and mental handicap.

With the increasing use of tape-recorded police interviews in England it has become possible to study more objectively than before police–suspect interactions and behaviour. During contemporaneous note-taking, both the police and the suspect had time to think whilst questions were being transcribed. Moston (1990b) argues that contemporaneous note-taking resembles dictation, whereas tape-recorded interviews resemble a conversation. According to Moston, the transition from contemporaneous note-taking to tape-recording has resulted in major changes in police interviewing techniques.

Moston analysed over 400 taped police interviews which had been conducted by detectives in the Metropolitan Police Force. He found that the interviews typically began in one of two ways, which are referred to as "inquisitorial" and "accusatorial" strategies, respectively.

Inquisitorial strategies are aimed at general information gathering, whereas the accusatorial strategy focused on obtaining a confession. The choice of the initial strategy used appeared to relate to the interviewer's skills in interviewing as well as to the interrogator's assumptions about the suspect's guilt or innocence.

The purpose of the inquisitorial style of questioning at the beginning of interviews is to establish rapport with the suspect and to find out more about the suspect's general demeanour and reactions. Asking background questions, which are unrelated to the alleged offence, generally achieves these objectives.

Moston found that surprisingly few of the interrogators employ the inquisitorial style of questioning. Rather, the interrogator typically uses the confrontational (accusatorial) style of questioning where the emphasis is not to establish what happened, but to obtain a confession. There are three main ways in which the interrogator confronts a suspect. Firstly, there is "direct accusation", where the interrogator straightforwardly asks the suspect about his guilt or innocence (e.g. "Did you stab Joe Smith?"). Secondly, the evidence against the suspect is presented and an explanation is required, which takes the form of either an admission or a denial. Moston refers to this as the "evidence strategy". Thirdly, the interrogator combines the "evidence strategy" with "direct confrontation". This is referred to as "supported direct accusation" and is the most persuasive way of obtaining a confession.

Moston suggests that the "supported direct accusation" strategy can lead to false confession among suggestible or compliant suspects. Furthermore, if details of the crime have been communicated to the suspect at the beginning of the interview, which Moston argues is commonly the case, than it becomes virtually impossible to establish whether or not the suspect is simply echoing the earlier information given to him by the police. In other words, it becomes much more difficult to validate the confession because the suspect was not given the opportunity of spontaneously providing information which could be used to corroborate his confession.

Moston concludes that the manipulative police interviewing techniques identified by Irving (1980) 10 years previously have largely disappeared. He argues that this has occurred because of legal restrictions which make it more difficult for police officers to offer inducements as well as greater awareness about what constitutes psychological coercion. Not mentioned by Moston is the possibility that the tape-recording procedure itself has had an effect on police behaviour.

Moston argues that the manipulative form of interrogation used previously in England has been replaced by a confrontational style of questioning where suspects are directly accused of the alleged offence at the beginning of the interview and informed of the evidence against them. This, Moston suggests, indicates that present-day interrogators are seeking self-incriminating admissions rather than information of a more general kind. He further asserts that interrogators commonly lack the necessary skills to cope with suspects who do not readily come forward with a confession.

CONCLUSIONS

The main conclusion from this Chapter is that the tactics and techniques recommended in police interrogation manuals, like that of Inbau, Reid and Buckley (1986), are based on "psychological principles" which can be immensely effective in influencing the beliefs and decision-making of suspects during interrogation. The basic ingredient of the techniques involves the interrogator being able to "read" the signs of suspects' lying and "guilt", which forms the justification for manipulating them into confessing by playing on their vulnerabilities and using trickery and deceit.

There are five potential problems with these techniques. The first relates to the nature and extent of psychological coercion involved. There is no doubt that these techniques are inherently coercive in the sense that their objective is to overcome the suspects' resistance and will-power not to incriminate themselves. In other words, suspects are manipulated and persuaded to confess when they would otherwise not have done so.

It is, of course, perfectly true that no police interrogation is completely free of coercion, nor will it ever be. Furthermore, a certain amount of persuasion is often needed for effective interrogation. The real issue is about the extent and nature of the manipulation and persuasion used.

The second problem relates to ethical and professional issues. Many of the tactics and techniques recommended encourage the police officer to employ trickery, deceit and dishonesty. Although such measures are commonly allowed in American Supreme Court judgements, they raise very serious questions about the ethical nature of this form of interrogation. Public awareness of this kind of police behaviour must inevitably lose the public's respect for the professionalism of police officers. In addition, recent evidence from my own research (Gudjonsson and Petursson, 1991a) indicates that when suspects feel that they have been induced to confess by unfair means they retain strong feelings of resentment towards the police, even many years afterwards.

The third problem is what may happen when interrogators misread the "lie signs" of suspects, assuming them to be guilty of a crime of which they are totally innocent. Indeed, many interrogators appear to have "blind faith" in the use of non-verbal signs of deception. The empirical evidence clearly shows that non-verbal signs are very unreliable indicators of deception (Ekman, 1985). Innocent suspects may be manipulated to confess falsely, and in view of the subtlety of the techniques utilized innocent suspects may actually come to believe that they are guilty. Inbau, Reid and Buckley state that their techniques, when applied in accordance with their recommendations, never result in a false confession, but they provide no evidence for this. Their failure to accept the possibility that false confessions can occur shows a limited insight into the potentially deleterious effects of their techniques.

The fourth problem relates to the ways in which psychological manipulations during interrogation may adversely influence the perceptions of judges and jurors when they listen to the police evidence in court.

Finally, police manuals are based on experience rather than objective and scientific data. Experience is invaluable to police work and its usefulness is illustrated by the effectiveness of the techniques recommended. However, relying solely upon experience in determining procedure may create serious pitfalls (e.g. untested assumptions) and fail to bring to light important facts about human behaviour, such as the susceptibility of some suspects to give erroneous information when placed under interrogative pressure. What is needed is more research into the effectiveness and pitfalls of different interrogation techniques.

Police interrogators in England are not trained in the tactics and techniques recommended by Inbau, Reid and Buckley. Nevertheless, it appears that some of the tactics are to a certain extent used by English police officers. Irving (1980) believed that these tactics were effective in producing confessions, even when they did not appear to be well tuned in to the suspects' personality and weaknesses. With the implementation of the Police and Criminal Evidence

Act in January 1986, manipulative tactics appear to have been markedly reduced, except perhaps in the most serious crimes. With the introduction of routine tape-recording their use may be further reduced. It seems that the persuasive interrogation style of the past has been replaced by a confrontational type of questioning which is less manipulative in nature. The effect on the confession rate among criminal suspects is unclear at present.

CHAPTER 4

Why Do Suspects Confess?

There are typically serious consequences that follow a self-incriminating admission or confession. The more serious the crime, the more severe the consequences are likely to be for the offender concerned. Commonly, the offenders' self-esteem and integrity are adversely affected, their freedom and liberty are at stake, and there may be financial and other penalties. Bearing in mind the potentially deleterious consequences of confessing to the police, it is perhaps surprising to find that a substantial proportion of all suspects confess during custodial interrogation. Zimbardo (1967) goes as far as to suggest that more than 80% of all crimes are solved by the suspect making a confession, and once a confession has been made defendants are seldom acquitted. Even though Zimbardo's comments are unsubstantiated, and probably exaggerated, they emphasize the fact that confessions are commonly made and form an important part of the evidence brought against the defendant when the case goes to court.

The objective of this Chapter is to provide the reader with empirical findings and theoretical models which help to explain why people confess to crimes, either spontaneously or for which they are being interrogated. It will become evident that there are varied reasons why suspects confess, and often a combination of factors needs to be considered. These relate to the circumstances and characteristics of the case, police behaviour and custodial factors, and the attitude, personality and experiences of the suspect.

HOW COMMONLY DO SUSPECTS CONFESS?

There are several studies which indicate that the many suspects interrogated at police stations sooner or later confess to the crime of which they are accused. A further proportion of suspects make self-incriminating admissions which do not quite amount to a full confession. The admission or confession may be obtained orally ("verbal admissions"), in writing ("written admissions"), or both orally and verbally. As we saw in Chapter 3, police interrogations in Britain are increasingly being tape-recorded.

"Verbal confessions" which are not accompanied by written confessions can be problematic, unless they are tape-recorded, because understandably subjects more readily retract such confessions, sometimes denying that they ever made them in the first place. The police, by knowledge of the previous record of the suspect, and by their perception of the total circumstances of case, which may not be admitted as evidence, could easily become convinced of the guilt of the suspect whilst appreciating the absence of hard evidence required to secure a conviction. In such cases, some officers may be tempted to secure what they regard as justice by "fitting up" suspects; that is, augmenting the existing evidence by claiming that suspects made verbal admissions which they subsequently refused to put into writing (e.g. Kirby, 1989; Graef, 1990; Miller, 1990).

Confessions may also consist of offenders confessing to "unsolved" offences whilst interrogated. Such offences may be "taken into consideration" (commonly referred to as "TIC") when the suspect's case eventually goes to court. Police officers may encourage such confessions in order to improve their clear-up rate.

What we are discussing in this Chapter are primarily confessions, oral, written or tape-recorded, which are obtained by the police during custodial interrogation.

The reported frequency with which suspects confess to crimes during interrogation varies somewhat from study to study. One reason for this is that definitions of a "confession" may vary. For example, many self-incriminating admissions may fall short of a full-blown confession. In one study they may be pooled together with full confessions. In another study they may be kept separate. However, in spite of the difficulties involved in comparing confession rates across studies, it is useful to have some approximation of the frequency with which suspects "confess" to crimes, or make serious self-incriminating admissions, during interrogation. Table 4.1 gives the proportions of suspects who made confessions in different studies.

Evaluating the results purely in terms of full confession, the highest confession rates are found in the Zander (1979) and Mitchell (1983) studies, and the lowest in the Neubauer (1974), Softley (1980), and Moston, Stephenson and Williamson (1990) studies. This means that the confession rates for the different studies range from 42 to 76%. In addition to these confessions, a certain proportion of suspects made self-incriminating admissions which fell short of full confessions. For example, in the Mitchell study 14% of the subjects had made self-incriminating admissions in addition to the 71% who had fully confessed. This means that 85% of the defendants had some kind of damaging self-incriminating statements in the committal papers when the case went to court. Similarly, in the Softley study 14% of the defendants had made admissions which fell short of full confession. This brings their self-incriminating-statement rate up to nearly 61%.

There are problems in evaluating the findings of Zander (1979), Irving (1980) and Irving and McKenzie (1989), in that no clear distinction appears to have

Table 4.1. The proportion of suspects who confess or make admissions during custodial interrogation

Study	Exercised rights to silence (%)	Country of origin	Type of study	Sample size	Proportion of suspects who make admissions or a confession (%)
Baldwin and McConville (1980)	5	England	Crown Court files	282	76
Irving (1980)	?	England	Observational	60	68
Irving and McKenzie (1989)	?	England	Observational	68 (1986 sample)	65
				68 (1987 sample)	46
Moston, Stephenson and Williamson (1990)	16	England	Observational/ from tape-recordings	1067	42
Mitchell (1983)	?	England	Crown Court files	394	71
Neubauer (1974)	?	USA	Case files	248	47
Softley (1980)	12	England	Observational	187	48
Zander (1979)	4	England	Crown Court files	282	76

been made between full confession statements and self-incriminating admissions. The authors seem to use the terms "confession" and "admission" interchangeably. The confession rates given in Table 4.1 for their studies may therefore be somewhat inflated when compared with the rates for the other studies, because they include admissions as well as full confessions.

There is one further factor which should be taken into account when evaluating the data in Table 4.1. The studies with the highest confession rates may be biased in that they included only suspects who were subsequently charged and committed to the Crown Court for trial. The Mitchell (1983), Baldwin and McConville (1980), and Zander (1979) studies fall into this category. The Mitchell study was concerned with cases heard at the Worcester Crown Court in 1978, Baldwin and McConville looked at Crown Court cases in London and Birmingham, and Zander looked at a sample of cases heard at the Old Bailey. It could well be that the proportion of defendants who are charged and committed for trial is higher for those who confess than for those who make no self-incriminating admissions or confessions. In fact, it would be expected that the great majority of those suspects who confess are likely to be charged because of the increased likelihood of securing a conviction when the case goes to court. Irving and McKenzie (1989) found that suspects who made self-incriminating admissions are about three times more likely to be charged than those who made no admissions. Similarly, Neubauer (1974) found that a confession affects the disposal of cases and how suspects plead.

Moston, Stephenson and Williamson (1990) used three types of outcome in their study: *confession, denial,* and *neither confession nor denial.* In the study, 177 suspects (17%) chose to remain silent and make neither a confession nor a denial. The importance of this study is that it was conducted after the implementation of the Police and Criminal Evidence Act (PACE) in England and Wales, and consists of tape-recorded interviews conducted by Metropolitan police officers. Comparing the 42% confession rate in this study with rates in the Softley (1980) and Irving (1980) studies indicates that somewhat fewer suspects are now confessing in England than previously. Irving and McKenzie (1989) found some marked differences in the admission rate for the years 1986 and 1987, as is evident from Table 4.1. These authors note that the admission rate has fallen most for serious offences, where in fact the most persuasive interrogation techniques are generally found to be used.

These findings indicate that with the introduction of PACE, and the more recent use of tape-recordings, somewhat fewer suspects are confessing. This change could be attributed to at least two different factors. Firstly, the implementation of PACE and the increased use of tape-recordings could mean that police officers are more restricted in the type of interrogation techniques they use (Irving and McKenzie 1989), and this in turn may influence the frequency with which suspects confess. Secondly, Moston, Stephenson and Williamson (1990) argued that there appears to be a general mistrust of police questioning, which may reduce the number of suspects who make confessions. If true, this may be related to changes in social attitudes towards the police, which encourage protests about wrongful conviction and resistance to interrogation.

THE CHARACTERISTICS OF SUSPECTS WHO CONFESS

It is evident from this discussion that not all suspects interrogated by the police confess to the crimes of which they are accused. Undoubtedly, some do not confess because they are innocent of the alleged offence. Others, probably a very small minority, confess to crimes they did not commit. This small subgroup of suspects is discussed in detail in Chapters 10, 11 and 12.

Are certain types of suspect more likely to confess than others? There is evidence from various studies that this is indeed the case. It is the purpose of this section of the Chapter to review the evidence for some of the most noticeable characteristics that separate those who confess during interrogation from those who are able to resist doing so.

1. Age and Confessions

Age is often considered as an indirect measure of maturity and, as Neubauer (1974) points out, more mature suspects would be expected to cope better with the unfamiliarity and demands of police interrogation than less mature suspects. Is there a relationship between age and the readiness to confess? Yes, there is some evidence that younger suspects are more likely to confess to the police during interrogation than older suspects, but this has not been found in all studies.

Leiken (1970) found in Colorado that 42.9% of suspects under the age of 25 had made confessions under police interrogation, compared with 18.2% of older suspects. Softley (1980), in an English study, found that 53% of suspects over 21 years of age made admissions or confessions, compared with 68% of those below the age of 21. The difference was statistically significant. Most important, however, was the frequency with which juveniles confessed. Of 38 juveniles in the study, 30 (79%) made admissions or confessions.

The clearest example of a negative linear relationship between frequency of confessions and age comes from the British study of Baldwin and McConville (1980). The study was carried out in two major English cities, London and Birmingham. The samples comprised Crown Court cases. It is clear from the figures given by Baldwin and McConville that there is a consistent and significant trend for suspects to confess less the older they are. This trend was the same in the two cities studied and for both verbal and written confessions.

What are the interpretations that can be drawn from these findings? First, the younger the suspect, the easier it is to obtain a confession from him or her. Second, there appears to be no clear cut-off point with regard to age. That is, it is not the case that after a certain age (e.g. 21 years) suspects have reached their ceiling of resistance. In fact, they continue to become increasingly more resistant as they grow older. Presumably, there is an upper age limit, after which suspects' ability to resist the pressures of interrogation begins to decline again. In other words, it is likely that age will reach its peak in terms of resistance. For example, the very old and frail suspect would be expected to cope less well with interrogation than the younger suspect.

What are the factors that make suspects become less likely to confess with age? A number of different factors could be responsible. One factor suggested by Leiken (1970) is that older suspects are better equipped psychologically to cope with the demand characteristics of the interrogative situation, because of greater life experience. This interpretation is consistent with the results of a study by Gudjonsson (1988a), who found a highly significant relationship between the type of coping strategy utilized by people and their ability to resist interrogative pressure. It is possible that natural maturation and experience of life help the suspect to cope with a demanding situation such as a police interrogation.

Another explanation, provided by Baldwin and McConville (1980), is that older suspects are more likely to understand and assert their legal rights during interrogation. This could be investigated by looking at the differences between younger and older suspects in the extent to which they insist on their legal rights during interrogation. For example, younger suspects may be more likely to waive their right to have access to a solicitor than older suspects.

Temperamental differences related to age may also be important. For example, such factors as neuroticism, impulsiveness and venturesomeness are negatively correlated with age (Eysenck and Eysenck, 1978; Gudjonsson and Adlam, 1983) and these are the types of factor that may make some suspects confess more readily.

There have been studies which have not found age to be a significant factor. For example, Mitchell (1983) found no significant variation in the confession rate for defendants up to the age of 50 years. After the age of 50 markedly fewer defendants confessed. Neubauer (1974) gathered data on 248 criminal defendants in Prairie City and found no significant difference in confession rates between minors (16–20 years) and adults (21 years or older). The confession rates for the two age groups were 50 and 44%, respectively. More recently, Moston, Stephenson and Williamson (1990) found no simple relationship between age and the frequency with which suspects confess. However, taking the evidence against them into account some interesting findings emerged, which indicates that younger suspects tended to deny involvement in offences more frequently when the evidence against them was strong, whereas this trend was reversed when the evidence against them was only moderate.

Older suspects more commonly used their right to silence when the evidence against them was strong. The authors concluded that juveniles tend to rely on inappropriate "escape" strategies when faced with strong evidence against them.

The differences between the studies with regard to age are difficult to interpret. Whether they are caused by differences in the measurement of "confession" or sampling bias, as Neubauer (1974) speculates, remains to be seen. The findings of Moston and his colleagues indicate that age should not be considered in isolation from other salient variables; which may act as important intervening variables in their association with confession.

2. Type of Offence and Confessions

Do suspects confess more readily to some types of offence than others? There is some evidence that this may be the case.

Neubauer (1974) found that suspects interrogated about property offences (e.g. theft, burglary, forgery) confessed more often (56%) than those suspected of non-property offences (e.g. violent offences) (32%).

Mitchell (1983) found that suspects interrogated about sexual offences confessed most readily. With an overall confession rate of 70% in the study, the rate for suspected sexual offenders was 89.3% in contrast to 52.5% for non-sexual offenders. Suspects also appeared to confess more readily to property offences (76%) than to violent offences (64%), which is consistent with the findings of Neubauer (1974).

Neubauer (1974) argues that the main reason for the greater number of confessions among alleged property offenders than other offenders relates to the nature of the evidence that the police have at the time of the interrogation. He states that with regard to property offences there is more often forensic evidence (e.g. fingerprints) to link the suspect with the alleged offence than in non-property offences. This means that during interrogation the police have more persuasive evidence to convince the suspect that denials are futile. The position may be somewhat different with regard to sexual offenders, in that there could be special psychological reasons that facilitate their confession-making behaviour. This point will be taken up again later in this Chapter when discussing the results from a recent Icelandic study into factors that may facilitate or inhibit confessing among criminals.

3. Previous Convictions and Confessions

It would be expected that the more experience suspects have had of police interrogation, the less likely they are to confess. In other words, suspects who have had several previous convictions would: (a) be expected to be more likely to know and to assert their legal rights; (b) be expected to be more familiar with the probable consequences of making self-incriminating admissions; and (c) be more familiar with the police environment and interrogations.

Supporting the above expectancy, Neubauer (1974) found that suspects with previous convictions were less likely than first offenders to: (a) sign the custody interview form advising them of their legal rights; and (b) confess to the alleged offence. This indicates that first offenders are more compliant at the police station than offenders with previous convictions.

Further support comes from an important observational study in four English police stations. Softley (1980) found a significant difference in the rate of confession among suspects who had previous convictions at the time of the interrogation and those without previous convictions. Among suspects without previous convictions, 76% had made either a self-incriminating admission or a full confession, compared with only 59% of those suspects with a criminal record.

Moston, Stephenson and Williamson (1990) found a bivariable interaction of the strength of evidence between previous convictions and confession, relating to both conviction number and evidential strength. That is, generally confessions rise steadily in accordance with the strength of evidence that the police have against the suspect, but the rate of increase in the frequency of confessions is related to previous convictions. For example, there was no overall difference in the rate of confession between those with and without previous convictions. Yet when the evidence against the suspect was strong, those without previous convictions were significantly more ready to confess (78%) than those with previous convictions (59%).

One American and one English study have found no significant relationship between previous convictions and the rate of confession among criminal suspects (Leiken, 1970; Zander, 1979), and two English studies found an unexpected positive relationship between the rate of confession and previous confessions (Baldwin and McConville, 1980; Mitchell, 1983).

Baldwin and McConville (1980) found that suspects with previous convictions were more likely to make verbal or written confessions than suspects who had no previous convictions. This was particularly true in their London sample. Similarly, Mitchell (1983), in his Worcester study, found that suspects with previous experience of the criminal process tended to confess more readily than those without such experience.

What factors account for the discrepancy between these findings? Mitchell (1983) suggests two possible explanations for the positive relationship he found. Firstly, he speculates that suspects with previous convictions may more readily appreciate the advantages of confessing. Secondly, suspects with previous convictions may be less equipped to cope with police interrogations.

With regard to the first point, Mitchell does not spell out what advantages he has in mind for those who confess. For most suspects it is unlikely to be in their own interest to confess. The second point Mitchell makes seems rather strange, because it is not at all clear why suspects with previous convictions should find it more difficult to cope with the demands of police interrogation. There are a number of possible reasons for this. They include:

1. Suspects with previous convictions having been "traumatized" by their previous interrogation experiences and subsequently giving in more easily (I have seen such cases but it is doubtful that it holds for the majority of suspects);

2. Those suspects who persist in crime possess certain idiosyncratic characteristics (e.g. low intelligence) that make them generally less able to cope with interrogative pressure;
3. Suspects with previous convictions believing it is futile to deny their involvement in crimes;
4. Confessions may be easier to make after suspects have confessed once; e.g. first offenders may find it particularly inhibiting to confess because their reputation is at stake and they do not wish to be labelled as a criminal. "Labelling", of course, has been argued by Matza (1967) to be an important factor in the development of a criminal career. It could be applied to confessions in the sense that once labelled as a criminal, the suspect has less to "lose" in terms of his reputation than he did during his first interrogation.

An important factor raised by Firth (1975) is that the potential resistance effect of previous convictions may be offset by the more persistent and determined interrogation of suspects with previous convictions. In other words, a previous conviction may make police officers more convinced of the suspect's guilt, which results in more determined and persistent interrogation.

If Firth's suggestion is correct, one might expect to find least confounding effects of previous convictions during interrogations that are under observation by researchers. The reason for this is that police officers may control their interrogation tactics and techniques more when their behaviour is being observed. This is likely to result in more uniform methods of interrogation, irrespective of the number of previous convictions. This is exactly what one finds. For example, the strongest negative relationship between previous convictions and confessions was found in the Softley (1980) study. One possible interpretation is that direct observation affects the behaviour of the interrogators, which prevents or inhibits them from placing relatively more pressure on suspects with previous convictions.

There are, of course, important methodological issues that need to be considered when evaluating the outcomes from different studies. For example, different interrogation techniques, the duration and intensity of the interrogation, the policies adopted at different police stations, and the nature of the alleged offence, may potentially confound the results from the various studies quoted above and lead to inconsistent results. The study of Moston, Stephenson and Williamson (1990) provides a beginning, and an important methodology, for addressing these issues in future studies.

LEGAL ADVICE

In recent years there has been increasing emphasis on informing suspects of their legal rights. The most important of these are the right to silence (i.e. suspects are not obliged to say anything to the police unless they wish to do so and therefore can refuse to answer a question put to them) and the right to legal advice prior to and during interrogation. Being informed of these rights does not mean that suspects necessarily understand them (Grisso, 1980; Gudjonsson, 1991b), and even if they do understand them they may choose or be persuaded by the police to waive their legal rights (Leiken, 1970). The purpose of these legal rights is to protect the suspect against self-incrimination.

Some authors of police interrogation books and manuals seem to view the rights to silence and legal advice as a hindrance to successful police interrogation (Inbau, Reid and Buckley, 1986; Macdonald and Michaud, 1987). For example, the latter authors make the following recommendation to interrogators:

> "Do not make a big issue of advising the suspect of his rights. Do it quickly, do it briefly, and do not repeat it" (p. 17).

What proportion of suspects exercise their legal right to silence? According to Irving (1980):

> "To remain silent in a police interview room in the face of determined questioning by an officer with legitimate authority to carry on this activity requires an abnormal exercise of will" (p. 153).

It is perhaps for this reason that suspects have been traditionally reluctant or unable to exercise their right to silence.

Softley (1980), in an early observational study in four English police stations, found that of 187 suspects interrogated, 12% exercised their right to silence to a certain extent. Four per cent refused to answer all salient questions pertaining to the alleged crime. Older suspects were significantly more likely to exercise their right to silence, although it is worth noting that the great majority of suspects in all age groups did not exercise their right to silence. Similarly, suspects with previous convictions more frequently exercised their legal right to silence than those without previous convictions.

Other early studies support the infrequent use of the right to silence prior to or during custodial interrogation. Zander (1979) found that 4% of his sample had used their right of silence. Baldwin and McConville (1980) found that about 5% of their two samples made no statements of any kind to the police. Mitchell (1983) found that less than 1% of their sample made no statement of any sort.

There is some evidence that suspects are increasingly requesting, and being allowed access to, legal advice prior to custodial interrogation. In England, PACE markedly strengthens the suspect's right to legal advice during custodial interrogation (Irving and McKenzie, 1989). Irving and McKenzie, in their observational studies at an English police station in 1986 and 1987, found that of the 136 suspects observed about 30% had had legal advice prior to the interrogation. Unfortunately, in the original study at Brighton Police Station, Irving (1980) made no mention of the number of suspects who had legal advice prior to or during their custodial interrogation. It is surprising that such an important factor as legal advice played no part in the original study. Similar omission was made in the study conducted by Baldwin and McConville (1980). One possible explanation for this apparently serious omission, which is supported by other English studies (Zander, 1972; Softley, 1980; Mitchell, 1983), is that legal advice was infrequently requested or allowed before the implementation of PACE in 1986.

Marked hindrance by the police in allowing suspects access to a solicitor is reported by Walsh (1982), who conducted a study of arrests and interrogation practice in Northern Ireland. Fifty per cent of the sample studied reported that they had requested a solicitor. Of these 76% claimed that they were refused access to a solicitor and the 12% who were eventually allowed to see a solicitor had to wait more than 48 hours. In other words, no suspect was allowed access to a solicitor within 48 hours of arrest! Similar findings are reported for the USA by Leiken (1970), who found in a reasonably comprehensive study, that after the implementation of the "Miranda" warning (i.e. a formal warning against self-incrimination), 67% of suspects claimed to have requested a solicitor, but only 6% were allowed to have one. Leiken concluded that:

> "The police are able to somehow effectively frustrate the right to counsel, despite the suspects' knowledge of their rights and their attempts to assert them" (p. 27).

The recent study by Moston, Stephenson and Williamson (1990), which involved the analysis of tape-recorded police interrogations in the London Metropolitan area, supports the findings of Irving and McKenzie (1989) that in recent years suspects are more frequently being allowed access to a solicitor. In their study, which involved 1067 subjects, 41% had had legal advice prior to the interrogation. This sometimes involved being given legal advice over the telephone. It is also noteworthy that 177 suspects (16%) used their right to silence.

Moston, Stephenson and Williamson (1990) looked at "The incidence, antecedents and consequences of the use of the right to silence during police questioning" (p. 1). The study followed two previous reports into rights to silence following the implementation of PACE (Home Office, 1989; Williamson, 1990), where it had been found that in London and West Yorkshire, 23 and 12% of suspects, respectively, had used their rights not to answer at least some questions. The figures went up to 46 and 23%, respectively, for subjects who had had legal advice prior to the interrogation.

Moston, Stephenson and Williamson (1990) assessed various aspects of right to silence by having detectives at 10 Metropolitan police stations complete a questionnaire about each interview conducted on suspects. Seven key background variables were additionally recorded:

- Strength of evidence against the subject;
- The seriousness of the offence;
- Type of offence;
- Age of suspect;
- Sex of suspect;
- Criminal history;
- Use of legal advice.

A total of 1117 cases were recorded, which was about 90% of the cases intended for the study. The outcome of each case was also monitored and showed that 16% of the subjects had used their right to silence. Of those, half refused to answer any questions and the remainder refused to answer some. Great variation was found between different police stations in the use of silence; e.g. at Holborn only 8% of suspects used their right to silence, in contrast to 25% at Uxbridge. The authors suggest that both police tactics and the behaviour of solicitors may vary from station to station and affect the extent to which suspects exercise their right to silence.

Moston and his colleagues found that certain case and background variables predicted the use of the right to silence. The use of right to silence was associated with the seriousness of the offence, previous convictions and access to legal advice, but it did not adversely affect the decision to prosecute or their plea of "guilty" when the case went to court. Those who used their right to silence were more likely to be convicted than those who denied the offence during interrogation. The authors suggest that the use of silence may not always be to the advantage of the suspect.

A recent study by Sanders and Bridges (1989) looks at the operation of the legal advice provisions of PACE. They found that about 25% of suspects actually request legal advice prior to or during interrogation. Of those requests, about 80% are successful, which indicates that about 20% of the suspects in the study are actually allowed access to a solicitor. According to the authors, their figures are very similar to those previously obtained in a Home Office survey.

The studies reviewed above indicate that, at least as far as England is concerned, more suspects are now being allowed access to a solicitor prior to interrogation than 10 years ago. This is undoubtedly due to the influence of PACE, and the gradual introduction of tape-recording which became standard police practice in England and Wales in 1991 (Home Office, 1988).

THEORETICAL MODELS OF CONFESSION

There are a number of theoretical models that have attempted to explain the mechanisms and processes that facilitate a confession during custodial interrogation. Five different models or theoretical orientations are reviewed in this Chapter. Each model looks at confessions from a different perspective, and taken together the models provide an important insight into the reasons why suspects tend to confess during custodial interrogation.

1. The Reid Model of Confession

Jayne (1986) provides an informative model for understanding the process which results in a confession during interrogation. The model is based upon the "nine steps" of interrogation discussed in detail in Chapter 3. Jayne refers to the model as the "Reid model" because it was developed by John E. Reid and Associates of Chicago. The model attempts to explain why the "nine steps" of interrogation are successful in eliciting confessions.

The model construes interrogation as the psychological undoing of deception. Criminal deception is primarily motivated by avoidance behaviour; that is, avoiding the likely or possible consequences of being truthful. The two types of consequence of being caught in deception are labelled "real" and "personal". *Real* consequences generally involve loss of freedom or financial penalties. *Personal* consequences involve lowered self-esteem and damaged integrity. Having to admit to criminal behaviour is embarrassing to most people and this makes it difficult for them to confess.

Successful deception is reinforced in accordance with operant conditioning principles. Thus, undetected lying is rewarding and increases the chances of further lying. However, successful socialization teaches people that it is wrong to lie and when lying occurs people may experience an internal conflict, comprising feelings of frustration and anxiety. The increased level of anxiety associated with lying induces the person to confess. Least internal anxiety is generated by telling the truth. The level of anxiety is assumed to increase linearly from omission to evasion to blatant denial. As the level of anxiety increases, the person copes by the operation of defence mechanisms which function to reduce anxiety and restore self-esteem. The two main defence mechanisms relevant to interrogation are "rationalization", which serves to help the offender by avoiding full responsibility for the offence (i.e. the offender somehow rationalizes the offence), and "projection", which means that the offender attributes blame for the offence to some external source (e.g. the victim). Both rationalization and projection serve to distort the account of what really happened.

According to the model, a suspect confesses (i.e. tells the truth) when the perceived consequences of a confession are more desirable than the anxiety generated by the deception (i.e. denial). The perceived consequences and perceived anxiety can be manipulated psychologically by the interrogator. Thus:

> "[the] goal of the interrogation . . . is to decrease the suspect's perception of the consequences of confessing, while at the same time increasing the suspect's internal anxiety associated with his deception" (Jayne, 1986, p. 332).

Jayne (1986) argues that there are three basic concepts relevant to the interrogator's manipulation of perceptions of consequences and anxiety.

These are "expectancy", "persuasion" and "belief". *Expectancy* refers to what is perceived by the suspects as desirable. At the beginning of an interrogation confessing is generally construed as highly undesirable. *Persuasion* is a way of changing the suspect's view of what is desirable ("expectancy" change) and his basic "beliefs in the structure of internal messages that tend to support or refute an expectancy" (p. 333).

According to the model, there are four essential criteria for changing the suspect's expectancies and beliefs:

1. The information provided by the interrogator must be perceived as credible; this is made up of perceived sincerity and trust which is communicated through subtle means to the suspect.

2. The interrogator develops insight into the suspect's attitudes and weaknesses. It is particularly important to assess what consequences the suspect thinks he is avoiding by denial and what his propensity for anxiety tolerance is. Thus:

   > "The goal of the interrogation is to affect perceived consequences and anxiety, this information directs the selection of themes, the timing of alternatives, and the identification of the most appropriate anxiety-enhancement statements" (p. 335).

3. The suspect needs to internalize the interrogator's suggestions. This involves a three-stage process. First, the suspect must comprehend the interrogator's ideas (this is called "relating"). Second, the suspect must accept the message communicated by the interrogator (called "accepting"). Third, the suspect must internalize or believe the interrogator's suggestions.

4. The interrogator must constantly observe whether or not the suspect is accepting the theme suggested, whether the suspect needs more anxiety-enhancement, and if the timing of presentation of an alternative is right. Persuasion is construed as a dynamic process that needs to be regulated according to the strengths and vulnerabilities of the suspect. Jayne states that it is most difficult to elicit a confession from suspects with high tolerance for anxiety and guilt manipulation.

Jayne recommends a number of manipulative ploys that can be used by interrogators to reduce the perceived consequences of confessing during interrogation. This is mainly achieved by presenting the suspect with themes that increase self-deception and cognitive distortion through the use of two principal psychological mechanisms called "rationalization" and "projection". These two "defence mechanisms" enable the person to deal with threatening experiences by a form of self-deception of which he or she is unaware. In the case of interrogation either or both of these processes can reduce anxiety by altering the suspect's perceptions of the likely consequences of self-incriminating admissions. In Chapter 2 we saw that self-deception enhances psychological well-being and that cognitive distortion operates by making offenders rationalize and justify their criminal act. What the interrogator is doing is enhancing the natural tendency of offenders to employ defence mechanisms to justify their crimes and maintain their self-esteem.

Jayne states that, in general, rationalization and projection are most effective in reducing the perceptions concerning the *real* consequences for the criminal behaviour, whereas the ploy of using sympathy and compassion are relatively more effective in overcoming inhibitions about the perceptions of *personal* consequences.

Increasing perceived anxiety about persisting with denials is achieved through psychological manipulation that concentrates on making the suspect turn his anxiety inwards rather than outwards. Outwardly turned anxiety (e.g. suspiciousness, anger, hatred) inhibits confession-enhancing behaviours, whereas playing on the suspect's feelings of guilt and shame increases the kind of anxiety that commonly results in a confession.

2. A Decision-making Model of Confession

Hilgendorf and Irving (1981) present an interesting conceptual model for understanding some of the factors that make suspects confess to the crime of which they are accused. The foundation for their model derives from an extensive review of the interrogation process, which was commissioned by the Royal Commission on Criminal Procedure (Irving and Hilgendorf, 1980). Hilgendorf and Irving argue that one of the main advantages of their model is that it is "closely linked to the legal concepts of voluntariness and oppression" (p. 81).

The basic premise of the model is that when suspects are interrogated they become engaged in a complicated and demanding decision-making process. Some of the basic decisions that the suspect has to make relate to:

- Whether to speak or remain silent;
- Whether to make self-incriminating admissions or not;
- Whether to tell the truth or not;
- Whether to tell whole truth or only part of the truth;
- How to answer the questions asked by the police interrogator.

Applying the decision-making model of Luce (1967) to the police interrogation situation, Hilgendorf and Irving argue that decisions are determined by:

1. Perceptions of the available courses of action. The assumption here is that the suspect has more than one course of action open to him and has to choose between them.

2. Perceptions concerning the probabilities of the likely occurrence of various consequences attached to these courses of action. These are referred to as "subjective probabilities".
3. The utility values or gains attached to these courses of action.

These factors indicate that suspects have to consider the kind of options there are available to them. They have then to evaluate the likely consequences attached to these various options. For example, if they confess, are they likely to be charged with the offence of which they are accused? If they insist on their innocence, is the interrogation likely to continue?

The decision-making of the suspect is governed by the *subjective probabilities of occurrence of the perceived consequences*. In other words, decisions are not based on what is objectively, or even realistically, likely to happen. It is what the suspect *believes* at the time to be the likely consequences that influences his behaviour. This means that one cannot assume that the suspect objectively considers the serious legal consequences of making a self-incriminating confession. An innocent suspect may confess under the misguided belief that, since he or she is innocent, no court will bring in a guilty verdict and that the truth will eventually come out.

The suspect has to balance the potential consequences against the perceived value ("utilities") of choosing a particular course of action. For example, would a confession inevitably lead to cessation of interrogation and would the suspect be allowed to go home? After confessing would visits from the family be allowed? Hilgendorf and Irving argue that threats and inducements, even when slight and implicit, can markedly influence the decision of the suspect to confess because of the perceived power the police have over the situation and the apparent credibility of their words.

Following the work of Janis (1959), Hilgendorf and Irving draw our attention to the important finding in the literature that decision-making is not just influenced by perceptions of utilitarian gains or losses; factors related to self- and social approval and disapproval can also be very important psychologically. Indeed, some authors, particularly those with psychoanalytic orientation (e.g. Reik, 1959; Rogge, 1975), emphasize the role of social and self-approval utilities in eliciting confessions. One illustration of the reasoning underlying the utilities of approval and disapproval is as follows. In general crime does not meet with social approval. Therefore confession involves the admission of a socially disapproved act. However, for the suspect not owning up to an offence allegedly committed by him can result in strong self and social disapproval. Conversely, being able to "get it off your chest", and accept punishment for what one has done, activates potential approval utilities.

Hilgendorf and Irving postulate that there are a number of social, psychological and environmental factors which can affect, or indeed seriously impair, the suspect's decision-making during police interrogation. On occasions these factors can undermine the reliability of the suspect's confession. The most salient factors are as follows:

1. The police can manipulate the social and self-approval utilities during interrogation in order to influence the decision-making of the suspect. In particular, the suspect's feelings of competence and his self-esteem are readily susceptible to manipulation. In view of the legitimate authority of police officers,

    ". . . the interrogation situation contains pressures on the suspect to give excessive emphasis in his decision-making to the approval or disapproval of the interrogator, and to be extremely sensitive to all communications, both verbal and non-verbal, which he receives from the interrogator" (p. 81).

2. The police interrogators can manipulate the suspect's perceptions of the likely outcome concerning a given course of action. One way of achieving this is by minimizing the seriousness of the alleged offence and by altering perceptions of "cost" associated with denial, resistance and deception.
3. The police interrogators can impair the suspect's ability to cope with information processing and decision-making by various means. For example they can, through social, psychological and environmental manipulation, increase the suspect's existing level of anxiety, fear and compliance. Personal threat is seen as an inherent part of any custodial interrogation and it can by itself raise levels of anxiety. Unfamiliarity and uncertainty are further anxiety-inducing factors. Social and physical isolation are seen as potentially powerful influences.

    "The situation of physical confinement by the police supports and facilitates these pressures and the effect becomes more pronounced the longer the total period of detention in police custody" (p. 81).

The Hilgendorf and Irving model relates to decision-making of suspects during custodial interrogation. It is not, strictly speaking, a model of false confession. However, the model highlights a number of important factors which can potentially render a confession unreliable.

3. A Cognitive-behavioural Model of Confession

I have argued elsewhere (Gudjonsson, 1989b) that confessions are best construed as arising through the existence of a particular relationship between the suspect, the environment and significant others within that environment. In order to understand that relationship it is helpful to look closely at the *antecedents* and the *consequences* of confessing behaviour within the framework of behavioural analysis. This represents a social learning theory approach to confession. Table 4.2 shows typical antecedents to a confession and the immediate and long-term consequences.

"Antecedents" refers to the kind of events that occur prior to interrogation. These are the factors that may trigger or facilitate the forthcoming confession. A large number of different factors may be relevant, such as fatigue, illness,

Table 4.2. The antecedents and consequences of confessions

Antecedents	Consequences	
	Immediate	Long-term
Social		
Isolation	Police approval, praise	Disapproval
Police pressure		
Emotional		
Distress	Feelings of relief	Feelings of guilt, shame
Cognitive		
"The police know I did it"	"It's good to get it off my chest"	"What is going to happen to me now?"
"The truth will come out in the end"	"My solicitor will sort it out"	"This is very serious"
"Perhaps I did do it, but I can't remember it"	"How could I have done such a dreadful thing?"	"I'm now certain I had nothing to do with it"
Situational		
Nature of the arrest	Charged, allowed access to a solicitor	Judicial proceedings
Confinement?		
Solicitor present?		
Caution understood?		
Familiarity with police procedures?		
Physiological		
Aroused physical state, inhibitions reduced by alcohol or drugs; drug withdrawal	Arousal reduction	Arousal returns to base level

deprivation of food and sleep, stress, social isolation, feelings of guilt and bereavement.

There are two major types of consequence, which are referred to in Table 4.2 as "immediate" (or "short-term") and "long-term" consequences. The immediate or short-term consequences occur within minutes or hours of the suspects confessing to the alleged crime. The long-term consequences take place within days, weeks or years of the suspects confessing. The types of consequence, whether immediate or delayed, depend on the nature and circumstances of the case and the psychological characteristics of the individual concerned.

The types of antecedents and consequences are construed in terms of *social, emotional, cognitive, situational* and *physiological* events. These types of events have been used to explain other types of behaviour, including delinquent behaviour (Stumphauzer, 1986).

Social Events

Table 4.2 gives two main types of social event that may trigger a confession. The first event refers to being isolated from one's family and friends. It was noted in Chapter 3 how much emphasis police manuals place on isolating the suspect from any external influence that may reduce a willingness to confess. The second type of social influence relates to the nature of the interrogation itself. The social process, as is so well illustrated by the Reid model described earlier in this Chapter, is an important factor in obtaining a confession from suspects.

The immediate consequence of confessing is social reinforcement by the police interrogators. The police may praise the suspect for owning up to what he has done. Visitors such as relatives may be allowed, and in some cases the suspect is allowed to go home. The long-term consequences commonly involve the defendant having to come to terms with social disapproval from the media and from the general public.

Emotional Events

Being arrested and brought to a police station is undoubtedly stressful for most suspects. Generally suspects can be expected to experience considerable levels of anxiety and distress. Some of the anxiety is caused by the uncertainty of the situation, the fear of what is going to happen at the police station, the fear of being locked in a police cell, and fear of the consequences regarding the alleged offence. A suspect who has committed a serious offence, possibly on impulse, may also be distressed by the fact of the conduct itself. Suspects who are experiencing bereavement at the time of their arrest are likely to be particularly vulnerable to emotional distress. For example, most suspects would find difficulty in coping with being interrogated in connection with the death of a close friend or family member.

There are two distinct emotional experiences that are particularly relevant to confessions; these are the feelings of *guilt* and *shame*. Within the context of confessions, shame is best viewed as a degrading and humiliating experience and it often accompanies a sense of exposure. In contrast, guilt is linked to the concept of conscience (i.e. it is associated with some real or imagined past transgression which is inconsistent with the person's internalized values and standards). There are theoretically marked motivational and behavioural differences between guilt and shame (Tangey, 1990). Whereas a feeling of guilt motivates people towards reparative action (i.e. confessing, apologizing, making amends), a feeling of shame has the reverse effect; it makes the person want to hide from others and not reveal what happened.

After confessing, suspects may experience a sense of emotional relief as the immediate pressure is lifted and there is greater certainty about their immediate future (Irving, 1980). Guilty suspects may in addition experience a relief from being able to talk about their offence. The police are often the first people suspects talk to about their crime. Before long, a feeling of shame sometimes sets in or becomes exacerbated, especially as the suspect may have to cope with unfavourable publicity about the case and begins to talk to friends and relatives about the crime.

Cognitive Events

Cognitive factors comprise the suspect's thoughts, interpretations, assumptions and perceived strategies of responding to a given situation. This kind of factor can very markedly influence behaviour. What is important to remember is that the suspects' behaviour during the interrogation is likely to be more influenced by their perceptions, interpretations and assumptions about what is happening than by the actual behaviour of the police. Table 4.2 lists the kind of self-statements that suspects may make during interrogation. Suspects who "talk" themselves into believing that the interrogators are not going to give up until they have given a confession, or believe that the police have sufficient evidence to "prove" that they committed the offence, may be greatly influenced by such thoughts and beliefs. For innocent people, the thought that the "truth" will eventually come out, even if they give in to persistent interrogation, can facilitate a false confession. Similarly, innocent suspects who begin to doubt their own recollections of events because they are confused during interrogation, may agree with the unfounded suggestions of the interrogator, and come to believe that they committed a crime of which they are in fact innocent. These are the so-called "coerced-internalized" false confessions discussed in detail in Chapters 10 and 11.

The immediate cognitive consequences may relate to thoughts associated with the easing of the pressure. For innocent suspects the thought (or hope) that their solicitor is going to sort everything out may predominate. Suspects who mistakenly come to believe that they have committed the offence of which they are accused may come to wonder how they could have committed such a terrible crime and have no recollection of it. Within days, after their confusional state has subsided, they may become fully convinced that they had nothing to do with it.

The most striking cognitive events associated with the potential long-term consequences of confession undoubtedly relate to suspects' thoughts about what is going to happen as the result of their self-incriminating confession. They begin to think about the seriousness of their predicament and this may make them inclined to retract their previously made confession.

Situational Events

Situational events are of many different kinds. The circumstances of the suspect's arrest (e.g. being arrested suddenly in the early hours of the morning) may affect the suspect's ability to cope with the subsequent interrogation, especially since this coincides with the nadir (i.e. lowest point) of the physiological cycle. Similarly, being locked up in a police cell for several hours or days may "soften up" suspects (i.e. weaken their resistance) and make them more responsive to interrogation. On the other hand, familiarity with police procedures and interrogation is likely to provide suspects with knowledge and experience which make them more able to understand and assert their rights.

The immediate situational consequence commonly associated with a confession is that the suspect is charged with the alleged offence, after which he is allowed access to a solicitor when this has been previously denied. The long-term consequences relate to possible prosecution and judicial proceedings.

Physiological Events

The physiological antecedent to a confession is undoubtedly heightened arousal, which includes increased heart rate, blood pressure, rate and irregularity of respiration, and perspiration. These occur because suspects are commonly apprehensive, worried and frightened. Once the suspect has confessed there is likely to be a sharp reduction in his level of physiological and subjective arousal because of greater certainty about the immediate future. Physiological arousal may then return to its normal level, although it should be noted that uncertainties about the pending court case and outcome may lead to an increased subjective and physiological state of arousal.

4. Psychoanalytic Models of Confession

Various psychodynamic models of the "need to confess" have been proposed. Such models rest upon the assumption that the feeling of guilt is the fundamental cause of confessions and false confessions. These psychoanalytic models are highly controversial, as the theses upon which they are based have limited acceptance in the scientific community.

Undoubtedly, the most detailed formulation is that offered by Reik (1959), which is based on books and papers written in Germany in the 1920s. Reik's work attempts to show that the unconscious compulsion to confess plays an important part in religion, myths, art, language and other social activities, including crime.

Reik relies heavily on Freud's concepts of the id, ego and superego. Within this framework a confession is construed as "an attempt at reconcilitation that the superego undertakes in order to settle the quarrel between the ego and the id" (p. 216). Here the superego is seen to play a very important part in the need of the individual to confess. If the superego remains silent, there develops a strong feeling of guilt and need for self-punishment. This may result in a "compulsion" to confess, and on occasion false confession.

The development of the feeling of guilt after transgression and the unconscious need for self-punishment are seen as universal characteristics of the individual and have an important impact upon his or her emotions and behaviour. It is only after the person has confessed that the ego begins to accept the emotional significance of the deed. For the criminal this is different to the intellectual acceptance of the deed, which always precedes its emotional acceptance. According to Reik's psychoanalytic model, emotional acceptance of the criminal act may take years to process. It is only after having confessed that the offender has made the first step back into society. A confession serves the function of relieving the person from the feeling of guilt.

Rogge (1975), like Reik, argues that confessions are based on feelings of guilt. He goes a step further and suggests that guilt feelings are made up of two components, fear of losing love and fear of retaliation.

"Those who are guilty of some criminal offense are under such anxiety lest they have lost love and lest there will be retaliation that they usually confess" (p. 227).

Berggren (1975) presents a psychological model which highlights the need of the individual to confess to his or her transgression of social norms. People's knowledge of their transgression produces a sense of guilt which is experienced as oppressive and depressing. The confession produces a sense of relief which has important cathartic effects. For a satisfactory cathartic effect to occur the confession has to be to a person in authority, such as a priest or policeman.

Until recently, no empirical studies had looked at the role of feelings of guilt in facilitating a confession among criminals. A study carried out by myself into the electrodermal reactivity of Icelandic criminals, policemen and clergymen during a "lie detection" experiment (Gudjonsson, 1979a), indicates that there may be important group differences in relation to guilt following transgression. Criminals were found to be least physiologically responsive to deception and clergymen the most. This suggests that criminals, perhaps by virtue of early conditioning or by habituation, no longer suffer the pangs of conscience following the committing of an offence. Psychoanalytic formulations seem to overlook the importance of individual and group differences in remorse following transgression.

In a small early study, Redlich, Ravitz and Dession (1951) found that people with a strong generalized feeling of guilt and anxiety were less able to resist interrogation whilst under sodium amytal. The authors argued that the findings supported Reik's formulation that guilt is a fundamental cause of confessions.

5. An Interaction Process Model of Confession

Moston, Stephenson, and Williamson (1990) recently outlined a model which helps us explain how the background characteristics of the suspect and the case can influence the interrogator's style of questioning, which in turn affect the suspect's behaviour and the outcome of the interview. The model postulates that the suspect's response to an allegation, irrespective of his or her involvement in the crime under investigation, is influenced by the interaction of two main groups of factors: (a) background characteristics of the suspect and the offence (e.g. type of offence, the severity of the offence, age and sex of suspect, and the suspect's personality); and (b) contextual characteristics of the case (e.g. legal advice, the strength of the police evidence and the interrogation techniques utilized). A distinction is drawn between the suspect's initial reaction to the accusation and his or her subsequent responses.

The model emphasizes the importance of looking at the interaction of a number of case-related variables, rather than viewing them in isolation. Thus, the outcome of the interview is dependent upon an interaction process comprising a number of factors. One important implication of the model is that background characteristics of the suspect and the case, in conjunction with contextual factors, influence the interrogator's beliefs, attitudes and style of questioning, which in turn influence the suspect's behaviour. In addition, case characteristics may strongly influence the behaviour of *both* the suspect and the interrogator.

FACTORS INHIBITING CONFESSION

There are a number of factors which may make it difficult for people to confess to crimes they have committed. This is not surprising when one considers the potential consequences of confessing for the offender and his family. Some of the most important potential consequences of confessing to a crime are as follows:

1. *Fear of legal sanctions.* All crimes carry the possibility of a certain penalty. The range of penalties and sentencing options varies considerably from one country to another, but in general the more serious the offence the greater the punishment is likely to be (Eysenck and Gudjonsson, 1989). Most criminal offences carry the possibility of a prison sentence, which means the loss of liberty for a certain amount of time. In many countries the most serious offences are subject to a mandatory prison sentence or even the death penalty. Another consequence of a criminal conviction, which may inhibit some first-time offenders from confessing, is the thought of having a criminal record. A criminal record may make it more difficult for the offender to obtain employment in the future.

2. *Concern about one's reputation.* Some offenders are reluctant to confess because they are very concerned about what effect it may have upon their reputation in the community. The higher a person's standing in the community, the more he perceives he has to lose, and the greater his reluctance to confess. It is, of course, the suspects' perceptions of their own standing in the community that are important in influencing their behaviour, rather than the objective reality of the situation. In some instances a relatively minor offence, such as being apprehended for shoplifting or drunken driving, may be such a devastating experience for some people that they may become depressed and suicidal after being convicted. This reaction may be even more evident when the convicted person holds a senior position, or has led an otherwise exemplary life in the community.

3. *Not wanting to admit to oneself what one has done.* After committing an offence people may "suppress" the memory of the offence, because what they did is totally unacceptable to them (i.e. they push the memory out of conscious awareness). Being able to "forget" what happened probably functions to protect the psychological well-being and self-esteem of the offender. The mechanism for this phenomenon is discussed in Chapter 5 in relation to psychogenic amnesia. As we saw in Chapter 2, the more reprehensible the offence, the more offenders are likely to exercise denial when being interviewed.

4. *Not wanting one's family and friends to know about the crime.* Some offenders may be concerned that if their family and friends knew about the crime they had committed they might be adversely affected. In many cases the offender is undoubtedly right in thinking that his family and friends would be hurt, shocked and disappointed when learning about the crime. In reality, many families of suspects undoubtedly suffer from such tangible pain as adverse publicity via local newspapers, being shunned by neighbours, and becoming the subject of much local gossip. Not wanting to hurt loved ones, and the possible fear of being rejected by them because of what one has done, are powerful emotions which may inhibit the willingness of the offender to confess.

5. *Fear of retaliation.* When an offender confesses to a crime he may implicate others, and the fear of possible retaliation by them may act to inhibit his confessing. Indeed, the fear of retaliation may in some instances be much stronger than the fear of penal sanctions if convicted.

Reluctance to Confess: A Case Example

Sometimes the unwillingness or inability of people to confess to a crime they have committed can take extreme proportions. A case in point is that of Mrs R. She was a woman in her mid-50s who was tried at the Central Criminal Court in London for the horrific murder of her best friend, a murder of which she claimed to have no recollection whatsoever.

Mrs R's friend had been bludgeoned to death in her own home with a heavy object during what appeared to be a frenzied attack. The murderer then tied a scarf around the deceased's neck and repeatedly stabbed and mutilated her body with a bread knife. At first sight the murder had many of the signs of a sexually motivated killing, which meant that the police would have been looking for a male suspect. As things turned out, the case was even more bizarre than it initially appeared.

Shortly after the discovery of the murdered woman's body, fingerprinting was carried out on friends and neighbours so that they could be excluded from the inquiry. Mrs R, who was the victim's closest friend, was discovered during fingerprinting to have lacerations on her hands. The police also noticed what looked like blood on her handbag. A search in her handbag revealed an even more surprising discovery, a piece of the established murder weapon!

A conventional blood group analysis was carried out on the cross-matching of blood between the two women. The evidence suggested, but was not conclusive, that the victim's blood was on Mrs R's handbag and the rims of her glasses. Conversely, the blood of Mrs R's group was found on the dead woman's clothing and mixer taps within the victim's flat. Mrs R strongly denied any involvement in the murder and instructed her solicitor to have various blood specimens analysed by the newly developed DNA profiling technique, so that she could once and for all prove her innocence. This was done and the results were conclusive. The blood on Mrs R's handbag and glasses did belong to the deceased woman and the blood found on the victim was that of Mrs R, who continued to insist that she had no recollection whatsoever of having killed her best friend. In fact, in spite of all the forensic evidence, which was clearly overwhelming, Mrs R could not contemplate the thought that she had murdered her friend in a most horrific way. In view of the forensic evidence, Mrs R pleaded guilty to manslaughter on the grounds of diminished responsibility, but she never "admitted" that she could possibly have been responsible for the murder. In her own words, "I could never have killed my closest and dearest friend, no matter what the forensic evidence says". It is probable that the inability of Mrs R to "admit" to the murder, was primarily caused by the difficulties she had in accepting that she had committed a brutal and horrific act of violence against her best friend.

Psychological assessment showed Mrs R to be of average intelligence, but she had a strong tendency to deny painful and undesirable emotional experiences, particularly those relating to anger and hostility. She was a proud and strongly willed woman who found self-confrontation difficult. Her psychological profile was that of an "overcontrolled personality" (Megargee, 1966), i.e. the type of person who has rigid inhibitions about the appropriate self-expressions of anger and frustration, and may suddenly lose control and act extremely explosively when provoked.

Medical evidence sought by the defence indicated that Mrs R suffered from some brain damage, possibly caused by forceps delivery at birth. This information, in conjunction with her overcontrolled personality, led to a successful defence against the murder charge, which resulted in a conviction for manslaughter and committal to hospital for treatment.

EMPIRICAL STUDIES OF CONFESSIONS

Very few studies have actually researched the precise reasons why suspects confess to crimes they have committed. It is easy to understand that suspects would generally be resistant to confessing, considering the adverse consequences of doing so. Nevertheless, many guilty suspects eventually confess to the crime. Some confess readily and without much external pressure, whereas others take a long time to confess or only confess when the evidence against them is overwhelming.

It is to be expected, from the five theoretical models discussed above, that suspects are likely to confess to the police for a number of different reasons. One way of studying the reasons why suspects confess during custodial interrogation is by the use of self-report questionnaires. That is, offenders can be systematically asked questions about what made them confess to the police and these can be correlated with other measurements, including those associated with intelligence, attitudes, attribution of blame and other personality dimensions. Another method is to analyse the social interaction between the interviewer and suspect from tape-recordings of real-life interrogation, or by observation at the time of the interrogation. These two methods complement each other, as can be seen from the following empirical studies.

Irving (1980) and Irving and McKenzie (1989) have researched the evidence for some of the hypotheses generated by the Hilgendorf and Irving (1981) decision-making model of confession. The main implication of the model is that there are a number of social, psychological and environmental factors that can affect the suspect's decision-making during custodial interrogation. These include confinement prior to interrogation, abnormal mental state, and interrogative tactics and ploys.

The research by Irving which relates to police interrogation techniques was reviewed in Chapter 3. The main finding is that in 1979 (Irving, 1980), the police were employing manipulative and persuasive interrogation techniques with some frequency and this was thought to have been at least partly responsible for the reasonably high confession rate. Following the implementation of the Police and Criminal Evidence Act (PACE), Irving carried out two further studies, in 1986 and 1987, at the same police station (Irving and McKenzie, 1989).

It was found that in 1986 the interrogators at Brighton Police Station had dramatically reduced the extent to which they used manipulative and persuasive interrogation techniques, but the confession rate was very similar to that found in the 1980 study. One tantalizing finding was that out of 10 serious cases investigated in the 1979 study, all had resulted in a confession. In 1986 only five out of 11 serious cases (45%) had resulted in a confession. The conclusion reached by Irving and McKenzie was that the effects on admissions were confined to serious cases.

In the 1987 study, which comprised 68 suspects as in the 1986 study, it was found that interrogators were more frequently using manipulative and persuasive techniques, particularly in the more serious cases, than in the previous year, but the frequency with which these techniques was used was still only about half of its 1979 level.

Moston, Stephenson and Williamson (1990), whose Interaction Process Model of police interrogation was reviewed earlier in this Chapter, provide some valuable findings about an association between case characteristics and the outcome of a police interrogation. They carried out a careful analysis of tape-recorded interviews concerning 1067 cases which were being investigated by the Metropolitan Police. Out of the total sample, 446 suspects (41.8%) made self-incriminating confessions, 444 suspects (41.6%) denied any involvement in the offence, and a further 177 subjects (16.6%) neither admitted nor denied the alleged offence. The authors then proceeded to determine which of several case characteristics (i.e. criminal history, age and sex of suspect, offence category) and context variables (i.e. legal advice, strength of the evidence against the suspect) were related to outcome, using the techniques of hiloglinear analysis which partitions out any associations among variables in a similar way to multiple regression.

Three case characteristics had a significant impact on the outcome of the interrogation. First, the strength of the evidence against the suspect was strongly associated with the outcome. That is, confessions were rare (i.e. less than 10% of cases) and denials common (i.e. 77% of cases) when the evidence against the suspect was weak. On the other hand, when the evidence against the suspect was viewed by the police as strong, then confessions were common (67% of cases) and denials infrequent (16% of cases).

Second, the outcome of the interrogation varied according to the severity of the offence. That is, the more serious the offence the more likely suspects were to make neither admissions nor denials. One reason for these findings is that the more serious the offence, the more likely suspects are to use their right of silence (Moston, Stephenson and Williamson, 1992).

Third, suspects who had legal advice confessed significantly less often than those who had no legal advice. That is, over 50% of those who had no legal advice confessed, in contrast with less than 30% of those who had had legal advice. Moston, Stephenson and Williamson (1990) conclude, on the basis of their findings, that confessions fall by about 20% once suspects have contact with a legal representative. An alternative explanation is that the suspects who requested a solicitor were different in their personality, or in their experiences, than those who did not request a solicitor. An important question to ask is why some suspects requested and were allowed to seek legal advice, while others did not? This question was not addressed by Moston and his colleagues.

The study found no significant differences in confession rates between offence types (offences against the person versus property offences), age and previous criminal convictions, which is in contrast with the findings of Neubauer (1974), Softley (1980), and Baldwin and McConville (1980). Moston, Stephenson and Williamson (1990) argue that the previous significant findings may be an artefact of the studies' faulty methodology, because they did not take into account possible inter-associations between case characteristics. In other words, correlating isolated variables with interrogation outcome may produce plausible, yet erroneous, results. This is undoubtedly a very valid point and should be carefully considered in future research into confessions.

One conclusion to be drawn from the study is that it may be the strength of the police evidence and access to legal advice that determine the outcome of the interrogation, rather than interrogation techniques *per se*.

With my psychiatrist colleague Hannes Petursson (Gudjonsson and Petursson, 1991a), I recently investigated the reasons for confessing among Icelandic prisoners (the study has been replicated in Northern Ireland with very similar results; see Gudjonsson and Bownes, 1991). We looked at a number of factors that could be associated with the reasons for the confession, such as the type of offence committed, the offenders' intelligence, attitudes, personality, and the way they attributed blame for the crime they had committed.

We hypothesized that confessions are predominantly elicited by three types of facilitative factor. These are:

1. "Internal pressure" to confess, where suspects experience a great deal of guilt about the crime they committed and consequently need to relieve themselves of the guilt by confessing;
2. "External pressure" to confess, which is associated with persuasive police interrogation techniques, police behaviour, and fear of confinement;
3. "Proof", where suspects believe that there is no point in denying the offence because the police will eventually prove they did it.

We administered a specially designed "Confession Questionnaire" to Icelandic prisoners who had been convicted of various offences, which included violent, property and sexual offences. Factor analysis of the Confession Questionnaire revealed the three *facilitative* factors listed above and one *inhibitory* factor (see below). Six items loaded on a factor labelled "external pressure". The components of this factor were associated with the police environment, e.g. subjects indicated they had confessed because of the fear of being locked up and as a result of police persuasion. In terms of frequency, fear of being locked up was rated as having been a very important reason for the confession in over 20% of the cases. Fear of the police or threats of violence were only rated as important in 5% of cases.

The second factor, "internal pressure", comprised four items which were related to feelings of guilt about the commission of the offence and the relief associated with the confession. Over 42% of the subjects said they had experienced considerable relief after confessing. About one-third (34%) said they had confessed because they had wanted to get the offence "off their chest". The findings indicate that talking about the offence to a person in authority was important in many cases because people were distressed by what had happened and wanted to give their account of what had occurred.

The third facilitative factor, "proof", consisted of only two items, which were associated with the subjects seeing no point in denying the offence, as the police would sooner or later prove their involvement in it. With regard to frequency, 55% of the subjects said that they had confessed because they strongly believed at the time that the police would be able to prove they had committed the crime.

The principal conclusion that can be drawn from these results is that the most frequent and important reason suspects confess is the strength of their belief in the evidence against them. Both internal and external (police) pressure are important in many cases where the police have little or no proof. This is due to the fact that there are a number of strong forces which make it difficult for suspects to confess to their crimes. These "inhibitory factors" include not wanting to admit to oneself the responsibility for the crime, not wanting others to know about what one has done, and not wanting to be viewed as a "criminal". Not wanting to face the "real" or "personal" consequences associated with the criminal act means that the resistance often has to be overcome by either internal or external pressure.

We found some indication that the reasons offenders give for having confessed to the police during interrogation are related to the type of offence committed. For example, sex offenders confessed more frequently than other offenders because of a strong internal need to confess. This was in spite of the finding that sex offenders were the most inhibited of all groups about confessing because of the potential "real" or "personal" consequences of so doing.

We looked at a number of variables that might be associated with the reasons why offenders confess. These included intelligence, extraversion, neuroticism, psychoticism, age, coping abilities, the offenders' attitudes and how they attribute blame for their crime.

We found that a confession which resulted principally from external pressure was associated with a perceived inability to cope with the police interrogation. It is of interest to note that both external pressure to confess, and the inability to cope with it, were associated with anxiety proneness (i.e. trait anxiety), age and intelligence. One possible explanation is that the brighter, older and more emotionally stable offenders are better able to cope with interrogative pressure than other offenders.

Internal pressure correlated most strongly with feelings of remorse concerning the offence committed and the perception that the offence had resulted from mental causes, such as sudden loss of self-control rather than criminal disposition. The main implication is that if the crime is seen as being inconsistent with the persons' views about themselves (i.e. it is "out of character") then they are more likely to have an internal need to confess.

There were clear indications from the study that the offenders' views and attitudes about their confessions were related to the reasons they gave for the confessions. Confessions that resulted primarily from external pressure were associated with the greatest amount of dissatisfaction and regret. The subjects in this group considered, retrospectively, that they had confessed far too readily at the time of the interrogation and they had not fully appreciated the consequences of their confession. They subsequently began to regret bitterly having made the confession and wished they had not confessed.

In marked contrast, the stronger the perceived proof and internal pressure to confess at the time of the police interrogation, the happier the offenders remained about having confessed. The implication is that the reason why offenders confess significantly affects how they subsequently view their confession. Offenders who remain bitter and dissatisfied because their confession resulted from police pressure may be less able to come to terms with the "real" and "personal" consequences of their crime than other offenders.

Dissatisfaction with the confession was also found to be correlated with personality scores. Extraverts and those with antisocial personality characteristics reported greatest initial resistance during interrogation and they were the types of offenders who most strongly regretted having confessed.

The finding that the subjects who are most disordered in terms of their personality are also most resistant to confessing is consistent with the findings of an earlier study we carried out in Iceland (Gudjonsson and Petursson, 1982). We found that offenders with the diagnosis of "personality disorder" in homicide cases had tried hardest to cover up their crime and to avoid detection. In contrast, it was uncommon for those who were mentally ill to try to avoid detection. The defendants who had no diagnosable abnormality fell in between the other two groups in terms of avoidance of detection.

Another important finding from our Icelandic study is the importance of the role of solicitors. Very few of the subjects in the study had had a solicitor present during the interrogations, and 25% of the sample stated that they would definitely not have confessed if they had had access to a solicitor.

HOW IMPORTANT ARE CONFESSIONS?

How important are confessions for solving a crime and in securing a conviction in a court of law? Zimbardo (1967) states that "more than 80% of all criminal cases are solved by confession" (p. 17). Are Zimbardo's claims exaggerated? The available evidence suggests that they probably are.

The importance of a confession to the police depends on the strength of the other evidence against the suspect (Softley, 1980). When the evidence against suspects is strong then they are much more likely to confess (Softley, 1980; Irving and McKenzie, 1989; Moston, Stephenson and Williamson, 1990), even though in such cases the confession may add little to the overall strength of the case. When the evidence against suspects is weak then a confession may be sufficient on its own to convict them.

On occasions a confession can lead to important further evidence to incriminate a suspect, such as the discovery of a murder weapon or the body of a victim. Such evidence can be used to corroborate the validity of the confession made. The extent to which detectives attempt to corroborate pieces of information contained in the confession varies considerably. Ideally, the validity of the confession should be carefully investigated.

One might expect that where there is a legal corroboration requirement, as in the United States of America, detectives would be motivated to seek evidence to support the validity of the confession. According to Ayling (1984), this does not always appear to be the case. In other words:

> "Contrary to the assumptions behind the corroboration rule, the rule does not motivate police to gather independent evidence" (p. 1193).

Studies that have attempted to assess the importance of confession evidence as a part of the prosecution case are scarce. The critical research question is, in what proportion of cases do interrogations provide the police with substantial evidence against the suspect which was not available prior to the interrogation? The empirical findings on this point are somewhat contradictory, but suggest that confession evidence may be either crucial or important to the police in about 20% of cases. Furthermore, once a confession has been made, even if it is subsequently retracted, the defendant is convicted in the great majority of cases.

In a major English study, Baldwin and McConville (1980), analysed the committal papers among 1474 Crown Court cases. They found that confessions provided the single most important evidence against the suspect. In about 30% of cases the self-incriminating admission or confession was crucial to the prosecution case. Forensic evidence was only important in about 5% of cases. Furthermore,

> "No more than seven of the defendants who had made written confessions in London (5.2%) and 23 in Birmingham (2.4%) were eventually acquitted at trial. These figures thus provide striking confirmation of the hypothesis that to obtain a written confession from a suspect is tantamount to securing his conviction in court" (p. 19).

Three other English studies warrant a brief mention. Softley (1980), in an observation study in four police stations, found that detectives claimed that they would have dropped about 8% of the cases if a confession or an admission had not have been forthcoming.

In two separate observational studies, Irving and McKenzie (1989) considered that the strength of evidence against suspects prior to interrogation was "strong" in about 50% of cases and "fair" in a further 30% of cases. This means that in about 20% of cases there was no tangible evidence against suspects prior to the interrogation.

Moston, Stephenson and Williamson (1990) analysed 1067 tape-recorded police interviews and classified the strength of evidence against suspects prior to interrogation as either "weak" (26%), "moderate" (34%) or "strong" (40%). The weaker the evidence against suspects the less likely they were to confess.

In an important American observational study, conducted in New Haven, Wald et al. (1967) assessed the importance of confessions in solving crime, apprehending accomplices and clearing up other crimes. Having observed the interrogation of 127 suspects and interviewed the detectives involved, the authors found that interrogation was only necessary for solving the crime in about 17% of cases (Wald et al., 1967, Table F-6, p. 1585). They concluded:

"Thus, even in a force as scientifically advanced as Los Angeles', there is strong evidence that confessions are of small importance, since arrests can be made only where the crime is for the most part already solved because such substantial evidence is available before interrogation" (p. 1588).

CONCLUSIONS

From the evidence presented in this Chapter, it seems that until recently over 60% of suspects made self-incriminating admissions or confessions during custodial interrogation. As far as England is concerned, the rate seems to have dropped to between 40 and 50% in recent years, following the implementation of the Police and Criminal Evidence Act (PACE). The two most significant factors may be changes in police interrogation techniques and the increased use of solicitors. The effect of tape-recording on confessions, which is to become standard practice in England in 1991, is uncertain and will require careful research.

Factors such as age and previous convictions appear to be related to readiness to confess, but these variables should be studied in conjunction with other variables, such as the seriousness of the offence, the strength of the evidence against the suspect, and access to legal advice. Recent research at the University of Kent indicates that many case and background variables are inter-related, and that studying these in isolation may give potentially misleading results.

Five different models or groups of model about confessions were discussed in this Chapter. These are:

1. "The Reid Model of Confession", where interrogation is construed as a subtle psychological way of overcoming resistance and deception;
2. "A Decision-making Model of Confession", where an attempt is made to draw attention to the kind of factors that influence the suspects' decision-making during interrogation;
3. "A Cognitive-behavioural Model of Confession", where confessions are viewed in terms of their "antecedents" and "perceived consequences";
4. "Psychoanalytic Models of Confession", where confessions are seen as arising from internal conflict and feelings of guilt;
5. "An Interaction Process Model of Confession", where the outcome of interrogation is seen as resulting from the interaction of background variables and contextual characteristics.

Each of the models makes somewhat different assumptions about why suspects confess during custodial interrogation, although there is considerable overlap between some of the models. It is only recently that empirical studies have attempted to test out specific hypotheses generated by the models. Two studies have been conducted so far and some general conclusions can be drawn about the reasons why suspects confess to crimes about which they are interrogated.

The available evidence indicates that suspects confess due to a combination of factors, rather than to one factor alone. Three general factors appear to be relevant, in varying degree, to most suspects. These relate to an *internal* pressure (e.g. feelings of remorse, the need to talk about the offence), *external* pressure (e.g. fear of confinement, police persuasiveness), and perception of *proof* (e.g. the suspects' perceptions of the strength of evidence against them). The findings from two different studies indicate that the strongest incentive to confess relates to the strength of the evidence against suspects. Furthermore, those who confess because of strong evidence against them, and where there is an internal need to confess, appear to be subsequently most content about their confession. Confessions that result from police persuasiveness and pressure seem to leave suspects disgruntled, even years afterwards.

CHAPTER 5

The Role of Perception and Memory in Witness Testimony

Police interviewing is primarily concerned with the gathering of accurate and complete information. Perception and memory form an essential part of this information-gathering process. For this reason it is important to provide the reader with information about the basic psychological processes of memory within which the reliability of interviewees' testimony needs to be evaluated. Detailed recent reviews of these memory processes are provided by Loftus, Greene and Doyle (1990) and Yarmey (1990). The legal issues concerning the testimony of children are discussed in detail by Spencer and Flin (1990).

There will be separate sections on child witnesses and amnesia (i.e. pathological forgetting) at the end of the Chapter. These areas are discussed in some detail in view of their importance to police interviewing.

THE MEMORY PROCESS

Memory is generally considered to be an active and distortion-prone process (Bartlett, 1932; Loftus, 1979a). It can be described theoretically within a three-stage sequential framework (Crowder, 1976; Loftus, 1979a). The first stage, *acquisition*, involves the perception and encoding of the original event which is placed and interpreted in the context of a person's previous knowledge and experience. This involves transferring the information from "short-term" (working memory which holds information for a few seconds) to "long-term" (more permanent) memory. The second stage, *retention*, consists of the period of time between the observed event and eventual recollection. The final stage, *retrieval*, involves the person bringing back the memory into awareness.

A number of factors can affect the accuracy and completeness of memory at the three stages and it is important to deal with these in turn. Broadly speaking, these three stages can be influenced by such factors as the person's abilities, past experiences, beliefs, personality, and his or her mental and physical state, in addition to a host of environmental stressors and interrogational factors (Buckhout, 1974; Hollin, 1989). Errors in memory typically involve both *errors of omission* and *errors of commission* (Yarmey, 1990). The former includes the failure to pay attention to stimulus material or deciding to focus on selected material, whereas the latter involves some interference with the memory process by thoughts, emotions and external stimuli.

Acquisition

The acquisition stage can be affected by three types of factor, described by various authors as:

1. "Event" and "witness" factors (Loftus, 1979a; Loftus, Green and Doyle, 1990);
2. "Stimulus" and "subject" factors (Clifford, 1979);
3. "Situational" and "individual" factors (Hollin, 1989).

Event factors are related to the nature and circumstances of the incident itself, whereas witness factors relate to the characteristics and limitations of the witness.

The length of time people have to observe a particular incident or event may affect the accuracy of their subsequent recall. Generally, the longer the observation time the more accurate the subsequent memory (e.g. Laughery, Alexander and Lane, 1971; Clifford and Richards, 1977; Ellis, Davies and Shepherd, 1977). Similarly, the more often people view a particular detail or incident the more likely they are to recall it (e.g. Burtt, 1948).

Lighting conditions and the time of day when an incident is witnessed have been shown to be important. Kuehn (1974) found that when an incident was observed at twilight people had less complete recollection of it then when it took place in the daytime or at night. Yarmey (1986) found that accuracy of recall was better in daylight and at the beginning of twilight than at the end of twilight or at night. The salience of a particular detail has been shown to be important in the registration and encoding of information. For example, Marshall, Marquis and Oskamp (1971) found that subjects gave more accurate and complete recall of information judged by them to be salient. This seems to relate to the observation of Gardner (1933) that unusual, extraordinary and interesting details more readily catch our attention than the insignificant and commonplace details. In addition there is the finding that unexpected details or an event are better remembered than details that are consistent with expectations (Pezdek et al., 1989).

The type of information perceived may affect the ease with which the information is remembered. Following the early work of Cattell (1895), many researchers have found that inaccuracies commonly occur with the reporting of time, speed, and distance (Loftus, 1979a). Time estimates, such as the duration of an event, are frequently highly inaccurate. The consistent error that people make is to *overestimate* the time that an event took (Cattell, 1895; Marshall, 1966; Buckhout, 1974; Loftus et al., 1987). In general, females overestimate duration more than males (Loftus et al., 1987). This persistent tendency to overestimate duration is further exacerbated when people are under stress (Sarson and Stroop, 1978). Thus, the errors made with regard to duration tend to be in one direction.

The judgement of speed, for example involving a moving vehicle, is commonly flawed (Gardner, 1933; Marshall, 1966). Great variation occurs between people observing the same event (Loftus, 1979a).

A number of studies have shown that the nature of the incident witnessed may significantly affect the subsequent accuracy of recall. The consistent finding is that events containing violent scenes are more poorly recalled than non-violent scenarios (Clifford and Scott, 1978; Clifford and Hollin, 1981; Hollin, 1981; Loftus and Burns, 1982). However, this does not necessarily imply that there is a direct and simple relationship between the seriousness of the crime observed and memory performance. For example, in one experiment Leippe, Wells and Ostrom (1978) found that the value of the object stolen affected the subsequent identification of the thief by "witnesses". When subjects knew that the object stolen was valuable they more readily identified the thief than when the object was inexpensive. One possible explanation for this finding is that when subjects believe they are viewing a serious crime, they pay more attention to the details of crime. However, this only seems to be the case when "serious" crime does not as well contain an element of violence. It could be, as Deffenbacher (1983) suggests, that the Leippe et al. study caused only a moderate level of arousal, and thereby enhanced attention optimally in accordance with the Yerkes-Dodson Law (Yerkes and Dodson, 1908). On the other hand, studies utilizing a violent scenario are more arousing and may impair memory performance.

The work of Easterbrook (1959) demonstrated that in situations of high stress people concentrate selectively and more intensively on fewer features of the environment. Clifford and Hollin (1981) suggest that high arousal, caused by the witnessing of a violent event, results in the narrowing of the person's attention to the details of the incident. Evidence for this narrowing of attention comes from the work of Loftus, Loftus and Messo (1987) concerning "weapon focus". It was found that during an armed robbery the subjects' attention was focused overwhelmingly on the weapon the assailant was carrying during the crime. Undue attention being paid to the weapon may reduce the witnesses' ability to recognize other features of the incident, such as the identity of the assailant.

Christianson and Loftus (1991) have demonstrated in five recent experiments that the relationship between emotional stress and memory is complicated, and statements that emotional events either lead to an impairment *or* enhancement in memory, depending on the circumstances, is an oversimplification. These authors have drawn a clear distinction between memory for *central* as opposed to *peripheral* detail. Their research shows that emotional stress tends to enhance memory associated with central detail whilst memory for peripheral detail is reduced.

The role of chronic anxiety, independent of the stress associated with the witnessed event, can cause preoccupations so that people pay insufficient attention to their environment (Loftus, Greene and Doyle, 1990). This may affect their ability to give an accurate and detailed account of events and the appearance of people.

Interest may also play a crucial role in memory. For example, females have been found to be more accurate in their memory recall than males with regard to "female-oriented" details, whereas the reverse is true concerning "male-oriented" details (Powers, Andriks and Loftus, 1979). Therefore, gender may significantly influence the type of details that are remembered from an incident.

Brown and Kulik (1977) put forward the idea that major and surprising events (e.g. the assassination of a president) can result in exceptionally vivid, detailed and accurate memory traces of everything that was observed at the time. They labelled this type of memory as a "flashbulb " memory. Although the memory for central details can be enhanced by a strong emotional experience, there is currently no evidence of a special "flashbulb" memory mechanism (McCloskey, Wible and Cohen, 1988).

Haward (1963) makes the point that people see what they *expect, desire* or *need* to see and these influences are affected by their past experiences, attitudes and beliefs. Loftus (1979a) gives numerous illustrations of the importance of the effect of expectations on our perception and actions. She identifies four different types of *expectation* that can affect our perceptions: cultural expectations or stereotypes, expectations from past experience, personal prejudices, and temporary expectations. Each type of expectation can seriously distort people's judgements, and in some instances even cause fatal accidents (e.g. Sommer, 1959). Yarmey (1990) argues that social expectations and stereotypes are particularly likely to adversely affect perception and memory when the event observed is complex and of short duration.

A number of experimental studies have shown that the elderly have poorer memory than younger subjects (Burke and Light, 1981). This has also been shown within the context of eyewitness testimony (Yarmey, 1984). Yarmey believes that the memory problems of the elderly may be exacerbated by such factors as the brevity and complexity of the event observed.

Retention

In the intervening period between acquisition and retrieval, memory generally becomes less complete and accurate. There are at least two types of factor that can cause this to happen. These are referred to as the "retention interval" and "postevent interference" (Yarmey, 1990).

1. Retention Interval

Memory tends to deteriorate and become less accurate with time for a witnessed event (Loftus, 1979a). This appears to be due to normal forgetting, which is most rapid shortly after acquisition and then declines more slowly (Yarmey, 1990). However, the decline in memory and accuracy may be to a certain extent related to the type of material observed. For example, Yarmey (1990) recommends that voice identification beyond 24 hours should be treated with "utmost caution" (p. 321). A similar caution, but for different reasons, has been advocated by Clifford (1983) about the reliability of voice identification.

Face recognition, on the other hand, seems less affected by delay than most other types of witness testimony (Loftus, 1979a). Ellis, in his review paper on "Practical aspects of face memory" (1984), concludes that the recognition for faces may be quite accurate and resistant to distortions over a period as long as weeks or months. Similar conclusions were reached by Shepherd, Ellis and Davies (1982) with regard to person identification:

> ". . . in all three experiments involving delay, rates of identification of a target person from an identification parade remained remarkably stable over delays ranging from 1 week to 4 months. Furthermore, this stability was not associated with any marked increase in the rate of mistaken identity." (p. 113).

Shepherd, Ellis and Davies cogently point out that this does not mean that extended intervals, over several months or years, could not markedly affect correct identification. Indeed, they believe that long delays are highly undesirable because of the increased possibility of misidentification. Furthermore, they emphasize that the process of identification itself is highly distortion-prone. Mistaken identification often occurs in criminal cases (see Chapter 10 for details).

2. Postevent Interference

After witnessing an event a person is often exposed to new information. This may be communicated by the media, for example, when the witness reads about a crime in a newspaper. Similarly, discussing the crime with other people, including police officers, may affect subsequent accuracy and completeness of recall.

The danger with postevent information is that it

> ". . . can not only enhance memories but also change a witness's memory and even cause non-existent details to become incorporated into a previously acquired memory" (Loftus, 1979a, p. 55).

Loftus provides supportive evidence for the claim that postevent information can be non-verbal as well as verbal. After a while, witnesses may not be able to differentiate between their original perception of the event and the new information incorporated from "external" sources. Loftus also shows that the intervening and wishful thoughts of the witness may, in certain circumstances, be sufficient to affect how events are remembered.

It has been shown that misleading information most readily distorts memory when it is encountered by the witness after a long retention interval

(Loftus, Miller and Burns, 1978). In addition, peripheral details of the observed event are more easily interfered with by postevent information than the central features (Dristas and Hamilton, 1977, quoted by Yarmey, 1990). Leading questions which are based on unfounded premises and expectations can seriously distort the normal memory process (Loftus, 1979a). Smith and Ellsworth (1987) argue that misleading information is least likely to affect witnesses' statements during police questioning when witnesses believe that the police do not themselves know precisely what happened. This suggests that witnesses are most likely to be misled by the police when they have full trust in the knowledge base of the interviewing officers.

There are two further important factors that relate to postevent information. These are the effects of discussion among witnesses before they give evidence and the effects of being shown photographs or artist's drawings prior to making an identification. Both can potentially interfere with the memory process.

Alper et al. (1976) found that group discussion of a staged incident resulted in more complete information, but there was an increase in the number of non-existent details being reported. Warnick and Sanders (1980), using a similar methodology, came up with different findings. Those subjects who had discussed the incident in a group gave more accurate accounts of it than those who had not discussed what they had seen. Hollin and Clifford (1983) showed that it is quite easy to contaminate the recall of individual witnesses by prior group discussion. They recommend that attempts should be made to obtain uncontaminated accounts from witnesses before they have the opportunity of communicating with other witnesses.

There is evidence that showing witnesses photographs prior to a recognition task can impair successful recognition (Davies, Shepherd and Ellis, 1979). Similarly, an artist's drawing or an Identikit composite have been reported to interfere with subsequent identification of suspects (Bruce and Young, 1986; Comish, 1987). In view of potential memory contamination, Yarmey (1990) warns that

"Publication of police artist sketches or commercial composites in newspapers or on television could interfere with subsequent line-up identification" (p. 305).

Retrieval

Much of the failure in memory is the result of the inability of the witness to retrieve information rather than faulty acquisition or retention (Tulving, 1974). For this reason a distinction must be drawn between information which is potentially available in memory storage and that actually accessible at any one point in time (Tulving, 1983). Only a small proportion of all memories are accessible on a given occasion.

The two most commonly used memory tests to elicit retrieval are those that rely on *recall* or *recognition* (Gregg, 1987). A recall procedure typically means that witnesses are presented with the stimulus material and are subsequently requested to report all that they can remember about it. "Free recall" means that there are no constraints placed on the witness with regard to recall. "Cued recall" refers to witnesses being provided with specific cues to aid recall, and falls in between the free recall and recognition in terms of retrieval search requirement and sustained attention (Burke and Light, 1981). Recognition means that witnesses are given an explicit cue which comprises the actual physical stimuli and this generally involves effortless retrieval (e.g. having to identify a person from a photograph or a line-up). Therefore, free recall is a much more effort-demanding task than recognition.

Whether the witness can retrieve information by recall or recognition testing procedures depends on a number of factors. One very important factor is the retrieval strategies that the witness uses when attempting to recall an event from memory. There are a number of retrieval strategies available which can markedly facilitate access to memory. These are discussed in detail in Chapter 8 in connection with the "cognitive interview". Events that are encoded during high levels of emotional arousal tend to be initially more difficult to retrieve, but with time they may be successfully retrieved (Bradley and Baddeley, 1990).

Asking witnesses to give a free narrative account of events often results in reliable information being produced, but such accounts are typically incomplete and need to be followed up by either specific or general questions (Lipton, 1977; Dent, 1986). Following up initial free recall accounts by cued recall is common and acceptable police practice. However, cued recall can be potentially misleading because the scenario that the police have may be unfounded and uninformed. In addition, as illustrated in Chapter 4, the precise wording of the question asked may influence the witness's recollection of an event (Loftus, 1979a).

Context Effects

McGeoch (1932) raised the importance of the original learning context on subsequent memory and suggested that two contexts are always present:

1. The "intra-organic conditions" of the learner;
2. The stimulus properties of the "external environment".

Davies (1986) has reviewed the experimental evidence with regard to these external and internal context factors.

Studies relevant to demonstrating the importance of "intra-organic conditions" in facilitating memory can be described under the general heading of "state-dependent memory". This refers to the idea that people will find it easiest to recall an event when they are in a similar state of mind to that when the event was originally observed (i.e. the mood during the retrieval stage is congruent with that of the acquisition stage). In other words, if people are in a particular mood or under the influence of a particular drug during the acquisition of information, then retrieval is enhanced when the same mood or drug state is present. This has been demonstrated in a variety of contexts, including drugs (Overton, 1964;), alcohol (e.g. Weingartner and Faillace, 1971; Lisman, 1974) and mood (Schare, Lisman and Spear, 1984; Haaga, 1989).

Studies focusing on the influence of the "external environment" on eyewitness memory are reviewed in detail by Davies (1986). The findings lend strong support to the theory that memory can be significantly facilitated by reinstatement of context in which the event was originally observed. The implication is that taking witnesses to the scene of the crime, showing them photographs of the scene, or having them visualize it mentally, can enhance recognition and recall.

One way of explaining the powerful influence of internal and external contexts is within Bower's (1981) "associative network theory". The theory construes emotions as serving memory units that become associated with certain features of the observed and experienced event. By reinstating or re-living the original "state" or "context", retrieval cues are maximized. This assumption forms an important basis for the theory of "cognitive interviewing techniques", which is discussed in detail in Chapter 9.

Integration or Coexistence?

The work of Loftus and her colleagues (for a review see Loftus, 1979a), shows that postevent (misleading) information can seriously interfere with the original memory of an event. Greatest contamination occurs when the postevent information is introduced after a long delay that follows acquisition, but shortly before retrieval (Loftus, Miller and Burns, 1978). In other words, contamination is most likely to occur after the memory and confidence for the original event has markedly deteriorated, which means that misleading information is not so easily detected. The other important point is that postevent information has greatest impact when it is still fresh in a witness's mind (i.e. shortly before retrieval is attempted).

Other research indicates that misleading information is more likely to be accepted if it is trivial and peripheral rather than salient and central (Hammersley and Read, 1986). Furthermore, witnesses are least likely to be misled about events that they remember well (Hammersley and Read, 1986).

There is considerable controversy in the literature about whether postevent information replaces the original memory (i.e. it becomes permanently integrated into the memorial representation of the event) or whether it coexists with the original memory and leaves it relatively unconfounded in the long-term. The former theoretical position is advanced by Loftus (Loftus, Miller and Burns, 1978; Loftus, 1979a; Hall, Loftus and Tousignant, 1984). McCloskey and Zaragoza (1985) and Zaragoza, McCloskey and Jamis (1987) have advocated the "coexistence" theory, where it is argued that the original memory is not impaired or weakened by the postevent information and that it can possibly become accessible in the right retrieval environment. What seems to happen, according to these authors, is that the misleading information is accepted by witnesses who fail to remember original critical details. In other words, it fills a gap in their memory.

Recent research shows that exposure to misleading information may not necessarily make witnesses remember having seen the information suggested, even though they accept it when being misled (Zaragoza and Koshmider, 1989). In other words, they believe the misleading information is accurate because they have no recollection to suggest otherwise, but they do not subsequently develop a memory for events they have not seen. Whether such "pseudomemory" develops after a longer retention interval than was allowed in the present study needs to be investigated in future research.

Loftus and Hoffman (1989) make the point that, irrespective of whether "integration" or "coexistence" occurs, the fact remains that postevent information (e.g. the introduction of non-existent objects) does affect eyewitnesses' testimony, and this has important legal implications.

There is some tentative evidence that subtle but real qualitative differences may exist between perceived (real) and suggested memory descriptions (Schooler, Gerhard and Loftus, 1986), which implies that witnesses and legal advocates can be taught to differentiate between the two. Real memories were found to contain more sensory information (e.g. colour, size, shape) than suggested memories. Suggested memory descriptions, on the other hand, were likely to be long-winded (i. e. more words were used to describe the event) and they lacked the vividness of the real memories.

CHILD WITNESSES

Cohen, Eysenck and Levoi (1986) argue that childhood memories tend to be "sparse and incoherent" and that relatively "little is recalled of events occurring before the age of 7" (p. 53). The authors explain this "childhood amnesia" in terms of a young child not having developed the "general knowledge schemas" which are necessary for interpreting and organizing early autobiographical memories. The notion of schemas, which was first introduced by Bartlett (1932), is that our processing of information is strongly influenced by pre-existing knowledge and experiences; that is, what is encoded and stored in memory is interpreted and organized within the context of existng mental representations or "packets of stored knowledge". This is why meaningful and familiar material is easier to remember than material that cannot be easily interpreted or organized around previous knowledge and experiences. In other words, the more one knows about a particular area of knowledge the easier it is to retain new information about it.

The Vulnerabilities of Child Witnesses

Davies (1991) has recently reviewed the literature on child witnesses. He describes growth in three areas of knowledge that improves children's ability to remember as they become older. First, there is growth in general knowledge with age which helps children to place the new experience or observation in the context of what they already know. Secondly, with age, children learn certain "scripts" or routine sequences of action in their everyday living, which facilitate memory processing. Thirdly, as children become older they learn more efficient and effective strategies for encoding information (e.g. the use of rehearsal, visual imagery and associative links). Thus, children have more limited world knowledge and encoding strategies than adults, which makes them less able to take in and retain new information.

Davies (1991) points out that children do not only have more limited encoding strategies than adults. Their retrieval strategies are also less effective, but appear to improve markedly between the ages of 5 and 10 years (Kobasigawa, 1974; similar findings are reported by Davies, Tarrant and Flin, 1989). In view of this, young children may need considerable prompting and support by the interviewer for a complete account to be obtained (Davies and Brown, 1978). However, cued recall may be particularly dangerous with children and people with mental handicap, because these two groups are much more dependent on external cues than are adults (Dent, 1986).

The most difficult cases to assess are undoubtedly those that involve the interviewing of children who, it is suspected, have been sexually abused (Jones, 1988; Wakefield and Underwager, 1988; Underwager and Wakefield, 1990). Various interviewing techniques and approaches have been recommended, including the use of anatomically correct dolls, but there is a lack of consensus about the most satisfactory way of interviewing these children (Vizard, 1991).

Jones and McGraw (1987) argue that there are qualitative differences between the fictitious and genuine accounts of children who allege sexual abuse. Fictitious accounts were marked by the absence of appropriate detail, lack of accompanying emotion, and absence of description of coercion. The children who provided reliable accounts more often used personal pronouns and age-appropriate words. Wakefield and Underwager (1988) have similarly suggested certain criteria for distinguishing between genuine and false accusations.

Yarmey (1990) recommends that children should be interviewed by the use of free narratives and general questions (e.g. "What happens when Daddy dresses you?"). Specific and leading questions should be avoided. Tully and Tam (1987) recommend that police officers use "special care questioning" techniques, which are in three parts:

1. Assessing and preparing the child for the interview;
2. A special questioning protocol, where interviewers are taught to ask open and non-leading questions;
3. Careful examination of the child's statement after the interview.

Davies, Flin and Baxter (1986) and Jones (1988) argue that young child witnesses are often able to provide valuable and reliable testimony, provided they are interviewed carefully and sympathetically.

What are the specific problems with the reliability of children's testimony? Yarmey (1990) lists four problems that have been highlighted by other authors during this century. These relate to:

1. The relative inability of some children to distinguish reality from fantasy (Piaget, 1972);
2. Children's proneness to fantasize about sexual matters (Freud, 1940);
3. The inherent suggestibility of children (Binet, 1900); and
4. The tendency of children to confabulate (Saywitz, 1987).

With regard to fantasizing, there is no empirical evidence that children's testimony is generally prone to unreliability by strong tendency to fantasize (Spencer and Flin, 1990).

In spite of these potential problems, children as young as 6 years of age are able to give accurate descriptions during free recall, although they typically recall less than adults (Goodman, Aman and Hirschman, 1987). Very young children (i.e. 3 years or younger) are less accurate than older children (Goodman, Aman and Hirschman, 1987). However, Jones (1987) illustrates a case where a 3-year-old girl was able to provide a convincing account of a traumatic event that she had experienced. Her account, which deteriorated in detail quite rapidly with time, matched the defendant's eventual confession. It seems that with young children unfamiliar events are particularly easily forgotten with time (Johnson and Foley, 1984).

It seems that children of 12 years or older are able to provide as much free recall information as adults and they are no more likely to give in to leading questions than adults (Loftus, Greene and Doyle, 1990).

Davies, Tarrant and Flin (1989) argue, on the basis of their findings, that psychologists should make a more serious attempt to identify individual witness characteristics which are likely to discriminate between reliable and unreliable child witnesses, rather than focusing on age differences *per se*.

Unfortunately, according to these authors, no cognitive and personality factors have been found that can satisfactorily discriminate between reliable and unreliable witnesses. Eyewitness confidence in recall has consistently been shown to be a poor indicator of accuracy (Wells and Murray, 1984; Loftus, Greene and Doyle, 1990). However, there are different aspects to confidence-accuracy relationships and within-person ratings appear more promising than between-persons ratings (Stephenson, 1984).

Reality Monitoring

Johnson and Raye (1981) use the term "reality monitoring" to describe the ability of the person to distinguish between two different kinds of memories:

1. Those that result from external stimuli of experienced events through perceptual processes;
2. Those that are internally generated and relate to reasoning, planning, imagining and thinking.

The inability to distinguish between the memory of an experienced (real) as opposed to an imagined event (fantasy) is commonly seen in major psychiatric illnesses, such as schizophrenia. However, a breakdown in reality monitoring can occur in everyday life (Cohen, Eysenck and Levoi, 1986). For example, it is common for the memory of a planned act to be mistaken for the memory of an act that has been carried out.

Little research has been carried out into the reality monitoring of children. For example, do children find it more difficult than adults to distinguish reality from fantasy in their recollections? In general the answer seems to be no, unless one is dealing with very young children. Lindsay and Johnson (1987) found that children as young as 6 years of age have no serious problems with reality monitoring, although younger children under certain circumstances show some inferiority to older children in reality monitoring.

The Suggestibility of Children

Are children more susceptible to leading questions than adults? It is often assumed that they are and this commonly undermines the confidence legal advocates have in their testimony (Spencer and Flin, 1990).

Moston (1990a) discusses four potential sources of suggestibility among child witnesses:

1. Demand characteristics;
2. The credibility of the misleading information;
3. Repeated questioning;
4. The linguistic form of the question.

Even when children yield to leading questions, this tends to be with regard to peripheral rather than central detail (Goodman and Reed, 1986; Goodman, Aman and Hirschman, 1987).

However, children appear significantly more responsive than adults to expectations and instructions of people in authority (Gudjonsson and Singh, 1984a; Ceci, Ross and Toglia, 1987; Zaragoza, 1987; Singh and Gudjonsson, 1991; Richardson, 1991). Therefore, the fact that the questions are leading may be less important, once their memory for an event is controlled for, than the potential influence of the interviewer. Children generally recall less of observed events than adults and this makes them potentially more suggestible. The same holds true for the mentally handicapped (Tully and Cahill, 1984; Clare and Gudjonsson, 1991a). The work which Krishna Singh and I have carried out on the impact of negative feedback with delinquent and non-delinquent children will be discussed fully in Chapter 7. It illustrates the heightened susceptibility of children to negative feedback by people in authority, even when they are no more susceptible to leading questions than adults. Even the mere fact that questions are repeated, in the absence of explicit negative feedback, may communicate to the child that their first answer was wrong and that they should give another one (Moston, 1987; 1990a).

Moston and Engelberg (1991) discuss in detail the importance of social support for children as a way of reducing stress during interviewing. This is an area that has, until recently, been seriously neglected by researchers.

THE EFFECTS OF ALCOHOL ON MEMORY

The work that has been carried out into the adverse effects of alcohol on memory has focused on three aspects of memory, as follows:

1. Short-term retention;
2. The encoding and formation of new memories, which includes the transfer of short-term memory retention into long-term storage;
3. Retrieval.

The results from the various studies indicate that moderate quantities of alcohol impair the process of forming new memories, whilst short-term retention and retrieval are unaffected (Loftus, 1980). According to Loftus' review, marijuana has similar effects on memory, except that short-term retention may also be vulnerable to an impairment.

Only one study has looked at the effects of mild alcohol intoxication on eyewitness memory. Yuille and Tollestrup (1990) interviewed 120 subjects who had witnessed a staged crime. One group (the "alcohol group") had been given three alcoholic drinks, which gave an average blood alcohol level of 0.10 ml (range 0.06–0.12 ml). The legal limit for driving in the country where the experiment was conducted is 0.08 ml. The second group (the "placebo group") was given three non-alcoholic drinks which tasted similar to real alcohol. The third group (the "control group") consumed no drink. The memories of the three groups were tested by free recall (both immediate and after 1 week's delay) and recognition (i.e. photograph identification). Approximately half of all the subjects were tested with regard to both immediate and delayed recall, whereas the remaining half only gave delayed recall.

The results of the study gave strong support for the hypothesis that even a mild level of intoxication significantly impairs memory. The two control groups recalled over 20% more information on immediate recall than the alcohol group, and their recall was also more accurate. The superior recall of the control groups persisted at 1 week follow-up, indicating that both immediate and delayed recall are adversely affected by alcohol. In view of the finding that the impaired recall of the alcohol group persisted at 1 week follow-up, when they were no longer intoxicated, Yuille and Tollestrup concluded that the most likely explanation is that alcohol interferes with the acquisition and encoding of the observed event, rather than with retrieval. What is important is that all three groups, including those who had been given alcohol, retained their memory very well indeed over a 1 week period.

There were three further findings from this study. First, state-dependent effects were not found with regard to alcohol on immediate recall. That is, testing the subjects in the alcohol group under the same conditions as they observed the "crime scenario" (i.e whilst intoxicated) did not appear to facilitate their memory. Secondly, the fact of having given immediate recall significantly improved delayed recall, which highlights the importance of retrieval practice immediately after witnessing an event. The implication for the police is that, whenever appropriate and practicable, they should consider interviewing witnesses as soon as possible after they have witnessed an event, even if they are mildly intoxicated. Thirdly, alcohol appeared to have no significant effect on witnesses' ability to identify the assailant from photographs at 1 week follow-up, although they more often made errors when the assailant's photograph was not among those shown to the subjects.

In conclusion, even a moderate amount of alcohol impairs the acquisition of new information, although the overall effects are probably quite small. Retrieval appears to be facilitated when witnesses are interviewed as soon after the observed event as possible. This also holds true for witnesses who are mildly intoxicated at the time of information acquisition.

AMNESIA

Criminal suspects commonly claim amnesia after the commission of a violent crime (for reviews see Schacter, 1986a: Kopelman, 1987). Amnesia may also be claimed in cases of non-violent crimes, but its reported frequency is much less than that for violent crimes (Schacter, 1986a). "Amnesia" in this context means a general impairment in previously acquired memories, which is a pathological condition and can be either *organic* or *functional* in origin. It is not to be confused with normal forgetting in everyday life.

"Organic amnesia" refers to pathological forgetting, which is caused by some damage, temporary or permanent, to brain functions. The different types of organic amnesias are discussed in detail by Kopelman (1987). They include head injury, brain disease, epilepsy, drug toxicity and alcohol blackouts. "Functional amnesias" occur without any evidence of brain pathology (i.e. they are predominantly psychological or psychogenic in nature). This type of amnesia includes "fugue states" (i.e. loss of memory for one's personal identity, associated with a period of wandering) and situation-specific amnesia where the memory for specific episodes is lost (e.g. about a violent crime). Functional amnesias are commonly thought to result from emotional shock and psychological trauma (Schacter, 1986a), but they do appear to develop more readily in people with a previous history of brain damage (Kopelman, 1987).

Amnesia, whether organic or functional in nature, can be either *anterograde* or *retrograde*. The former refers to a pathological impairment in the remembering of facts and events after the psychological or organic trauma, whereas the latter entails forgetting before the onset of the trauma. Kopelman (1987) uses the term "post-traumatic amnesia" to describe memory loss following the trauma or shock (e.g murder, head injury) and ending when the memory is fully recovered. It differs from "anterograde" amnesia in that the amnesia for the crucial period may persist without impaired ability to learn new information.

Taylor and Kopelman (1984) examined 203 men during custodial remand and looked in depth at their offences, their mental states at the time, and their memories of the offences and their surrounding circumstances. Twenty-one (10%) claimed to be amnesic for their offence. Their amnesia was most commonly associated with acts of violence and when the victim was closely related to the offender. Out of 34 homicide cases, nine (36%) claimed amnesia, and in these cases the victim was, with one or two exceptions, a relative or a close friend. On the basis of their findings, Taylor and Kopelman suggest that there are three main ways in which amnesia for offences occurs:

1. As a result of the pharmacological effects of alcohol;
2. As part of a psychotic mental state (schizophrenia or depression);
3. As a psychological defence mechanism, such as repression or suppression.

Taylor and Kopelman assumed for research purposes that all their subjects' claims of amnesia were genuine.

In a recent Icelandic study (Gudjonsson et al., 1989), amnesia was found to have been claimed in nine out of 16 (56%) homicide or attempted homicide cases. All nine offenders had been intoxicated at the time of the offence. These findings are in broad agreement with those of O'Connell (1960), Bradford and Smith (1979), Taylor and Kopelman (1984) and Parwatikar, Holcomb and Menninger (1985), in that amnesia is claimed in a large proportion of homicide cases and alcohol intoxication is reported with high frequency in such cases.

Alcohol on its own does not cause amnesia, unless it is related to alcoholic "blackouts" (Goodwin, Crane and Guze, 1969). It is more likely that in some cases alcohol-induced brain dysfunction acts as a substrate which directs the way in which the person copes with severe emotional stress (Gudjonsson and Taylor, 1985).

Kopelman (1987) describes three possible mechanisms in psychogenic (functional) amnesia:

1. Faulty memory acquisition. The severe emotional stress or trauma that precedes the amnesia impairs the ability of the person to register and encode what is going on.
2. It is proposed that the trauma associated with the observed or participated event is unacceptable to the conscious mind of the person and is consequently "repressed" (i.e. pushed out of awareness). When this occurs salient information can possibly be detected by psychophysiological means without conscious awareness (Gudjonsson, 1979b; Lynch and Bradford, 1980). A detailed discussion of the role of "repression" in the development of amnesia is given by Pratt (1977).
3. Following the work of Bower (1981), psychogenic amnesia is viewed in the context of a state-dependent memory. Here the amnesia is construed as a primary retrieval deficit. It requires inducing in the person the same subjective state as that which occurred at the time of the amnesia.

What has never been established in the literature is the proportion of psychogenic amnesias that are actually genuine. Some authors are very sceptical about the genuineness of psychogenic amnesia and view most such amnesias as feigned (e.g. Price and Terhune, 1919; Bradford and Smith, 1979; Bronks, 1987). Such scepticism was highlighted in the English landmark case of R-Podola (Court of Criminal Appeal, October 1959). Others (e.g. Pratt, 1977; Taylor and Kopelman, 1984; Kopelman, 1987) are more accepting about genuine claims of amnesia. Schacter (1986b) suggests that there are two different methods of differentiating between feigned and genuine amnesia.

The first approach is to look at the psychiatric history of the amnesic person (Bradford and Smith, 1979), the current psychological profile (Parwatikar, Holcomb and Menninger, 1985), the premeditation of the crime (Power, 1977), and the response to drug-aided interviews and the polygraph (Bradford and Smith, 1979; Lynch and Bradford, 1980). These approaches are all without empirical support.

The second approach is to look at the nature of the amnesia and devise methods of differentiating between feigned and genuine amnesia. Schacter

(1986b) has provided some evidence from controlled laboratory studies that "feeling-of-knowing" ratings (i.e. the subjective feeling that one could retrieve the "lost" memory if given the right cues) can differentiate between genuine and feigned forgetting. The reason seems to be that people who feign the condition have insufficient understanding about the nature of genuine memory loss and this makes their faking open to detection. Whether similar methods of detecting malingering can be applied to cases of alleged amnesia, which after all is different to normal forgetting, remains to be seen.

In conclusion, amnesia is a pathological form of forgetting which is commonly reported by offenders following the commission of a violent crime. The condition may have both functional (psychogenic) and organic causes. Our understanding about the nature of amnesia and ways of establishing its genuineness are very limited at present.

CONCLUSIONS

In this Chapter I have discussed the nature and relevance of memory within the context of testimony. Memory is an active and constructive process and there are a number of factors that can interfere with the processes of *acquisition*, *retention* and *retrieval*. Broadly speaking, these three stages can be influenced by such factors as the person's abilities, past experiences, beliefs, personality, and physical and mental state, in addition to a host of factors associated with the custodial environment. We know a great deal about the type of event factors that can influence memory, but lack knowledge about factors related to individual differences, such as personality.

The acquisition of memory can be impaired by such factors as short observation period, the focus of attention, poor lighting conditions, lack of interest, alcohol intoxication, the nature and degree of violence contained in the stimulus material, and stress. The relationship between emotional stress and memory needs to be considered in the context of the nature of the detail observed. Whereas emotional stress appears to enhance memory for *central* detail, it reduces the amount of *peripheral* detail observed.

The retention of memory generally deteriorates over time, which can be caused by both normal forgetting and interference with memory by postevent information. Misleading information most readily distorts memory when it is encountered by the witness after a long retention interval. Peripheral details are more prone to distortion than the central features. The type of material stored in memory is also important. For example, voice recognition seems less reliably remembered than face recognition and is more affected by delay. Witnesses typically overestimate the duration of an event, particularly when it is emotionally stressful.

Much of the inability to remember is due to problems with retrieval rather than acquisition and retention. This is because the information that has been satisfactorily stored in memory is not always accessible, i.e. it cannot be readily retrieved. At any one time only a small fraction of all available memory is accessible. Memory retrieval can be enhanced by applying certain retrieval techniques. These are discussed in detail in Chapter 8.

There are special problems with child witnesses, because of their relatively poorer retrieval abilities and greater suggestibility under certain conditions. However, child witnesses, even very young ones, can give reliable accounts of events and people's appearance when they are carefully interviewed.

Psychogenic amnesia for salient events is often claimed in cases of violent crimes. It is alleged to occur in between one-third and half of all homicide cases and most commonly accompanies the killing of a close relative or a friend. There are no reliable psychological methods available at present for differentiating genuine from feigned amnesia.

CHAPTER 6

Suggestibility: Historical and Theoretical Aspects

My interest in "interrogative suggestibility" began in 1980 when I took a post as a Lecturer in Psychology at the Institute of Psychiatry, University of London. I was commonly being asked by defence and prosecution counsels to prepare court reports involving the assessment of the reliability of evidence. These referrals generally related to two types of cases:

1. Where mentally handicapped victims were going to be called to give evidence but there was concern about the likely reliability of their evidence;
2. Where defendants had retracted confessions made during police interviewing.

Cases of the former type were generally referred by the prosecution, and the latter by defence counsel. It soon became apparent that the legal advocates were particularly interested in the individual's levels of suggestibility.

In a pioneering single case study, Professor Gunn and I (Gudjonsson and Gunn, 1982) established a precedent at the Old Bailey in London (formally known as the Central Criminal Court). The case involved a 22-year-old mentally handicapped woman called Mary, who claimed that she had been sexually assaulted by a group of young men and women. The Director of Public Prosecutions requested an answer to three main questions:

1. Was Mary competent as a witness in a court of law?
2. If she was competent, was she reliable as a witness?
3. Was she severely subnormal as defined in the Mental Health Act 1959?

Being able to establish the likely reliability of Mary's statements was particularly important as her testimony was the main prosecution evidence against six defendants.

The psychological assessment, carried out by myself, focused on Mary's mental handicap and the likely reliability of her evidence. The assessment was carried out during two sessions on the same day. Mary obtained a Full Scale IQ of 47 on the Wechsler Adult Intelligence Scale. At the time of the assessment there was no standardized psychological test available which could be used to assess the reliability of Mary's testimony. For this reason I used (experimental) psychological procedures to assess Mary's general level of "suggestibility". These were as follows:

1. Did Mary have a tendency to claim perceptions that had no objective basis?
2. Did Mary have a tendency to answer questions with information that the interviewer suggested?

The first procedure related to possible distortions in Mary's *sensory* processing, whereas the latter was concerned with her *memory* processing.

Mary's suggestibility was tested in the afternoon, whereas the intellectual assessment had been completed in the morning. She was told that the purpose of the afternoon session was to establish how much she remembered about the morning session. During free recall Mary was able to give a reasonably accurate account of the morning session and even remembered several of the questions asked and tests administered. Subsequently an attempt was made to induce in Mary false perceptions, both olfactory (the smell of a cigar) and tactile (feeling a pencil she was holding becoming increasingly hot and reaching the point of burning her fingers). Mary uncritically accepted both suggestions and during the tactile experiment she suddenly dropped the pencil on the floor claiming that it had burned her finger.

With regard to interrogative suggestibility, a special test was constructed which consisted of leading questions. After each leading question I challenged her answer and asked her to provide a more accurate one. Mary proved highly suggestible in response to many, but not all, of the questions. She was particularly suggestible when confronted with sophisticated or abstract ideas and then readily gave observations which had no basis in her own observations. When uncertain about events, she tended to confabulate. However, she was able to resist attempts to alter her account of events she had experienced and clearly remembered.

The main conclusions from the psychological assessment, which were presented to the jury in the case, were that Mary had limited mental capacity, but she was capable of distinguishing between facts and fantasy when facts were clear to her. Her ability to distinguish between the two diminished markedly when she was unsure of facts. Then she became highly suggestible. However, those of her statements that had no objective basis could be easily altered under pressure, whereas those answers that were correct could not be altered. The psychological findings were presented to the jury in such a way as to provide them with some guidelines by which they could discriminate between the reliable and unreliable evidence as pertaining to the case being tried. Thus, although Mary was in general very suggestible, she was able to give reliable evidence about facts that she had witnessed and was certain about. It was suggested that the jury could differentiate between Mary's reliable and unreliable evidence on the basis of her answers to careful cross-examination; reliable evidence pertaining to simple and basic facts should not alter under cross-examination whereas unreliable evidence was likely to. Mary's evidence was subjected to this test. Although unable to identify any of the six defendants as being responsible for specific acts, she gave a general account of events which the jury found reliable. The outcome of the case was that five of the six defendants were convicted on at least one charge.

The most important lesson from this case is that moderately mentally handicapped people may well be able to give reliable evidence pertaining to basic facts, even when they are generally highly suggestible and prone to confabulation. A detailed psychological assessment of the handicapped person's strengths and limitations may be necessary in some cases in order to provide the jury with information which helps them evaluate the reliability of the person's testimony.

The present case provides a model of how this can be achieved. Davies, Flin and Baxter (1986) consider that an extension of the procedure pioneered in our case could provide a useful innovation in the case of children's testimonies.

There was an important legal distinction made in the present case between Mary's competence as a witness and the reliability of her evidence. The two were dealt with as separate issues. Competence was decided by the judge on the basis of Mary's understanding of the concepts of truth, God and contempt of court, whereas the issue of reliability, the judge decided, was for the jury to decide upon.

Mary's case provided a conceptual framework for assessing the reliability of evidence by way of psychological procedures. It resulted in the development of a standardized psychological test for measuring "interrogative suggestibility" (Gudjonsson, 1983a, 1984a), which formed the basis for the theoretical model of Gudjonsson and Clark (1986).

In this chapter the theoretical work that has been carried out into interrogative suggestibility will be reviewed in some detail. I will argue that it is a special type of suggestibility and it bears little resemblance to traditional classifications of suggestibility, such as that commonly associated with hypnosis. I shall endeavour to explain precisely how it differs from other types of suggestibility and what the implications are. Until recently, interrogative suggestibility has been a neglected area of research and much of the review literature into suggestion and suggestibility has failed to specifically mention this type of suggestibility.

THEORETICAL APPROACHES

There are two main theoretical approaches to interrogative suggestibility. Schooler and Loftus (1986) refer to these as the "individual differences approach" and the "experimental approach". According to these authors, the first approach is best illustrated by my own work (Gudjonsson, 1983a, 1984a), which was integrated into a detailed model (Gudjonsson and Clark, 1986; see below). The model has specific domains of applicability to police interrogation and views suggestibility as being dependent upon the coping strategies people can generate and implement when confronted with the *uncertainty* and *expectations* of the interrogative situation. The emphasis of the model is on explaining *individual differences* in interrogative suggestibility.

The "experimental approach" is illustrated by the work of Loftus and her colleagues (Loftus, Miller and Burns, 1978; Schooler and Loftus, 1986). Here the emphasis is on understanding the conditions under which leading questions are likely to affect the verbal accounts of witnesses. Individual differences do not feature prominently in this approach and interrogative suggestibility is viewed as being mediated by a central cognitive mechanism, labelled "discrepancy detection".

There is no doubt that the two approaches—the individual differences and the experimental—are complementary to each other and they will feature extensively in the rest of this Chapter. The emphasis in this Chapter is on *theoretical* aspects of suggestibility. The procedural implications of the two theoretical approaches will be discussed in Chapter 7.

SOME CHARACTERISTICS OF SUGGESTION AND SUGGESTIBILITY

There is an important distinction to be drawn between the concepts of "suggestion" and "suggestibility". These two concepts, although clearly linked, have been poorly defined and differentiated in the literature. In fact, in the early literature there seems to have been no distinction made between suggestion and suggestibililty (Gudjonsson, 1987a).

With regard to the concept of suggestion, Gheorghiu (1989a) refers to the early definition of McDougall (1908) as still being of great influence. McDougall defined suggestion as:

> "A process of communication resulting in the acceptance with conviction of the communicated proposition in the absence of logically adequate grounds for its acceptance" (p. 100).

McDougall thought that his definition covered all "varieties" of suggestion and suggestibility. There are two major problems with McDougall's definition.

First, it implies that a particular suggestion inevitably results in the acceptance of the suggestion. As Gheorghiu (1989a) points out, this is not necessarily the case. In fact, he argues elsewhere (Gheorghiu, 1972) that an essential prerequisite is that in every suggestible situation the person must have the alternative for a suggestible or a non-suggestible reaction; if there is no opportunity for an alternative response then the response elicited is forced or coerced rather than selected.

The second problem with McDougall's definition of suggestion is that it fails to draw a distinction between suggestion as a stimulus and the reaction of the individual to the suggestion. Rather than construing suggestion as a complicated process, as McDougall does, it is operationally much simpler to conceptualize it as a *stimulus* which provides an individual with a certain message to respond to. This message may be variously referred to as a hint, a cue or an idea. Viewing suggestion as a stimulus, which has the potential to trigger or elicit a reaction, makes it easier to separate it conceptually from the concept of suggestibility.

Suggestibility refers to the *tendency* of the individual to respond in a particular way to suggestions. Therefore, whereas suggestion refers to the properties contained in a stimulus, suggestibility refers to characteristics of the person who is being incited to respond. The suggestion only has the potential to elicit a reaction; whether it does or not depends on the susceptibility of the person, the nature and characteristics of the suggestion and the person offering it, and the context in which the suggestion occurs.

Gheorghiu (1989b) makes the important differentiation between *direct* and *indirect* suggestion procedures, a distinction he attributes to Sidis (1898). A *direct* procedure involves the subject being told openly and explicitly what is expected of him or her. In other words, the intention of the influence is *overt*. *Indirect* suggestion procedure is more subtle and implicit. The experimenter does not make it clear or obvious that he or she is attempting to influence the responses of the subject. This typically means that the subject is not informed of the actual purpose of the test or procedure.

Gheorghiu (1989b) argues that the effects of suggestions can sometimes become compulsive. He gives as an example people whose lives become unwittingly influenced by the prediction of a fortune-teller. Similarly, he argues, "people can autosuggestively talk themselves into thoughts of suicide and then more or less compulsively surrender to them" (p. 101). The idea of autosuggestion implies that people can generate their own suggestions; that is, spontaneously suggest things to themselves.

Gheorghiu (1989b) has drawn attention to the lack of unitary definitions of the concepts of suggestion and suggestibility. He cogently argues that, because of the complexity and varied nature of the phenomena, collective theoretical and empirical input from specialists of different disciplines is required.

BRIEF HISTORICAL BACKGROUND TO SUGGESTIBILITY

Coffin (1941) stated that the early principle and theory of suggestion came from hypnotists in the nineteenth century, although the phenomena of suggestion were recognized long before that time. Coffin quotes the work of Noizt, who pointed out in 1820 that the fundamental psychological law at work is that every idea might become an action (the phenomenon was later labelled as an "ideo-motor" response). Thus, the suggested idea is transformed into action because the idea of the action has reached the respondent's consciousness. This shows how the concept of suggestion was originally developed as a way of explaining hypnotic phenomena, and replaced the "fluidistic" theories that were prevalent at the time, such as those relating to "animal magnetism". Those theories viewed hypnosis as arising from physical influences, and the psychological forces at work were either not recognized or minimized at the time. According to Gheorghiu (1989b), the concept of suggestion began to play a significant part in hypnosis when early workers, such as Bertrand (1823) and Braid (1846), began to consider hypnosis from a more psychological perspective.

Bernheim (1910) expanded the meaning of the term suggestion and considered it to be a normal phenomenon that might take place in a waking state as well as during hypnosis. He described a range of phenomena which he considered were related to suggestion, such as the daily influence of one person upon another resulting in changes in beliefs and attitudes, and the phenomena observed in hypnotized individuals. It is important to note that Bernheim provided no evidence that these different phenomena were fundamentally related. Indeed, they probably were not related at all.

Gheorghiu (1989b), p. 3) argues that Bernheim's (1888, reprinted 1964) work was particularly important in drawing attention to the concept of suggestion as "a fundamental principle for the explanation of hypnosis itself" rather than considering it only as "a vehicle for the induction of hypnotic phenomena". This extended interpretation of the concept of suggestion meant that suggestion was seen as an important feature of hypnosis, where hypnosis was itself characterized by heightened suggestibility. Thus, no longer was suggestion only seen as a medium for inducing hypnosis; people who had been successfully hypnotized were seen as optimally susceptible to suggestions.

Interest in individual differences and experimental psychology at the turn of the nineteenth century resulted in many tests of suggestibility being developed. Here the term suggestion was operationally defined in tests and experimental procedures. These were initially limited to producing simple motor and sensory reaction, but they gradually included more complex phenomena, such as changes in judgement, opinion and attitude. The tests and procedures used were not based on clear theoretical foundations, and it is for this reason that the theoretical work on suggestion and suggestibility has greatly lagged behind the experimental and applied work.

Most of the early tests of suggestibility measured the influence of suggestion upon the sensory system (visual, tactile, auditory, olfactory, etc.). Commonly the procedure consisted of the subject being presented with a real sensory stimulus which was then omitted without informing the subject, whose reactions were monitored. In one test a small electric current was passed into the subject's hand which made it slightly warm. The procedure was subsequently repeated without the current being on, but the subject was not informed about this. The subject was considered suggestible if he or she reported warmth the second time, and the faster the response was elicited the more suggestible the subject was considered to be. Similar tests were developed by Binet (1990), which dealt with suggestively produced illusions of change concerning progressive weights and lines. In all these tests the suggestions were presented *indirectly*, in that the subject did not know that he or she was being influenced.

Several tests of motor suggestibility have been developed and these are generally construed as *direct* tests, in the sense that the subject is told that he or she is being influenced. Examples of these tests are the "hand rigidity" test of Aveling and Hargreaves (1921) and Hull's (1933) well-known "body sway" test. With regard to the former test, the subject is told that his arm is gradually becoming rigid like a steel poker, whereas in the "body sway" test the subject is told that he is falling forwards or backwards and the distance he slopes in the suggested direction is carefully monitored.

THE CLASSIFICATION OF SUGGESTIBILITY

Eysenck's early and influential work into the nature of suggestibility was to establish, by the use of factor analysis, to what extent the range of different suggestibility tests were functionally related (Eysenck, 1943; Eysenck and Furneaux, 1945). The result of these studies was to demonstrate that there are at least two independent types of suggestibility, labelled by Eysenck and Furneaux as "primary" and "secondary". The primary type consisted of so-called "ideo-motor" tests, whose phenomena are characterized by non-volitional movements following the experimenter's repetitive and monotonous suggestion. The best single test of primary suggestibility is the "body sway" test discussed earlier, which has been consistently shown to correlate highly with hypnotizability. Eysenck and Furneaux (1945) showed that primary suggestibility correlated significantly with neuroticism. Gibson (1962) subsequently looked closely at personality variables associated with susceptibility to hypnosis, and suggested that it was more meaningful to look at the combination of personality scores rather than individual correlations.

The evidence for a stable factor of secondary suggestibility is less clear than for primary suggestibility. It seems to embrace much more varied and complex phenomena than primary suggestibility. Eysenck (1947) associates it with "indirection" and "gullibility" and defines it as:

> "The experience on the part of the subject of a sensation or perception consequent upon the direct or implied suggestion by the experimenter that such an experience will take place, in the absence of any objective basis for the sensation or perception" (p. 167).

Eysenck gave the "ink blot" and "odour" tests as examples of the kind of tests measuring secondary suggestibility. Secondary suggestibility did not correlate with hypnotizability and there was a negative correlation with intelligence.

Eysenck and Furneaux (1945) raise the possibility of "tertiary" suggestibility, which involves attitude change resulting from persuasive communication originating from a prestige figure. Evans (1967) argues that the empirical evidence for this type of suggestibility is lacking, but the idea was nevertheless found to be meaningful in the work of Gibson (1962). The "tertiary" type of suggestibility bears some resemblance to interrogative suggestibility.

Evans (1967, 1989) argues that the traditional distinction between primary and secondary suggestibility has been made without sufficient empirical evidence. He suggests that three types of suggestibility are identifiable, which he refers to as "primary" (passive motor), "challenge" and "imagery" (sensory) suggestibility, respectively. A fourth factor was vaguely identified which related to "dissociative" behaviour and this was not thought to be related to "waking" suggestibility dimensions.

Evans (1967, 1989) recognizes that factor-analytic studies following the work of Eysenck and Furneaux (1945) have consistently confirmed the existence of primary suggestibility, but much less support has been found for a single factor of secondary suggestibility of the kind described by Eysenck and Furneaux.

Evans (1989) discusses two further findings which are important in relation to the classification of suggestibility. Firstly, a placebo response, which has important implications for various therapies, has no relationship with suggestibility or hypnotizability. It seems directly related to expectancy variables, particularly those found in a doctor–patient relationship. Secondly, the ability to produce meaningful behavioural responses to suggestion during REM ("rapid eye movement") sleep is significantly correlated with hypnotizability and "dissociative" phenomena.

It is interesting to note that the detailed work of Evans (1967, 1989) completely ignores any mention of a suggestibility factor relevant to interrogation, although Binet (1900) and Stern (1910, 1938) had produced interrogative procedures which could well have been included in factor analytical studies into the classification of suggestibility.

The only early work that does highlight the importance of interrogative suggestibility in the classification of suggestibility is that of Stukat (1958). He carried out a number of factor-analytical studies with children and adults in Sweden as a classification device for generating hypotheses and understanding the nature of suggestibility. Unlike the previous research, Stukat included in his research tests intended to measure "personal" and "prestige" types of suggestibility, and two "leading question" tests. The results of his factor analysis revealed a secondary suggestibility factor of rather wide scope, which was somewhat dissimilar to that of Eysenck and Furneaux and represents tests:

"... in which different subjective influences, such as set expectations and need for conformity, direct the individual's perceptions, memory and judgement" (Stukat, 1958, p. 239).

The kind of tests that had the highest factor loadings on Stukat's secondary suggestibility factor were:

1. "Contradictory suggestion" tests (the examiner contradicts the subject's judgement in a discrimination task);
2. "Co-judge" suggestion tests (a tendency to be influenced by co-judge suggestion in making one's judgement in a discrimination task);
3. "Weight and line pairs" tasks (the subject has to classify non-identical weights and lines after a suggestion that they are identical).

The two "leading question" tests had rather low loadings on this factor and correlated poorly with the secondary suggestibility tests described above. Stukat thought that the contradictory and co-judge tests were most clearly characterized by personal influence and pressure from one individual upon another, so that the individual's need for conformity was the most significant functional determinant in the secondary suggestibility process. Results from group comparisons supported Stukat's theory. That is, groups thought to have the strongest need for conformity (e.g. young children, anxious people) were found to be most suggestible. The findings were interpreted as showing that "functional determinants", such as needs, attitudes, values and differential reinforcement, influence perception, memory and judgement, particularly in an unstructured situation.

It is evident from the above discussion that there are several different types of suggestibility. According to Gheorghiu (1989a), suggestion procedures have traditionally been used to influence three unrelated processes— motor processes, sensory processes and memory processes. We have seen that motor processes are commonly associated with *primary* suggestibility, which in turn is related to hypnotizability. *Secondary* suggestibility is found to cover a range of different test phenomena, which are mostly but not exclusively associated with sensory processes and perceptual judgements. Unfortunately, the tests that seem to make up the secondary suggestibility factor are not always closely interrelated. A broad definition of secondary suggestibility seems to have some theoretical implications for interrogative suggestibility, but it is the influence upon memory processes which is clearly most relevant.

After reviewing the literature on suggestibility I concluded that there were good theoretical and empirical reasons for construing interrogative suggestibility as a distinct type of suggestibility (Gudjonsson, 1987a). This view has been recently reinforced by Gheorghiu (1989b) in his critical review of the development of research on suggestibility. Indeed, interrogative suggestibility bears little resemblance to traditional definitions of suggestibility, whether classified into "primary" and "secondary" phenomena as Eysenck proposes (Eysenck and Furneaux, 1945; Eysenck, 1943) or "primary", "challenge" and "imagery" suggestibility, as argued by Evans (1967). In particular, on conceptual grounds no relationship would be expected between interrogative suggestibility and primary suggestibility.

THEORIES OF SUGGESTIBILITY

A number of theories have been put forward in order to explain primary and secondary suggestibility. These have been extensively reviewed by Stukat (1958). Primary suggestibility is most commonly explained in terms of an ideo-motor response, which is fundamentally related to theories of conditioning. These seem of no relevance to interrogative suggestibility and will not be discussed in detail.

Various theories have been proposed to explain phenomena relevant to the elusive entity of secondary suggestibility. For example, Binet's (1900) tests of progressive weights and lines, as well as his "prestige" and "interrogatory" tests, were assumed by him to include:

1. Obedience to mental influence from another person;
2. The tendency to imitate;
3. Influence of a preconceived idea that paralysed the individual's critical sense;
4. Expectative attention.

Stukat (1958) found some support for Binet's theoretical formulation from his factorial studies, where the first two categories (1 and 2 above) were quite similar to Stukat's "need for conformity" factors and the last two (3 and 4) corresponded to an "expectative" factor.

McDougall (1908), whose definition of suggestion was given earlier, associates suggestibility with four distinct conditions:

1. Abnormal states of the brain (e.g. as during hypnosis, sleep and fatigue);
2. Deficiency and poor organization of knowledge regarding the subject matter being communicated;
3. The impressive character of the person communicating the suggestion (i.e. "prestige" suggestion);
4. The character and disposition of the subject.

McDougall thought of the relative strengths of "instincts", "assertion" and "subjection" as the most crucial conditions determining the individual's level of suggestibility. For example, an individual with a strong impulse of self-assertion when communicating with others of lower status makes the former non-suggestible to the influence of the latter. McDougall also emphasized the importance of the person's knowledge, and confidence in his knowledge, as mediating variables in the susceptibility to suggestion. McDougall's emphasis on both *motivation* and *cognitive* factors in determining suggestibility is fundamental to the understanding of secondary suggestibility, including interrogative suggestibility.

Another theoretical model of relevance to secondary suggestibility is that of Sherif (1936). He argues that a stimulus is never reacted to in isolation. It is always experienced, perceived, judged and reacted to in relation to other stimuli, present or past, to which it is fundamentally related. Sherif used the term "frame of reference" to denote these functionally related factors that influence perceptions and judgements.

Coffin (1941) has expanded Sherif's theory. He regards suggestion as a framework response, determined by internal factors (e.g. attitude) and external features of the stimulus situation. When a situation is "well structured" in terms of either attitudinal or situational factors, only those suggestions which accord with the existing frame of reference are likely to be accepted. The advantage of the *cognitive* model of Sherif and Coffin is that it is conceptually simple and seems to explain many experimental findings. A possible weakness is the strong emphasis on the cognitive aspects of internal factors, because even though suggestions may well function as a frame of reference, usually there are emotional and motivational factors involved in the suggestion process which "drive" the subject towards accepting or rejecting the suggestion.

A similar cognitive emphasis is evident in the work of Asch and his colleagues on prestige suggestion (Asch, Block and Hertzman, 1938; Asch, 1952; Crutchfield, 1955; Krech, Crutchfield and Ballachey, 1962). In accordance with Gestalt psychology, Asch (1952) argues that subjects' reactions in "prestige" experiments such as those of Bridge (1914) and Moore (1921) are reasonable and rational and quite different from the uncritical automatic reactions of hypnotized subjects. One of Asch's most important contributions to the suggestibility literature is to point to a distinct cognitive difference between hypnotic suggestion and "prestige" suggestion on the basis of qualitative analysis. Within this theoretical framework, man is seen as a rational creature who searches logically for meaning and coherence. The emphasis on the rational character of suggestible behaviour is in contrast to a more sociological view, where the emphasis is placed upon the passive and uncritical nature of the reaction in social situations.

Milgram (1974) has researched the effects of authority, status and power on such behaviour as obedience. He defined obedience as the action of a subject "who complies with authority" (p. 113). He investigated the extent to which subjects were prepared to obey the instructions of an experimenter when it involved behaviour ordinarily regarded as unreasonable and socially unacceptable (e.g. seemingly administering a strong electric shock to helpless victims). Milgram concluded that the extensive willingness of subjects to uncritically obey the experimenter was due to the special relationship which developed between the experimenter and the subject. Most subjects reported that they felt under strong pressure to obey the experimenter, believing that disobeying would ruin the experiment and upset the experimenter. This raises an important point about the extent to which the implicit etiquette in a particular situation can influence human behaviour. Milgram discusses this point within the framework of Goffman's (1959) influential book *The Presentation of Self in Everyday Life*.

Milgram makes four important distinctions between obedience to authority and conformity to peer group pressure as described by Asch (1951), as follows:

1. Obedience, unlike conformity, occurs within a hierarchical structure;
2. Conformity means that people imitate the behaviours and values of others. In contrast, obedience refers to compliance without imitating the source of influence;
3. The message that results in obedience is typically direct (i.e. an order or a command), whereas it is implicit or indirect in the case of conformity;
4. In Milgram's obedience research, subjects admitted that they were complying with a force external to themselves, whereas it is evident from conformity studies that the subjects are largely unaware of the pressure acting on them to conform.

Irving and Hilgendorf (1980) have applied Milgram's findings to police interrogation situations and point out that during interrogation some subjects may obey instructions that ordinarily they would resist.

It is important to realize that the studies of Asch and Crutchfield are concerned with influence in the context of group pressure, whereas obedience research focuses on how subjects react to pressure from a person in authority. However, the behaviour of the subject in each setting may be mediated by similar factors, such as a desire to be liked, eagerness to please, the need to maintain self-esteem, the need to fulfil role obligations and expectations, and avoidance of conflict and confrontation.

The powerful influence of perceived authority on behaviour has not just been demonstrated by laboratory studies, such as those of Milgram. For example, Bickman (1974) studied the effects of uniform on people's compliance in a natural social setting. He found that when the experimenter was dressed in a guard's uniform, 83% of pedestrians obeyed his instruction to give a confederate a "dime" for a parking meter, in contrast to 46% when he was dressed in civilian clothing.

Within the field of social psychology, the term "conformity" is used to refer to a change in behaviour or belief as a result of pressure, real or imagined, from a group or a person (Kiesler and Kiesler, 1970). According to Kiesler and Kiesler, there are basically two types of conformity which correspond to the terms "compliance" and "private acceptance". With regard to compliance, people behave as others wish them to behave but without their believing in what they are doing. Kiesler and Kiesler argue that obedience studies, like those of Milgram, give a good illustration of compliance without private acceptance. Private acceptance, on the other hand, is more commonly seen in studies into suggestibility.

Reinforcement and Suggestibility

The effects of prior reinforcement upon suggestibility (e.g. Kelman, 1950) have important implications for interrogative suggestibility. The general finding is that individuals who experience success in a task when they are first examined tend to be more resistant to subsequent suggestions than those who experience failure. Such findings can be interpreted along both *motivational* (e.g. strength of the anxiety drive) and *cognitive* (thought processes) lines. The work of Kelman is particularly supportive of motivational factors in that certain personality factors (e.g. traits of submissiveness, inferiority feelings, anxiety) seem to interact with differential reinforcement. Related to this is the work of Seligman and his colleagues on "learned helplessness" (Abramson, Seligman and Teasdale, 1978).

Suggestibility: a State or a Trait?

There is a considerable disagreement in the literature about whether suggestibility should be viewed as a "trait" or a "state". Implicit in the concept of suggestibility is the idea that it refers to some stable tendency of the individual to respond in a particular way to a given situation. Prideaux (1919) viewed suggestibility as a general trait of the individual. The work of Eysenck (1947) into different types of suggestibility very much relies on the trait hypothesis. Critical advocates of the trait hypothesis, such as Krech and Crutchfield (1948), Baxter (1990) and Moston (1990a) emphasize that suggestibility is greatly affected by situational factors. Indeed, Krech and Crutchfield reject the trait hypothesis and are pessimistic about developing individual measures of suggestibility. They construe suggestibility as being dependent upon the "total psychological situation" (p. 337).

Krech and Crutchfield put forward two reasons for rejecting the trait hypothesis. First, they point to the poor correlations between different suggestibility tests, and between suggestibility and personality type. Hence, the specific nature of the test situation is assumed to be more important than a person's psychological make-up. Secondly, even if consistently high correlations were found between different suggestibility tests this does not necessarily give support for the trait hypothesis, because subjects may consistently accept or reject suggestions for very different reasons.

Stukat (1958) is critical of the reasons put forward by Krech and Crutchfield against the trait hypothesis, but concedes that:

> "No analysis of suggestion and suggestibility can omit the actual needs and attitudes of the subject, the personal relationship between experimenter and subject, or the characteristics of the stimulus situation" (p. 32).

Stukat argues that Krech and Crutchfield go too far in their emphasis on situational factors by denying the existence of suggestibility as a trait. He provides evidence from his own extensive research to support the trait hypothesis and states:

> "Therefore we conclude that, in view of the fact that the situational variation was maximized in our investigations, there have appeared suggestibility factors that were not situationally caused. It then seems reasonable to refer the factors to relatively constant tendencies in the individual to be more or less suggestible, irrespective of the situation" (p. 92).

DEFINITION OF INTERROGATIVE SUGGESTIBILITY

One of the earliest experiments conducted into human testimony is that of Cattell (1895). He asked college students a number of questions that were potentially misleading and they had to indicate their degree of confidence in each answer. However, the idea of interrogative suggestibility appears to have been first introduced at the turn of the century by Binet (1900, 1905), whose contribution to the understanding and measurement of the various types of suggestibility has been quite outstanding. Unfortunately, his book *La Suggestibilité* has never been translated into English and it is undoubtedly for this reason that his work has not been as influential as it should have been. Binet's procedure for measuring interrogative suggestibility involved asking leading questions concerning a picture which subjects had been shown previously. This kind of "interrogatory" procedure, which is of relevance to the effects of questioning upon memory recall and testimony, was subsequently used by other workers, such as Stern. The classical experimental work of Stern (1910, 1938, 1939) demonstrated that leading questions can produce distorted responses because they are phrased in such a way as to suggest the wanted response, whether correct or incorrect. Several subsequent studies have employed a similar or modified procedure to that of Stern in order to elicit this type of suggestibility (e.g. Burtt, 1948; Trankell, 1958; Powers, Andriks and Loftus, 1979; Cohen and Harnick, 1980).

Davies, Flin and Baxter (1986) make the interesting observation that both Binet and Stern used static pictures rather than simulated incidents as stimulus material, although Stern (1910) did call for "event tests" (i.e. studies of incidents). Davies et al. argue that static pictures may limit the forensic relevance of the material. This problem was overcome by the early innovative British study of Pear and Wyatt (1914), who used a realistic simulated incident as stimulus material.

Not all authors agree on a definition of interrogative suggestibility. Powers, Andriks and Loftus (1979) define it as:

> ". . . the extent to which they [people] come to accept a piece of postevent information and incorporate it into their recollection" (p. 339).

This definition highlights the importance of *memory processing* as an integral part of interrogative suggestibility, and it is for this reason that the fundamental processes of perception and memory were discussed in Chapter 5.

There are two main problems with the above definition of interrogative suggestibility. First, as highlighted in Chapter 5, it has not been proved that people necessarily *incorporate* the suggested information into their recollection, although the information may be accepted by the individual. Secondly, the definition is too vague to provide the researcher with operationally testable hypotheses.

A more focused definition is provided by Gudjonsson and Clark (1986), who define interrogative suggestibility as:

". . . the extent to which, within a closed social interaction, people come to accept messages communicated during formal questioning, as the result of which their subsequent behavioural response is affected" (p. 84).

This definition comprises five interrelated components which form an integral part of the interrogative process:

1. A social interaction;
2. A questioning procedure;
3. A suggestive stimulus;
4. Acceptance of the stimulus;
5. A behavioural response.

The first component relates to the nature of the social interaction involved. Many of the social aspects of the police interview were discussed in Chapter 3. It is evident from that discussion that the police interview is a closed social interaction. For example, in his observation of police interviews with the Brighton CID, Barrie Irving noted:

"The interview is a closed social interaction: the room is closed, the participants close to each other, interruptions are avoided as far as possible" (Irving, 1980, p. 122).

Similarly, Inbau, Reid and Buckley (1986) comment:

"The principal psychological factor contributing to a successful interrogation is privacy—being alone with the person under interrogation" (p. 24).

The second distinguishing component of the police interview is that it involves a questioning procedure. There may be two or more participants, and the questions asked typically relate to some factual material that the interviewer wishes to obtain about what the person has heard, seen or done. Feelings and intentions may also be enquired about. In most instances the questions asked are concerned with past events and experiences. This means that the memory recollections of the respondent are particularly important. Anything that interferes with the memory process makes it more difficult for the interviewer to obtain valid information from the respondent.

The third component relates to the nature of the suggestive stimulus. This was discussed in detail in Chapter 2 where it was shown that questions can be "leading" because they contain certain premises and expectations, which may or may not be informed and well founded. It was also shown that questions can be leading because of the context in which they appear.

The fourth component makes it explicit that there must be some kind of *acceptance* of the suggestive stimulus. This does not necessarily mean that the person incorporates the suggestive information into his or her memory. Rather, the suggestion must be perceived by the respondent as being plausible and credible.

The final component states that the respondent must give some kind of a behavioural response to the suggestive stimulus. It is not sufficient for the interviewer that the respondent believes or accepts the suggestion privately. The respondent must indicate, either verbally or non-verbally, whether or not he or she accepts the suggestion. On occasions the respondent may accept the suggestion offered by the interviewer but is reluctant to commit himself or herself to a definite answer.

The Gudjonsson and Clark (1986) definition of interrogative suggestibility provides the framework for a theoretical model which helps to further our understanding of the process and outcome of the police interview. It was mentioned earlier in this Chapter that interrogative suggestibility bears little resemblance to other types of suggestibility. Elsewhere (Gudjonsson, 1989c), I take this argument further and show that, from a conceptual point of view, there are four main features of interrogative suggestibility which differentiate it from other types of suggestibility. These have been incorporated into the Gudjonsson and Clark (1986) theoretical model, which will be discussed in detail later, and comprise the following:

1. Interrogative suggestibility involves a questioning procedure within a closed social interaction.
2. The questions asked are mainly concerned with past experiences and events, recollections and remembered states of knowledge. This makes it different from suggestibility of those types that are concerned with the motor and sensory experiences of the immediate situation.
3. Interrogative suggestibility contains a strong component of uncertainty which is related to the cognitive processing capacity of the individual.
4. An important feature of interrogative suggestibility is that it commonly involves a highly stressful situation with important consequences for a witness, victim or suspect (there are, of course, also important consequences for the interviewer and the police investigation).

THE GUDJONSSON AND CLARK THEORETICAL MODEL

There are two distinctive types of suggestibility important to police work (Gudjonsson, 1983a). The first type relates to the pioneering work of people like Binet (1900) and Stern (1910, 1939) into the reliability of human testimony. Here the emphasis is on the impact of leading or suggestive questioning on testimony. The second type of suggestibility relates to the extent to which interrogators are able to "shift" unwanted but perhaps accurate answers by challenge and negative feedback. This aspect of the interrogation process is implicit in some of the theories of interrogation discussed in Chapter 3, but until my own work (Gudjonsson, 1983a) it had never been formally or systematically studied. I argued that these two aspects of suggestibility are conceptually distinct, showing subsequently (Gudjonsson, 1984a, 1991a), by the use of factor analysis, that the two types of suggestibility are indeed reasonably independent of each other.

The importance of negative feedback during interrogation is described as follows:

> "One type of instruction that may markedly distort individual responses is criticism or negative feedback. An interrogator who communicates negative feedback to a suspect, witness or victim, may through an interrogative pressure shift unwanted, but perhaps true, responses in favour of untrue or distorted ones. For example, repeating the same questions several times because the answers given are not acceptable to the interrogator may make the S adapt himself to the expectations reflected in the interrogator's manner and style of questioning" (Gudjonsson, 1984a, p. 303).

The importance of the last sentence is to emphasize the fact that negative feedback may be *implicit* rather than explicit; that is, negative feedback need not necessarily be stated explicitly or openly. It can be implied, for example, by the interrogator repeating the same question several times. In other words, repeated questioning may act as a form of negative feedback when interviewees begin to believe that the interrogator is not accepting their previous answers.

I make the point that the two distinct types of suggestibility lead to different inferences and practical implications:

> "Knowledge of the types of suggestive questions Ss are particularly susceptible to, and the extent to which they can be misled by such questions, may give useful practical information about the potential reliability of witness testimony. Applications of critical feedback. . . represent relatively greater pressured suggestibility and may therefore be more linked with anxiety and coping processes" (Gudjonsson, 1984a, p. 311).

A psychometric instrument for measuring these two types of suggestibility was developed (Gudjonsson, 1983a, 1984a). The content of this scale, and the parallel form (Gudjonsson, 1987b), will be described in Chapter 7. The early work into the validity of the first scale helped refine and extend the earlier theoretical conceptualization of interrogative suggestibility.

The Gudjonsson and Clark (1986) theoretical model is shown in Figure 6.1. The model integrates the "leading questions" and "negative feedback" aspects of suggestibility discussed by Gudjonsson (1983a, 1984a). It construes suggestibility as arising out of the way the individual interacts with others within the social and physical environment. The basic premise of the model is that interrogative suggestibility is dependent upon the coping strategies that people can generate and implement when faced with two important

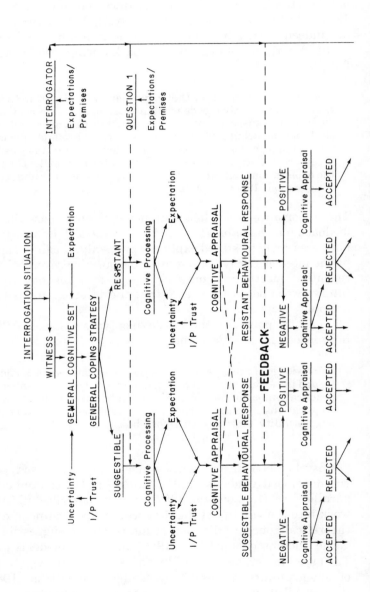

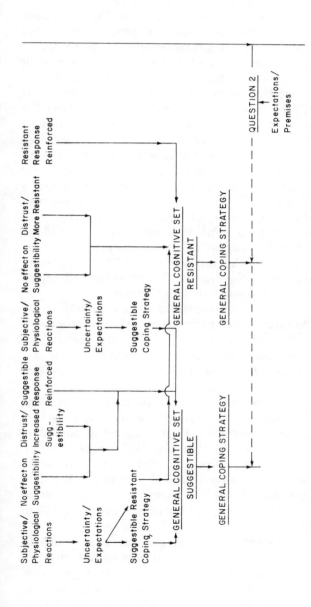

Figure 6.1. A theoretical model of interrogative suggestibility. I/P=interpersonal (Reproduced by permission from Gudjonsson and Clark, 1986).

aspects of the interrogative situation—*uncertainty* and *expectations*. The model begins by defining the social situation and the participants involved. The general cognitive set of the interviewee is then defined and this results in the interviewee adopting a "general cognitive strategy", which can facilitate either a *suggestible* or *resistant* response repertoire. The police then begin asking a question which undergoes cognitive processing by the interviewee, who then employs one or more strategies of general coping. As can be seen from Figure 6.1, this process involves the interviewee having to deal with *uncertainty* and *interpersonal trust* on the one hand and certain *expectations* on the other. These three components are seen as essential prerequisites for the suggestibility process. The cognitive processing of the question results in "cognitive appraisal", which in turn results in either a *suggestible* or a *resistant* behavioural response.

Uncertainty means that the interviewee does not know for certain the right answer to a question. This may occur, for example, when his memory for events is incomplete or non-existent. Sometimes interviewees may accept a suggestion contained in a leading question, knowing that it is wrong, because they are eager to please the interrogator or are reluctant to disagree with the suggestion openly. When this happens the interviewee should be considered to be *compliant* rather than *suggestible*. Interviewees can only be described to be truly suggestible when they privately accept the suggestion offered or at least believe it to be plausible. This is inherent in the definitions of interrogative suggestibility given earlier in this Chapter.

Interpersonal trust is another important prerequisite for yielding to suggestions. It means that the interviewee believes that the interrogator's intentions are genuine and that there is no trickery involved in the questioning. Interviewees who are suspicious of the interrogator's intentions will be reluctant to accept suggestions offered, even under conditions of increased uncertainty.

It is evident from the above discussion that uncertainty must be present in order for a response to suggestion to occur. In addition, leading questions must be sufficiently subtle so that they are perceived as being plausible, believable and without trickery; otherwise, they are likely to be rejected. There is a link between uncertainty and interpersonal trust in that the latter may depend on the extent to which interviewees are able to detect that they are being misled. The better the interviewee's memory for events, the more readily he or she is likely to detect an attempt by the interrogator to mislead or influence the responses given.

Expectation of success is an essential prerequisite for a response to suggestion to occur. This is because uncertainty and interpersonal trust are necessary but not sufficient on their own to make people yield to suggestions. Indeed, if interviewees are uncertain about the correct answer to a particular question, then they can declare their uncertainty by giving a reply of "I don't know", "I am not sure", or "I can't recall". However, many people are reluctant to declare their uncertainty because they believe that:

1. They must provide a definite answer;
2. They should know the answer to the question;
3. They are expected to know the answer and be able to give it.

The theory postulates that most people would be susceptible to suggestions if the necessary conditions of uncertainty, interpersonal trust and heightened expectations are present. The extent to which the interviewees yield to suggestion is a function of their cognitive appraisal of the interrogative situation and the coping strategies they are able to adopt. A coping strategy that helps interviewees resist suggestions involves being able to look objectively and critically at the situation and not commit oneself to an answer unless one is absolutely sure of the facts. A coping strategy that is amenable to suggestion involves an unrealistic appraisal of the situation and the reluctance to admit the fallibility of one's memory when uncertain.

Figure 6.1 shows that *feedback* is an important part of interrogative suggestibility. This is conceptualized by Gudjonsson and Clark (1986) as:

> ". . . a signal communicated by an interrogator to a witness, after he/she has responded to a question or a series of questions, intended to *strengthen* or *modify* subsequent responses of the witness" (pp. 93-94).

The signal may be positive (i.e. reinforcing a previous response) or negative (i.e. tending to modify an unwanted answer). Feedback, whether positive or negative, may be communicated implicitly or explicitly. Repeated questioning is one example of implicit negative feedback. Implicit positive feedback may consist of providing interviewees with refreshments, praise or sympathy after they begin to give wanted answers. Explicit negative feedback consists of the interrogator openly stating that he or she thinks the interviewee has made a mistake or is lying. What is communicated is that the answer given is not acceptable and that a different one is required. Explicit positive feedback may consist of the interrogator reinforcing wanted or accepted answers by utilizing such utterances as "good", "that's right", or "now we're getting somewhere".

Gudjonsson and Clark argue that feedback, and particularly negative feedback, may have quite dramatic effects upon the subsequent behaviour of an interviewee. This is clearly illustrated by the work of Gudjonsson (1984a, 1984c), where negative feedback is shown to have two distinct effects: (a) it makes interviewees change or *shift* their previous answers; and (b) it heightens their responsiveness to further leading questions. The latter aspect of suggestibility is of greater theoretical relevance to the Gudjonsson and Clark model but, as we will see in later Chapters, the *shift* aspect of suggestibility has important forensic implications.

During interrogation negative feedback may be given after each answer, when the answer is unacceptable to the interrogator, or at the end of a series of questions. Gudjonsson and Clark argue that negative feedback with regard to specific questions is easier for interviewees because they know precisely which questions require changing. Negative feedback after a series of questions is likely to affect the interviewee more because they may be unclear as to which answers they are required to change. For theoretical simplicity, Figure 6.1 focuses on feedback, positive and negative, given question-by-question.

Following a behavioural response by the interviewee, which may be yielding or resistant, the interrogator provides either positive or negative feedback which needs to be adequately processed and understood for it to have its proper effects. According to the model, the processing outcome of feedback is related to the previous behavioural responses of the interviewee, and these are differentiated as follows:

1. *Suggestible behavioural response followed by positive feedback.* Here previous yielding to suggestions is reinforced by the interrogator, which results in a general cognitive set that is more susceptible to suggestions during subsequent questioning.
2. *Resistant behavioural response followed by positive feedback.* Here positive feedback is accepted and reinforces the resistant behavioural response of the interviewee. This results in the general cognitive set of the interviewee becoming more resistant. This kind of positive feedback probably does not happen often during interrogation.
3. *Resistant behavioural response followed by negative feedback.* Gudjonsson and Clark consider this feedback aspect of the model to have the most important practical implications. Here negative feedback can be either "accepted" or "rejected". Not all interviewees will "accept" negative feedback. If negative feedback is rejected then it will have no major effects upon subsequent susceptibility to suggestions, but Gudjonsson and Clark point out that negative feedback can on occasions make some interviewees more resistant to subsequent suggestions. The reason for increased resistance is due to interviewees developing a suspicious cognitive set (e.g. thinking that they are being tricked) as the result of the negative feedback.

When negative feedback is accepted it may result in strong emotional and physiological reactions which will further increase uncertainty. Self-esteem is most readily affected, followed by increased anxiety, both subjective and physiological. Lowered self-esteem results in debilitating thoughts and coping strategies, which means that interviewees are more likely to seek external cues rather than relying on their own judgement and internal frame of reference. The outcome of this process is assumed to influence the general cognitive set and coping strategies of the interviewee during subsequent questioning.

According to the model, negative feedback, if accepted by the interviewee, does not automatically lead to a suggestible general cognitive set, although this most commonly happens. For example, some interviewees may perceive negative feedback constructively as a form of challenge to improve, which as a result makes them take a more critical view of the situation.

4. *Suggestible behavioural response followed by negative feedback.* Gudjonsson and Clark argue that negative feedback is unlikely to be given after the interviewee has yielded to a suggestion because it would confuse the person and serve no useful purpose for the interrogator. However, there are at least two circumstances where this situation may arise. Firstly, where the interrogator has asked several leading questions and the interviewee has only yielded to some of them. The interrogator then attempts to elicit more yielding answers by giving negative feedback about the interviewee's overall performance. This approach is used with the administration of some suggestibility scales, and will be discussed in the next Chapter. Secondly, the interviewee may have yielded to a suggestion contained within a false alternative question (i.e. more than one alternative is suggested); he or she fails to give the desired alternative because the question was not structured to explicitly indicate the wanted alternative answer. The model predicts that highly suggestible interviewees most readily respond to negative feedback by changing their answers to false alternative questions, as opposed to closed yes–no answer questions, because their response alternatives are more limited. The reason for this is that an individual who has yielded to nearly all of the yes–no type questions during interrogation is reaching a "ceiling effect" in terms of suggestibility. Since false alternative questions give people more than one suggestible option, it would be easier for them to alter their answers to those questions than yes–no type questions and still remain highly suggestible in terms of affirmative answers.

Implications of the Model and Hypotheses

The best way of evaluating the merit of a theory is by finding out how well hypotheses derived from the theory are supported by empirical findings. A number of hypotheses can be predicted from the model, and to what extent these have been supported will be discussed in the next Chapter. Some of the main hypotheses derived from the model are as follows:

1. Implicit in the model is the assumption that interrogative suggestibility is a distinct type of suggestibility. In particular, it would not be expected to correlate with *primary* suggestibility as found in a hypnotic context.
2. The model views suggestibility as a dynamic process that is potentially *situation-bound*. This is particularly true of negative feedback, whose impact is expected to vary according to the intensity, quality and nature of the feedback, in addition to the interviewee's past experiences. However, the model recognizes that suggestibility can be reasonably stable over time because of the cognitive (e.g. memory, intelligence) and personality (e.g. self-esteem, method of coping with stress, anxiety proneness, dependence upon social approval) factors that mediate suggestibility. Therefore, stable individual differences in suggestibility

can be measured reliably and these can predict how people are likely to cope with real life interrogation.

3. The three components of suggestibility—*uncertainty, interpersonal trust* and *expectation*—can be manipulated to a certain extent by an interrogator to alter the interviewee's susceptibility to suggestions.

4. Interviewees who enter the interrogation with a *suspicious* cognitive set are likely to be less suggestible than those with a trusting cognitive set.

5. The type of coping strategies people are able to use during interrogation affects their level of suggestibility. For example, avoidance coping is likely to facilitate acceptance of suggestions, whereby interviewees give answers that to them seem plausible and consistent with external clues provided, rather than only giving definite answers to questions they clearly remember. In contrast, a non-suggestible coping strategy involves a critical analysis of the situation and a facilitative problem-solving action.

6. Interviewees with poor memory recollections and those of low intelligence are generally more suggestible than those of higher cognitive abilities.

7. Suggestibility is related to certain personality variables, such as low self-esteem, anxiety proneness, lack of assertiveness and fear of negative evaluation.

8. Negative feedback can markedly affect interviewees' mood (e.g. self-esteem, anxiety) and heighten their acceptance of suggestions.

9. There are significant differences between the response alternatives of suggestible and non-suggestible individuals in response to negative feedback.

External Evaluation of the Model

There have been two publications which give detailed external evaluation of the Gudjonsson and Clark theoretical model. The first critique was by Schooler and Loftus (1986) and the second by Irving (1987). The editor of the journal *Social Behaviour*, where the theoretical paper was published, invited the two distinguished scientists, Loftus and Irving, to provide an objective critique of the model. The work of Elizabeth Loftus in the field of eyewitness testimony (e.g. Loftus, 1979a) is well known internationally. Barrie Irving has been an influential figure within the British criminal justice system (Irving, 1990). These two distinguished scientists make somewhat different points and their critiques will therefore be discussed separately. The Schooler and Loftus critique is particularly important because it highlights certain differences and similarities between the "individual differences" and "experimental" approaches to interrogative suggestibility. These two approaches are clearly complementary to each other, as indeed Schooler and Loftus have pointed out, and taken together they further our understanding of interrogative suggestibility substantially.

Schooler and Loftus review in some detail the different components that make up the model and its theoretical implications. They conclude that the model:

". . . represents a formidable attempt to make sense of a multi-faceted phenomenon. The emphasis on the role of individual differences in interrogative suggestibility complements the more experimental approach to the influence of post-event suggestions. For example, experimental studies of post-event suggestions have usually ignored the ways in which various personality variables may influence suggestibility. . . . At the same time the individual differences approach is relatively devoid of detail regarding the precise cognitive mechanisms that may mediate the incorporation of post-event suggestions. Throughout their discussion, Gudjonsson and Clark hint at plausible mechanisms without explicitly describing them" (p. 107).

Schooler and Loftus then proceed by discussing how Gudjonsson and Clark could enrich their model by considering some of the central cognitive mechanisms, such as "discrepancy detection", that experimental research has identified as mediating suggestibility. The importance of the principle of discrepancy detection is that it helps to explain the process whereby people accept and integrate inconsistent information into their memory (.e.g. Tousignant, Hall and Loftus, 1986). According to this principle:

"Recollections are most likely to change if a person does not immediately detect discrepancies between post-event suggestions and memory for the original event" (Schooler and Loftus, 1986, pp. 107–108).

Discrepancy detection is assumed to be affected by two factors: (a) "the strength of the original information in memory"; and (b) "by the manner in which the post-event suggestion is influenced" (p. 108).

Studies providing evidence for the influence of memory on discrepancy detection have manipulated the interval between viewing the event and subsequent suggestions being offered (Hertel, Cosden and Johnson, 1980; Loftus, Miller and Burns, 1978). The results from these studies indicate that subjects are more likely to incorporate misleading suggestions into their recollection when there is a long interval between viewing the original event and the presentation of post-event suggestions. Schooler and Loftus argue that one interpretation is that the more memory deteriorates over time, the less subjects are able to detect discrepancies between what they observed and what is subsequently erroneously suggested to them. This implies that post-event suggestions are least likely to impair discrepancy detection when encountered very close to viewing the original event.

According to Schooler and Loftus, studies that have varied the sentence construction of misleading suggestions provide evidence that discrepancy detection is influenced by the manner in which the post-event suggestion is presented. For example, Loftus (1981) found that explicitly directing subjects' attention to the misleading information made them more willing or able to scrutinize their memories and detect discrepancies. Similarly, Greene, Flynn and Loftus (1982) advised subjects, prior to their reading a narrative containing misleading post-event information, to be on the look-out for misleading information. This resulted in the subjects reading the passage more slowly and detecting more discrepancies between factual information and misleading post-event suggestions. Tousignant, Hall and Loftus (1986) found that just asking subjects to read post-event narratives slowly increases discrepancy detection.

Schooler and Loftus conclude that incorporation of post-event suggestions is influenced by a number of factors, but they are all mediated by the general principle of discrepancy detection. These authors then go on to explore to what extent the various components of the Gudjonsson and Clark model can be explained in terms of discrepancy detection. They argue that several of the salient components can be explained by the principle of discrepancy detection. These are *uncertainty, interpersonal trust,* and *negative feedback.*

According to Schooler and Loftus:

> "Uncertainty facilitates suggestibility by reducing the likelihood that a witness will experience a discrepancy between the original event and the subsequent suggestion" (p. 107).

Applying the principle of discrepancy detection to individual differences in memory capacity these authors argue:

> ". . . presumably people who tend to be less certain as a result of poor memory abilities are less able to catch discrepancies between the original event and subsequent suggestions" (p. 110).

With regard to interpersonal trust between a witness and an interrogator, Schooler and Loftus argue that a suspicious cognitive set makes witnesses scrutinize the interrogator's questions more closely, and this helps them identify discrepancies between what they originally observed and what has been subsequently suggested to them. They cite the work of Dodd and Bradshaw (1980) as evidence for this phenomenon.

According to Schooler and Loftus, negative feedback can be interpreted in relation to discrepancy detection because:

1. Negative feedback reduces subjects' confidence in their own memories and this makes them less likely to compare the suggestions of the interrogator with their own recollection;
2. Increased anxiety caused by negative feedback may decrease the subjects' ability and/or motivation to scrutinize adequately the content of the interrogator's questions.

Schooler and Loftus acknowledge that positive feedback poses a problem for discrepancy detection. They state that people are most likely to incorporate inaccurate details into their recollection when "they do not carefully attend to the inaccurate facts" (p. 109). Related to this is the tendency of people to be most influenced by "unmemorable suggestions"; that is, pieces of information that they do not take much notice of at the time they are suggested. Accordingly, blatant and obvious suggestions are less likely to influence people than subtle suggestions (Loftus, 1981). For positive reinforcement to work, the suggestions have to be obvious so that people know what they are being reinforced for. This poses problems for the principle of discrepancy detection. Schooler and Loftus overcome this by suggesting two conditions where people may be influenced by obvious suggestions:

1. There may be situations where people do detect discrepancies between what they observed and what is suggested to them, but they nevertheless decide to *comply* with the interrogator.
2. Obvious suggestions may be accepted and incorporated into recollections when people have little memory for the original detail. Where memory is very poor for a particular detail the suggestion may be quite obvious without the person detecting any kind of a discrepancy.

> "Here, witnesses may recall having accepted a suggestion and may, in response to positive feedback, become increasingly suggestible in the future" (p. 109).

Schooler and Loftus make no attempt to explain the *expectation* component of the Gudjonsson and Clark model in terms of discrepancy detection. The reason for this is undoubtedly that this component of the model cannot easily be explained by the principle of discrepancy detection. Indeed, the Gudjonsson and Clark model would predict that failure in discrepancy detection is a *necessary* but not a *sufficient* condition for people to yield to suggestions. This limitation or weakness of the discrepancy detection principle appears to be completely overlooked by Loftus and her colleagues. In other words, people may fail to detect discrepancies between what they observed and what is subsequently suggested to them, but this does not inevitably mean that they accept misleading information and incorporate it into their memory. After all, people can state that they do not know a particular answer after failing to detect a discrepancy.

In my view, the main advantage of the principle of discrepancy detection is that it highlights a central cognitive mechanism which has an important function in mediating suggestibility. However, as this discussion demonstrates, there is more to interrogative suggestibility than discrepancy detection. The implication of Schooler and Loftus, that Gudjonsson and Clark could have been more economical in the description of their model, is intuitively attractive, but in reality interrogative suggestibility is a more complex phenomenon which probably requires more than one model for complete understanding. It seems that by attempting to explain interrogative suggestibility comprehensively in terms of one cognitive mechanism, Schooler and Loftus are over-ambitious and overlook the complexity of the phenomenon. The main theoretical difference between the Gudjonsson and Clark model and the conceptual framework of Schooler and Loftus is that

Gudjonsson and Clark postulate that suggestibility is mediated by a number of cognitive and personality variables, rather than relying on one central mechanism.

Irving (1987) describes his own approach to police interrogation as "interrogation watching" (p. 19). This reflects his observational study of interrogation techniques at Brighton Police Station (Irving, 1980). His comments on the Gudjonsson and Clark model are therefore more empirical than theoretical, although his comments have theoretical implications.

Irving echoes the comments of Schooler and Loftus that the model could have been more simply described, but his reasoning is somewhat different. He states:

> ". . . would it not be more parsimonious to propose that the phenomenon which Gudjonsson and Clark want to label suggestibility, when it does occur, is merely an extreme form of a compliant reaction? All that is required to incorporate this suggestion into Gudjonsson and Clark's scheme is to postulate that, at low levels of amplitude, compliant responses (for example involving confabulation) do not obscure the original memory signal (i.e. are not sufficient to interfere with recall either at the time or after interrogation) but more extreme compliant reactions produce noise so intense that original memory signals (recall) are obscured" (Irving, 1987, p. 20).

Irving continues:

> "All the elements in Gudjonsson's model are reducible or functionally equivalent to the factors described as being pertinent to obtaining responses in suspects during interrogation" (p. 21).

The strength of Irving's argument lies in highlighting the potential overlap between the concepts of "suggestibility" and "compliance", and this point will be dealt with in Chapter 7 in a discussion about the relationship between the two concepts, in terms of both theory and empirical findings.

The weakness of Irving's argument lies in his overlooking the main theoretical difference between the concepts of suggestibility and compliance. The difference relates to the *personal acceptance* of the information provided (e.g. Wagstaff, 1981). Unlike suggestibility, compliance does not require personal acceptance of the information provided or request made. In other words, a compliant individual behaves as others wish him to behave without believing in what he is doing. In this respect, compliance is similar to Milgram's (1974) concept of obedience. Irving's comment concerning extreme compliant responses interfering with memory does not coincide with traditional definitions of compliance. In other words, it is not easy to see how extreme compliance, which Irving indeed relates to such work as that of Milgram (1974), can seriously affect memory. This does not mean that compliance cannot under certain circumstances affect memory. Indeed, the work of Bem (1966, 1967) indicates that "saying can become believing", but this is more likely to occur at low levels of amplitude responses rather than at extreme levels of compliance.

Irving makes the point that individual differences are likely to be of little importance during real-life police interrogation, because interrogators are able to neutralize their effects by applying various tactics and ploys. He then goes on to state, on the basis of his own observational studies, that tactics aimed at individual differences may be "no more than the icing on the cake" (p. 25). The implication is that the reasons why people confess during custodial interrogation are due to factors that have nothing to do with the personality of the suspect. To Irving's credit, he does not argue that individual characteristics are never relevant or important. In his view, personality characteristics, like intelligence, are only important when extreme.

Irving draws our attention to the potential importance of the seriousness of the crime:

> "In practice, as long as the crime involved is relatively serious, then *all* suspects, regardless of their individual proclivities, will tend to produce a level of attention sufficient to the task (Treisman, 1969), except where mental handicap or drug intoxication makes that impossible for them. Custodial interrogation does tend to focus the mind" (p. 23).

Irving's bold assertion is based on an assumption rather than empirical facts. It is not clear why he refers to Treisman's (1969) article in support of his argument, because the article only deals with attention in the context of subjects being presented with more information than they can handle. The article does not deal with the critical components of attention which are relevant to police interrogation, such as vigilance, arousal and motivation.

CONCLUSIONS

The early experimental work of Cattell (1895) demonstrated the influence of suggestion upon human testimony. However, it appears to have been Binet (1900) who first introduced the idea of interrogative suggestibility and provided a conceptual framework for testing it. Before his work both French and German psychologists had known about the effects of suggestion upon sensation and perception, particularly in connection with hypnosis.

Many tests were developed to measure different types of suggestibility. Most of these appear to have had no clear theoretical base or rationale. Later workers factor analysed the results from these tests in an attempt to understand the nature of suggestibility. They discovered that there were at least two types of suggestibility, referred to by Eysenck and Furneaux (1945) as "primary" and "secondary". "Primary" suggestibility consisted of so-called "ideo-motor" tests and correlated highly with hypnotizability. "Secondary" suggestibility appeared to measure much more varied and complex phenomena and was shown to be less stable and reliable. All the factor-analytical studies, with the exception of those conducted by Stukat (1958), failed to include tests of interrogative suggestibility. This resulted in interrogative suggestibility being a neglected area of research.

Interrogative suggestibility is a special type of suggestibility and differs from other types of suggestibility in several important ways. Most significantly, it involves a questioning procedure which is typically concerned with past experiences and events, recollections and remembered states of knowledge. This makes it very different to suggestibility concerned with motor and sensory experiences of the immediate situation.

There are two main theoretical approaches to interrogative suggestibility. These are called the "experimental" and "individual differences" approaches. The "experimental" approach is principally concerned with the conditions under which leading questions are likely to affect the verbal accounts of witnesses. Here suggestibility is viewed as being mediated by a central cognitive mechanism, which is labelled "discrepancy detection". The "individual differences" approach, on the other hand, views suggestibility as being mediated by a number of different cognitive and personality factors, rather than by one central mechanism. This implies that witnesses and criminal suspects respond differently to interviewing and interrogation according to their cognitive abilities, mental state and personality.

The principal reason for the differences between the two approaches relates to the nature of the subjects studied, which formed the basis of the theoretical ideas behind the models. The "experimental" approach has relied extensively on college students as their experimental subjects, whereas the "individual differences" approach is based on research with varied and heterogeneous samples, which include normal subjects, criminal subjects, prisoners and psychiatric patients. This Chapter has highlighted the strengths and weaknesses of each approach and shows how the two radically different approaches complement each other in furthering our theoretical understanding of interrogative suggestibility.

CHAPTER 7

Interrogative Suggestibility: Empirical Findings

Until the development of the Gudjonsson Suggestibility Scale (GSS 1; Gudjonsson, 1983a, 1984a) there were no measures of interrogative suggestibility available that could be used to assess an individual case. Certain laboratory procedures were available for measuring people's responses to leading questions, following the work of Loftus and her colleagues, but these were unsatisfactory and impractical for forensic application. I developed the GSS 1 because there was a need for such an instrument to assess pre-trial criminal cases involving retracted confessions. The purpose of this Chapter is to look at the testing of interrogative suggestibility and its empirical aspects. Most of the work reported is that carried out on the GSS 1 and its parallel form, the GSS 2.

Can interrogative suggesibility be reliably measured? Is there empirical evidence that interrogative suggestibility differs from suggestibility described in a hypnotic context? How does suggestibility relate to the constructs of "compliance" and "acquiescence"? These are basic types of questions that are addressed in this Chapter before the more empirical findings are discussed in relation to the Gudjonsson and Clark (1986) model. Many of the theoretical questions raised in Chapter 6 are dealt with experimentally in this Chapter.

The best way of testing the merit of a particular theory is on the basis of how well the various hypotheses derived from the theory can be supported by empirical findings. A number of hypotheses derived from the Gudjonsson and Clark model were listed in Chapter 6 and I now examine how well the theory has stood up to empirical investigations.

THE GUDJONSSON SUGGESTIBILITY SCALES

After laying the foundations for the theoretical work on interrogative suggestibility, which was discussed in detail in Chapter 6, the construction and early validation of a suggestibility scale were used to assess the individual's responses to "leading questions" and "negative feedback" instructions, when being asked to report a factual event from recall. The scale, referred to as the Gudjonsson Suggestibility Scale (GSS 1), is particularly applicable to legal issues, such as police officers' questioning of witnesses to crime and interrogation of criminal suspects. It employs a narrative paragraph describing a fictitious robbery, which is read out to the subject. He or she is then asked to report all that can be recalled about the story. After the person has given free immediate and delayed recall to the story (the delay is generally about 50 minutes), he or she is asked 20 specific questions, 15 of which are subtly misleading. After answering the 20 questions the person is told that he or she has made a number of errors (even if no errors have been made), and it is therefore necessary to ask all the questions once more. The person is asked to be more accurate than before. Any change in the person's answers from the previous trial is noted as *Shift*. The extent to which people give in to the misleading questions is scored as *Yield 1*. Yield 1 and Shift are typically added together to make up *Total Suggestibility*.

The internal consistency of the 15 Yield 1 and 15 Shift items on the GSS 1 was measured by Cronbach's alpha coefficient for 195 subjects (Gudjonsson, 1984a). The coefficients were 0.77 and 0.67 for Yield 1 and Shift, respectively. Singh and Gudjonsson (1987) recommended some modifications in the scoring of Shift, which increased the internal reliability of the measure to 0.71. This consisted of slight modification in the scoring of Shift and increased the number of items from 15 to 20. This means that a distinct change in the answers given after "negative feedback" applies to all the 20 items on the GSS 1, and not just to the 15 "leading" items as had been used in the original work.

Following the early development of the GSS 1, and a comprehensive external review on the Scale's validity by Grisso (1986), I constructed a parallel form, labelled GSS 2 (Gudjonsson, 1987b). The two scales are identical except for the content of the narrative paragraph and interrogative questions. The content of the GSS 1 reflected the forensic objectives of the instrument; that is, the narrative stimulus has a criminal content. However, since there is no reason to suppose that criminal vs. non-criminal narrative stimuli would affect the suggestibility scores (Grisso, 1986), the GSS 2 narrative has a non-criminal content. The GSS 2 was validated by correlating the scores obtained by subjects with the scores derived from the GSS 1. The correlations between the two scales within the same session were 0.90 and 0.92 (Total Suggestibility), for normal and forensic subjects respectively (Gudjonsson, 1987b). For a group of forensic patients tested on two separate occasions the correlation was 0.81. The correlations were consistently slightly lower for Shift than Yield 1, which is consistent with the prediction from the Gudjonsson and Clark model. The findings give strong support for the test-retest reliability of interrogative suggestibility, even when people are tested many months apart. Therefore, interrogative suggestibility, as measured by the Gudjonsson Suggestibility Scales, appears to be reasonably stable over time when the experimental conditions are similar.

The early validation studies on the GSS 1 were reviewed by Grisso (1986), who concluded:

> "Construct validation research with the GSS has placed the forensic examiner in a good position to use GSS scores when considering questions of an examinee's decreased resistance to suggestion or subtle pressure in interrogations by law enforcement officers" (p. 147).

The GSS 1 and the GSS 2 have very similar norms (Gudjonsson, 1987b) and can be used interchangeably. The Cronbach alpha coefficients for the GSS 2 appear to be somewhat higher than for the GSS 1. In a recent study (Gudjonsson, 1991a), which comprised 130 subjects, the alpha coefficients were 0.87 and 0.79 for Yield 1 and Shift, respectively (Gudjonsson, 1991a). The coefficient for *Yield 2* (see below for definition) was 0.90. Factor analysis of the Yield 1 and Shift items on the GSS 2 indicated two factors, with Yield 1 items loading on the first factor and Shift items on the second factor. This finding is identical to that found for the GSS 1 (Gudjonsson, 1984a) and indicates that there are two reasonably independent types of interrogative suggestibility, which correspond to the extent to which people give in to misleading questions (Yield 1) and how they respond to interrogative pressure (Shift).

Register and Kihlstrom (1988) argue, on the basis of their work on a modified version of GSS 1, that there are three possibly independent types of interrogative suggestibility:

1. Responses to negative feedback;
2. Responses to leading questions;
3. Responses to repeated questions.

These authors found that, even when no negative feedback was given, their subjects would nevertheless alter some of their answers when re-interrogated on the GSS 1. One possible reason for this is that repeated questioning may act as a form of implicit negative feedback. That is, subjects assume that they have made errors and this is why they are being re-interrogated. Further work needs to be carried out in order to establish if responses to repeated questions are independent of responses to negative feedback.

The GSS 1 and GSS 2 were developed for two different purposes. Firstly, the scales were intended to be used for research in order to further our understanding of interrogative suggestibility and its mediating variables and mechanisms. Secondly, the scales were intended for forensic and clinical applications. The primary application was to establish an instrument that could identify people who were particularly susceptible to erroneous testimony during questioning.

Much of the early work on the GSS 1 was concerned with validating the scale and developing the theoretical basis for the Gudjonsson and Clark model. More recently, various experiments have been carried out to test the various hypotheses derived from the model (Gudjonsson, 1989b, 1989c). As will be shown later in this Chapter, many of the hypotheses derived from the Gudjonsson and Clark model have been tested and supported experimentally.

Types of Clinical Information Derived from the Scales

Most of the research with the GSS 1 and GSS 2 has been concerned with two types of information which can be readily derived from the Scales. These correspond to Yield 1 and Shift. However, the following information can be obtained for clinical and research purposes:

1. Immediate Recall

This measures immediate verbal recall on the GSS narrative and gives an indication of the subject's attention, concentration and memory capacity. The maximum number of "ideas" that subjects can recall is 40. The mean score for people of average IQ is about 21, with a standard deviation of 6. Therefore, a score of 11 falls at the 5th percentile rank for "normal subjects" (i.e. it falls outside the normal range). Clinical groups, such as forensic patients, typically score more than one standard deviation below the mean for normal subjects (i.e. a score about 15 with a standard deviation of 8), even when their intellectual functioning is not known to be impaired.

2. Delayed Recall

Delayed recall of the GSS narrative is usually obtained about 50 minutes after immediate recall. As with immediate recall, the maximum number of correct "ideas" is 40. Memory on the GSS narratives typically deteriorates by about 1 point for normal subjects and 1.5 points for forensic patients, which gives mean delayed memory scores of 20 and 13.5 for normal and forensic subjects, respectively. This means that verbal memory deteriorates between 5 and 10% within 1 hour. However, among normal subjects about 75% of the immediate recall is retained at 1-week follow-up (Singh and Gudjonsson, 1984; Tata and Gudjonsson, 1990). Gudjonsson (1983a) found that the rate at which memory deteriorated within 50 minutes was significantly correlated ($r=0.52$; $p<0.001$) with Shift on the GSS 1. That is, those subjects whose memory deteriorated most, irrespective of their level of free recall, alter their answers most after negative feedback.

3. Yield 1

Yield 1 refers to the number of suggestions the subject yields to on the GSS 1 and GSS 2 prior to negative feedback. The maximum score the subject can obtain is 15. The mean score for normal subjects is about 4, with a standard deviation of 3. This means that a Yield 1 score of 9 or above falls outside the normal range (i.e. the 95th percentile rank). Forensic patients, including court referrals, typically obtain a Yield 1 score of between 6 and 7, with a standard deviation of 3.5.

4. Shift

Shift refers to the number of times there has been a distinct change in the subject's answers following negative feedback. The wording of the negative feedback, which is administered immediately after the 20 questions have been asked (Yield 1), is:

> "You have made a number of errors. It is therefore necessary to go through the questions once more, and this time try to be more accurate."

This should be stated *firmly*. Subjects typically change some of their answers after they have been told that they have made a number of errors during the 20 questions. The direction of the change is irrelevant in the scoring of Shift. The highest possible Shift score on the GSS 1 and GSS 2 is 20 (i.e. all 20 questions are included in the scoring of Shift, unlike Yield 1 and Yield 2). The mean Shift score for normal subjects is about 2.5, with a standard deviation of 2.2. This means that a score of 7 or above falls outside the normal range. The mean score for forensic patients, including court referrals, is about 4, with a standard deviation of 3.

5. Yield 2

Yield 2 refers to the number of leading questions which the subject yields to after the negative feedback has been administered. Therefore, Yield 2 represents the number of suggestions accepted after interrogative pressure. Yield 2 indicates the type of change that has occurred as a result of the negative feedback. Usually, the change (i.e. Shift) is in the direction of *increased* suggestibility. That is, after negative feedback and repeated questioning subjects tend to yield more to the leading questions than they did before (Gudjonsson, 1984a; Register and Kihlstrom, 1988). Typically Yield 2 is about one point higher than Yield 1, which means that a score of 10 or above falls outside the normal range.

Yield 2 has been used in some of the more recent research with the GSS 1 and GSS 2. It provides additional information in that it tells the examiner precisely how interrogative pressure, which is administered in the form of negative feedback, affects the subsequent susceptibility of the subject to suggestive questions. Yield 2 is more highly correlated with Shift than Yield 1 among normal subjects, forensic cases and children (Gudjonsson, 1984a), which means that it gives a better indication than Yield 1 of the subjects' vulnerability to yielding to leading questions when placed under interrogative pressure.

6. *Total Suggestibility*

This is the sum of Yield 1 and Shift. This gives an indication of the subject's overall level of suggestibility. The mean Total Suggestibility score for normal subjects is about 7, with a standard deviation of 5. This means that a score of 15 or above falls outside the normal range (i.e. 95th percentile rank). The mean score for forensic patients, which includes court referrals, is about 10, with a standard deviation of 5.5.

7. *Confabulation*

Confabulation refers to problems in memory processing where people replace gaps in their memory with imaginary experiences which they believe to be true. Confabulation can be measured on the memory part of the GSS 1 and GSS 2 stories. This includes any pieces of information which have been added to the story, or major distortions in the story's content. The mean number of confabulations on the GSS 1 narrative for immediate and delayed (50-minute) recall is about 0.5 (Smith and Gudjonsson, 1986). This means that three or more confabulations on either immediate or delayed recall will fall outside the normal range. Very similar mean scores for confabulation to that found by Smith and Gudjonsson were obtained by Register and Kihlstrom (1988), in a study that utilized the GSS 1.

Confabulations at 1-week follow-up were studied by Tata and Gudjonsson (1990). The number of confabulations clearly increases as memory deteriorates over time, but factors such as the severity of negative feedback administered during the interrogation have a significant effect on the subsequent rate of confabulation (Tata and Gudjonsson, 1990). Normal subjects, who have not been subjected to negative feedback, typically have one or two confabulations after 1 week. The rate doubles when subjects have previously been given negative feedback during the interrogative part of the GSS 1. The type of negative feedback given in the Tata and Gudjonsson study was more severe than that given as part of the standard GSS 1 procedure. Even when no negative feedback is given, as in the Register and Kihlstrom (1988) study, repeated questioning and misleading interrogative questions significantly increase subsequent confabulations during free recall.

SUGGESTIBILITY AND HYPNOTIC SUSCEPTIBILITY

I argued in Chapter 6 that the susceptibility to hypnosis is related to *primary* suggestibility, using Eysenck's conventional classification, whereas interrogative suggestibility is a special type of suggestibility which is unrelated to suggestibility of the primary type and only relates to the more elusive category of secondary suggestibility.

Evidence that interrogative suggestibility differs from susceptibility to hypnosis comes from three empirical studies. In the first study, Hardarson (1985) found no significant correlation ($r=0.15$) between scores on the Harvard Group Scale of Hypnotic Susceptibility and interrogative suggestibility, as measured by the GSS 1, among 40 Icelandic university students.

In two different experiments, comprising university students and psychiatric patients respectively, Young et al. (1987) correlated the GSS 1 Total Suggestibility score with the Barber Suggestibility Scale (Barber and Calverley, 1964). The Barber Suggestibility Scale consists of eight test suggestions which are theoretically related to primary suggestibility. None of the three scores on the Barber Suggestibility Scale, which comprised the subjects' responses to suggestions, their rated subjective involvement in the tasks, and their verbalized resistance to the suggestions, correlated with interrogative suggestibility.

Register and Kihlstrom (1988) used a variant of the GSS 1 during an experiment into hypnosis. The subjects were 40 college students who had all completed the Harvard Group Scale of Hypnotic Susceptibility. No significant difference in interrogative suggestibility was found between hypnotizable and non-hypnotizable subjects. The authors concluded that the results:

". . . support Gudjonsson's (1987a) hypothesis that interrogative suggestibility is independent of suggestibility as measured in a hypnotic content." (p. 556)

The three studies quoted above all indicate that there is no correlation between interrogative suggestibility and hypnotic suggestibility.

COMPLIANCE

In Chapter 6 I offered a theoretical distinction between suggestibility and compliance. The main difference, it was argued, was that suggestibility, unlike compliance, implies personal acceptance of the information provided or request made. In this Chapter the concept of compliance, as it is relevant to interrogation, is explored in greater detail, particularly in relation to testing and empirical findings.

In its broadest sense, compliance refers to the tendency of the individual to go along with propositions, requests or instructions for some immediate instrumental gain. The person concerned is fully aware that his or her responses are being influenced, and an affirmative or a compliant response does not require personal acceptance of the proposition. In other words, people may disagree with the proposition or request made, but they nevertheless react in a compliant way. This is different to suggestibility, where there is personal acceptance of the proposition offered by the interrogator. This kind of distinction between suggestibility and compliance is also evident in the literature on suggestibility in relation to hypnosis (Wagstaff, 1981).

I have argued elsewhere (Gudjonsson, 1989a), that compliance has two major components to it. Firstly, there is an eagerness to please and the need of the person to protect his or her self-esteem when in the company of others. Secondly, there is avoidance of conflict and confrontation with people, and particularly those perceived as being in a position of some authority. These two components of compliant behaviour overlap extensively with Milgram's (1974) construct of "obedience to authority". Indeed, my compliance scale (GCS; Gudjonsson, 1989a) is more closely associated with Milgram's work than that of Asch (1951). The reason for this is that highly compliant subjects appear fully aware of their difficulties in coping with pressure when in the company of people in authority. As was mentioned in Chapter 6, the subjects in Asch's experiments were not aware that they were being influenced by the subtle suggestions introduced.

How can compliance be measured? There are two main ways of measuring compliance, which are based on behavioural observation and self-report procedures, respectively.

Milgram's (1974) experiments and the work of Asch (1952) were based on behavioural observation. Conformity studies typically use count data, such as the number of people who conform in a given condition or to a given suggestion. Other studies have used continuous measures, such as a Likert scale, to assess the degree of conformity or changes in conformity (Beins and Porter, 1989).

The second method for studying compliance is by way of a self-report questionnaire. I have constructed a 20-item compliance scale which is relevant to police interrogation (GCS; Gudjonsson, 1989a). The scale was intended to complement my work into interrogative suggestibility. It consists of 20 statements, which are answered as either "true" or "false". Factor analysis of the scale revealed two main factors making up the scale. Statements loading significantly on the first factor indicated uneasiness or fear of people in authority and avoidance of conflict and confrontation (e.g. "I tend to become easily alarmed and frightened when I am in the company of people in authority"; "I tend to give in to people who insist that they are right"; "I give in easily to people when I am pressured"). Statements loading on the second factor indicated an eagerness to please ("I try hard to do what is expected of me"; "I try to please others"; "I generally believe in doing as I am told").

The GCS appears to have satisfactory reliability. The internal reliability of the scale, as measured by Cronbach's alpha coefficient, is 0.71, which is on the low side. Test–retest reliability was measured by administering the scale twice, 1-3 months apart, to forensic patients. The test–retest reliability obtained was 0.88.

The GCS has been less extensively researched than the GSS 1. However, the research work that has been carried out so far gives support for the validity of the GCS. The construct validity of the GCS is supported by the fact that performance on the GCS has been found to correlate with other variables with which it should be theoretically related.

I found that compliance, as measured by the GCS (Gudjonsson 1989a), correlated significantly ($r=0.35$; d.f.$=123$; $p<0.001$) with social desirability as measured by the Marlowe–Crowne Social Desirability Scale (Crowne and Marlowe, 1960). A low but significant correlation ($r=0.27$; d.f.$=59$; $p<0.05$) was found between compliance and neuroticism, as measured by the Eysenck Personality Questionnaire (EPQ; Eysenck and Eysenck, 1975). A moderately high correlation ($r=0.54$; d.f.$=66$; $p<0.001$) was found between compliance and the Social Conformity Scale of Pettigrew (1958).

I have provided evidence for the validity of the GCS in terms of *group differentiation* (Gudjonsson, 1989a). I looked at the normative GCS scores of different groups of subjects and hypothesized that alleged false confessors should score higher than, for example, those criminal suspects or defendants who had been able to resist confessing whilst being interrogated by the police. The results from the study clearly indicated that this was the case. This type of validation will be mentioned later in this Chapter in relation to more recent studies of the GCS.

Situational Determinants of Compliance

The GCS, to a certain extent, overcomes problems with compliance being potentially situation-bound, because the subject is rating how he or she generally reacts to interpersonal pressure, rather than referring to any one particular situation. This does not, however, exclude the possibility that subjects may fill in the GCS differently according to their situational circumstances. For example, since many of the GCS items give a fair indication of what the scale is measuring, some criminal suspects, when this seems favourable to their case, may endorse items in such a way as to exaggerate their compliance scores. Similarly, it is possible that suspects who previously gave in to police pressure and confessed when they did not really want to have biased perceptions of their own compliance, which becomes reflected in their self-report scores. In other words, because the suspect gave in to the police pressure, he thinks he must be compliant and fills in the scale accordingly.

A number of situational factors have been shown to influence compliance in a particular experimental setting. The type of factors that can increase compliance are: happy mood state (Milberg and Clark, 1988); touch and gaze (Kleinke, 1977, 1980; Hornik, 1988); demand for eye contact (Hamlet, Axelrod and Kuerschner, 1984); the prestige of the communicator (Kelman and Holland, 1953); the perceived power of the experimenter (Bandura, Ross and Ross, 1963); agreement with a smaller request previously (Freedman and Fraser, 1966); the gender of the experimenter (Heslin, Nguyen and Nguyen, 1983; Stier and Hall, 1984); the manipulation of self-esteem (Graf, 1971); and feelings of guilt (Freedman, Wallington and Bless, 1967; Carlsmith and Gross, 1969; Konoske, Staple and Graf, 1979).

The feeling of guilt is undoubtedly one of the most important factors that increase the individual's likelihood of complying with a request.

Freedman, Wallington and Bless (1967) manipulated guilt feelings in two different ways in three studies. In all studies there was marked increase in subsequent compliance. The authors put forward two possible mechanisms for this. First, complying with a request after experimental guilt manipulation helps the individual expiate the guilt by doing something "good" to compensate for what he or she had done "wrong" previously. Konoske, Staple and Graf (1979) construe this as the subjects' attempt to restore their lowered self-esteem. Second, compliance may be a way of punishing oneself for the action that caused the guilt feeling in the first place.

Another important finding in the Freedman, Wallington and Bless study is that guilt may strongly motivate people to avoid being confronted with the person they have allegedly harmed. Therefore, there appear to be two conflicting motivations as a result of guilt: people are motivated to engage in altruistic behaviour as a way of alleviating guilt feelings and restoring self-esteem, but there is a strong tendency towards avoidance behaviour when this means actually meeting the person allegedly harmed. The implication is that guilt feeling manipulation is most effective in increasing compliant behaviour when the subject does not subsequently have to be confronted with the victim. This is, however, unlikely to be a problem when the subject is already interacting with the victim. The most likely explanation is that subjects are too embarrassed to "face" the victim.

One of the most important findings with regard to guilt manipulation research is that, once guilt is induced in the subject, it can be directed into greater compliance with requests that are completely unrelated to the original source of guilt. This has important implications for police interrogation, because guilt induction is recommended in manuals on police interrogation (see Chapter 3).

Few studies have looked at the type of situational factors that reduce compliance. The most important one appears to be anger (Milberg and Clark, 1988), which will be discussed in detail later in this Chapter.

ACQUIESCENCE

Acquiescence refers to the tendency of an individual to answer questions in the affirmative irrespective of the content (Cronbach, 1946). It shares with suggestibility the fact that both concepts are concerned with information obtained in response to questions or statements, and when in doubt subjects may give affirmative answers. The main difference between the two concepts is that, with regard to acquiescence, the questions are not structured in such a way as to specifically suggest the wanted or expected answer, which is the case with suggestibility.

It is conceptually possible to break an acquiescent response into three stages (Gudjonsson, 1990d). First, the person has to read or listen to the question or statement. This links acquiescence with such factors as attention, interest, reading ease and powers of observation. Second, the person has to understand the words, concepts and meaning of the question. Here conceptual judgements, comprehension, general knowledge, vocabulary and concept formation are likely to play an important part. If the question asked is too difficult for the person to read or to understand, then uncertainty or doubt is created, which is a prerequisite for an acquiescence response to occur (Gudjonsson, 1986). Third, when subjects are uncertain about how to answer the question they have three choices of action:

1. They can refuse to give simple yes–no or true–false answers;
2. They can give the answers they consider most plausible;
3. They can guess and give answers at random.

Out of the three available options, option 2 is most closely associated with an acquiescent response.

How can acquiescence be measured? The best, and most common, way of measuring acquiescence is by way of an item-reversal technique (Sigelman et al., 1981; Winkler, Kanouse and Ware, 1982). This consists of employing matched pairs of logically opposite items or statements. The degree of acquiescence is then measured by the number of items or statements in which the person agrees affirmatively with both. For example, the statement "I am happy most of the time" is logically opposite to the statement "I am sad most of the time". If the person answers both statements affirmatively, then his response is acquiescent. If he answers both statements negatively, then he is being *inconsistent* but not acquiescent.

CORRELATIONS BETWEEN SUGGESTIBILITY, COMPLIANCE AND ACQUIESCENCE

Do suggestibility, compliance and acquiescence scores correlate with one another? The evidence indicates that suggestibility and compliance are modestly correlated and that there is a weak, but significant, relationship between suggestibility and acquiescence. There is no significant relationship between acquiescence and compliance.

Two studies have investigated the relationship between suggestibility and acquiescence. Both correlated GSS 1 scores with the acquiescence scale of Winkler, Kanouse and Ware (1982). The first study (Gudjonsson, 1986) comprised a group of 30 male volunteers. A low but a significant correlation ($r=0.33$; $p<0.05$) was found between Total Suggestibility and acquiescence. I suggested that a state of uncertainty and low self-esteem, which arises when subjects are in doubt how to answer a question, produces an unpleasant feeling. This negative state motivates subjects to reduce uncertainty and to restore their self-esteem. Affirmative answers function to facilitate this process because they are seen as being more acceptable to the interviewer.

I subsequently failed to find a significant relationship ($r=0.13$) between Total Suggestibility and acquiescence in a study comprising 60 forensic patients (Gudjonsson, 1990c). It seems that suggestibility does have some relationship with acquiescence but the relationship is very weak and may not be found in all studies. In the same study, acquiescence was not found to correlate significantly ($r=0.11$) with compliance, as measured by the GCS.

There appears to be a certain overlap between the constructs of suggestibility and compliance. In fact, suggestibility and compliance may be mediated by similar factors, such as avoidance coping, eagerness to please, and certain anxiety processes associated with how the individual copes with pressure. In one study (Gudjonsson, 1990c), I correlated the GSS 1 scores with the GCS score among 119 subjects. Yield 1, Shift and Total Suggestibility correlated significantly with compliance, the correlations being 0.40, 0.53 and 0.54 for the three suggestibility scores respectively ($p<0.001$).

On theoretical grounds, compliance should be less correlated with intelligence than are acquiescence and suggestibility (Gudjonsson, 1990c).

Acquiescence is probably best construed as predominantly comprising intellectual and educational components rather than temperament or personality variables. This interpretation is consistent with the finding that highly acquiescent individuals tend to come from poorer educational backgrounds (Ware, 1978) and are often mentally handicapped (Sigelman et al., 1981). Compliance, on the other hand, is best construed as a personality measure. Suggestibility probably falls in between the other two measures, but it is clearly much more akin to compliance than acquiescence.

In one study (Gudjonsson, 1990c), comprising 139 subjects who had completed the GCS and the Wechsler Adult Intelligence Scale (WAIS-R), there was no significant correlation between compliance and intelligence ($r<0.08$). In contrast, both acquiescence and suggestibility have been found to have modest negative correlations with intelligence. Factor analysis (Varimax rotation) of the WAIS-R subtests, the GSS 1 Total Suggestibility score, the GCS score and acquiescence, revealed three main factors. These factors are best construed as verbal intelligence, non-verbal intelligence and compliance. Acquiescence had clear loading on the first two factors, whereas suggestibility and compliance loaded highly on the third factor (-0.67 and -0.81 respectively). Compliance had particularly low loadings on the two intelligence factors.

SUGGESTIBILITY AND GENDER

With regard to the GSS 1, there seems to be some general tendency for females to score slightly higher on suggestibility than males, but the difference, which is about one point for Total Suggestibility, has not been found to be significant (Gudjonsson, 1984a; Gudjonsson and Lister, 1984).

Powers, Andriks and Loftus (1979) found that female subjects were significantly more suggestible than male subjects. An interesting finding was that sex differences in accuracy were related to the type of information at which a question was aimed. Women were significantly more accurate than men on questions dealing with female-oriented details (e.g. women's clothing and actions), whereas men were more accurate with regard to other details (e.g. the thief's appearance and the offence's surroundings).

The authors conclude that males and females tend to be accurate on different items, which suggests that each sex pays more attention to those items which are of interest to them and most relevant to their own sex. One consequence of this is that there is a difference in the ease with which misleading information can be made to influence the subjects' memory and answers about specific items. The authors of the above study quote the work of Eagly (1978) in support of their conclusions. Eagly's study indicates that people's attitudes can be more readily influenced when they have little information about the subject area or regard it as trivial and unimportant.

SUGGESTIBILITY AND AGE

The research into the effects of age on suggestibility is discussed in Chapter 5 in relation to children. For the purposes of this Chapter I shall briefly mention the data available on the relationship between age and GSS and GCS scores.

No significant relationship has been found between GSS 1 and age for different groups of adult subjects (Gudjonsson, 1984a; Gudjonsson and Lister, 1984). Similarly, no significant correlation was found between age and compliance, as measured by the GCS, among 369 adult subjects (Gudjonsson, 1989a).

No published study has yet looked at GSS scores among children below the age of 11. Two studies have investigated the suggestibility scores of boys between the ages of 11 and 16. The results from both studies indicate that youths are no more suggestible than adults, unless their answers are subjected to negative feedback (i.e. interrogative pressure). Then they become markedly more suggestible than adults. In the first study (Gudjonsson and Singh, 1984a) we compared the GSS 1 scores of 31 delinquent boys with those of 20 normal males who had similar memory scores on the GSS 1. No difference emerged between the two groups with regard to Yield 1, whereas the Shift and Yield 2 scores were significantly higher among the youths. An identical pattern of GSS 1 scores has been found among 40 normal youths (Singh and Gudjonsson, 1991).

SUGGESTIBILITY AND INTELLIGENCE

Gudjonsson and Clark (1986) suggested two reasons why there should be a negative relationship between intelligence and suggestibility. Firstly, it is argued, suggestibility is related to uncertainty, which itself depends to a certain extent on the memory capacity of the individual. Memory, in turn, is to a significant extent correlated with intelligence. Secondly, suggestibility is considered to be influenced by the person's ability to cope with the uncertainty, expectations and pressure associated with interrogation. Persons of low intelligence would have more limited intellectual resources to assist them to cope with an unfamiliar task, such as interrogation.

There appears to be a significantly negative relationship between interrogative suggestibility and intellectual functioning, which has been demonstrated in a number of studies with different groups of subjects. However, there is strong evidence that the relationship between suggestibility and intelligence is significantly affected by range effects. That is, it is only in studies utilizing subjects of average intelligence or below, or where a large range of IQ scores are used, that significant results emerge. An IQ range of average or above appears to have no significant correlation with suggestibility. That is, subjects with IQs above average are no less susceptible to suggestive influences than subjects of average IQ, but subjects with IQs well below average, such as those who are borderline or mentally handicapped, tend to be markedly more suggestible.

Two early studies suggested that there was a relationship between intelligence and the ability to give accurate recall. Howells (1938) found a small but positive correlation ($r=0.27$) between accuracy during an eyewitness experiment and intelligence. In other words, there was a slight tendency for the more intelligent subjects to give more accurate accounts of events.

The second study is that by Burtt (1948). He found a correlation of -0.55 between intelligence and suggestibility, which indicated that subjects of lower intelligence tended to be more suggestible than those of higher intelligence.

In the first ever study on the GSS 1, I found that IQ, measured by the WAIS, correlated negatively with both Yield 1 and Shift (Gudjonsson, 1983a). The correlation with Full Scale IQ was -0.55. Similar correlations were found for Verbal ($r=-0.47$) and Performance ($r=-0.50$) IQs.

Tully and Cahill (1984) found a correlation of -0.69 between intelligence, measured by Raven's Coloured Matrices and the Crighton Vocabulary Test, and suggestibility, which was measured by the GSS 1. The correlation is exceptionally high because the authors, unwisely in my view, pooled together for their analysis the scores of 15 normal control subjects and 30 mentally handicapped subjects. Some of the subjects in the mentally handicapped group had IQs of 50 or below, which is likely to have seriously skewed the distribution of IQ scores.

In one study I analysed the relationship between suggestibility and IQ among 60 normal subjects and 100 forensic patients (Gudjonsson, 1988b). The correlations with Full Scale IQ were -0.52 and -0.58 for the normal and forensic patients, respectively.

However, in spite of the highly significant negative correlations between IQ and suggestibility, the relationship between the two variables was dependent upon the range of IQ scores. That is, IQs above 100 in the two groups did not correlate significantly with suggestibility, whereas IQs below 100, as well as the entire IQ range, correlated significantly with suggestibility. These findings have important implications for studies that have relied on subjects whose IQs fall in the average range or above.

More recently I looked at the types of intellectual skills that most highly correlated with suggestibility among 60 forensic referrals (Gudjonsson, 1990c). The subjects had all completed the WAIS-R (Wechsler, 1981). A negative correlation of -0.44 was found between Full Scale IQ and total suggestibility on the GSS 1. The subtests that had highest correlations with suggestibility were Picture Arrangement ($r=-0.48$), Similarities ($r=-0.43$) and Comprehension ($r=-0.40$). Lowest correlations were with Digit Span ($r=-0.24$) and Information ($r=-0.30$). Thus, I concluded that suggestibility is, as far as intelligence is concerned, most strongly associated with the capacity for logical reasoning, sequential thought, and social awareness and sophistication. In other words, people who can quickly size up a social situation are more able to critically evaluate the interrogative situation and adopt a facilitative problem-solving action.

Sharrock and Gudjonsson (1991) argue that the relationship between intelligence and suggestibility among criminal suspects may be affected by their previous convictions. They suggest that previous convictions may act as a "suppressor variable" (Wiggins, 1973) in that they tend to reduce the correlation between intelligence and suggestibility.

Tata (1983) found no significant correlation between IQ, which was estimated from the National Adult Reading Test (Nelson, 1982), and suggestibility scores on the GSS 1. The mean IQ for the subjects in the study was 117, with the range of scores falling between 106 and 125.

Powers, Andriks and Loftus (1979) conducted an eyewitness experiment on 25 undergraduate students at the University of Washington. Suggestibility scores did not correlate significantly with nine intelligence-related subtests of the Washington Pre-college Test. The authors had expected a negative correlation between suggestibility and intelligence, and explained the lack of a significant correlation on the basis of their subjects being of higher than average intelligence. They point to the possibility of range effects:

"It is entirely possible that an experiment conducted with subjects possessing a wider range of cognitive abilities would produce very different results" (p. 344).

What are the main implications of the above findings concerning range effects? There are two broad implications. One implication relates to the nature of the subjects studied, and the other to the type of factors that facilitate a suggestible response.

Schooler and Loftus (1986) state in their review of the Gudjonsson and Clark (1986) model:

"It appears that individual differences in cognitive abilities may not always be as directly related to suggestibility as Gudjonsson and Clark would have us believe" (p. 110).

The reason why Schooler and Loftus came to this conclusion is that American research has failed to find a significant relationship between suggestibility and cognitive variables associated with intelligence and memory. I have argued that the reason why American studies have failed to find the expected significant relationship is due to the homogeneous nature of their samples as far as cognitive abilities are concerned (Gudjonsson, 1987c).

The "experimental approach" to suggestibility relies almost exclusively on college students as subjects, which seriously limits the type of inference that can be drawn about the cognitive variables that mediate suggestibility. The theory of "discrepancy detection" was developed on the basis of studies utilizing American college students, where the range of intellectual functioning of the samples is typically very restricted. Therefore, generalizing the findings from such studies to some kind of general mechanism that is applicable to heterogeneous samples may not be warranted.

Intellectual functioning appears to affect the person's cognitive appraisal of the interrogative situation and the coping strategies that can be adopted. Adequate cognitive appraisal of the interrogative situation seems possible to achieve by the majority of people at the average level of intellectual functioning (Gudjonsson, 1988a). It is possible that with this minimum level of intellectual ability, other factors besides intelligence, such as anxiety, assertiveness and self-esteem, become more prominent. The advantage of this "individual differences" approach is that it highlights the fact that suggestibility is undoubtedly mediated and affected by a range of factors, rather than by one factor alone. Intellectual functioning is only one of several factors that are likely to mediate suggestibility and its overall influence may be comparatively modest.

SUGGESTIBILITY AND MEMORY

Suggestibility has been shown in a number of studies to correlate significantly with memory capacity. In other words, the poorer the subject's memory the more suggestible he or she is likely to be.

Verbal recall on the GSS 1 and the GSS 2 has been found to correlate negatively with suggestibility as measured by these scales but, as with IQ, the correlation is somewhat affected by range effects (Gudjonsson, 1988b). The correlation between memory on the GSS and suggestibility is similar to that found for IQ. That is, correlations of between −0.5 and −0.6 for normal subjects. The correlations are considerably lower among forensic patients (Gudjonsson, 1987c, 1988b).

Schooler and Loftus (1986) rightly point out that the significant correlation between memory and suggestibility on the GSS could be confounded by item similarities on the two within-scale measures. In other words, the significant relationship between the two variables could be an artefact due to the memory recall being based on the same items to which the misleading suggestions are later directed. This is an important point, because one does not know whether it is memory capacity *per se* which makes subjects more susceptible to suggestions, or the fact that they have poor recall about the subject matter on which they are questioned.

I attempted to solve this issue by comparing the correlations between memory and suggestibility from independent tests as well as those from within a test (Gudjonsson, 1987c). I administered the GSS 1 and GSS 2 to three groups of subjects with the sequence of administration being counterbalanced. I then correlated memory and suggestibility both within and between tests. The correlations were very similar for the within and between measures, which indicates that the correlation between suggestibility and memory on the GSS is not markedly affected by item similarities on the two measures. Furthermore, the findings indicate that suggestibility does correlate negatively with the memory capacity of the individual and with a magnitude similar to that found between memory and IQ. These findings are consistent with those of Gudjonsson and Singh (1984a), who discovered that memory recall on the GSS 1 correlated negatively with observers' independent ratings of suggestibility.

Considering the moderate correlation between memory and intelligence, the question arises as to what extent the two cognitive measures overlap in their relationship with suggestibility. The available evidence suggests that, in spite of a considerable overlap in the variance explained, memory and intelligence also do contribute separately to the subject's susceptibility to suggestions. For example, I have found that both immediate and delayed recall on the GSS 1 add to the variance in suggestibility after IQ had been controlled for (Gudjonsson, 1983a). Similarly, Sharrock and Gudjonsson (1991) found, by way of a "path analysis", that both delayed memory and IQ contribute individually, as well as jointly, to the variance in suggestibility.

An interesting finding from the first study on the GSS 1 (Gudjonsson, 1983a), but not researched further, is the importance of the rate at which memory deteriorates over time, as opposed to absolute memory levels. I found a highly significant negative correlation between suggestibility and the percentage of delayed vs. immediate recall. In other words, the more rapidly memory deteriorated over a 40- or 50-minute period, the more suggestible normal subjects tended to be, irrespective of their absolute levels of memory. One possible explanation is that people whose memory deteriorates rapidly over time learn to distrust their own judgement and rely more on cues provided by others.

SUGGESTIBILITY AND ANXIETY

Interrogative suggestibility appears to be significantly mediated by anxiety processes. Whether anxiety is generated through instructional manipulation or by other means may not be of critical importance. The general finding is that situational stress (i.e. "state" anxiety) is more important than "trait" anxiety.

The empirical evidence indicates that there is a poor relationship between suggestibility and trait anxiety as measured by self-report questionnaires. For example, Haraldsson (1985) found no significant correlation between GSS 1 suggestibility scores and neuroticism, which was measured by the Icelandic version of the Eysenck Personality Questionnaire (EPQ; Eysenck and Haraldsson, 1983). The sample consisted of 54 Icelandic university students.

In the first study on the GSS 1 (Gudjonsson, 1983a), I found a low but significant correlation ($r=28$, $p<0.05$) between total suggestibility and neuroticism, as measured by the English version of the EPQ (Eysenck and Eysenck, 1975).

There is some evidence that suggestibility is more strongly associated with "state" anxiety than "trait" anxiety. The former is typically construed as a transitory emotional state that is characterized by subjective feelings of apprehension and heightened autonomic nervous system reactivity. Trait anxiety, on the other hand, refers to relatively stable individual differences in anxiety proneness.

In one study (Gudjonsson, 1988a), I set out to investigate the hypothesis that state anxiety is more strongly associated with suggestibility than is trait anxiety. I administered the Spielberger State Anxiety Inventory (SSAI; Spielberger, 1969) twice to the subjects in the study. The subjects first completed the SSAI prior to the GSS 1 interrogation and then after they had been interrogated and given the standard negative feedback. In contrast to studies utilizing trait anxiety, some highly significant correlations emerged. The correlations were consistently higher with the second administration of the SSAI than the first. In addition, Shift and Yield 2 correlated significantly more highly with state anxiety, during both administrations of the SSAI, than with Yield 1. The correlations with Shift were 0.42 and 0.69 for the two SSAI tests, respectively.

The findings from this study support the hypothesis that suggestibility is strongly associated with state anxiety. This indicates that it is how apprehensive subjects feel at the time of the interrogation which is important rather than their more generalized anxiety proneness. In addition, state anxiety is clearly most strongly associated with how subjects react to interrogative pressure, rather than to leading questions *per se*. This supports my theory (Gudjonsson, 1984a) that Yield 2 and Shift scores on the GSS are more linked to anxiety and coping processes than Yield 1. The findings complement those of Tata (1983), who found that negative feedback on the

GSS 1 is accompanied by increased electrodermal reactivity as well as changes in mood, as measured by the Multiple Affect Adjective Checklist (Zuckerman and Lubin, 1965).

In an early study (Gudjonsson and Singh, 1984a), we attempted to validate the GSS 1 by administering the scale to 31 delinquent and adolescent boys (aged 11–16 years) who had been independently rated by two teachers on measures of suggestibility and self-esteem. The teachers' behavioural ratings of suggestibility correlated highly significantly with the GSS 1 Shift score. Furthermore, one of the items from the Coopersmith Behaviour Rating Form (Coopersmith, 1967), which is a measure of self-esteem rated by independent informants, correlated highly significantly with the GSS 1 Shift score. The question asked was, "Does this child become alarmed and frightened easily?" (rated on a 5-point Likert scale). This finding suggests that Shift is a measure of how readily the person becomes frightened when in the company of others.

Further evidence that Shift is related to how subjects cope with pressure comes from a study (Gudjonsson, 1984d), where it was found that Shift correlated negatively ($r = -0.37$; d.f. $= 48$; $p < 0.05$) with the Ego score, as measured by the Arrow-Dot Test (Dombrose and Slobin, 1958). No significant correlation was found for Yield 1. The Arrow-Dot Test is a perceptual-motor task which requires the solution of 23 simple graphic problems whilst subjects are placed under time pressure.

Studying anxiety from a different perspective, I investigated the relationship between suggestibility and social-evaluative anxiety (Gudjonsson, 1988b). The latter was measured by the Fear of Negative Evaluation (FNE) and Social Avoidance and Distress (SAD) scales of Watson and Friend (1969).

In view of the fact that people who score high on the FNE are prone to become apprehensive in evaluative situations and attempt to avoid social disapproval, it would be expected that they are more susceptible to suggestive influences than low FNE scorers. The theoretical reasoning for a relationship between the SAD and suggestibility is less clear, except that social distress may relate to how people respond to negative feedback.

It was found that the FNE scores correlated significantly with all the GSS 1 suggestibility scores, whereas no significant correlations were found for the SAD scale. The results support the view that interrogative suggestibility is more strongly associated with fear of negative evaluation than social distress.

Hansdottir et al. (1990) attempted to study the effects of anxiety and instructional manipulation on suggestibility by a way of experimental manipulation. Forty subjects were divided into four experimental groups. At the beginning of the experiment half the subjects were instructed to imagine as vividly as they could a stress-provoking situation and immediately afterwards listened to Stravinsky's *Rite of Spring* to further their anxiety. The other half of the subjects listened to neutral music only. The "anxious" and "neutral" subjects were then divided into two further groups and given either a low or a high expectation about their performance on the GSS 1.

It was found that situational stress only had a significant effect on suggestibility in the low expectation group. The authors point out that one explanation for this finding is that the high expectation instruction created performance anxiety in the subjects, which was similar to the anxiety generated by the anxiety manipulation. Administering the anxiety manipulation in addition to the high expectation instruction had no significant effect. Similarly, instructional manipulation did not significantly increase suggestibility among subjects who had been previously aroused by anxiety manipulation.

SUGGESTIBILITY AND INSTRUCTIONAL MANIPULATION

The expectation component of the Gudjonsson and Clark (1986) model indicates that suggestibility can, to a certain extent, be influenced by the type of instruction given prior to interrogation. For example, telling subjects that they should be able to answer all the questions asked raises their expectation about performance and may increase their susceptibility to suggestions. Conversely, telling subjects that they are not expected to know all the answers to the questions asked makes them more cautious about guessing the answers.

Evidence that subjects' suggestibility can be affected by the type of instruction given prior to interrogation comes from two studies. In one study we administered the Yield 1 part of the GSS 1 to medical students (Gudjonsson and Hilton, 1989). One group of subjects were told that they should be able to remember most of the story read out to them and give definite answers to all the questions asked about it. The second group was given the standard GSS 1 instruction which mentions no particular expectation about performance. The subjects are basically told to be as accurate as possible. The third group were told that they were not expected to be able to give a definite answer to all the questions asked. A one-way analysis of variance showed the difference between the three groups to be highly significant and there was a significant linear trend across the three conditions as predicted. Tests on the mean scores indicated that it may be somewhat easier to lower than to raise suggestibility by giving instructions to manipulate expectations about performance.

The second study into the effects of instructional manipulation on suggestibility is that by Hansdottir et al. (1990), which was described earlier with regard to anxiety. This study was similar to that carried out by us except that there were only two instructional manipulation conditions, "high" and "low" expectations. The findings are consistent with those found in our study and give support for the theoretical model of Gudjonsson and Clark.

SUGGESTIBILITY AND THE EXPERIMENTER EFFECT

Are the scores on a suggestibility test influenced by the characteristics of the experimenter? In one paper I raised some concern about the consistency with which negative feedback could be administered on the GSS 1 and stated:

"It is generally more difficult to present pressured instructions in a systematic and uniform way than suggestive questions. The emphasis that is placed on the negative feedback may influence the response elicited. In addition, if Ss do very well on the first trial and make no or few errors, then it can be embarrassing to inform them that they have made a number of errors. Such embarrassment may be unwittingly communicated to the S and affect subsequent responses" (Gudjonsson, 1984a, p. 311).

There are two important points to consider with respect to the administration of the negative feedback. Firstly, it is imperative that the precise wording is used when one is relying on the existing normative data for interpretation of the results. I have come across clinicians and researchers who actually changed the wording, either because they had forgotten the actual wording or had found it too embarrassing to tell the subject that a number of errors had been made. Secondly, the negative feedback should be stated firmly.

Evidence for an experimenter effect with regard to Shift comes from an Icelandic study which was conducted by six University students (Haraldsson, 1985). Whereas Yield 1 was not influenced by the experimenter, there was a trend, which was almost significant, for this to be the case with Shift. Haraldsson (1985) stated when interpreting this trend:

"Some of the experimenters commented that they had found it difficult and embarrassing to give negative feedback to Ss. Such an attitude may be communicated to the S and affect the resulting Shift scores" (p. 766).

A similar trend to those found by Haraldsson was found in a study I conducted in 1984 (Gudjonsson and Lister, 1984). Here the male experimenter (myself) obtained higher Shift scores than the female experimenter (Lister). Although the difference between the experimenters was not quite significant in both of these studies, they are worth reporting because they highlight potential problems with the measurement of Shift. Researchers and clinicians should be aware of the importance of paying careful attention to the way they administer negative feedback and ensure that they follow the proper instructions.

SUGGESTIBILITY AND SOCIAL DESIRABILITY

Both suggestibility and compliance correlate with social desirability, but the correlation is small and may not prove to be significant in all studies. Social desirability is commonly associated with "lie scales", such as those measured by the EPQ (Eysenck and Eysenck, 1975) and the Marlowe-Crowne scale (Crowne and Marlowe, 1960). A high "lie" score is generally construed as an attempt by subjects to present themselves in a socially favourable light (Gudjonsson, 1990b).

In an early study (Gudjonsson, 1983a), I found that the GSS 1 Total Suggestibility score correlated very modestly ($r=0.34$; d.f.$=43$; $p<0.01$) with social desirability as measured by the EPQ Lie Scale. Similarly, low but significant correlations between GSS 1 suggestibility scores and social desirability have been reported by other authors (Tata, 1983; Haraldsson, 1985).

As far as compliance is concerned, I have found a low but significant relationship with social desirability (Gudjonsson, 1989a).

SUGGESTIBILITY AND COPING STRATEGIES

The Gudjonsson and Clark (1986) model emphasizes the importance of coping strategies in the suggestion process. The findings from one study strongly support the view that suggestibility is significantly related to the coping strategies subjects can generate and implement when faced with the demands of the interrogative situation.

The study investigated the impact of coping on suggestibility among 30 normal subjects (Gudjonsson, 1988a). All subjects completed the GSS 1 and were afterwards asked about the coping strategies they had utilized during the GSS 1 interrogation. The subjects' descriptions of their coping strategies, both behavioural and cognitive, were classified according to the "methods of coping" described by Billings and Moos (1981) and Moos and Billings (1982). These fell into three groups:

1. "Active-cognitive" methods (i.e. the subjects try actively to manage their thoughts and appraisal of the situation);
2. "Active-behavioural" methods (i.e. behavioural attempts by the subjects to deal directly and critically with the situation);
3. "Avoidance coping" (i.e. the subjects avoid a critical appraisal of the situation).

It was hypothesized that the "avoidance coping" would be associated with heightened suggestibility, whereas "active-cognitive" and "active-behavioural" methods facilitate a critical analysis of, and coping with, the situation and therefore make the subject more resistant to suggestions.

A highly significant relationship between suggestibility and coping strategies was found. That is, subjects who reported having utilized "avoidance coping" had much higher suggestibility scores (i.e. Yield 1, Yield 2 and Shift) than the subjects who had been able to use the active-cognitive/behavioural methods.

A typical coping strategy of a suggestible subject was to give answers that to them seemed plausible and consistent with the external cues provided, rather than attempting to critically evaluate each question, and only give definitive (affirmative) answers to questions they could clearly remember.

Typical self-statements of this group were: "I gave plausible answers"; "I didn't want to look stupid"; "It is always best to give a definite answer even if it is wrong"; "I changed answers I wasn't sure about".

Non-suggestible coping strategies involved a critical analysis of the situation and a facilitative problem-solving action. Common self-statements of this group were: *Cognitive*—"I can't be expected to know all the answers"; "Some of the questions were not in the story"; "I am sure I have done as well as anyone else": *Behavioural*—"I tried to stick to what I remembered"; "I looked critically at each of my answers"; "I tried to look at the situation objectively".

SUGGESTIBILITY AND ASSERTIVENESS

According to the Gudjonsson and Clark (1986) model, it would be expected that assertiveness would correlate negatively with the GSS suggestibility scores. The reasoning for this is that unassertive individuals will find it difficult to implement facilitative coping strategies when faced with the uncertainty and expectations of the interrogative situation. One study, conducted by myself, has looked at this issue (Gudjonsson, 1988a).

The correlations between suggestibility, as measured by GSS 1, and assertiveness, which was measured by the Rathus (1973) Assertiveness Scale, were all significant. The correlations in a group of 30 normal subjects were as follows: Yield 1, $r=-0.42$; Yield 2, $r=-0.49$; Shift, $r=-0.40$; Total Suggestibility, $r=-0.46$.

I found a significant negative correlation (-0.53) between assertiveness and FNE (Fear of Negative Evaluation). One possible explanation is that high FNE inhibits assertive behaviour (Lohr et al., 1984), as well as the coping strategies that subjects can implement during interrogation.

SUGGESTIBILITY AND SELF-ESTEEM

Three studies have found a negative relationship between self-esteem and suggestibility, which supports the theoretical model of Gudjonsson and Clark. The results indicate that feelings of powerlessness and incompetence are particularly effective in inducing suggestibility. Furthermore, the findings suggest that manipulating suspects' self-esteem during interrogation may markedly increase the risk of uncritical acceptance of misleading information.

In the first study (Gudjonsson and Singh, 1984a), we correlated the Yield 1 and Shift scores from the GSS 1 with self-esteem, as measured by the Coopersmith Behavior Rating Form (BRF; Coopersmith, 1967). The subjects were 31 delinquent boys who were in an assessment centre. The BRF was filled in by members of staff who knew the boys well. Each boy was rated by two teachers and the average score was used for the statistical analysis. Self-esteem correlated negatively with Shift $(r=-0.40;$ d.f.$=29; p<0.05)$, but no significant correlation was found for Yield 1 $(r=-0.14)$.

Singh and Gudjonsson (1984) administered the GSS 1 to 30 subjects twice, 1 week apart. After each "interrogation" the subjects completed a number of Semantic Differential Scales (Osgood, Suci and Tannebaum, 1957) related to self-concept. Three "concepts" ("Myself as I am generally", "Myself during the experiment", and "The experimenter") were rated on 12 bipolar scales. Each bipolar scale consisted of a pair of bipolar adjectives. Factor analysis revealed three distinct factors in relation to each concept, which corresponded to Osgood's *Evaluative*, *Potency* and *Activity* dimensions.

The main findings of the study were that suggestibility (Yield 1 and Shift) correlated significantly with a low score on the Potency dimension but not with the other two dimensions. The correlations were significant with regard to the concepts "Myself as I am generally" and "Myself during the experiment". The correlations between Potency and suggestibility were lower during the second interrogation than the first. Singh and Gudjonsson (1984) state:

> "The implication of this is that the impact of self-esteem upon suggestibility is particularly likely to occur when Ss are unfamiliar with interrogative tasks and procedures. It also suggests that manipulation of self-esteem may be potentially more harmful to the reliability of testimony when naive and inexperienced Ss are employed who are unfamiliar with the nature of the task in hand" (p. 208).

Lister and I (Gudjonsson and Lister, 1984), administered the GSS 1 to 25 males and 25 females and asked them afterwards to complete the Semantic Differential Scales used in the Singh and Gudjonsson study. The subjects also completed the Rotter (1966) Locus of Control Scale. The Semantic Differential concepts rated by the subjects were, "Myself during the experiment" and "The experimenter". Three factors emerged from factor analysis, which were called "Potency", "Competence" and "Evaluative". It was found that the greater the perceived distance between the self and the experimenter in terms of Potency and Competence, the more suggestible the subjects were, both in terms of Yield 1 and Shift. The correlations were higher among the male subjects. The authors concluded from their findings that interrogation techniques aimed at manipulating confidence and self-esteem can increase subjects' susceptibility to suggestive influences.

SUGGESTIBILITY AND LOCUS OF CONTROL

There are theoretical and empirical grounds for expecting a relationship between suggestibility and the perception of control over the environment. Rotter (1966) described a questionnaire which measures attribution style along the dimension of *internal–external locus of control*. People with a high internal locus of control attitude perceive reinforcement as being contingent on their own behaviour. Conversely, people high on external locus of control view reinforcement as being contingent on environmental factors, such as fate and chance. One theoretical reason why locus of control would be expected to correlate with suggestibility is that people who perceive themselves as having strong control over environmental events (i.e. they have an internal locus of control) commonly describe themselves as potent and powerful (Hersch and Scheibe, 1967). From this perspective, people with high external locus of control would be expected to be more suggestible than those with internal locus of control.

In our study quoted above in relation to self-esteem (Gudjonsson and Lister, 1984), we found that suggestibility correlated significantly with external locus of control among the male subjects, but the correlation was not quite large enough to be significant for the female sample.

The findings from this study are consistent with a number of other studies which have shown that people with an internal locus of control tend to be more resistant to influence and pressure than those with external locus of control (Biondo and MacDonald, 1971; Ryckman, Rodda and Sherman, 1972; Eisenberg, 1978).

Brehm and Brehm (1981) point out that the greatest effect of internal vs. external locus of control is noted in those studies where there was greatest threat to the subjects' freedom to choose or act. What differentiates external locus of control subjects most from those with internal locus is the strong tendency of the latter to exhibit "reactance" arousal when faced with threat. Reactance arousal is probably best construed as a counterforce which motivates the subject to react forcefully to perceived threat or loss of freedom to act. If the task they are confronted with is perceived as having low threat value, then there appears to be much less difference between "internals" and "externals" in their reactions. The implication is that reactance arousal, which is generally activated when the individual's sense of freedom is threatened, is more readily activated in "internals" than "externals", which makes them particularly resistant to pressure under high threat conditions. This does not, however, exclude the possibility that the type of threat individuals are faced with may affect their reactance arousal in idiosyncratic ways.

RESISTERS AND ALLEGED FALSE CONFESSORS

My colleague Dr MacKeith and I recently reviewed the legal, psychological and psychiatric aspects of alleged false confessions (Gudjonsson and MacKeith, 1988). We concluded that the two most relevant endurable psychological characteristics in the assessment of such cases were *interrogative suggestibility* and *compliance*. We further discussed the importance of these two psychological characteristics with reference to a proven case of false confession (Gudjonsson and MacKeith, 1990).

Two studies have compared the suggestibility scores of alleged false confessors and resisters in criminal trials. In 1984 I compared the GSS 1 scores of 12 alleged false confessors and eight resisters (Gudjonsson, 1984c). The resisters comprised a group of defendants who had all persistently denied any involvement in the crime they had been charged with, in spite of forensic evidence against them. The alleged false confessors consisted of defendants who had retracted confessions they had previously made during police interrogation. The resisters were found to be significantly more intelligent and less suggestible than the alleged false confessors. A particularly significant finding was the difference between the two groups in the type of suggestibility which related to the ability to resist interrogative pressure. These were the Shift and Yield 2 scores on the GSS 1.

I identified two limitations with the study. First, the number of subjects in each group was very small. Secondly, part of the difference in suggestibility between the two groups could have been influenced by the differences in IQ between the two groups. Sharrock (1988) goes further and states that the differences in the IQ between the two groups "accounts for most of the difference in their suggestibility" (p. 220). Sharrock's bold statement seems to have been based on the erroneous assumption that, since there is a certain negative relationship between IQ and suggestibility, this is likely to have mediated the differences in suggestibility between the alleged false confessors and resisters. I take the view that suggestibility is mediated by a number of factors, intelligence being only one of them. However, Sharrock raised an important point which warranted a study where the IQs of the two groups are controlled for.

In an attempt to investigate Sharrock's observation, I recently extended and replicated the 1984 study (Gudjonsson, 1991c). The resisters and alleged false confessors were different to those used in the 1984 study and the number of subjects in each group was much larger than in the previous study. Perhaps most importantly, however, the two groups of subjects were matched with respect to age, sex, intelligence and memory capacity. The study also had the advantage over the 1984 study that the subjects had all completed both the GSS 1 and the GCS. Thus, both suggestibility and compliance were measured. It was hypothesized that, even with intelligence and memory capacity controlled for, the two groups would still show significant differences with regard to suggestibility and compliance, the main difference being related to the ability of subjects to resist interrogative pressure, as measured by the GCS and the Yield 2 and Shift parts of the GSS 1.

The most important finding was that highly significant differences emerged between alleged false confessors and resisters after their intelligence and memory capacity had been controlled for. This has important implications for the assessment of retracted confession cases. First, it demonstrates that the assessment of suggestibility and compliance, which are theoretically construed as overlapping characteristics (Gudjonsson, 1989a), contribute to discriminating between the two groups and that this is largely independent of the subjects' level of intelligence. In other words, intelligence may be an important factor in differentiating between alleged false confessors and retractors, but other factors, such as suggestibility and compliance, are also important and should not be underestimated. Secondly, the present findings are a clear warning to clinicians carrying out a forensic assessment. That is, even though suggestibility and intelligence are modestly correlated, it is erroneous to assume that differences in suggestibility and compliance are largely or necessarily mediated by differences in intelligence, as Sharrock (1988) postulated.

The mean suggestibility scores in this recent study are very similar to those found in the 1984 study for alleged false confessors and resisters. Furthermore, consistent with the previous findings, the most striking difference between the two groups is in relation to Yield 2 and Shift, which links confessing behaviour primarily with the suspects' ability to cope with pressure, rather than their tendency to give in to leading questions *per se*.

It is worth noting that, whereas alleged false confessors as a group are markedly higher on suggestibility and compliance than the average male in the general population, the resisters are, in contrast, unusually resistant to suggestions and interrogative pressure. Having said that, it should be borne in mind that we are dealing with group means, and there are clear individual differences within the respective two groups. For example, not all of the alleged false confessors proved highly suggestible or compliant; similarly, but less striking, not all of the resisters were low on suggestibility and compliance. This raises an important point which should always be carefully considered by the psychologist or psychiatrist when carrying out a forensic assessment in cases of alleged false confession. The suspect's ability to resist the police interviewer's suggestions and interrogative pressure, when these are present, is undoubtedly due to the combination of situational and interrogational factors on the one hand, and the suspect's mental state, motivation, personality and coping ability, on the other.

Figure 7.1 gives the suggestibility and compliance scores of three groups of subjects (Gudjonsson, 1991d). Here I compared the suggestibility and compliance scores of 76 alleged false confessors, 38 forensic patients who had not retracted their confession and still maintained their involvement in the crime, and 15 criminal suspects or defendants who had been able to resist police interrogation in spite of other evidence against them on which they were subsequently convicted. The subjects had all completed the GSS 1, the GCS and the WAIS-R. The three groups differed highly significantly in their suggestibility and compliance scores after IQ and memory recall on the GSS 1 had been controlled for by an analysis of covariance.

Figure 7.1 shows that there is a linear relationship between the three groups with regard to suggestibility (total score) and compliance. The alleged false confessors had the highest suggestibility and compliance scores and the resisters the lowest. The other forensic cases obtained scores which fell right between the other two groups on the two measures. Therefore, suggestibility and compliance differentiate between "false confessors", "forensic patients" and "resisters" in their own right and irrespective of differences in IQ.

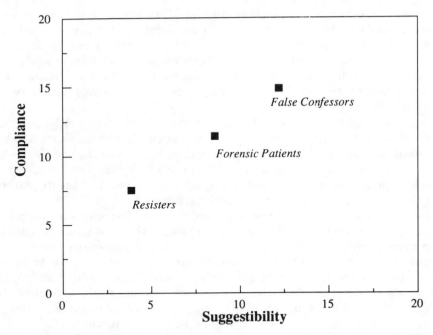

Figure 7.1. Mean suggestibility and compliance scores of "false confessors", "forensic patients" and "resisters"

It is interesting to note in this study that differences between the three groups were more marked with regard to the suggestibility and compliance scores than intelligence. This suggests that personality, as measured by suggestibility and compliance, may be a better indicator of how people cope with police interrogation than intellectual functioning.

Irving (1987) makes the interesting point that whether or not defendants were able to cope with police interrogation may predict GSS 1 scores, but this does not necessarily mean that GSS 1 scores will predict prospectively how people will cope with police interrogation. This is a valid point to make, because it is only by implication that one can suggest from the above-mentioned studies that the resisters' low suggestibility and compliance scores and the alleged false confessors' high scores influenced their behaviour at the time of the police interrogation. No study has examined prospectively how low and high suggestibility and compliance scorers are able to cope with police interrogation.

POLICE INTERVIEWING AND SUGGESTIBILITY

A study by Tully and Cahill (1984) suggests that the GSS 1 is able to predict, to a certain extent, the accuracy of witnesses' testimony during police interviewing. Forty-five subjects, 30 of whom can be loosely defined as mentally handicapped, took part in an experiment involving a staged scenario incident concerning the removal of some plants. The subjects were not aware at the time that 1 week later they were going to be asked questions about the incident. Prior to the staged scenario the subjects had completed a number of psychological tests, which included the GSS 1. One week later the subjects were all brought back to the testing centre and told that they were to be interviewed by police officers about the previous week's incident concerning the flower pots. The subjects' interviews with the police were video-recorded and analysed for accuracy and details of information.

Tully and Cahill analysed the interview material in terms of the number of *accurate* and *erroneous* recollections given by the subjects. The authors do not correlate these with suggestibility as measured by the GSS 1 but, as they give all the necessary raw scores in their book, such an analysis is possible. I have worked out these correlations. Suggestibility correlated negatively ($r=-0.63$; $p<0.001$) with the number of items of accurate information provided by the subjects and positively with the amount of erroneous information given ($r=0.39$; $p<0.01$). These results suggest that the more suggestible the subjects were, the less accurate information they gave, and the more errors they made when interviewed as witnesses to a staged scenario by the police 1 week later. This indicates that interrogative suggestibility, as measured by the GSS 1, can to a certain extent predict the reliability of information given by witnesses when interviewed by the police.

The police officers who interviewed the subjects in this study had been asked to elicit "accurate" information from the subjects, and they knew that most of the subjects were mentally handicapped. In addition, they were aware that their interviews were being video-recorded. This means that they would probably have been trying not to lead or mislead their "witnesses", although it is inevitable that they had to ask some specific questions in order to direct the focus of their questioning to the type of information they had been requested to obtain by the researchers.

Unfortunately, Tully and Cahill give no information about the police officers' interviewing techniques or the extent to which they may have been leading or misleading in their questioning. This is a major weakness in the study, especially since the authors had the data from the video-recorded interviews to study the effects of police interviewing styles on the reliability of the information obtained.

SUSPICIOUSNESS AND ANGER

I suggested in Chapter 3 that interrogators are intuitively aware of the need to induce a positive mood in the suspect in order to build up rapport and trust. Without rapport and trust being successfully achieved, self-incriminating admissions will be less forthcoming. In particular, negative emotional states, such as suspiciousness and anger, are viewed as undesirable emotional states which can potentially adversely affect the interrogative process and outcome.

Similarly, the Gudjonsson and Clark (1986) theoretical model indicates that *trust* is an essential component of the suggestion process. Lack of trust and suspiciousness are seen as seriously reducing the individual's receptiveness to suggestions. This is because the suspect or witness enters the police interview with a "suspicious cognitive set", which seriously influences the way he or she copes with the demand characteristics of the situation. Anger is not specifically mentioned by Gudjonsson and Clark, but it can function to make the suspect more critical and suspicious of the interrogator and his motives.

What do empirical and experimental findings tell us about the effects of suspiciousness and anger upon suggestibility? There is growing evidence that the intuitive view of experienced interrogators about the effects of mood is well founded. What has been shown is that certain negative moods affect compliance and suggestibility in a rather predictable way, and theoretical explanations can be put forward to explain such findings.

Loftus (1979b) found in her research into eyewitness testimony that if the questions asked are too blatantly misleading, then subjects commonly react by subsequently becoming less receptive to suggestions. The reason seems to be that when subjects become suspicious of the experimenter they will then scrutinize the interrogator's questions more carefully and readily identify when they are being misled. Further evidence for this comes from a study by Dodd and Bradshaw (1980) into the effects of pragmatic conditions on the acceptance of misleading information. For example, subjects were more guarded about accepting accounts from informants who were not perceived as "neutral". In other words, if communicators appear to have something to gain from giving a particular account, then subjects become suspicious of the reliability of the information provided and less readily incorporate it into their memory.

I noted in my forensic work in some major criminal cases (Gudjonsson, 1989d) that sometimes defendants were highly inconsistent in their GSS suggestibility scores when tested on two separate occasions. As a standard clinical practice, I always keep detailed notes of the defendants' mood and mental state during testing, as well of their attitudes towards the tests administered. Some interesting and striking observations were made with regard to the inconsistencies on the GSS. On the occasion when defendants proved highly suggestible their behaviour during testing was invariably associated with reasonable rapport and cooperation. In contrast, when these defendants were highly resistant to suggestions, there had been expressed indication of either suspiciousness and/or anger.

It can be tentatively suggested on the basis of this small anecdotal study, and some further cases, that in order for anger to encumber suggestibility it has to be directed *outwards* towards some third person or object, rather than towards the self. The anger need not necessarily be felt towards the interrogator, but it will still seriously reduce the person's susceptibility to suggestions. In other words, an angry suspect is probably difficult to interrogate at the best of times, even if the anger is not directed towards the interrogator. Suspiciousness, on the other hand, appears to have a more specific focus. It has to be directed towards either the experimenter or the tests themselves.

Stricker, Messick and Jackson (1967) discuss the implication of suspiciousness for conformity research. They found strong evidence that subjects' suspiciousness about the experiment they were participating in was related to lack of conformity and cooperation. In other words, those subjects who expressed ideas indicating suspiciousness about the testing procedure were much less conforming than those who expressed no such suspicions. The authors offered two possible explanations for their findings. Firstly, the subjects' generalized suspicious cognitive set predisposes them to seek evidence of deception and makes them more able to identify it when it does occur. Secondly, when subjects, for whatever reason, happen to become suspicious during a particular experiment, they develop a resistant cognitive set which helps them resist pressure and suggestions.

Milberg and Clark (1988) examined the effects of different moods, which were experimentally induced, on compliant behaviour. Three different mood states were induced: a happy mood, a neutral mood, and an angry mood. Significant differences in compliance were noted according to mood. Subjects in the happy mood condition were subsequently significantly more compliant than subjects in the neutral mood condition. Furthermore, far less compliance was noted among the subjects in the angry mood condition than in the neutral condition.

The authors concluded that happiness not only increased compliance; in this experiment it was necessary in order for anybody to comply with a subsequent task request. Similarly, anger induction not only decreased compliance; it resulted in significant changes taking place to the extent that subjects took the *opposite* view to that communicated by the experimenter. In other words, they reacted in quite an extreme way. The implication for real-life interrogation is that making suspects angry can badly backfire and result in a so-called "boomerang" effect (Brehm, 1966; Brehm and Brehm, 1981). This principle is based on "reactance theory", which is a counterforce which motivates people to assert themselves when their freedom to choose or act is threatened (Brehm and Brehm, 1981).

Another implication for real interrogations is that suspects who are interviewed by the police whilst in a negative emotional state, such as when suspicious or angry, need to be interviewed very carefully because they may be more likely to misinterpret interactional cues and attribute negative qualities to the interrogator and his or her messages. If this happens, the suspects are less likely to be forthcoming and open to suggestions, it will be more difficult to establish satisfactory rapport with them, and the likelihood of reactive arousal will be greatly enhanced.

The studies reviewed indicate that mood does, under certain circumstances, influence susceptibility to suggestions. An individual who is in a positive mood is more likely to cooperate with requests and accept suggestions than a person who is in a negative mood. However, as Milberg and Clark rightly point out, when the mood of the subject is self-focused its effects on compliance may be quite different to those mentioned above. For example, a self-focused positive mood may make people feel more confident in their own judgement and abilities. This is likely to reduce their reliance on external cues when asked misleading questions or requested to do things they would rather not do. Indeed, earlier in this Chapter it was shown how a sense of "competence" and "potency" in relation to perceptions of the self made subjects more resistant to misleading questions and interrogative pressure.

SUGGESTIBILITY AND PREVIOUS CONVICTIONS

Gudjonsson and Singh (1984b) argue that there are at least two theoretical reasons why criminals with previous convictions should be less suggestible than those with no previous convictions. First, offenders with extensive experience of police interrogation may develop increased resistance to interpersonal pressure applied during interrogation. Second, criminal recidivists may be characteristically more prone to resist interpersonal pressure than less habitual offenders.

Two studies have found a negative relationship between suggestibility, as measured by the GSS 1, and previous convictions. Gudjonsson and Singh (1984b) correlated the number of previous convictions among 35 delinquent adolescent boys and their suggestibility scores obtained on the GSS 1. All but two of the boys had previous convictions and the mean number of previous convictions for the group as a whole was 3.2 (range 0-9). The correlations with the GSS 1 were -0.21, -0.36 ($p < 0.05$), and -0.38 ($p < 0.05$) for Yield 1, Shift and Total Suggestibility, respectively. The findings indicate that the extent to which delinquent boys resist interrogative pressure during interrogation is significantly correlated with their previous convictions.

Sharrock and Gudjonsson (1991) extended the study quoted above, by investigating the effect of previous convictions on suggestibility whilst controlling for memory and intelligence. The subjects were 108 defendants who had been assessed by the authors as part of a pre-trial assessment. The findings were very similar to those of Gudjonsson and Singh (1984b). Shift was more highly negatively correlated with previous convictions than Yield 1, although both were significant. The authors concluded that interrogative experience, which was assessed by the presence of previous convictions, had a causal bearing on both Yield 1 and Shift independent of intelligence.

CONCLUSIONS

In this Chapter I have reviewed the psychometric and testing aspects of interrogative suggestibility. The evidence presented indicates that interrogative suggestibility can be reliably and validly measured. The GSS 1 and GSS 2 are based on a theoretically sound suggestibility construct and the scoring can be objectively quantified. The advantage of these tests is that they involve the person being subjected to "interrogation" under experimental conditions, and the answers are recorded in a standardized way. This overcomes self-report bias, which may be a problem when we have to rely exclusively on suspects' own account of their behaviour.

The scales have conceptual roots in both the legal notions of reliability of testimony and psychological notions of individual differences in susceptibility to suggestions. Both scales have satisfactory internal consistency and correlate highly with each other. The GSS 1 has been more extensively researched than the GSS 2, but the two scales are parallel forms which can be used interchangeably.

There is now substantial evidence that there are at least two kinds of interrogative suggestibility which are only modestly correlated. These are referred to in this Chapter as Yield 1 and Shift, respectively. Yield 1 measures the extent to which people give in to misleading questions, whereas Shift is more a measure of how people respond to interrogative pressure, which links it particularly to anxiety and coping processes. Shift seems more akin to the concept of compliance than Yield 1, because people are making a conscious decision to alter their answers in an attempt to improve their performance. Shift is less stable as a measure than Yield 1 and it is more susceptible to an experimenter effect. However, both Yield 1 and Shift have been shown to be fairly stable over time and are valid measures of interrogative suggestibility. The most impressive findings relate to the ability of the Scales to differentiate between defendants who allege that they made false confession and those who made no self-incriminating admissions during police interrogation.

The GSS 1, and to a lesser extent the GSS 2, has been used to test a number of hypotheses raised by the Gudjonsson and Clark (1986) theoretical model of interrogative suggestibility. A number of studies have supported hypotheses derived from the model. Interrogative suggestibility is clearly distinct from that found in a hypnotic context. It has been shown to be correlated with a number of cognitive and personality measures, including those measuring intellectual functioning, self-esteem, anxiety, assertiveness and locus of control. Of particular importance seems to be the ability of the person to cope with the demands, expectations and pressures of the interrogative situation.

Suggestibility is, to a certain extent, influenced by situational factors and experience. Mood variables, such as anger and suspiciousness, have been shown to markedly reduce people's susceptibility to suggestions and their willingness to comply with requests. Suggestibility in a given situation can be influenced by the type and nature of instructions given prior to interrogation, such as those related to expectations about performance.

One of the most difficult questions with regard to suggestibility relates to the extent to which one can generalize from a GSS test score to a trait concept of interrogative suggestibility. This is not a new issue, but is nevertheless a very important one, and will be taken up in the final chapter of this book when all the evidence, theoretical, empirical, and anecdotal, has been assessed.

CHAPTER 8

Psychological Techniques for Enhancing Memory Retrieval

There are three major psychological techniques available for enhancing memory retrieval among witnesses, victims and suspects. These are: investigative hypnosis, the cognitive interview and drug-aided interviews. The use of hypnosis as a way of improving memory retrieval has been extensively used in the United States of America and in Israel and it has attracted considerable research. More recently, special clinical interview techniques (the cognitive interview) have been advocated as a way of increasing the accuracy and completeness of eyewitness accounts. The other development, which was first advocated in the 1930s, consists of using drugs as a way of enhancing memory retrieval (drug-aided interviews). With increasing research the potential and limitations of these aids have become apparent. The purpose of this Chapter is to review the literature on each of these techniques and discuss their potential and limitations.

INVESTIGATIVE HYPNOSIS

The Nature of Hypnosis

There is considerable controversy in the literature about the nature of hypnosis and there appears to be no one satisfactory definition available. In fact, nobody seems to know what hypnosis is, in spite of the fact that a large number of theories exist on the process and mechanisms involved. Modern theorists are divided into two main schools, "state theorists" and "non-state theorists", which reflect somewhat different assumptions and conceptualizations about the nature of hypnosis (Fellows, 1986).

Most authors, whether "state" or "non-state" theorists, describe the nature of hypnosis in terms of subjects' overt behaviour or in terms of what they are experiencing. State theorists typically view hypnosis as an altered state of consciousness (or "trance") which is characterized by heightened suggestibility. For example, Waxman (1986), who views hypnosis as a special state, defines it as:

"An altered state of awareness effected by total concentration on the voice of the therapist" (p. 23).

Wagstaff (1988) considers Hilgard's (1974) "neo-dissociation" theory as the best state theory for explaining the hypnotic process. The theory states that during hypnosis imaginative involvement enables the subject's mind to split off or dissociate from what else is going on.

Non-state theorists do not view hypnosis as a special state; rather they see it as a form of role-play or a goal-directed action. Spanos (1986), who is a non-state theorist, defines hypnosis as:

"A purposeful, goal-directed action that can be understood in terms of how the subjects attempt to interpret their situation and the self-presentations they attempt to convey by their actions" (p. 449).

According to Wagstaff (1988) there are three main differences between the state and non-state approaches to hypnosis. Firstly, although non-state theorists agree that hypnosis may involve an altered state of consciousness, they do not see it as being unique to hypnosis. Secondly, unlike the state theorists, non-state theorists do not believe the subjects lose conscious control during hypnosis, but only act as if they do. Thirdly, non-state theorists view hypnosis as a "waking" behaviour, as opposed to behaviour dissociated from consciousness, which has major implications for the type of mechanisms that are seen as being responsible for the hypnotic effects observed and reported.

Temple (1989) has drawn attention to recent attempts to bring together apparently conflicting theories under a new theory, labelled a "Connectionist Theory of Hypnosis". The theory, which looks at hypnosis from a "system" point of view, has its basis in neuroscience and computer technology. It views hypnosis as a process of complicated and hierarchical energy transformation at different levels in the brain, which can be activated or deactivated by external stimuli. The advantage of the theory is that it recognizes the important interactions between structurally different response systems (e.g. cognitive, affective, motivational).

Applications

Hypnosis, irrespective of its theoretical base, has a number of different applications (Temple, 1989). Hypnosis has a long history as a therapeutic tool (Waxman, 1986) and has been shown to be effective with a number of psychological and psychosomatic conditions (Gibson and Heap, 1991).

". . . [it] is not itself a therapy but a set of adjunctive procedures which may be applied to a wide variety of therapies" (Heap, 1988, p. 9).

Wagstaff (1983) defines *forensic hypnosis* as:

"Hypnosis applied to the collection of evidence for judicial purposes" (p. 152).

Haward (1990), on the other hand, defines it as:

"Hypnotic techniques applied to information-gathering for evidential purposes" (p. 60).

Reiser (1980) prefers to use the term "investigative hypnosis" to describe the information-gathering aspects of hypnosis. Reiser makes the point that investigative hypnosis is a subspeciality within hypnosis which requires special training and experience. The hypnotic process and the objectives are different from those found in the therapeutic uses of the techniques. Rather than being an adjunct to therapy, investigative hypnosis is an adjunct to information-gathering and any therapeutic benefits are incidental (e.g. victims of rape or disasters reporting that they feel a great deal better after undergoing investigative hypnosis).

Haward (1988) mentions two main applications of hypnosis to forensic work. Firstly, anxious witnesses can be prepared for giving evidence in court by different hypnotically related procedures, such as relaxation, desensitization and post-hypnotic suggestion. Secondly, hypnosis can be used for information-gathering either in relation to *mens rea* (i.e. establishing criminal intent and mental state) or *actus reus* (the nature of the criminal act itself). The present Chapter only deals with *actus reus*-related issues, because this is where investigative hypnosis has its greatest potential. Here hypnotic techniques either aim at overcoming resistance in psychogenic amnesia, especially in the case of rape victims who have been traumatized by the experience, or they attempt to improve the recall of less traumatized witnesses where no major repression of memory traces has taken place (Haward, 1988). Readers who are interested in other forensic applications are recommended the work of Udolf (1983) and Haward (1988).

Investigative hypnosis is typically used with witnesses and victims of major crimes (Reiser, 1980; Haward, 1980, 1990). In exceptional circumstances it has been used with the defendants (Coons, 1988; Haward, 1990). According to Haward (1990), "forensic" hypnosis has been used in the Netherlands since the nineteenth century and in the United States of America since 1907. In the United States of America and in Israel, police officers are trained in investigative hypnosis, which is a highly controversial practice (e.g. Orne, 1979; Laurence and Perry, 1988). In the United Kingdom investigative hypnosis is normally conducted by qualified psychologists and never by police officers (Haward, 1980; Mottahedin, 1988).

Hypnosis may result in a confession when used with criminal suspects and this may cause ethical problems for the hypnotist. In a recent case a woman who was accused of killing her children confessed falsely to the crime under hypnosis (Coons, 1988). The confession was not allowed in evidence by the judge.

Stages in the Hypnotic Process

The process of investigative hypnosis in relation to memory enhancement consists of a number of distinct stages. Reiser (1980, 1990) describes seven main stages. Stage 1 involves careful preparation of the case prior to the hypnosis session, where the relevant information about the case and the subject is obtained. This leads on to a pre-induction stage of the actual hypnosis session (Stage 2). Here the hypnotist establishes rapport with the subject and explains the procedure. The pre-induction interview and the entire hypnosis session are audio- or videotape-recorded.

Stage 3 consists of the hypnotic induction. The purpose is to induce in the subject a hypnotic state by having him or her concentrate on a particular physical or mental activity (e.g. fixing the eyes on a certain spot) whilst certain suggestions are offered (e.g. that the eyelids are becoming very heavy). A number of different induction techniques are available for this purpose (e.g. Reiser, 1980; Udolf, 1983).

Once the initial induction has been achieved, the hypnotic stage has to be deepened (Stage 4) and this can be done in several different ways. Counting is sometimes used where it is suggested that the subject will go into a deeper and deeper state of relaxation with each number mentioned. The use of imagery (e.g. asking subjects to imagine that they are in some very relaxing setting) is another useful way of achieving deep relaxation and increased concentration. As people become more absorbed in the imagery, and subsequently in memory-enhancing exercises, the less distracted they are likely to be by extraneous noises or worrying thoughts.

Stage 5 involves formal attempts at enhancing memory which could be potentially useful for the police in obtaining investigative leads. A number of different memory retrieval techniques are available for this purpose. Two commonly used techniques are "age regression" (for a review, see Orne, 1979) and the so-called "television technique" (for a review, see Reiser, 1980). Direct suggestions that memory will improve can also be used (Orne, 1979; Udolf, 1983). "Age regression" involves taking the subject back in time to the situation towards which recall is being directed. This means that the subject may actually re-experience or relive the original experience. The "television technique" involves the subject watching an imaginary television screen on which is shown the scene of the crime and the events that took place. The idea is to distance the subject from the traumatic event and therefore make it less painful to recall. This may have certain advantages when the session is conducted by hypnotists, such as police officers, who are without any clinical training and qualifications (Udolf, 1983).

After the memory retrieval procedure is completed, the subject enters Stage 6. Here post-hypnotic suggestions are given whilst the subject is still in the hypnotic state. These typically involve telling the subject that his or her memory, at which the hypnosis is directed, will improve with time and during further sessions.

The final stage (Stage 7) involves the subject coming out of the hypnosis. This can, for example, be achieved by counting slowly whilst telling the subject that the hypnotic state is becoming lighter and lighter. Occasionally subjects may be resistant about coming out of hypnosis and fall into natural sleep (Weitzenhoffer, 1957).

Can Hypnosis Enhance Memory?

There is considerable anecdotal case-history evidence to suggest that hypnosis can enhance memory in criminal cases (Arons, 1967; Reiser, 1980, 1990) and disaster cases (Raginsky, 1969; Hiland and Dzieszkowski, 1984). The enhanced memory may result in new leads which prove significant in solving the case. Investigative hypnosis seems to be most effective in very serious cases, such as murder, robbery, rape and terrorism, where the arousal created by the experience leads the mind to block out the painful emotional experience. The main conclusion one can draw from the anecdotal evidence is that hypnosis can be a highly effective tool in criminal investigations, even in cases where there has been no obvious psychological trauma.

Early controlled laboratory research into hypnotic memory enhancement consistently failed to corroborate the successful findings of the anecdotal studies (Smith, 1983; Wagstaff, 1984). There were some exceptions, of course, but the successful studies were very small in number (Stalnaker and Riddle, 1932; Griffin, 1980). How can such marked discrepancy between the laboratory and real-life anecdotal findings be explained? One possible explanation raised by both Smith (1983) and Wagstaff (1984), and more recently by Reiser (1990), is that experimental studies may simply lack ecological validity (i.e. they are far too removed from the real-life situation). Indeed, many experimental studies in the past have used relatively non-meaningful stimuli and have lacked the type and amount of emotional arousal that are commonly found in real-life situations. The more realistic and meaningful the memory enhancement context, the more favourably the outcome is likely to be (Timm, 1981; Relinger, 1984; Orne et al., 1988). There is some evidence to suggest that lack of ecological validity has been at least partly overcome by some recent studies and this has improved the results of the studies with regard to memory enhancement (e.g. Geiselman, et al., 1985; Yuille and Kim, 1987). The conclusion to be drawn is that more ecologically valid experimental studies need to be carried out before definite scientific conclusions can be drawn about the true benefits, and limitations, of hypnosis for memory enhancement.

Potential Problems

Haward (1988) lists three potential problems with the use of investigative hypnosis. The first problem relates to the scientific validity of the techniques used, which was discussed above. The second problem involves the possible inadmissibility by the courts of evidence obtained during hypnosis. This issue has been discussed by a number of authors (e.g. Orne, 1979; Diamond, 1980; Haward and Ashworth, 1980; Udolf, 1983; Morris, 1989; Reiser, 1990; Haward, 1990) and need not be discussed in any detail here. The legal admissibility concerning whether or not to allow pre-hypnosis recollections varies between jurisdictions in the United States of America and, in a recent English case cited in Haward (1988, 1990), the evidence of witnesses to a violent crime was not allowed by the judge because of the possibility that their memory for events had been interfered with by the hypnotic process. The third problem discussed by Haward relates to the possibility that hypnosis contaminates the memory of witnesses. For example, Wagstaff (1984) makes the important point that a clear distinction must be drawn between the *volume* and the *accuracy* of the memory elicited during hypnosis. Hypnosis may, for example, markedly increase the amount of information generated, but this may be at the expense of accuracy.

Reviewing the scientific literature on the use of investigative hypnosis, the normal memory process seems to be potentially interfered with in three respects. Firstly, subjects may be particularly prone to confabulate whilst under the influence of hypnosis. Some authors prefer to use the term "pseudomemory" instead of confabulation to describe the type of "fantasy" material generated during the hypnosis process. Secondly, hypnosis may heighten some subjects' susceptibility to leading questions. Thirdly, the hypnotic process may actually make subjects feel overconfident in their recollections (i.e. it hardens their confidence in their memory without an objective basis for it).

Orne (1961, 1979) argues that during hypnosis subjects tend to confabulate as a way of coping with their perceived expectations of the situation. Similar arguments have been put forward by Diamond (1980) and Temple (1989). Relinger (1984) and Reiser (1985) argue that increased confabulation is by no means inevitable in hypnosis. Indeed, a certain amount of confabulation is a common feature of memory retrieval and is partly related to the amount of interrogative pressure the person is placed under (Eugenio et al., 1982; Tata and Gudjonsson, 1990). That is, the more the subject is pressured to recall, the greater the amount of confabulation. What needs to be asked is whether hypnosis is more likely to facilitate or generate confabulation than other memory retrieval techniques.

The experimental evidence is somewhat equivocal on this point. A number of studies have shown memory under hypnosis to be specially susceptible to confabulation (Stalnaker and Riddle, 1932; Laurence and Perry, 1983; Spanos and McLean, 1986; McCann and Sheehan, 1987; Register and Kihlstrom, 1988), whereas others have failed to find evidence for this (Spanos et al., 1989). Geiselman et al. (1985) compared memory recall and confabulation among three experimental groups: those receiving hypnosis, a standard police interview, and a "cognitive interview". Although not quite significant, the hypnosis group had the largest number of confabulations.

It has been argued by some authors (e.g. Hull, 1933) that hypnosis is primarily a state of heightened suggestibility. Suggestibility in this context is seen as a personality trait which is augmented by hypnotic induction techniques. A number of studies have shown that during hypnosis some subjects may be particularly susceptible to leading questions (Putman, 1979; Zelig and Beidleman, 1981; Sanders and Simmons, 1983), but contrary results have also been reported (Yuille and McEwan, 1985).

Orne (1979) argues that hypnosis makes subjects more confident in their recall, irrespective of whether it is accurate or erroneous, even though there is no objective basis for the increased confidence. Temple (1989) goes so far as to suggest that:

> "This subjective feeling of certainty and unshakeable conviction is what makes hypnotic recall so extremely dangerous. And it is what can transform a witness in court into an extremely convincing one who will sway both judge and jury by giving false testimony. . . ." (p. 281).

There is some evidence that hypnotic subjects report greater confidence in their incorrect recall than control subjects (Wagstaff, 1982; Sheehan and Tilden, 1983; Nogrady, McConkey and Perry, 1985). Other studies have failed to find a difference in confidence between hypnotized subjects and controls (Putman, 1979; Sanders and Simmons, 1983; Gregg and Mingay, 1987).

Investigative Hypnosis: Brief Summary

Investigative or forensic hypnosis has been extensively used as an information-gathering tool. It is commonly used by police officers in the United States of America and Israel, although in recent years the technique has come under severe criticism from academics, because of lack of empirical findings in experimental studies. The technique appears to be of greatest value with witnesses and victims in cases where memory recall is inhibited because of emotional trauma.

THE COGNITIVE INTERVIEW

The "cognitive interview" was recently developed by Geiselman et al. (1984) as a way of enhancing memory retrieval during interviewing of victims and witnesses. It owes its theoretical underpinning to experimental research on memory, from which three general principles evolved. First, a particular memory trace is made up of several specific features, such as shape, size and colour. Second, the effectiveness of a particular cue in eliciting retrieval depends on how many similarities it has with the encoded event (Flexser and Tulving, 1978). Third, there may be several different paths to the retrieval of a particular piece of information, which means that one cue may be more effective in gaining access to a particular memory trace than another.

The Techniques

Developing these theoretical ideas, Geiselman and his colleagues developed the cognitive interview as a way of potentially enhancing the ability of eyewitnesses to retrieve stored memory traces (Geiselman and Fisher, 1989). The techniques employed in the interview utilize four general methods of facilitating retrieval. The first two methods aim at increasing the similarities between the encoding and retrieval contexts, whereas the last two methods focus on utilizing more than one retrieval path.

There were two recommended ways of increasing the similarities between the encoding and retrieval contexts. Firstly, witnesses should be encouraged to "reinstate the context" in which the observed incident occurred. This involves the witnesses focusing their minds on the context surrounding the incident (e.g. some specific features of the physical environment, their thoughts and feelings experienced at the time). This technique works well in facilitating recall in the laboratory (Bower, Gilligan and Monteiro, 1981; Malpass and Devine, 1981). Secondly, the witnesses are instructed to report everything they can think of, no matter how trivial it may seem to them. They are encouraged to make several attempts at retrieval when this is necessary. This is based on the general principle that the more witnesses try to remember a particular event the more they will recall (Roediger and Thorpe, 1978).

Geiselman et al. recommend two methods for increasing the number of retrieval paths utilized. Firstly, witnesses are instructed to recount the incident in more than one order (Whitten and Leonard, 1981). For example, the witnesses may attempt to go through the incident in reverse order, or focus on those aspects which impressed them most. Secondly, witnesses are instructed to report the incident from a variety of perspectives (Anderson and Pichert, 1978). This includes trying to see the incident from the point of view of some other person present, or the interviewer may ask about a particular matter in different ways in order to facilitate the retrieval process.

How does the effectiveness of the cognitive interview compare with other interviewing techniques, such as those found in a standard police interview? The studies that have addressed this issue indicate that the cognitive interview elicits significantly more accurate information than a standard police interview, and without an accompanying increase in incorrect information or confabulation (Geiselman et al., 1984, 1986). The realistic laboratory experiments carried out in these studies indicate that the cognitive interview elicited between 25 and 35% more material than the standard police interview, without producing more inaccurate information. It seems from these promising results that all four methods of enhancing retrieval are important and should be utilized.

More recently Fisher, Geiselman and Raymond (1987) and Fisher, Geiselman and Amador (1989) recommend one additional technique for retrieval enhancement. This involves motivating witnesses to concentrate adequately on retrieval attempts. Poor concentration lowers the ability of the witness to retrieve information. Increased concentration can be facilitated in a variety of ways. These include:

1. Witnesses should be made to feel relaxed and comfortable;
2. There should be no obvious distractions;
3. Witnesses should be encouraged to focus their attention on internal mental images;
4. Witnesses should not be rushed to retrieve information.

Police Interviews

Fisher, Geiselman and Raymond (1987) analysed tape-recorded police interviews in order to identify some of the problems evident in such interviews with regard to inhibiting retrieval. Three commonly used techniques seemed to hinder memory retrieval. These were:

1. Frequent interruptions of witnesses' descriptions;
2. Asking them too many short-answer questions;
3. Inappropriate sequencing of questions.

Frequent interruptions by police interviewers seemed to reduce the witnesses' ability to concentrate on the retrieval process. This was particularly detrimental when witnesses were attempting to concentrate on mental images which generally require considerable effort. The second problem with frequent interruptions is that they come to be expected, which increases the likelihood that witnesses will adopt superficial retrieval efforts.

Asking direct questions that require short answers can be fruitful as a way of eliciting relevant information. However, Fisher and his colleagues found two main problems when too many short-answer questions are being asked. First, this type of question generally elicits less concentrated retrieval than open-ended questions. The second problem is that short-answer questions elicit information which is tied to the specific request. This narrows down the type of information gathered and prevents potentially important but unsolicited information from being revealed.

Inappropriate sequencing of questions was found to be a major problem in most of the police interviews analysed. This commonly involved follow-up questions which were incompatible with the witnesses' mental image of the crime, which resulted in less than optimal tapping of the witnesses' memory of the event. Three types of inappropriate sequencing were found, referred to as "predetermined", "lagging" and "arbitrary" order, respectively. The disadvantage of the predetermined order was that it lacked the flexibility required to match the specific questioning with the ongoing and dynamic mental representation that the witnesses had of the crime. Asking follow-up questions in a lagging order often interrupted the flow of conversation. The authors recommend that follow-up questions should either follow immediately after the witnesses' original statement or should be left until the witnesses have completed their description of the event. There were two types of arbitrary order questions. First, questions related to the incident had unrelated features, which in some instances meant that witnesses were required to alternate between different sensory modalities (e.g. visual vs. verbal). Concentrating on one modality at a time appears to markedly facilitate retrieval. Secondly, it was not uncommon for interviewers to interject general knowledge questions in the middle of witnesses' reports of the details of the incident, which seriously distracted the witnesses' train of thought.

It was particularly striking from findings of the Fisher, Geiselman and Raymond (1987) study that police officers vary considerably in their interview styles and techniques. Furthermore, they appear to have limited awareness of the limitations of their interviewing practices and have no proper rationale or reasoning for the way they interview witnesses.

In a recent study involving real-life witnesses and victims, Fisher, Geiselman and Amador (1989) trained seven experienced police detectives in the cognitive interview techniques and compared the results of 47 subsequent police interviews with those of six experienced detectives who had had no training in the clinical interview techniques. The training given to the six detectives consisted of four 60-minute group sessions. Highly significant differences emerged between the two groups of detectives in the amount of accurate recall elicited. The results give further support for the superiority of the cognitive interview over the standard police interview. In fact, the detectives trained in the cognitive interview produced 63% more information than did the detectives who used a standard police interview.

Roy (1991) has recently discussed the potential application of cognitive interview techniques for the British police service. He argues that the police have not yet fully recognized the value and range of applications of these techniques, but their role in police interviewing is currently under consideration by the City of London Police and the Metropolitan Police.

Implications

What are the main implications of the principles and research findings concerning the cognitive interview? Firstly, the techniques described, which are based on scientific research into memory, can markedly increase the accuracy and completeness of witnesses' accounts of a crime they observed. This has been demonstrated both in realistic laboratory and field studies. The techniques clearly have the greatest contribution to make in cases that are heavily dependent on eyewitness accounts (e.g. cases of robbery and assaults). The techniques appear to increase recall without any accompanying increase in incorrect information or confabulation (Geiselman and Fisher, 1989).

Secondly, as Fisher et al. (1989) point out, on theoretical grounds the cognitive interview techniques can be used in a variety of settings other than police interviewing, for example, in education, clinical practice and research. In a police setting it is of greatest potential use with witnesses and victims, but there is no reason why the techniques could not be used, on occasions, with cooperative suspects to enhance their recollection of events.

Thirdly, there are important lessons to be learned for the training of police officers in interviewing techniques. Police officers in many countries receive little or no formal training in interviewing techniques and they appear to have little awareness of the limitations of their existing practices. Greater awareness of what precisely they are doing when interviewing people, and why they are doing it in that particular way, is the first step to improved efficiency and effectiveness. The second step would be to train them in the techniques of cognitive interviewing. The two main advantages of training police officers in the use of the cognitive interview are:

1. The techniques can be taught fairly quickly and do not require extensive training;
2. The cognitive interview techniques do not pose the legal problems surrounding the use of hypnosis for memory-enhancement (Morris, 1990).

Are there any foreseeable problems with the use of the cognitive interview techniques in actual police practice? Clearly there are some factors to consider. For example, according to Fisher, Geiselman and Amador (1989), the cognitive interview may require more time, and greater concentration and flexibility on the part of the interviewer, than the standard police interview. This has resource and manpower implications for the police. Some police interviewers may not be sufficiently adaptable and flexible in their style and personality to utilize the cognitive interview to its maximum potential, whilst others may not have the necessary motivation and patience required.

Geiselman and Fisher (1989) have begun to train police officers in the use of cognitive interview techniques. There appear to be fewer objections to police officers utilizing these techniques than has been the case with hypnosis. Considering that the cognitive interview has similar objectives to investigative hypnosis, but fewer legal and practical problems, it may in the future replace the need for investigative hypnosis, except in cases of psychogenic amnesia. In the future, forensic psychologists may be increasingly called upon to train police officers in cognitive interview techniques, and in some instances involving particularly complicated cases, they may be requested by the police to conduct the interview themselves.

The Cognitive Interview: Brief Summary

The cognitive interview is a new procedure or technique for enhancing memory retrieval. It is based on a sound theoretical foundation from the experimental literature on memory. A number of studies have been conducted into its validity with promising results. The technique appears to minimize the risk of interfering with the memory process and there is scope in the future for training police officers in the use of the technique.

DRUG-AIDED INTERVIEWS

Many drugs, including alcohol, have been used to facilitate talkativeness (Gottschalk, 1961; Naples and Hackett, 1978). However, their use has been less formal and systematic than that of barbiturates which are normally administered intravenously during the drug-aided interview.

The literature on drug-aided interviews covers two overlapping areas of application. These are best described as forensic and clinical applications, respectively. The purpose of both applications is to overcome inhibitions and increase communication. The procedure is invariably carried out or supervised by medical practitioners.

Forensic Application

The first attempt to use drug-aided interviews for forensic purposes was reported by House (1931), who had been using scopolamine as an anaesthetic drug during childbirth. House noticed that some of the women injected with the drug became talkative and verbally uninhibited. This encouraged him to inject scopolamine into two prisoners before interviewing them. Both men denied the charges brought against them and were subsequently acquitted in court. House concluded on the basis of these two cases that under the influence of scopolamine people cannot lie. House's bold and naive statement led to the misconception in the public's mind that under the influence of scopolamine, or similar drugs, people are not capable of lying, hence the terms "truth serum" and "truth drug" were coined.

Before long it was realized that scopolamine had serious side-effects in some instances, such as hallucinations (Freedman, 1967). It was therefore replaced by barbiturates, which appeared to have fewer undesirable side-effects. The most frequently used drugs were sodium amytal and sodium pentothal. Barbiturates are hypnotic (i.e. sleep-inducing) drugs which act as sedatives on the central nervous system. The forensic purpose of these drugs is to make the person more relaxed and open in order to facilitate communication.

Drug-aided interviews originally had two main forensic applications (Dession et al., 1953). First, during the 1940s and 1950s narcotic drugs were used by some psychiatrists as an aid to understanding the personality and motives of defendants facing criminal charges. The findings were then used to make judgements about issues such as psychiatric diagnosis, fitness to plead and stand trial, criminal responsibility, and disposal in terms of the most appropriate sentencing or treatment. Second, the objective was to obtain information about criminal activities and to assess the truthfulness of any statement given. Dession et al. (1953) provide detailed examples of the application of "narcoanalysis" in forensic practice and discuss the legal implications of the procedure. Gottschalk (1961) gives a somewhat more scientific appraisal of the early use of drugs in interrogation.

Clinical and experimental work carried out in the 1940s and early 1950s destroyed the early belief that people cannot lie under the influence of certain drugs. All that could be said is that in many instances drugs like barbiturates help people relax, which can improve communication, but the information obtained had to be interpreted with the greatest caution (Dession et al., 1953; Gottschalk, 1961). For example, in one study the fantasies of subjects under the influence of drugs frequently could not be differentiated from the factual material produced (Gerson and Victoroff, 1949). In another study, malingerers were able to remain uncommunicative during drug-aided interviews (Ludwig, 1944).

In a recent review, Haward (1990) describes six different uses that have been made of drug-aided interviews. These are:

1. "To prove *facts in issue*";
2. "To prove *mens rea*, or its absence";
3. "To demonstrate the truth of the victim's testimony";
4. "As evidence of character";
5. "As evidence of witness credibility";
6. "To facilitate obtaining a *confession*".

Haward (1990) points out that the admissibility of drug-aided interview material has varied considerably with the courts, both in Britain and in the United States, but the evidence allowed has tended to be related to a mental state examination (*mens rea*). According to Haward, drug-aided evidence has not been admitted when it aims to demonstrate witness credibility or truthfulness.

Haward (1974) argues that drugs are ineffective for eliciting the "truth" and they should only be used in certain cases (e.g. where there has been psychological trauma) to lower mental resistance and defensiveness. Danto (1979) describes the use of sodium brevital in police interrogations and claims, without any scientific justification, that suspects under its influence are more likely to tell the truth.

Clinical Application

Drug-aided interviews have been formally used since the early 1930s, either to aid therapy or as a way of obtaining information. Horsley (1936, 1943), who first introduced the term "narcoanalysis" to describe barbiturate-aided interviews, has described in detail how he began to use barbiturates in the early 1930s as an aid to psychotherapy and hypnosis. Horsley saw barbiturates as having similar behavioural effects to that of hypnosis, that is, drowsiness and relaxation which was allegedly accompanied by heightened receptiveness to suggestion. He favoured the use of barbiturates over hypnosis for diagnostic and therapeutic purposes because he thought that their effects were quicker, more predictable and generally more effective.

Following the work of Horsley (1936, 1943) and Bleckwenn (1930a, 1930b) psychiatrists began to experiment with the use of barbiturates as an adjunct to therapy, which included the treatment of post-traumatic stress disorder, or "war neurosis" as it was named at the time (Sargant and Slater, 1940; Grinker and Spiegel, 1945; Janis, 1971), and psychogenic amnesia (Herman, 1938; Sargant and Slater, 1940; Lambert and Rees, 1944). Some promising work was carried out in these two areas, which are both relevant to forensic psychiatry. The work of Grinker and Spiegel on abreaction and psychotherapy for traumatic war experiences has relevance to peacetime traumas, including rape (Janis, 1971). Lambert and Rees found that a barbiturate-aided interview was the most effective way of treating psychogenic amnesia; 82% of their amnesic patients so treated fully recovered their memory. The procedure thus offers both therapeutic and investigative value to victims of criminal conduct who suffer psychogenic amnesia.

The interest of psychiatrists in the use of barbiturate-aided interviews declined sharply in the early 1960s. Patrick and Howells (1990) attribute this decline to the increased recognition of barbiturate dependence and to major changes in psychiatric practice which followed the introduction of major tranquillizers and tricyclic antidepressants in the 1950s. However, some psychiatrists still use barbiturate-aided interviews for therapeutic purposes. Perry and Jacobs (1982) are probably the strongest recent advocates for the use of barbiturate-aided interviews and conclude, on the basis of their literature review, that sodium amytal can serve as a valuable adjunct to diagnostic assessment and treatment. Patrick and Howells (1990), in a more recent but less detailed review, are more circumspect in their evaluation of barbiturate-aided interviews for clinical purposes. Nevertheless, they consider its value particularly fruitful in two clinical areas. Firstly, they quote evidence from three studies to support the view that patients with genuine brain damage, in contrast to those with "functional disorders", exhibit temporary deterioration in cognitive functioning in response to the barbiturate amylobarbitone. In other words, the damaged brain is sensitive to the effects of the drug and temporarily impairs cognitive functioning, whereas this is not the case where the cause for the disorder is more psychologically determined. Secondly, some inaccessible and unresponsive patients become communicative after the administration of amylobarbitone and this helps markedly with the assessment of their mental state.

In spite of the potential value of barbiturates in reducing inhibitions and enhancing communication, it is worth bearing in mind that these drugs can result in fantasies in some vulnerable individuals that cannot be differentiated by the patient from reality. Dundee (1990) describes a number of cases where intravenous midazolam and diazepam, administered to female patients as a sedation, resulted in unsubstantiated allegations of sexual assault against the doctor concerned. There was a clear relationship between the dosage and the frequency of complaints. That is, the higher the dosage the greater the number of complaints.

Individual Differences

One major problem with the use of drug-aided interviews is that the person is not merely responding to the effects of the drug itself. Besides the pharmacological tolerance of the person to the drug, there are a number of non-pharmacological factors that can influence the person's responsivity to the drug. These include the personality of the individual concerned (e.g. emotional stability and suggestibility) and his or her perceptions, expectations and attitudes (Dession et al., 1953; Gottschalk, 1961). One study aimed at establishing whether barbiturates can facilitate the retrieval of new information better than a placebo substance (saline); sodium amylobarbitone was found to improve memory but so did the placebo substance (Dysken et al., 1979).

The importance of personality variables on the outcome of drug-aided interviews has been investigated in a small number of studies, which have tended to fall into two groups:

1. Those concerned with the effects of personality on the ability of people to withhold information under "narcoanalysis";
2. Studies focusing on the effects of drugs on suggestibility.

In an interesting study, Redlich, Ravitz and Dession (1951) attempted to establish whether people can withhold information during barbiturate-aided interviews. Although only a small number of subjects were used in the study, the results indicated that those subjects who "confessed" most readily under the influence of sodium amytal were prone to depression and feelings of guilt and anxiety. The authors concluded that people with strong self-punitive tendencies may give in readily during drug-aided interviews and even confess to crimes they had never actually committed.

Two types of study have investigated the effects of drugs on suggestibility. These relate to differences in suggestibility between drug addicts and "normal" controls, and to the more interesting studies where drugs are administered to subjects experimentally and their specific effects on suggestibility are carefully tested.

Glaus (1975) investigated the suggestibility scores of 19 drug addicts and those of 20 non-drug addicts by using a specially designed paper and pencil test. No significant differences in suggestibility were found between the two groups. There is a serious methodological problem with this study in that the suggestibility test utilized had not been standardized or validated.

Baernstein (1929) tested 19 college students on the "body sway" test, which measures the extent to which subjects move their trunk either forwards or backwards upon verbal instructions. There were two experimental conditions: (a) after the injection of sterile water, and (b) after injection of scopolamine. There was marked increase in suggestibility among eight highly suggestible subjects from the first to the second condition. However, there was no significant increase in suggestibility between conditions among the eleven most resistant subjects.

Eysenck and Rees (1945), in a more methodologically rigorous experiment, studied the effects of narcotic drugs (sodium amytal and nitrous oxide gas) on suggestibility as measured by the "press–release test", which is a test of primary suggestibility and measures the effect of the verbal suggestion that the subject is either releasing his hold on an object or grasping it more firmly. The type of suggestibility measured by the test correlates highly with the "body sway" test. The subjects were 20 neurotic patients, 10 of whom had previously scored very low on the "body sway" test. The remaining 10 subjects had scored very high on the test. The results of this study indicated that narcotic drugs only affected the suggestibility scores of already suggestible subjects, whereas the drugs left non-suggestible subjects unaffected.

The results from the studies of Baernstein and Eysenck and Rees strongly suggest that scopolamine and barbiturates only increase the degree of suggestibility in already vulnerable subjects and have little or no effect on those subjects who are resistant in a normal state.

Drug-aided Interviews: Brief Summary

Barbiturate-aided interviews have been used since the 1930s as an aid to memory retrieval and for diagnostic and therapeutic purposes. Their main purpose is to overcome inhibitions and make people more talkative. Although potentially valuable in some cases, the scientific validity of the procedure has not been demonstrated and its forensic application is very limited at present. There are serious problems with the reliability of information obtained during the procedure due to increased confabulation, fantasy and suggestibility among vulnerable subjects.

CONCLUSIONS

Three different techniques to aid police interviewing have been discussed in this Chapter. Each operates to *enhance* or *elicit* memory retrieval in order to provide a more complete account of facts and events. The limiting factor is the extent to which these techniques may increase inaccuracy of information, confabulation and suggestibility whilst enhancing memory retrieval.

Investigative hypnosis is an information-gathering tool that is commonly used in the United States of America and in Israel to enhance the memory retrieval of witnesses and victims. The validity of hypnosis for this purpose in real-life cases is well supported by anecdotal cases. However, the laboratory evidence for the effectiveness of hypnosis in enhancing memory is limited. Part of the problem with much of the experimental evidence is that it lacks ecological validity. Some of the more recent contextually relevant studies provide support for the validity of investigative hypnosis, particularly in cases of high emotional arousal where attempts are made to elicit meaningful material.

There are legal complications to using hypnosis with witnesses and victims of crime. This is due to the commonly held belief that hypnotic procedures interfere with normal memory processing. That is, hypnosis may increase the amount of information elicited, but this may be at the expense of accuracy. In particular, hypnosis is thought to increase confabulation and susceptibility to suggestions, and harden confidence in erroneous recall. The scientific evidence indicates that these can be potential problems with investigative hypnosis, but it should be emphasized that none of these problems inevitably occur, either in or out of hypnosis.

In recent years Geiselman, Fisher and colleagues, have developed special interviewing techniques, which they call "the cognitive interview". The cognitive interview consists of four general memory enhancement techniques which, like investigative hypnosis and drug-aided interviews, aim to increase the completeness of witnesses' memory recall for observed events. The techniques need further research and replication, but they are based on a sound theoretical foundation and their effectiveness has been empirically demonstrated in both laboratory and field studies. The advantage of these techniques is that they seem to interfere less with the memory process than hypnosis and drug-aided interviews. Furthermore, the techniques do not appear to result in legal problems with regard to the admissibility of the material elicited.

A number of different drugs have been used over the years as an aid to interviewing, diagnosis and treatment. Barbiturates are most commonly used. Their purpose is to overcome resistance or inhibition by a method of slow intravenous injection in order to facilitate talkativeness and communication. The scientific validity of the procedure has not been established, but from the available evidence it seems that drugs can in some cases increase the amount of information obtained. In addition, barbiturate-aided interviews appear to have some value in the recovery of memory in cases of psychogenic amnesia and for clinical and diagnostic purposes.

However, information obtained from drug-aided interviews cannot be relied upon as being accurate, as it often consists of confabulated as well as factual material. There is a great deal of individual variation in the way people respond to drug-aided interviews, and they can successfully lie and resist giving away information they do not wish to reveal. People with anxiety and depressive problems appear most responsive, but they are also most vulnerable to giving confabulated information. Suggestibility, at least of the primary type, seems to increase in vulnerable individuals (i.e. those who are prone to suggestions in a normal mental state) whilst they are under the influence of certain drugs, such as scopolamine and barbiturates.

An important factor that has never been investigated, clinically or experimentally, is the effect of drug and alcohol withdrawal on the accuracy and completeness of testimony. This is an area that requires urgent attention because many criminal suspects interrogated at police stations may be particularly distressed when they are withdrawing from substances on which they are physically and psychologically dependent.

CHAPTER 9

Psychological Techniques for Evaluating Testimony and Documents

A number of psychological procedures, techniques, tests and instruments have been devised this century which can be used to assist the police in evaluating the accuracy, reliability and truthfulness of evidence. The oldest and best known of these is the polygraph for detecting deception ("lie detection"). More recent developments include techniques which can be used for verifying the authenticity of written documents (stylometry) and special analysis of witnesses' statements for evaluating the truthfulness of such statements (Statement Reality Analysis).

Each of these topics will be discussed with reference to the relevant literature and anecdotal case material will be used as appropriate to illustrate specific points.

THE POLYGRAPH

The polygraph is an instrument that records simultaneously a number of physiological responses, which typically comprise heart rate, blood pressure, respiration and electrodermal reactivity. These physiological modalities can be influenced by a number of environmental and psychological factors unrelated to deception. For example, physical and mental exertion and changes in environmental temperature can affect all these physiological modalities. Similarly, stress, however caused, can lead to marked changes in heart rate, blood pressure, electrodermal reactivity and the pattern of respiration. Thus, the physiological measures that are used to detect deception can be affected by a number of factors, only one of which relates to lying itself. No physiological response unique to lying has ever been discovered.

The polygraph examiner has to make inferences about possible deception or truthfulness after comparing the physiological responses of the person to crime-related or "relevant" questions, as opposed to "control" questions. If the person consistently responds more strongly physiologically to the "relevant" than "control" questions or items, then he or she is typically designated *deceptive*. Conversely, if the responses to the "control" questions are consistently higher than those to the "relevant" questions, then the person is designated *truthful*. When the differentiation, in terms of physiological responses, between the "relevant" and "control" questions is not very clear or marked, then the outcome is labelled *inconclusive*.

The above description indicates that in order to be able to detect deception four conditions must be met:

1. There have to be certain tests which include "relevant" and "control" questions or items.
2. There has to be an instrument available which measures the person's physiological responses to the questions asked.
3. An examiner is required to construct the lie detection tests, to administer them, operate the polygraph and evaluate the polygraph charts.
4. Generally speaking, there has to be a subject who is either going to be telling the truth or be deceptive. Levey (1988) makes the point that the application of the polygraph is not restricted to detecting conscious deception: potentially, it can be used to detect information that is out of conscious awareness.

The four parts of the polygraph examination take place within a given context. There are three main contexts in which the polygraph is traditionally used: for employment screening, for security screening, and in the case of criminal investigation (Office of Technology Assessment, 1983).

The main discussion in this brief review is about the application of the polygraph as a tool in a criminal investigation. The polygraph is an instrument that measures physiological reactions that are potentially applicable in a variety of forensic settings as an information-gathering tool. It is the purpose of this review to give the reader some insight into these applications. The legal aspects of the use of the polygraph are not specifically discussed in this Chapter. Direct polygraph techniques, such as the control question technique, are not admissible in English law (Gudjonsson, 1983b). In the United States of America, the states have taken varied positions with respect to evidence derived from the use of the polygraph (Morris, 1990).

The Techniques

Several reviews about the application and effectiveness of polygraph techniques in criminal investigation have appeared (i.e. Reid and Inbau, 1977; Lykken, 1981; Raskin, 1982; Office of Technology Assessment, 1983; Levey, 1988). Most of the research conducted has been concerned with two polygraph techniques, known as the "Control Question Technique" (CQT) and the "Guilty Knowledge Technique" (GKT).

The CQT was originally developed by Reid (1947) and represents a formidable attempt to overcome the serious inadequacies that had been identified with the existing "Relevant-Irrelevant Technique" (RIT). The RIT had grown out of the work of Marston (1917), was developed by Larson (1932) and Keeler (1933), and consisted of two types of questions, *relevant* and *irrelevant* questions. Relevant questions pertained to the crime under investigation (e.g. "Did you take the missing money?"), whereas the irrelevant questions were concerned with some neutral items (e.g. "Are you sitting down now?"). The assumption made by polygraph examiners was that deceptive suspects would react substantially more strongly to the relevant than to the irrelevant questions. This was a very naive assumption because of the inherently emotionally arousing nature of the relevant questions for both deceptive and truthful subjects.

Reid's idea was to develop a technique where the physiological responses to the relevant questions could be compared with some emotionally arousing "control questions". These so-called "control questions" are constructed during a pre-test interview with the suspect. They are deliberately vague in nature and comprise a denial of some minor transgression. They are introduced by the polygraph examiner in such a way as to maximize their salience value and emotional arousal for truthful subjects.

The "Guilty Knowledge Technique" (GKT; Lykken, 1959, 1981), or "Concealed Information Test" as Raskin (1982) prefers to call it, is best described as an *indirect* test for measuring deception. In fact, the purpose of the technique is to detect concealed information rather than lying *per se*. That is, in contrast to the CQT, subjects are not asked direct questions about a specific offence where a "yes" or a "no" answer is required. Rather the GKT attempts to detect if subjects have a particular piece of information about the crime under investigation that only "guilty" subjects would be expected to have. For each crime, several tests may be constructed. Each test employs one relevant item having some association with the alleged crime, and several (usually five) control items. All the items are presented in a multiple-choice format whilst the subject's physiological responses are monitored. If the subject responds, physiologically and consistently, more strongly to the relevant than to the control items, then he or she is considered to possess certain knowledge about the crime. By implication this probably means direct or indirect involvement in the commission of the crime.

A case illustration of the application of the GKT to a mock crime, in a case of pseudologia fantastica, is given by Powell, Gudjonsson and Mullen (1983). The case involved a 36-year-old man who had spent over 20 years of his life engaging in extensive lying in order to obtain a more desirable persona and pecuniary advantage. The purpose of the experiment was to establish if he could withhold concealed information without it being detected by a polygraph. The man's deceptive answers were easily detected from his physiological responses.

The CQT and the GKT have been shown to be highly effective in detecting deception in an experimental situation, but the precise degree of accuracy in field studies is controversial (e.g. Levey, 1988). The CQT is the main technique used in criminal investigation, because it is easy to apply to most situations and, unlike the GKT, it does not require detailed knowledge about the crime in order to construct the polygraph test. Furthermore, often there is a great deal of public knowledge about the crime which makes it difficult, and in many instances impossible, to identify salient items of knowledge that could not be known to innocent subjects. The GKT would be inappropriate to use unless the polygraph examiner is completely confident that only the guilty subject would be able to differentiate the relevant items from the control items. It is undoubtedly true that field examiners could more often apply the GKT to criminal cases than they do, but the fact remains that it requires a great deal more work and sophistication than the CQT, and the necessary "concealed" information required to make up the test is often not available. This means that for practical purposes polygraph examiners have to rely on the CQT, in spite of its inherent limitations.

The main problem in evaluating the effectiveness of the CQT is the extraordinarily high claims for its accuracy by professional field examiners, which are not supported by scientific evidence. For example, some professional polygraph examiners claim an accuracy rate of 97% or above, whereas the scientific evidence indicates a more modest accuracy of about 85% (Levey, 1988). There is general agreement in the literature that the CQT is more prone to false-positive than to false-negative errors. This means that the main weakness of the CQT is that it tends to identify innocent subjects as guilty (false-positive error), whereas it is better at identifying deception in guilty subjects. In contrast, the GKT produces very few false-positive errors, but this may be at the expense of more false-negative errors (Raskin, 1990). Therefore, the GKT is better at protecting innocent subjects from being erroneously labelled deceptive than the CQT. However, it may be somewhat easier to defeat by deceptive subjects. Raskin (1990) argues that the relatively high false-negative error rate among deceptive subjects on the GKT is likely to be due to the fact that they may not, at the time of the crime, have adequately processed the specific information that is used to formulate the multiple-choice items.

Factors Influencing Outcome

There are a number of factors that affect the accuracy and outcome of a particular polygraph test. Some of the more important factors have been discussed by Raskin (1982, 1990) and Levey (1988). These include the personality of the subject and the type of countermeasures deceptive subjects deliberately use in order to defeat the polygraph test. The training, competence and experience of the examiner is also an important factor, but I shall not be dealing with that aspect in this brief review and refer the interested reader to a recent paper by Elaad and Kleiner (1990).

The personality of the subject taking the polygraph test may be relevant to the outcome. Levey (1988) suggests three personality characteristics that can affect the accuracy of the polygraph test:

1. Interrogative suggestibility;
2. Psychopathy;
3. Trait anxiety.

Levey argues for the possible importance of *interrogative suggestibility* in influencing the outcome of the polygraph, but he does not specify in what ways it could be important. No study has actually investigated its role in relation to the polygraph. One possibility is that suggestible subjects are particularly responsive to the examiner's instructions and psychological manipulation prior to actual polygraph testing. In fact, subtle psychological manipulation of the subject is part of the procedure of the CQT (Raskin, 1982, 1990) and the extent to which the subject believes the examiner may very well influence the outcome of the test.

There is no evidence that *psychopathic* criminals are more able to defeat polygraph tests than other criminals. Raskin (1982, 1990) reviews a number of studies which indicate that poorly socialized and antisocial people are as easily detected by the polygraph, when they are being deceptive, as are other deceptive subjects. However, there is some evidence that criminals and people diagnosed as personality-disordered are less responsive electrodermally than normal subjects to questions that raise moral issues (Gudjonsson, 1979a). Whether this is likely to influence the outcome of the polygraph test in a real-life situation is not clear.

Bradley and Janisse (1981) have argued, and provide some supportive evidence for their claim, that lies told by extraverts are more readily detected by the polygraph than lies told by introverts. Their argument is that extraverts are likely to find only the relevant questions cortically arousing, whereas introverts are more easily aroused in general and would therefore respond more strongly to both the relevant and control questions.

In 1982 I wrote a paper (Gudjonsson, 1982), in response to the Bradley and Janisse article, arguing on theoretical grounds that the relevance of the introversion–extraversion dimension would depend upon the technique and the nature of the stimulus questions used. In other words, these two authors seemed to have oversimplified the relevance of extraversion in the detection of deception, because different techniques can employ various types of control items with different "threat" value.

There is some evidence that emotional lability, which is also commonly referred to as *trait anxiety* or neuroticism, can affect the polygraph's false-positive and false-negative error rates (Gieson and Rollinson, 1980; Waid and Orne, 1980; Waid, Wilson and Orne, 1981). The findings from these studies indicate that stable subjects may react in a way that leads the examiner to make false-negative errors, whereas emotionally labile subjects more commonly react in a way that results in false-positive errors. This means that emotionally labile subjects can lose out in two ways. First, if they are innocent, they are more likely than stable subjects to be erroneously diagnosed as deceptive. This finding is consistent with an early study by Heckel et al. (1962), where it was found that emotional and psychiatric disturbance markedly increased the chances of an innocent person being erroneously classified as deceptive. Second, if they are genuinely being deceptive, then they are likely to be more readily detected than stable subjects.

Countermeasures are deliberate techniques that some subjects use in order to appear truthful when they are taking a polygraph test. Such techniques can seriously challenge the accuracy of the polygraph in detecting deception. There are a number of techniques that have been reported in the literature and they comprise three different ways of beating the polygraph test (Gudjonsson, 1988c).

1. Subjects may attempt to suppress their physiological responses to the relevant questions, e.g. by relaxation, biofeedback or some kind of mental distraction.
2. Subjects may attempt to reduce their overall level of physiological reactivity during the polygraph test, e.g. by taking drugs prior to the examination.
3. Subjects may attempt to augment their physiological responses to the control questions as a way of reducing the discriminative power of the relevant question. This can be achieved by inflicting physical pain or producing muscle tension.

A considerable amount of research has been carried out into the use of countermeasures as a way of defeating the polygraph tests (for reviews, see Gudjonsson, 1988c; Levey, 1988). The results do show that under certain circumstances the accuracy of the polygraph in detecting deception can be seriously undermined by the use of countermeasures. Generally speaking, it is more effective to beat the polygraph tests by attempting to augment the physiological responses to the control questions than by attempting to reduce the reactivity to the relevant questions. In addition, physical countermeasures are typically most effective, although this may depend on the individual concerned. Two conditions appear to increase the effectiveness of physical countermeasures. First, employing multiple countermeasures simultaneously improves the person's chances of beating the polygraph test. Second, physical countermeasures appear to be relatively ineffective unless people are given special training in how to use them.

Orne (1975) introduced the concept of the "friendly polygrapher" to argue that guilty defendants are more likely to beat the polygraph test if tested at the request of the defence rather than the prosecution, because under defence conditions the setting is likely to be more relaxed and less threatening. There is no evidence to support this notion, either theoretically or empirically (Raskin, 1986).

The polygraph is most commonly used with criminal suspects or defendants. In certain circumstances it is used with victims and witnesses. The control question technique may be invalid when used with victims of crime (e.g. rape victims), because the emotional trauma associated with the critical questions is likely to lead to false-positive error.

Examples of the Indirect Measures of Deception

Early in my psychology career, I used a variant of the GKT to detect the identity of a young woman who claimed to be amnesic for her background (Gudjonsson, 1979b). The woman, who was in her mid-twenties, had been admitted to hospital after a suicide attempt involving a drug overdose. On admission to hospital she was aggressive and suicidal and claimed to have only the haziest recollection of her own past. No abnormality was found on physical examination and an electroencephalogram (EEG) showed normal activity. A few days after her admission to hospital the woman was referred to me for a diagnostic assessment. A police investigation had failed to establish the woman's identity. Similarly, a photograph of the woman in a local newspaper failed to identify her. Having previously worked as a police detective, and having done some research into the use of the polygraph, I decided to make an attempt to discover her identity by using an electrodermal apparatus.

An interview with the woman revealed that she remembered going on a bus to Banstead, which is a small village in southern England, with the intention of killing herself there. She claimed not to recall why she had to die in Banstead and claimed that she had no recollection of having ever been there before. My initial hypothesis was that Banstead was a significant place to her because she probably had lived there as a child. When presented with the names of the local primary schools in the area, whilst her electrodermal responses were being monitored, a clear reaction was evident with regard to one of the schools. I visited the school and borrowed the school register. I then presented her with a selected number of christian and surnames from the school register (I had previously been able to identify her month of birth on the basis of her electrodermal responses which narrowed down the possible names). She responded to a christian name and a surname that matched. Both names proved later to be accurate and led to the woman's identity being fully established.

In the early stages of her amnesia the woman seemed preoccupied with death, which was stress-related as measured by the Dektor Psychological Stress Evaluator (Gudjonsson and Haward, 1982). During subsequent weeks the woman's amnesia gradually lifted, but simultaneously she became markedly suicidal. She made several serious suicide attempts before eventually discharging herself from hospital. Several months later the woman was found in another part of the country in a fugue state. In view of the apparently inverse relationship between the woman's claims of amnesia and her suicide attempts, Professor Haward and I speculated that her amnesia functioned as an alternative to suicide (Gudjonsson and Haward, 1982).

Another indirect way of using the polygraph as a way of detecting deception is illustrated by a court case I was involved in 1982 as an expert witness (Gudjonsson and Sartory, 1983). A young man had been referred to me by a firm of solicitors because of alleged blood-injury phobia.The man had been stopped late at night by the police for a speeding offence. He admitted to having consumed three pints of beer that evening. He failed two breathalyser tests and was asked to provide a specimen of blood, which he refused to give on the basis that he was mentally unable to provide a specimen. The man was subsequently convicted in a Magistrates' Court of drunken driving because he failed to provide a specimen of blood without a reasonable excuse. The case was referred for appeal and I was asked to address the question of whether or not the defendant suffered from genuine blood phobia, to the extent that at the time of being asked for a specimen he had been mentally incapable of consenting to provide it.

This case presented me with an ideal opportunity of applying recent knowledge about blood-injury phobia and polygraph technology to a forensic context, and this could inadvertently establish legal precedence in England. At the time it was known that cardiac reactions (i.e. heart rate and blood pressure) could be distinguished between blood phobias and other types of phobias. That is, blood-injury phobia is associated with lowered heart rate (bradycardia) in contrast to the usual cardiac acceleration to other phobic stimuli (e.g. Sartory, Rachman and Grey, 1977).

My colleague Gudrun Sartory and I set up an experimental paradigm where the defendant had to look, from a distance of about three yards, at some potentially fear-inducing objects for 15 seconds; these consisted of a bottle containing human blood and two syringes that differed in size. Other similarly shaped objects were used as control items in order to establish a base level of physiological reactivity. The defendant's heart rate and the pattern of his respiration were recorded in response to the relevant and control items on a polygraph and analysed by a laboratory computer. Marked heart rate *deceleration* was repeatedly noted with regard to the blood container and syringes, which was not evident in response to the control items. Considering that the relevant stimuli constituted no threat of impending venepuncture, the findings supported the diagnosis of genuine blood-injury phobia. The physiological findings, which were supported by clinical data, were presented at his appeal. During the cross-examination I was mainly asked about the possibility that the defendant could have faked his physiological responses. I excluded this possibility on the basis that:

1. The defendant would have required detailed knowledge about the unique cardiac responses of blood-injury phobia; it was highly improbable that he would have had this knowledge available to him;
2. It would have been more difficult for the defendant to *lower* his heart rate to the relevant stimuli than to *raise* it. He could have attempted to lower his heart rate to the relevant stimuli by meditation or by holding his breath, but the polygraph recording indicated regular breathing throughout the experiment. In addition, the heart rate deceleration to the relevant stimuli was sharp, which is not characteristic of meditation or breath holding efforts;
3. The physiological finding was supported by convincing clinical interview data.

The judges accepted the psychological evidence, but they expressed concern about the case's legal implications; in particular, they did not want to "open the flood gates" to people who claimed phobic problems. Nevertheless, the case had to be considered on the basis of its individual merit and the judges came to the conclusion that at the time of his arrest the defendant "was mentally incapable of providing a specimen of blood". The conviction was quashed.

Confessions Elicited by the Polygraph

There is no doubt that the fear of taking a polygraph test, and perhaps more importantly, failing it, can act as a strong incentive to confess, as suspects may view further denials as futile. How effective is the polygraph in eliciting a confession from a suspect? In the opinion of one of the early pioneers in the use of the polygraph:

> "The instrument and the test procedure have a very strong psychological effect upon a guilty subject in inducing him to confess. . . . In actual practice, unsolicited confessions are sometimes given at the mere suggestion that a subject should submit a lie test, or after the subject is brought into the laboratory and sees the instrument. Others have likewise confessed after the instrument was attached but before the test was started, and still others immediately after the test was finished, without a word of inducement from the examiner. . . . Statistics indicate that from 60 to 85 per cent of those subjects indicated as guilty by the test eventually confess. The report of the Chicago Police Scientific Crime Detection Laboratory heretofore referred to shows that 70 per cent confessed at the laboratory, while 15 per cent confessed to officers after leaving the laboratory" (Lee, 1953, pp. 161–162).

The rate at which suspects confess after being requested to take a polygraph test seems dependent upon at least two factors: the perceptions the suspect has of the polygraph and its effectiveness and the skills of the examiner in eliciting a confession during a post-test interview. Normally what happens is that where deception is indicated, the examiner tells the subject that he has failed the test and then proceeds to interrogate him in an attempt to obtain a confession from him (Lee, 1953; Reid and Inbau, 1977; Inbau, Reid and Buckley, 1986).

The effectiveness of the polygraph in eliciting a confession from guilty suspects is recognized by Lykken (1981), one of the most vocal scientific opponents of the use of the polygraph for detecting deception. His view is that the guilty suspects who confess as a result of failing a polygraph test are the more naive, gullible and less experienced criminals. Lykken argues that whether or not suspects confess after failing a polygraph test has little or nothing to do with the true accuracy of the polygraph in detecting lies. What is important is the faith of the suspect and examiner in the polygraph, irrespective of its true validity. It is likely that the frequency with which suspects confess after failing a polygraph test reinforces the polygraph examiners' faith in the polygraph. This may partly explain the extravagant claims made by some polygraph examiners about the validity of the techniques.

Does the use of the polygraph ever lead to a false confession? Lykken (1981) argues that the polygraph, like other interrogation techniques that rely on trickery, manipulation and subtle psychological coercion, greatly increases the risk of eliciting false confessions. How often false confessions are elicited by the use of the polygraph is not known. Nevertheless, there are documented cases where this has occurred (Connery, 1977; Lykken, 1981; Gudjonsson and Lebegue, 1989). What seems to happen is that polygraph examiners use a deceptive outcome as a way of persuading the suspect that he must have committed the offence and that any denials are futile. In some instances the suspects are told that the polygraph is 100% effective, and they are subsequently made to believe that they are guilty even when they have no recollection whatsover of having committed the offence (e.g. Connery, 1977; Gudjonsson and Lebegue, 1989).

The case described by Gudjonsson and Lebegue (1989) illustrates the "blind faith" some polygraph examiners appear to have in the accuracy of the polygraph. The case is discussed in detail in Chapter 11, so it will only be briefly mentioned here. It involved a 27-year-old American airman who had confessed to killing his best friend after failing four polygraph tests, which had been administered by agents of the OSI (Office of Special Investigations). The agents testified before a Court Martial in England that they *always* "believed in their charts" and that no emotional reaction beside lying can possibly result in a deceptive outcome.

Such "blind faith" in the accuracy of the polygraph can easily make examiners over-confident in their results. As a result, they may feel well justified in coercing a confession out of a suspect, who may happen to be innocent of the crime he or she is accused of. In addition, "blind faith" in the accuracy of the polygraph can make suspects confused about their own recollections of events and they begin to believe that they may have committed a crime of which they have no memory.

The Polygraph: Brief Summary

The polygraph measures several physiological or bodily reactions that are enhanced by stress of different kinds. No physiological response has been found to be unique to lying. These bodily reactions are monitored whilst subjects are asked questions or presented with test items pertaining to a particular crime. The basic assumption is that deception elicits a physiological reaction which can be objectively monitored by the polygraph. Deception is indicated when subjects react consistently more strongly to crime-related questions than to specially designed "control questions".

There are two main techniques for detecting deception, labelled the "Control Question Technique" (CQT) and "Guilty Knowledge Technique" (GKT), respectively. These techniques are based on different theoretical assumptions, with the CQT being a more direct measure of lying than the GKT. The effectiveness of these techniques for detecting deception in experimental settings, including realistic mock crimes, is well documented. However, these techniques are not infallible and their precise validity in real-life settings is controversial. These techniques can be effectively used as investigative tools, particularly the GKT, which is less prone to false-positive error than the CQT, but caution must always be exercised in the interpretation of the polygraph chart. Having "blind faith" in the charts can result in a miscarriage of justice.

STYLOMETRY

Stylometry, or "statistical stylistics" as Bailey and Dolezel (1968) call it, is the branch of psycholinguistics and literary studies that attempts to *quantitatively* identify the ways in which the writings, or spoken words, of one individual differ from those of another. Stylometry comprises a number of techniques, or approaches, whose common objective is to identify the authorship of a particular document.

Stylometry began in the nineteenth century, but it was not until the 1930s that mathematicians and statisticians developed real enthusiasm for literary problems. Other disciplines have subsequently developed interest in stylometry; these include psychologists, linguists, biologists, literary critics and forensic scientists. With improved computer technology and sophisticated statistical methods, the scope for carrying out detailed and complicated analyses has been transformed. No longer is it necessary to rely on the simple arithmetic calculations which were typical of the period prior to the influential work of Yule (1938, 1944) and Wake (1957).

Bailey and Dolezel (1968) provide an early but detailed annotated bibliography of stylometry, which includes well over 600 publications. Only one of the papers (Osgood, 1960) is of direct forensic relevance. Osgood compared contrived and genuine suicide notes by analysing a number of linguistic parameters, which included the number of syllables per word, the noun-verb ratio, the type-token ratio, and the verb-adjective ratio. Osgood concluded that:

> "The non-suicidal person, asked to produce the note he might write just before taking his own life, *fails* to catch the true suicide's emphasis on simple, non-discriminative action statements, his demanding, commanding, pleading character, his exaggerated emotional ambivalence toward himself and significant others, and his somewhat disorganised or distracted approach to encoding, leading to more errors and shortened, explosive segments" (pp. 305-306).

Basic Principles

Wake (1957) set forth three basic principles of stylometry. The first principle is to count the most frequent linguistic features found in a given document. Writers share common conventions in a given language and it is therefore not the highly infrequent or most striking features that are normally important. What is important is the frequency with which he or she employs specific words. Thus, the repetition of certain words may indicate a certain habit which can be identified and scrutinized. The second principle is to make comparisons by the use of statistical analysis which help to identify variations and deviations. The third principle is that the method used has some general application to a specific problem.

A range of linguistic features can be used for the statistical analysis being carried out. These will depend upon the information that is required from the document, the theoretical orientation and methods used, and on the nature and limitations of the document. Broadly speaking, there are two main approaches to forensic stylometry (i.e. those linguistic features that may be relevant to the preparation of court reports).

First, the language structure used in the document can be analysed. This may include the use of vocabulary, grammar, syntax and spelling. An example of this type of analysis was carried out by Svartvik (1968) in the case of Timothy Evans (for details about the case see Chapter 11). Svartvik analysed some stylistic features in the four statements that Evans made to the police on 30th November and 2nd December 1949. His findings were submitted to the Public Inquiry held at the Royal Courts of Justice, London, between 22nd November 1965 and 21st January 1966.

Second, a statistical analysis can be carried out which measures word frequency, sentence length, number of syllables used per 100 words, prepositions and collocations. Examples of this kind of work include that of Flesch (1948) and Morton (1978; Morton and Michaelson, 1990). Various ratios can also be worked out, such as the proportion of verbs to adjectives, the noun-verb ratio, and the ratio of different words to total number of words (called the "type-token ratio").

The Work of Arens and Meadow

Arens and Meadow (1957) wrote a detailed paper on the use of stylometry (they use the term "psycholinguistics") as applied to confession statements. These authors wrote very positively about the application of psycholinguistics to confessions and argued strongly for the legal acceptance of such evidence. In fact they considered it to be "the first step in the quest toward an improved methodology in the scientific analysis of confessions" (p. 46).

Arens and Meadow identified two different types of forensic application of psycholinguistics. The first type of application was concerned with the mental state of the suspect at the time of the police interview. Here there was no dispute about the accuracy of what was reported during the interview, but the expert would, by way of psycholinguistic procedures, attempt to identify one of three things:

1. Physical and mental exhaustion in the suspect;
2. Suggestive questioning used by police interviewers;
3. The suspect's emotional instability or stress.

All of the methods recommended by Arens and Meadow appear to be based on crude clinical impressions rather than sound scientific principles. The only possible exception was the use of the verb-adjective ratio, which had been shown experimentally to change according to emotional arousal. Arens and Meadow recommended that:

> "If the verb-adjective quotient obtained from the confession is markedly greater than that obtained from other verbalizations of the defendant, an inference might be drawn that the confession was made in a state of marked emotional instability" (p. 28).

The second way of using psycholinguistics was in cases where it was alleged by defendants that their confession had been fabricated by the police. The following procedures were recommended:

1. The expert carries out a clinical interview in order to form an impression about the defendant's personality and level of intelligence;
2. The expert carries out an analysis of the alleged self-incriminating confession statement, using such linguistic features as sentence length and vocabulary. These could be then compared with clinical impressions of intelligence or results from IQ tests;
3. The expert studies the confession statement and forms an impression about the personality of the author and then compares this with the personality of the defendant;
4. When available, previous confessions made by the defendant can be compared with the disputed confession;
5. The disputed confession can be compared with the known writings of the interviewing police officers.

The above recommended procedures are highly subjective, unvalidated, and lack scientific rigour. However, some of the procedures and recommendations do appear to have potential for fruitful research. For example, the idea of comparing certain linguistic features (e.g. sentence length, vocabulary) in disputed documents with those found in undisputed documents or in comparison with the person's intellectual functioning seems potentially useful. Since the Arens and Meadow paper there have been marked scientific developments with regard to stylometry and it is to those that we now turn.

Cluster Analysis in Court

Niblett and Boreham (1976) describe a case that was heard at the Old Bailey in 1975, where "cluster analysis" (Everitt, 1974) was used to refute the authenticity of an alleged oral confession. The confession, which was disputed by the defendant who claimed that it had been fabricated by the police, was, according to the prosecution, a verbatim record of what the defendant had told the police. Fortunately, the stylistic experts had access to an undisputed police statement which had been made by the defendant during an interrogation concerning another case. The two sets of statements were of sufficient length to carry out meaningful statistical analysis on them. A computer programme was used to place the different words used, and their frequency, into natural clusters. The results showed that the two sets of documents fell into two distinct clusters, which suggested that the disputed and undisputed documents were unlikely to have originated from the same person. This evidence was presented to the jury, who acquitted the defendant of the charges that had resulted from the alleged self-incriminating oral admissions.

The Work of Andrew Morton

The work of Andrew Morton (Morton, 1978) has been influential in raising the profile of forensic stylometry. Morton, an international authority on stylistic analysis, has worked on a number of forensic cases, which include the case described by Niblett and Boreham (1976). He was critical of using frequency counts of verbs, nouns and adjectives *per se*, and proposed that it is more meaningful to look at "collocations", that is, the combinations and sequencing of words and their relative positions in the script. Morton's argument is that collocations are a better reflection of *habit* (i.e. less consciously determined) than the choice of individual words. Morton considered simple and frequently used words as being of greatest value for stylistic analysis. Infrequently used words would be of very limited use unless one was analysing exceptionally lengthy documents.

The basic assumption is that there is far greater variation in the use of collocations between different authors than found within documents written by the same author. The collocations analysed may be of varied type. An example of Morton's method of using collocations involves comparing the number of times the word "and" is followed by "the" with how often "and" is not followed by "the". Contingency statistics (Chi-square) can be used to compare the frequencies of each combination for the disputed and "control" documents, respectively.

There have been studies that question the validity of Morton's methods. Two papers were recently published in the *Journal of the Forensic Science Society* that are of particular interest. The first paper (Totty, Hardcastle and Pearson, 1987) was prompted by the work of Gudjonsson and Haward (1983).

Totty, Hardcastle and Pearson (1987), who have made a serious study of Morton's methods, question the validity of his methods, but conclude that they are certainly worthy of further forensic research. The authors argue that a number of complicated issues need to be resolved before one can apply the techniques developed in the literary field to forensic problems. These include unknown base frequency characteristics of certain styles and the unknown effects of context and stress on the style of speech and writing. In addition, Totty, Hardcastle and Pearson consider documents of less than 1000 words to be unsuitable for reliable stylistic analysis, because of the problem with finding habits (i.e. consistent styles) that are sufficiently frequent to give valid results when applied to statistical methods.

Totty, Hardcastle and Pearson (1987) carried out stylistic analysis in three criminal cases where statements had been disputed, which include those used by Morton in the well-known St. Germain case. (At his appeal hearing in 1977, Ronald St. Germain disputed statements he is alleged to have made to the police when interrogated.) Their results gave strong support for Morton's methods as used in the St. Germain case. One of the most striking findings was the consistency in the style of St. Germain's utterances in documents recorded 3 years apart. However, Totty, Hardcastle and Pearson are cautious about generalizing too broadly from these findings and argue for further validation.

Smith (1989) presents a theoretical analysis of Morton's work and points to various weaknesses, which to a certain extent undermine the foundations of his methods. Major criticisms include:

1. Incomplete experimental evidence used by Morton to develop his methods;
2. Absence of clearly defined linguistic patterns which can most powerfully differentiate between authors of documents.

Smith provides an alternative theoretical framework that seems to overcome some of the weaknesses in Morton's methods.

More recently, Morton and Michaelson (1990) have extended Morton's earlier work and provide a new technique for using cumulative sum charts as a way of reliably identifying authorships of documents. The technique, called "The Qusum Plot", relies on sentence length distribution, which is plotted on a graph and compared with known authentic manuscripts. What is plotted is the cumulative sum of the differences in sentence length in comparison with a sequence of values fixed at the average. The basic assumptions are that different authors organize the lengths of their sentences into groups in different ways and these can be readily identified. The technique has many promising applications for the analysis of disputed confession statements.

The Flesch Formula of Reading Ease

The Flesch Formula was developed to assess objectively the reading ease of a given piece of writing (Flesch, 1946, 1948). It is a statistical formula which can be used to estimate the proportion of the general population who are likely to understand a written document (Ley, 1977). Sherr (1986) suggests that the Formula is particularly useful in a legal setting for assessing the readability of letters, outlines of procedures, and other material given to clients. In this context I have analysed legal documents pertaining to the new Police and Criminal Evidence Act (PACE) and demonstrated their complexity (Gudjonsson, 1990e, 1991b).

The Formula assesses the reading ease and comprehension difficulty of given material by taking into account the average sentence length of the material (referred to as "S") and the number of syllables per 100 words (referred to as "W"). The readability scores can theoretically vary from 0 to 100, depending on the complexity of the material. A score of 0 would indicate that the material was "practically unreadable", whereas a score of 100 indicates that it can be read by "any literate person". A score below 50 indicates difficult material, such as that found in technical and academic documents. A score between 50 and 60 indicates fairly difficult material. Standard reading material typically falls between a score of 60 and 70. A readability score higher than 70 indicates fairly easy reading material. Scores between 90 and 100 indicate that the material can be read and understood by most people.

Farr and Jenkins (1949) provide tables which give accurate and easy determination of the Flesch index scores. This relieves the researcher or practitioner of having to work out the statistical values manually, which is very laborious and time-consuming.

Having derived a particular Flesch index score, one has to be able to interpret the score obtained. Ley (1977) provides a way of doing this. He has worked out a way of converting index scores into an estimate of the percentages of the general population who are likely to be able to read and understand a given piece of writing. In addition, he gives the estimated IQ required for understanding different index scores. For example, a Flesch score between 31 and 50 would only be understood by approximately 24% of the general population and requires an IQ of 111 or above for full comprehension of the material. In contrast, a score between 81 and 90 would be understood by about 86% of the population and requires an IQ of 84 or above.

My colleague Professor Haward and I (Gudjonsson and Haward, 1983) had been looking at ways in which stylometry and the Flesch Reading Ease Index could be used in the assessment of disputed confession statements. The former method, as we have seen, assesses individual differences in the style of writing, whereas the Flesch Index is a convenient way of evaluating whether or not the written material (e.g. a confession) is consistent with the alleged author's reading ability and comprehension. We described how these related methods had been applied to disputed confession statements and concluded that they seemed to have been of some value in selected cases.

Forensic Application of the Flesch Formula

There are two broad ways of applying the Flesch Formula to forensic problems. First, as the Formula gives an indication of the reading ease and complexity of a given document, the psychologist may be able to establish the extent to which the defendant would have been able to understand a given document. An example of this use is the recent work I have carried out into the complexity of the Notice to Detained Persons (Gudjonsson, 1990e, 1991b) and the way the results are compared with subjects' actual understanding of the document.

The second application relates to being able to estimate the cognitive capacity of the author of a given document. As the Flesch Formula comprises sentence length and the number of syllables per word used, it may give some indication of the cognitive capacity of the author of a particular document. For example, defendants of modest intellect would not be expected to be able to write long and complicated sentences spontaneously. Two illustrative cases are given to highlight this type of forensic application.

Several years ago I was asked to assess an 18-year-old man who was charged with murder. He had made some self-incriminating admissions to the police, which were considered inadmissible by the judge during a *voire dire* because of the limited cognitive capacity of the defendant. He had an IQ of 69 and a reading age of 6 years. The prosecution proceeded with the trial on the basis that they had a letter which had allegedly been dictated by the defendant whilst he was on remand in prison. The letter, which consisted of nearly 600 words, was addressed to the police officer in charge of the defendant's case. The prison inmate who wrote the letter told the police that the letter had been written word for word as dictated by the defendant. The defendant disputed the content of the letter when it was read to him by his solicitor, claiming that it was not the letter he had dictated to the police.

I was able to analyse the complexity of the letter by using the Flesch Formula and compare it with five other undisputed letters which the defendant had dictated on other occasions. The Flesch score obtained for the disputed letter was 73, which was in marked contrast to the average score of 86 which was found for the five undisputed letters. I reached the conclusion that the complexity of the five undisputed letters was more consistent with the defendant's limited intelligence than the disputed letter. The disputed letter had in my view been markedly influenced by the prisoner who wrote the letter to the defendant's dictation. I considered it unsafe to rely on the disputed letter as having been an accurate record of what the defendant had dictated.

The author of the disputed letter gave evidence in court. He was not an impressive witness. He said that he recognized the letter as being in his handwriting, but claimed he had no recollection of having written it. Furthermore, he stated that he had to his knowledge never met the defendant. Following this testimony the prosecution had no choice but to withdraw their evidence and the judge dismissed the case.

Another illustration of the use of the Flesch Formula relates to a case that I was working on with the police in an attempt to build up a profile of the criminal. Several letters had been written to various companies in an attempt to extort large sums of money from them. I analysed the various letters written by the blackmailer and it was clear that some of the letters were highly complex in the way they had been written (e.g. the first letter received gave a Flesch score of 40, which indicated very complex material). I concluded that the blackmailer was a highly intelligent person, probably with an IQ of 120 or above. A few months later the blackmailer was apprehended and proved to be a successful civil servant!

I should like to point out that although the Flesch Index is a valuable measure of reading complexity, the technique is quite crude in that it only measures two linguistic features relevant to readability: sentence length and number of syllables in the words used. Complexity is also a function of other important linguistic features, including coherence and the way words are grouped together.

Stylometry: Brief Summary

Stylometry is the branch of psycholinguistics and literary studies that attempts quantitatively to identify, using statistical analysis, the ways in which the writings or spoken words of one person differ from those of another. The basic assumption is that people differ markedly in the frequency with which they use certain words, or combinations of words. These distinguishing features can be objectively measured and compared across different documents.

Some promising work has been carried out in the field, particularly by Morton (1978) who has raised the profile of forensic stylometry. However, much more research is needed before stylometry can have real impact on the forensic assessment of cases. His most recent work (Morton and Michaelson, 1990) provides scientists with potentially important forensic tools relevant to disputed confession statements.

STATEMENT REALITY ANALYSIS

"Statement reality analysis" is a semi-objective technique for assessing the truthfulness of a witness statement. The technique was invented by a well-known German psychologist, Udo Undeutsch, whose work in the area of alleged sexual abuse has revolutionized the way the judicial system in Germany and Sweden deal with these types of cases. More recently, as we will see, scientists in the United States of America have at last realized the tremendous potential of Undeutsch's technique and are beginning to utilize it (Rogers, 1990).

Undeutsch began to work on the truthfulness of witness statements in the early 1950s (Undeutsch, 1989). His work derived an impetus from the fact that in 1954 the Supreme Court of the Federal Republic of Germany decided:

> ". . . that an expert psychiatrist or psychologist must be called upon to testify on the subject of truthfulness of the witness's account, particularly in sex cases, if the conviction hinges primarily or exclusively on the testimony of a witness under the age of majority or if the witness testimony is not substantially corroborated by other evidence" (Undeutsch, 1989).

Since that landmark decision German psychologists have given an expert opinion about the truthfulness of key witnesses' statements in over 40 000 cases (Arntzen, 1982). Over 60% of the cases are referred by the prosecution and the remaining cases are assessed at the request of trial judges. Undeutsch himself has assessed over 1500 cases involving alleged sexual abuse (Undeutsch, 1982). His extensive experience, and those of his German and Swedish colleagues (e.g. Trankell, 1958, 1972), has helped to develop and refine the criteria on which the technique is based. More recently, further developments and refinements have been provided by Steller and Koehnken (1990).

Theoretical Assumptions

Undeutsch's theoretical foundation for his technique was based on a number of basic assumptions about human behaviour (Undeutsch, 1982, 1989). First, Undeutsch assumes, on theoretical and empirical grounds, that it is more meaningful and valid to judge the truthfulness of a particular statement that the person has made on its own merits, rather than judging it on the basis of his or her personality and reputation. His main argument is that people of previously good character can, and do on occasions, tell lies when there is a great deal at stake. Similarly, people who are known to be unreliable informants can, and on occasions do, tell the truth.

The second basic assumption is that in spite of the general unreliability of eyewitness testimony, victims of sexual abuse can under most circumstances provide an accurate account of the basic details of the abuse or assault, even when they are very young or of low intellectual ability. The reasons for this, Undeutsch argues, are that illegal sexual acts are salient and simply-structured events whose central details are generally easy to remember.

The third basic assumption, which is undoubtedly the most important one in terms of the formal criteria utilized by Undeutsch and his followers, is that the recall of real events differs from fictitious accounts in terms of its structure, content and quality. For example, the content quality of the statement given by the witness is assumed to differ markedly between invented or distorted and genuine accounts. The latter are seen as superior in terms of their quality, which include greater spontaneity and subjective richness. These qualitative differences are built into the so-called "criteria of reality". These descriptive criteria were carefully developed by Undeutsch and his colleagues as a way of differentiating the salient features, at different levels of analysis, between truthful and invented statements. The criteria form the basis for determining the truthfulness of statements. The purpose of the criteria is to check the reality of a particular statement. When the criteria are met then this supports the assumption that the content of the statement is based on a real and a factual event.

Undeutsch's Reality Criteria

Undeutsch (1967, 1982, 1989) has described in some detail the criteria that he uses for identifying the objective "reality" of statements. These are

classified into "fundamental" and "secondary" criteria (Undeutsch, 1982).
The former require certain basic assumptions to be fulfilled and include the
following features in the complainant's statement:

- Originality;
- Clarity;
- Vividness;
- Internal consistency;
- Detailed descriptions which are specific to the type of offence alleged;
- A reference to specific detail that would under normal circumstance be
  outside the experience of the witness or victim;
- The reporting of subjective feelings;
- Spontaneous corrections or additional information.

Undeutsch's "secondary" criteria complement the "fundamental" criteria
given above, and include the extent to which content of the statement agrees
with known psychological and scientific phenomena and other facts and
findings that exist in the case. Any inconsistencies will need to be resolved
by interviewing the witness or victim.

If a witness statement meets several of the criteria, it has to be considered
as truthful. However, a truthful statement may not necessarily meet the
necessary criteria of truthfulness, because of limitations with the statement
itself (Undeutsch, personal communication). Therefore, a statement that is
judged as truthful gives a more meaningful outcome than one where the
criteria of truthfulness are not met.

Undeutsch emphasized that his criteria are not only applicable to the
statements of alleged victims; the technique can also be applied to suspects,
but this does not appear to happen so often (Rogers, 1990).

How effective is Undeutsch's technique? Undeutsch argues that out of 1500
sex abuse cases that he was personally involved with over a period of three
decades, about 90% of the victims were determined to be telling the truth.
In about 95% of these cases the defendants were convicted and none were
subsequently proved to have been wrongly convicted (Undeutsch, 1982, p. 50).
Undeutsch does not indicate how many of the remaining cases, where the
outcome of the Statement Reality Analysis was allegedly inconclusive or
deceptive, involved a conviction of the defendant.

Undeutsch's Followers

Undeutsch's original reality criteria have been extended and refined over
the years. Like any promising technique in science, Statement Reality
Analysis needed to be modified and refined in view of experience and
research. The late Arne Trankell had met Professor Undeutsch in the 1950s
and became interested in his new and innovative technique. He soon applied
the technique, with certain modifications and innovations of his own, to an

interesting case of a 5-year-old boy who had alleged that a neighbour indecently assaulted him (Trankell, 1958, 1972). Trankell developed some "reality criteria" of his own, one of which Undeutsch himself has included in his list given above. Trankell's basic assumption was that the psychologist should not only concentrate on the witness and his or her personality,

"... but be directed to the *crucial statements and the multifarious conditions under which these statements are formed* (Trankell, 1972, pp. 67–68).

Trankell's idea of considering the conditions under which the statement was obtained, in conjunction with analysing all the statements in the case, was quite a unique one. As a result, he developed a technique of his own, called "Formal Structure Analysis", which is based on certain basic rules of logical reasoning and hypothesis testing. The technique rests on very similar theoretical foundations to Undeutsch's Statement Reality Analysis technique and shares similar objectives and criteria. Since Trankell's untimely death, his technique has recently been applied to a sex abuse case by his student Astrid Holgerson (1990).

Following the First International Conference on Witness Psychology, which was held in Stockholm in 1981, the impressive work of Undeutsch and Trankell and their colleagues became better known by psychologists in Britain and America. Before long important developments were to take place which have resulted in scientific research into the validity of Statement Reality Analysis.

Steller and Koehnken (1989) criticize the previous work into Statement Reality Analysis on the basis that it lacked precise definition and systematic organization. Accordingly, they reorganized and renamed the criteria used by various German workers, including those of Undeutsch, and added some of their own. There were 19 criteria in all, organized into five groups. The first category consists of three criteria about the general characteristics of the statement under investigation. Here the logical structure of the statement and the quality of its content in broad terms are closely scrutinized. The second group of criteria, "Specific Contents", involves a detailed analysis of the content and this includes any mention of unforeseen complications and specific conversation with the assailant. The third group of criteria, "Peculiarities of the Content", refers to six individual criteria where an attempt is made to identify unusual accounts, such as a mention of the offender's mental state or subjective feelings. The fourth group of criteria, "Motivation-related Contents", cover features of the statement which may give an indication of the victim's specific motivation to deceive. The final group of criteria, "Offence-specific Elements", deals with the nature of the alleged offence. It relies on what is known about sexual offences generally.

The evaluation of the findings from the 19 content criteria have no objective scoring or cut-off points. The outcome is judged by the psychologist on the basis of a qualitative opinion, after taking into consideration the relative intellectual abilities of the witness and the complexity of the events described. Hopefully, at some future date the scoring can be made more objective.

Validation Studies

Steller (1989) argues that there are three types of validation study that can be carried out with regard to statement analysis techniques. The best type of study is a prospective field validation study. The next best type of study involves retrospective studies of concluded cases. The third type of study involves various simulations to test the assessment procedure.

Steller (1989) reports the results of one retrospective study, one field study and two simulation studies. The main objective of these studies was to test Undeutsch's hypothesis that there are certain qualitative differences in the contents of genuine and fictitious witness statements which can be identified by applying certain reality criteria analysis to the statements.

The results can be viewed in terms of false-positive and false-negative error rates. In this context a false-positive error occurs when an untruthful statement is classified as truthful. Conversely, a false-negative error occurs when a truthful statement is classified as untruthful. Error rates of this type have to be viewed in the context of the particular "base rate". For example, in the field of criminal lie detection a high base rate of deception is commonly assumed (i.e. most suspects who take polygraph tests are assumed to be guilty), whereas in the case of witnesses' accounts where Statement Reality Analysis is applied, the reverse may be true (i.e. most witnesses may be truthful). It is fair to say that the actual base rates of deception for witnesses and suspects are not known, but when interpreting the results from research studies some idea of the respective base rates is important.

Statement Reality Analysis: Brief Summary

Statement Reality Analysis is a semi-objective technique for assessing the truthfulness of a witness statement. It was developed by Professor Udo Undeutsch, a German psychologist, who specializes in the assessment of cases of alleged sexual abuse. The technique is based on a number of fundamental criteria, the most important being that the recall of real events differs qualitatively from the report of fictitious or fabricated ones. Certain "criteria" are offered by Undeutsch to establish the truthfulness of the statement given.

The results from recent studies give strong support for Undeutsch's hypothesis and provide validation data for his technique. Much research still remains to be done in terms of validation and in identifying the type of reality criteria and other types of information that are most discriminative in different types of cases.

CONCLUSIONS

Three different psychological aids to police interviewing have been discussed in this Chapter. All three have the common objective of assisting with the evaluation of testimony. Of these, the psychophysiological detection of deception (i.e. the "lie detector") has been most extensively researched. It relies upon two main types of deception technique, which I refer to as the direct approach and the indirect approach, respectively. The two techniques that best represent these approaches are the Control Question Technique (CQT) and the Guilty Knowledge Technique (GKT). Each technique has different strengths and limitations. Both techniques, when carefully applied in the appropriate circumstances, have been repeatedly shown to detect deception among criminal suspects well beyond chance. These techniques are nevertheless controversial and need to be used with great caution, particularly when used with victims of crime.

The polygraph can be used effectively as an information-gathering device irrespective of deliberate deception. Two examples are given in this Chapter, one referring to attempts to establish the identity of an amnesic patient, and the other telling how the polygraph can be used to diagnose genuine blood-injury phobia for forensic purposes.

Stylometry is the branch of psycholinguistics and literary studies that attempts to identify the authorship of a particular document. It consists of a number of techniques, some of which have been applied to forensic work. A number of different linguistic features have been used for statistical analysis, which will depend upon the information that is required from the document, the theoretical orientation and methods used, and on the nature and limitations of the document. The recent work of Morton and Michaelson is particularly promising.

Statement Reality Analysis is a semi-objective technique for assessing the truthfulness of a witness statement. It originates from the work of Undeutsch in West Germany and Trankell in Sweden and is typically used to assess the veracity of child witnesses in alleged sexual abuse cases. The technique is based on a solid theoretical foundation and early validation of the technique is promising.

The emphasis of the Statement Reality Analysis technique upon establishing truthfulness makes it similar, in its objectives, to the polygraph techniques. Statement Reality Analysis and the polygraph techniques are unlikely to contaminate the memory of witnesses and suspects. These two psychological aids are limited to the detection of deception, and do not, unlike hypnosis, drugs and the cognitive interview, potentially assist with memory retrieval.

CHAPTER 10

The Psychology of False Confession: Research and Theoretical Issues

In this Chapter the literature and review studies into false confession are discussed within the broader framework of the miscarriage of justice, to which false confessions commonly lead. How many false confessions occur in different countries is impossible to estimate. Self-incriminating admissions and confessions made to the police and subsequently retracted are common, and the psychological assessment of such cases will be discussed in detail in Chapter 14. Once a confession has been given to the police the likelihood of a conviction when the case goes to court is greatly enhanced, even if the confession is disputed at the trial. If defendants are wrongly convicted then they can appeal against their conviction in the Court of Appeal.

Why do people confess to crimes they have not committed, which is clearly against their self-interest? The reason is typically a combination of factors which are associated with the circumstances and nature of the custodial interrogation and the accused's psychological vulnerabilities. Various types of false confession, differing in their psychological implications, have been described in the literature and these are reviewed in detail in this Chapter. False confessions occur in a variety of settings, ranging from those obtained by "coercive persuasion" by the Russian and Chinese communists to the present-day interrogation techniques of Western police. A detailed theoretical appraisal of the different types of false confession is given. This Chapter serves as the theoretical foundation for Chapters 11 and 12, where case examples are given of the different types of false confession.

MISCARRIAGES OF JUSTICE

It is difficult to think of a judicial system which is likely to be free of miscarriages of justice. Indeed, all judicial systems, whether adversarial or inquisitorial, are inherently fallible and are likely to remain so until the means of invariably identifying the offender is discovered. The basic recognition of the inherent fallibility of judicial systems is essential if miscarriages of justice are to be properly identified and dealt with. Unfortunately, as Woffinden (1989) so rightly points out, too often people have a misguided faith in the infallibility of criminal justice. Miscarriages of justice can and do happen and there is no evidence that they are becoming less common. The situation is very serious in that people who are wrongly convicted may spend many years in prison before their conviction is quashed or they are pardoned. Woffinden goes as far as to suggest that the great majority of miscarriages of justice are never put right.

In its broadest sense, four different ways in which justice has miscarried can be identified:

1. It may occur because the defendant did not receive a fair trial, even though he may have committed the offence in question. Therefore, the defendant may be *legally innocent*, but *factually guilty*. For example, a defendant who is convicted on the basis of fabricated evidence, even though he committed the offence, is innocent in law as he was convicted by unfair means and violation of due legal process.
2. There are cases of defendants who were only marginally involved in the case but were convicted of a more serious charge.
3. There are cases where the wrong person may be convicted for the offence committed.
4. On some occasions the miscarriage of justice arises when the alleged crime for which the defendant was convicted was never committed. In other words, the *actus reus* of the alleged offence has not been correctly established.

As we will see later, there have been a number of cases where the alleged murder victim turned up very much alive after the defendant has been convicted or even executed. Generally speaking, research into miscarriages of justice has tended to focus on innocent people wrongly convicted, rather than on those only technically innocent because of an error in due process.

Most countries have some kind of a mechanism for reviewing potentially wrongful convictions. Typically, this consists of some kind of an "appeal hearing", which in Britain is referred to as the Court of Appeal (Criminal Division). The Court of Appeal confines itself to questions of law and the evaluation of "new" evidence if this is available; it does not deal directly with questions related to guilt or innocence. An appeal may be:

> ". . . with the leave of the Court of Appeal, on any ground which involves a question of fact alone, or a question of mixed law and fact, or on any ground which appears to the Court of Appeal to be a sufficient ground of appeal" (Mitchell and Richardson, 1985, p. 808).

If the application for leave to appeal fails (as in the Raghip case in 1988—see Chapter 14) or the appeal is dismissed by the Court of Appeal (as in the Birmingham Six case in 1987—see Chapter 12), then the next step is to refer the case to the Home Secretary for his consideration. This only happens in cases that continue to cause public concern and where there has been intensive campaigning. If the Home Secretary is sufficiently concerned about the case, he has the power to do one of two things. He can recommend the Royal Prerogative of Mercy, which means that the Queen will grant a pardon to the convicted person. The other alternative is that the Home Secretary can refer the case back to Court of Appeal, as he did in the case of the Guildford Four (see Chapter 12). If the Court of Appeal is favourably disposed towards the case, it can quash the conviction or order a new trial.

O'Connor (1990) provides an excellent background to the history and development of English remedies for miscarriages of justice. He argues that current review procedures in England, which are supposed to act as a safety net for potential miscarriages of justice, are seriously defective and threaten public confidence in the judiciary. O'Connor suggests that problems arise because the Court of Appeal is often hostile to the cases heard and, at the expense of other considerations, tries to protect the image and reputation of the judicial system.

O'Connor's main recommendation is the development of an independent review body, such as a Tribunal, which has different procedures from the Court of Appeal. The principal role of the Tribunal would be to advise the Home Secretary upon the exercise of the Royal Prerogative. This involves granting a pardon where innocence is established or where there exists serious doubt about the convicted person's guilt. According to O'Connor, the Court of Appeal should still retain an alternative jurisdiction in these cases, which is confined to ruling on questions of law and procedure.

What are the main reasons for wrongful conviction? This question is best answered by reviewing the studies of wrongful convictions that have been carried out.

Studies into Miscarriages of Justice

A number of books have been written about cases where there has been an alleged or proven miscarriage of justice. These have generally given anecdotal and descriptive accounts rather than being based on rigorous scientific study. Considering the serious implications and consequences of miscarriages of justice, it is perhaps surprising that so few empirical and scientific studies have been carried out. However, following the important study of Borchard (1932), which was the first systematic study conducted into wrongful convictions, a great deal has been learned about the types of error that result in innocent people being wrongfully convicted. It is to these that we now turn.

Borchard looked at 62 American and three British cases (Adolf Beck, William Habron and Oscar Slater) where defendants had been wrongfully convicted in the early part of this century. Twenty-nine (45%) of the cases involved defendants convicted of murder and a further 23 (35%) comprised offences of robbery and theft. The innocence of these defendants was principally established by:

1. The discovery of the alleged murder victim being very much alive (12% of cases);
2. Subsequent apprehension of the real culprit;
3. Discovery of some other new evidence that "proved" the defendant's innocence.

In a total of 13 cases (20%) it was eventually established that no crime had actually been committed.

Borchard found that the most common causes of error were mistaken identification, relying unduly on circumstantial evidence, perjury by witnesses, self-incriminating confessions, and unreliability of "expert" evidence. Mistaken person identification was responsible for 29 (45%) of the convictions. In only two cases did the defendant bear a striking resemblance to the real culprit, which highlights the potential unreliability of person identification. The importance of the behaviour of police officers and prosecuting officials in potentially causing miscarriages of justice is evident from Borchard's study:

> "In a very considerable number, the zealousness of the police or private detectives, or the gross negligence of the police in overlooking or even suppressing evidence of innocence, or the prosecution's overzealousness, was an operative factor in causing the erroneous conviction" (p. xv).

Another important finding in this study relates to the importance of deception by innocent defendants. Innocent defendants do sometimes resort to deception (e.g. lying about an alibi) in order to strengthen their case. The detection of such deception may be very damaging to the case as Borchard points out:

> "Proof that an alibi or collateral testimony offered by the accused was false was extremely prejudicial, if not fatal, in several cases" (pp. xx–xxi).

Borchard points out that in several cases false confession resulted from police pressure. However, there were confessions that appeared to have been elicited more by internal psychological factors than by clearly coercive police tactics or techniques. Borchard states with regard to such confessions:

> "The influence of a stronger mind upon the weaker often produces, by persuasion or suggestion, the desired result" (p. xviii).

Borchard speculates that defendants' low intelligence may be an important factor in many false confessions.

Radin (1964) attempted to look at the reasons for wrongful convictions in 25 American States and the District of Columbia, without duplicating the cases discussed by Borchard. He looked at some 300 cases and highlighted different causes by illustrations of over 70 individual cases. Radin listed the various causes for wrongful conviction under different headings, such as "The

Police", "The Prosecutor", "The Witnesses", "The Record", and "Hue and Cry". He considered that the most shocking miscarriage was caused by Public Prosecutors deliberately abusing their power because of their over-riding ambitions. This includes deliberately withholding evidence favourable to the defendant, smearing by innuendo the reputation of defence witnesses, and covering up deficiencies which existed among prosecution witnesses.

One important cause of wrongful convictions which is often overlooked is "Hue and Cry". This involves being a victim of gossip or public outcry due to the viciousness of the crime. Such an outcry may make the police act hastily in their attempts to respond to public pressure, which could result in their jumping to conclusions rather than carefully following the facts. Once a much needed suspect is identified, a subsequently inept police investigation may follow in which facts supporting the suspect's innocence are ignored and overlooked.

Another important work into miscarriages of justice is the study by Brandon and Davies (1973). These authors looked at 70 British cases of "wrongful imprisonment" where errors had been corrected by either the Home Secretary or the Court of Appeal between 1950 and 1970. These did not include defendants released because of some legal technicality. In the view of Brandon and Davies, all the cases they included in their study involved defendants who were considered innocent of the crime for which they were convicted. The defendants had either been given free pardon (52 cases) or their conviction had been quashed by the Court of Appeal (18 cases). The authors cogently argue that the cases they looked at comprised only "the tip of a much larger iceberg" (p. 20) of wrongful convictions.

Brandon and Davies found that, after mistaken identification, self-incriminating confessions were the most common cause of wrongful imprisonment. They categorized the defendants who had made false confessions as follows:

1. There were a number of mentally handicapped defendants, including the well-publicized case of Timothy Evans (see Chapter 11). Many were also illiterate. Brandon and Davies state that they came across several other cases in which the defendants had not been formally tested intellectually, but it was concluded from their behaviour that these individuals were probably mentally handicapped.
2. Many of the defendants who were pardoned were juveniles.
3. There were a number of defendants who were apparently of normal intelligence but were psychologically vulnerable or disturbed in some way.

Brandon and Davies concluded from their findings that people who confessed to crimes, for which they were subsequently pardoned or exonerated, were typically psychologically "inadequate" in some way, because of either low intelligence, psychological disturbance, or youth. They speculated that what the three groups of "inadequates" had in common was abnormal susceptibility to suggestion.

Rattner (1988) recently reviewed the American literature concerning cases of allegedly innocent people being wrongfully convicted. He looked at 205 cases gathered from books, documents or newspaper articles. Murder (43%), robbery (29%) and forcible rape (12%) were the most common offences for which convictions had occurred. Twenty-one (10%) of the defendants had been sentenced to death. The type of errors that resulted in wrongful conviction were varied, but mistaken eyewitness identification was by far the most common cause (49%). "Coerced confession" had been the cause of wrongful confession in 16 (8%) cases.

Huff, Rattner and Sagarin (1986) looked at the frequency and major causes of wrongful conviction from three sources:

1. Their database of almost 500 cases;
2. Survey of criminal justice officials;
3. Review of the literature.

On the basis of their findings, the authors estimated, conservatively in their view, that almost 1% of defendants in serious criminal cases are wrongfully convicted, with much higher rates for minor charges.

As far as the causes of wrongful conviction are concerned, Huff, Rattner and Sagarin found that there was generally more than one factor involved in each case, although eyewitness identification was the single most important reason (i.e. almost 60% of the cases involved such an error). The authors point out the increased risk of wrongful conviction in cases where the crime has resulted in a public outcry. Finally, the authors outline policy implications and recommendations for prevention, identification, exoneration and compensation.

The largest number of wrongful convictions is reported by Bedau and Radelet (1987). The authors presented 350 cases where innocent defendants were in this century wrongfully convicted of capital or potentially capital crimes in the United States of America. The sample consisted of 326 (93%) homicide and 24 (7%) rape cases. Of the sample, 139 (40%) were sentenced to death and 23 (7%) were executed before their innocence was established.

Bedau and Radelet identified four groups of errors that were cause of the wrongful convictions. These were as follows:

1. *Errors caused by police investigation prior to trial.* These kinds of error were present in 23% of the sample. The largest source of error was false confession, which was present in 49 (14%) cases. This typically involved the police "coercing" a confession out of suspects by subjecting them to rigorous interrogation techniques and tactics. However, there were cases of voluntary confessions. In one case an innocent man confessed to murder in order to "impress" his girlfriend. In another case, a woman confessed and pleaded guilty to a murder she had not committed in an attempt to hide the fact that at the time of the murder she was having sexual intercourse!

Other police errors involved negligence and over-zealous police work. There were also cases where the police had secured conviction of an innocent defendant by threatening witnesses who were prepared to testify in his favour.

2. *Errors caused by the prosecution prior to or during the trial.* This was evident in 50 (14%) cases and the most common type of error was the suppression of exculpatory evidence (35 cases).
3. *Errors caused by prosecution witnesses.* This type of error comprised perjury (117 cases) and mistaken person identification (56 cases).
4. *Miscellaneous sources of error.* These included misleading circumstantial evidence (9%), insufficient consideration of alibi evidence (13%), incompetence of defence counsel (3%), and public demand and outrage (20%). The fact that in 70 cases public outrage and pressure appeared to have seriously influenced the trials' outcome, highlights the difficulties involved in trying notorious cases.

This study indicates that in most cases wrongful convictions are caused by a combination of factors, rather than by any one factor acting exclusively.

How was miscarriage of justice discovered in the 350 cases? There were a number of ways in which the defendants' innocence was proven. In 20 (6%) cases it was eventually discovered that no crime had been committed at all. There were 47 (13%) cases where the real culprit eventually confessed, sometimes after being apprehended for another crime. In addition, a number of real culprits confessed on their deathbed.

What is very striking from this study is that the defendants themselves could do very little to have their case reopened. Almost without exception, the defendants were dependent upon the good will of others in proving their innocence. Almost one-third of the cases were reopened because of the persistence and hard work of people who believed in their innocence. These comprised defence solicitors (16%), journalists or authors (11%) and other well-meaning citizens, including the defendants' loyal friends and relatives.

This study clearly shows that the criminal justice system itself is deficient in discovering, admitting to, and doing something about, errors which they make. Once defendants have been convicted they can attempt to be vindicated by appealing against their conviction, but this can only happen when there appears to have been some procedural error at the trial, or where there has been some newly discovered substantive evidence. As Bedau and Radelet (1987) point out:

> "This leaves most erroneously convicted defendants with no place to turn to for vindication" (p. 71).

The studies reviewed above have all used very stringent criteria for selection of cases in their study. In other words, they include only cases where there has been solid tangible proof of innocence. What is striking about these cases is that so many of the defendants were proven innocent by sheer luck and good fortune. All the authors recognize that they were only dealing with a small proportion of all cases of wrongful conviction. There can be no doubt that for every proven case of wrongful conviction there are many more that remain unproven.

DEFINITIONS OF FALSE CONFESSION

Ayling (1984) suggests two ways of defining "false confession". First, there are those who are totally innocent of the crime they are alleged to have committed, and according to Ayling they are probably few in number. Secondly, there are those who were involved in the alleged offence, but overstated their involvement during custodial interrogation. Ayling suggests that overstating one's involvement in a crime is much more common than confessing to a crime one has had nothing to do with, although he provides no data to substantiate his claim.

Ofshe (1989) gives an interesting definition of false confession. He states:

> "A confession is considered false if it is elicited in response to a demand for a confession and is either intentionally fabricated or is not based on actual knowledge of the facts that form its content" (p. 13).

This definition implies that a false confession can, theoretically, be induced from both innocent and guilty suspects. Thus, within Ofshe's definition, it is possible for a guilty suspect who has no recollection of having committed the alleged crime to be considered to be a "false confessor" when he is manipulated into confessing to the details of something of which he has no memory.

THE BROADER CONTEXT OF FALSE CONFESSIONS

Although this Chapter principally covers false confessions within the context of police interrogation, it is very important to be aware of the broader context in which they may occur. In fact, false confessions may arise in a variety of social, religious and political contexts (e.g. Sargant, 1957; Berggren, 1975; Henningsen, 1980; Hepworth and Turner, 1980). Two contexts are particularly relevant to this book, because of the types of psychological coercion utilized by the interrogators in order to extract a confession. There are the "show" trials and public confessions in Stalin's Russia (Beck and Godin, 1951; Leites and Bernaut, 1954; Hinkle and Wolff, 1956) and the "coercive persuasion" of American military personnel and Western civilians by Chinese communists (Orwell, 1951; Hunter, 1951, 1956; Lifton, 1956, 1961; Schein, 1956; Schein, Schneier and Barker, 1961).

The importance of the interrogation techniques of the communists in eliciting false confessions is well expressed by Hinkle and Wolff (1956):'

"The Communists are skilled in the extraction of information from prisoners and in making prisoners do their bidding. It has appeared that they can force men to confess to crimes which they have not committed, and then, apparently, to believe in the truth of their confessions and express sympathy and gratitude toward those who have imprisoned them" (p. 116).

Beck and Godin (1951), whose book *Russian Purge and the Extraction of Confession* is based on their personal experiences of victimization during the Yezhov period, estimate that between 5% and 10% of the Soviet population was arrested between 1936 and 1939. The reasons for these arrests were political and served to overcome any opposition to the existing political regime. The extraction of confessions functioned to justify these arrests and were intended to reassure the public of these persons' guilt. The interrogation techniques applied were individualized according to the characteristics and resistance of the arrested person. Interrogations were typically carried out at night and combined beatings, extensive sleep-deprivation, deprivation of social contact, physical discomfort, threats and intimidation. Beck and Godin's book emphasizes the psychological aspects of these interrogations. *In many instances beatings were not required. Nevertheless, almost everybody confessed*:

"Years of experience had enabled the NKVD to develop a technique of protracted interrogation which practically no one was able to resist" (p. 53).

One of the authors of the book, who was a history professor at the time of his arrest, had been prepared for his arrest and was determined not to confess. After 50 days of interrogation he eventually broke down and confessed falsely to armed revolt and acts of terrorism:

"I had now found out why those involved in "show" trials so readily admitted every accusation, and the comparison with the medieval witch-trials no longer seemed to me to be amusing. There are circumstances in which a human being will confess to anything" (p. 161).

Lifton (1956, 1961) and Hinkle and Wolff (1956) use the term "thought reform" to describe the process of indoctrination by the communists. Similarly, Schein, Schneier and Barker (1961) use the term "coercive persuasion". These terms can be used in a general sense to describe programmes

". . . of social influence that are capable of producing substantial behaviour and attitude change through the use of coercive tactics, persuasion, as well as interpersonal and group-based influence manipulations" (Ofshe, 1991a).

The critical features of these kinds of programmes involve the extreme degree of social control imposed, the immense attack on the person's self-concept, and environmental and social manipulation utilized to maintain and reinforce the behavioural and attitude change achieved (Lifton, 1961).

Cunningham (1973), who worked as a psychologist with the British military, interviewed many of the 900 British prisoners who were repatriated from Korea. What was most striking about them was the finding that about 80% had been interrogated so subtly by the Chinese that they did not even realize that they had been interrogated! Cunningham argues that the Chinese used a combination of intelligence briefings and subtle interrogation techniques with intensive group pressure for change.

What were the main differences between the methods of the Russians and Chinese interrogators? Hinkle and Wolff (1956) and Lifton (1956) argue that the Chinese methods of extracting confessions were influenced by the experience and practice of the Russian State Police, but there were clear differences.

1. The Russian confessions associated with the purge formed a part of "the ritual of liquidation" (i.e. a way of fighting political opposition), whereas in China they were "more the vehicle of individual reform" (Lifton, 1956; p. 193). Both were intended to facilitate or uphold certain Governmental regimes.
2. The Chinese utilized extensive group re-education programmes in conjunction with confession extraction; a practice which had not been utilized previously by the Russians.
3. The Chinese utilized social and emotional isolation of prisoners more selectively than the Russians. In fact, Schein, Schneier and Barker (1961) argue that whereas Russian interrogators relied on *understimulation* (i.e. they tended to keep prisoners in social confinement), the Chinese interrogators tended to *overstimulate* their prisoners (i.e. they prevented any privacy).
4. Unlike the Russians, the Chinese were using confession extraction as a vehicle for much more extensive and lasting "thought reform" changes and indoctrination, where considerable emphasis was placed upon changing the prisoner's permanent values, attitudes and beliefs.
5. The Chinese used more subtle and manipulative strategies and tactics than the Russians, where the emphasis was on exploiting human interactions and psychological vulnerabilities rather than using physical violence. However, both the Russians and the Chinese exploited human vulnerabilities and weaknesses which had been induced or exacerbated by fatigue, sleep deprivation, insufficient or inadequate diet, uncertainty, pain, and general physical discomfort.
6. Hinkle and Wolff (1956) argue that the procedures used by the Chinese were much less standardized than those employed by the Russians.

The "Resisters" and "Cooperators" of the Communist Regimes

Not all prisoners of the Chinese communists made self-incriminating admissions, and those who did, did so for different reasons. Schein (1956) gives a reasonably detailed description of the "resisters" and cooperators". There were different types of resisters, but the majority seemed to have been "well-integrated resistance leaders" whose principal characteristics were their ability to form sound judgements in ambiguous or poorly defined situations and to handle the reactions of the Chinese and the other prisoners. Other types of resisters included those men who had a long history of rebellious resistance to all forms of authority and those whose religious faith demanded total non-cooperation with the Chinese.

The "cooperators" were of different types. There were those, labelled "the weaklings", who were unable to withstand any physical or psychological discomfort. They were highly susceptible to suggestions when placed under pressure. The prisoners who were most vulnerable "ideologically" were those who had poor standing in the social community prior to their arrest. These were labelled "the low status persons" and tended to be young and unintelligent. Then there were the "bored or curious intellectuals", who seldom became ideologically confused or converted, but who nevertheless cooperated with the Chinese for stimulation and instrumental gain (i.e. in order to gain a reward or avoid punishment).

Hinkle and Wolff (1956), in their discussion of the Russian and Chinese interrogation techniques, argue that the people most vulnerable to making false confessions were those of high moral standing because of their guilt proneness. Possession of such a trait made them susceptible to self-criticism which could easily be exploited by the interrogators. Conversely, some psychopathic individuals were seen as vulnerable in the sense that their behaviour could be easily influenced by rewards and immediate instrumental gain, rather than by self-criticism and guilt.

Theoretical Aspects of Communist Indoctrination

The most detailed model presently available on coercive persuasion in the context of communist indoctrination is that of Schein, Schneier and Barker (1961). The basis of their model has its origin in Lewin's (1947) dynamic theory of groups and organizations, where it is assumed that beliefs, attitudes and values are closely integrated with one another around people's self-concept or self-image. The integration is dynamic rather than static and there are constant internal (e.g. needs and motives) and external (requests, demands) "forces" acting upon people which push them in different directions. People are assumed to be principally motivated to maintain stable self-esteem and to reduce uncertainty in their environment. These two factors determine the extent to which people's beliefs, attitudes, values and behaviour can be influenced by psychological manipulation.

The process of change or influence gradually takes place over a period of time and consists of three basic stages, labelled as *"unfreezing"*, *"changing"* and *"refreezing"* (Schein, Schneier and Barker, 1961, pp. 117-139). *"Unfreezing"* refers to the process whereby the forces pushing people towards confessing are strengthened (e.g. persuading people that it is in their own interest to confess, that there is substantial evidence to link them to the crime) whilst forces maintaining resistance are weakened (e.g. by tiredness, lack of sleep, exhaustion, emotional distress). Unfreezing is seen as an essential prerequisite for any change to occur.

Whereas *"unfreezing"* is construed as being principally influenced by the needs and motives of the prisoner, "changing" is viewed by Schein, Schneier and Barker as being more cognitively determined. That is, it involves an active decision-making process which includes clear ideas about the direction in which prisoners are required to change. The basic mechanism involves the *"identification"* of the prisoner, in order to establish a new identity or frame of reference with the person (i.e. interrogator, cellmate) who constitutes the sources of influence.

"Refreezing" refers to the new information or belief being integrated into the prisoner's self-concept and value system. In order for this to be achieved successfully, the new beliefs, attitudes, values and behaviours need to be reinforced, at least temporarily, by significant others in the prisoner's environment. Ofshe (1991a) draws attention to the extent to which the maintenance of such changes in attitudes tends to be "environmentally dependent" rather than "enduring". That is, once people are removed from the social support system that reinforces the attitude change, then they are likely to revert to their original beliefs.

In summary, for influence or change to take place, there has to be an incentive or a motive to change, the prisoner must have some indication or an idea about the direction in which he is to change, and change needs to be rewarded and reinforced for it to be sustained.

Schein, Schneier and Barker (1961) consider that the main difference between coercive persuasion and other kinds of influence is the extent to which the prisoner is confined involuntarily, or coerced into remaining, for exposure to "unfreezing pressures" from which there is no escape and no alternative sources of influence (p. 139). The authors point to many parallels between coercive persuasion in communist China and that found in non-communist settings, such as prisons, hospitals and the military. The principal components involve placing subjects in a situation from which there is no escape, whilst weakening their resistance to influence, bombarding them with "new" ideas and information, and isolating them from outside influences that could counteract the impact of the change.

Although Schein, Schneier and Barker do not specifically discuss the parallels between false confessions extracted by communist interrogators and interrogators in Europe and the United States of America, theories about the former have important implications about the psychology of false confessions in general. Coercive persuasion is a sociopsychological phenomenon involving a social process which can take place in a variety of contexts. Understanding the basic mechanisms and processes involved in communist interrogations and indoctrination help to further our knowledge about some general principles which are applicable to a variety of interrogative situations.

Theoretically, the processes leading to attitude change and confession, respectively, may be independent, but Schein, Schneier and Barker found that the two processes were closely related; that is, making a confession facilitates an attitude change and vice versa. These findings are consistent with the more experimental results of Bem (1966, 1967) where it was found that making a "false confession" subsequently resulted in subjects believing in the truthfulness of the confession. In other words, saying may become believing.

Schein, Schneier and Barker provide an excellent review of different theoretical explanations for coercive persuasion within the context of communist indoctrination. They review four major theoretical orientations, which fall under the following general headings: "psychophysiological theories"; "learning theories"; "psychoanalytic theories"; and "sociopsychological theories". The authors argue that each theoretical orientation provides an important contribution to the understanding of the "unfreezing", "changing" and "refreezing" of the prisoners' beliefs, attitudes, values and behaviour during the indoctrination process. However, no one theory, or a group of theories with similar orientation, can satisfactorily explain all the mechanisms and processes involved. Nevertheless, each theory contributes in unique ways and, taken together, the various theories provide a good understanding of the overall processes involved.

The most noteworthy *psychophysiological theories*, according to Schein, Schneier and Barker (1961), are those of Hinkle and Wolff (1956), Sargant (1957) and Hunter (1951, 1956). The theory of Hinkle and Wolff is perhaps the most impressive. Here the psychological changes taking place in the prisoners are seen as the result of mental and physical exhaustion, which was brought about by a combination of psychological and physiological stress over a long period of time. The source of the psychological stress was isolation, dependency, uncertainty and induction of guilt. Physiological stress resulted from fatigue, deprivation of sleep, hunger, pain and low room temperature. The mental and physical exhaustion made prisoners more receptive to influence because they were confused, their thinking had become uncritical, and they were in a state of heightened suggestibility. Hinkle and Wolff argued that once the immediate pressure was relieved (i.e. the prisoner was released and free of the communist environment) then the effect of the conversion disappeared in a matter of weeks. However, they recognized that some prisoners' attitudes and behaviour appeared to be permanently changed.

Sargant (1957) relies heavily on Pavlov's experimental induction of neuroses in dogs as the basis for his explanation of coercive persuasion. Severe stress is viewed as producing cortical inhibition and emotional breakdown, which result in heightened susceptibility to suggestion. According to Sargant, similar outcome may arise in the case of other stressors, such as those associated with some hospital treatments (e.g. psychotherapy, drug treatment).

Hunter (1951, 1956) gives less formulated theoretical reasoning for the effects of coercive persuasion than Hinkle and Wolff and Sargant, but his theory, like those of the other authors, emphasizes the importance of the deleterious effects of mental and physical stress, which results in a state of confusion so that the prisoner is unable to distinguish between "what is true and what is untrue" (Hunter, 1956, p. 67).

According to Schein, Schneier and Barker, the three theories discussed above emphasize, in terms of a basic mechanism, the enhanced suggestibility and uncritical thinking that commonly result from mental and physical stress and exhaustion. Furthermore, the three theories imply that the "new" beliefs, attitudes, values and behaviour coexist with the previous ones, rather than becoming fully integrated into the personality of the prisoner. This has important implications because it suggests that attempts at indoctrination have no long-lasting or permanent psychological changes upon the prisoner once he is repatriated.

Schein, Schneier and Barker disagree that psychophysiological stress necessarily produces a state of uncritical thinking and high suggestibility. They prefer to argue that severe stress facilitates "unfreezing" and is an incentive to change. The problem with the Chinese interrogators, according to Schein, Schneier and Barker, was that they were not very clear or explicit about the ways in which the prisoners should change. In other words, there were no explicit or implicit suggestions given by the interrogators, although the prisoners were all subjected to immense pressure to change. They had to work out, by trial and error it seems, how precisely they were to change.

Schein, Schneier and Barker argue that the psychophysiological theories help explain how "unfreezing" was facilitated by severe stress and how resistance was weakened over time, but they do not at all address the processes of "changing" and "refreezing". For these important processes we need to look at learning, psychoanalytic and sociopsychological theories.

The Schein, Schneier and Barker review of *learning theories* identifies three main approaches, all of which rely in varying degrees on Pavlovian conditioning. First, Meerloo (1954) presents a rather loosely defined and poorly argued theory about Chinese interrogators, where the behaviour of prisoners is said to be controlled by "negative and positive stimuli" (p. 810). Negative stimuli included physical and mental pressure, fatigue and hunger, which resulted in mental submission. Positive stimuli for desired behaviour included food and verbal praise. Second, there is Sargant's (1957) extension of Pavlov's experimental theory of neuroses, which was discussed in relation to psychophysiological theories of stress. Third, there is the work of Santucci and Winokur (1955) and Farber, Harlow and West (1957). Here the principles of Pavlovian and instrumental conditioning are combined, and this is the learning approach favoured by Schein, Schneier and Barker. The argument is that anxiety and guilt are conditioned by threats and punishments and this eventually results in compliant behaviour as a way of reducing conflict. Once compliant behaviour occurs then it is selectively reinforced by the interrogators.

Schein, Schneier and Barker argue that *psychoanalytic* formulations of confessions obtained by Communists point to the importance of an authoritarian superego, in conjunction with a relatively weak ego, as a predisposition and proneness to being influenced easily by people in authority. Similarly, Meerloo's psychoanalytic formulations (1951, 1954), emphasize the importance of guilt. External pressures weaken the ego's ability to fight and cope with pressure, whilst dependency needs and childhood hostilities are reactivated by the prison environment and produce guilt, which acts as an internal pressure to confess.

Cunningham (1973) gives an excellent illustration of how unresolved childhood conflicts were identified and exploited by the Chinese. Each prisoner was required to write out a detailed autobiography of his or her childhood, from which psychological weaknesses and vulnerabilities were identified. These were subsequently used by the Chinese to create stress and induce feelings of guilt.

Schein, Schneier and Barker discuss a number of theories relevant to persuasive interrogation, which they believe fall under the general heading of *sociopsychological theories*. These include theories that focus on the self-concept and identity (Lifton, 1956), cognitive dissonance (Festinger, 1957), group pressure (Asch, 1951, 1952) and differences between "internalization", "identification" and "compliance" (Kelman, 1958).

According to Schein, Schneier and Barker changes in self-concept and identity are central to explaining "the breaking point" and why prisoners' beliefs and values changed, but theories relying on this explanation (e.g. Lifton, 1956) fail to specify how the change comes about. "Breaking point" is viewed by Schein, Schneier and Barker as a psychological phenomenon in which self-concept is central and where prisoners can be trained to resist interrogative pressure (p. 233).

Festinger's (1957) theory of dissonance has implications for confessions because it postulates that it is the behavioural commitment of the confession which produces dissonance (i.e. a special type of conflict), which is in turn reduced by change in belief and attitudes. Schein, Schneier and Barker point out several limitations of dissonance theory when it is applied to coercive persuasion. For example, they view the theory as oversimplifying the thinking process, because changes in attitudes and beliefs may precede as well as follow a confession.

Early workers in the field of social influence did not make a clear conceptual or theoretical distinction between private acceptance of information and compliance (McCauley, 1989). The experimental work of Kelman (1958) indicated three distinct processes of social influence, which he labelled "compliance", "identification", and "internalization". Compliance was said to occur when people agreed with propositions without private acceptance for some instrumental gain (i.e. in order to gain a reward or avoid punishment). Internalization implied that people privately accepted the proposition offered and it became integrated into their belief system. Identification occurred when people accepted influence because they desired to emulate the agent of influence.

Schein, Schneier and Barker consider Kelman's work as an important contribution to the understanding of coercive persuasion. Its main contribution is to highlight different mechanisms of change which lead to different types of outcome. The main problem seems to be that one does not know to what extent the three distinct processes may overlap or interact. For example, is it possible that compliance may lead to identification or internalization? Similarly, identification may lead to internalization or compliance.

Many of the theories discussed above in relation to communist interrogation and indoctrination are relevant to false confession within the context of police interrogation, as will become evident later in this Chapter.

RETRACTED OR DISPUTED CONFESSIONS

Dr MacKeith and I (Gudjonsson and MacKeith, 1988) have drawn a distinction between false and retracted confessions. A retracted confession consists of the suspect or defendant declaring that the self-incriminating admission or confession he made is false. As a result the confession may be disputed at the suspect's forthcoming trial. This does not necessarily mean that the confession that the suspect made is false, because guilty people as well as innocent people may retract their confession before the case goes to court.

In exceptional circumstances a confession may be disputed at the trial, even when the suspect has not formally retracted it. This probably happens more often in adversarial proceedings where the onus is on the prosecution to prove their case rather than establishing the suspect's guilt or innocence by inquisitorial means. In such a case the confession may be made inadmissible in court because of legal technicality (e.g. breaches of existing Codes of Practice). A suspect or defendant may also dispute that he actually made the confession in the first place. He may allege that the confession was fabricated by the police. In such instances the police may allege that the defendant made the confession but refused to sign it (Graef, 1990). Even if the self-incriminating statement is signed by the suspect he may allege that the police officers made the statement up and he just signed it.

Oral confessions, or so-called "verbals", pose great problems. These consist of the police alleging that the suspect stated orally that he had committed the crime or implying that he was somehow involved. Many instances of such "verbals" have been shown to be fabricated by the police, as was mentioned in Chapter 2. In the words of one British police officer:

> "There are lots of side-steps in the police. They rarely stick to testimony. The classic case is verbals. One of the magistrates actually said, 'Well, it's very hard for this court to believe that the PCs, Sergeants and Inspectors all collaborated to produce this evidence'. Of course, this is precisely what they'd bloody done" (Graef, 1990, p. 278).

Verbal confessions to people other than the police can be allowed in evidence and require no corroboration in English law. A good illustration of this is what happened in the recent trial concerning the attempted murder of the well-known English boxing promoter Frank Warren. Terry Marsh, a former world boxing champion, was charged with the attempted murder of Mr Warren. Marsh was alleged to have made a verbal confession about the attempted murder to another prisoner whilst on remand in prison. In the summing up the judge, Mr Justice Fennell, stated with regard to the prisoner's evidence about Marsh's confession:

> "As a matter of strict law, his evidence does not require corroboration. But in my judgment and my direction to you, it would be very wise indeed to look for independent support before you proceeded to act on the basis of his evidence" (*The Times*, 1990).

Establishing the "ground truth" is often difficult or impossible in cases where confessions have been retracted. The "ground truth" refers to factual matters that can either be incriminating or exonerate the suspect. In cases of false confession such evidence may include subsequent arrest or conviction of the real culprit, the discovery that no crime had been committed in the first place (e.g. the alleged murder victim turning up alive), or the discovery of some "new" evidence (e.g. new alibi witnesses, psychological or psychiatric findings).

The time of the retraction may vary greatly. Some suspects declare their innocence at the first opportunity (e.g. immediately the pressure is off, when a relative or a solicitor visits), while others retract days, weeks or even years afterwards. In some circumstances the suspect may never withdraw the confession, even though it is false.

It is worth bearing in mind that it is very unlikely that all genuine false confessions are eventually retracted. There could be a number of reasons for this, as follows:

1. The suspect falsely confessed to protect somebody else;
2. The suspect believes there is no point in retracting the confession;
3. The suspect wants to be punished for the crime he confessed to, even though he did not commit it;
4. Having confessed to the crime, the suspect prefers to plead guilty to the charge rather than dispute it, even though he is innocent;

5. The person believes that he has committed the offence, even though he has no memory of having carried out the act;

6. The suspect, or a prisoner serving a prison sentence, "confesses" to further offences in order to assist the police in improving their crime figures (Graef, 1990). Such confessions are referred to as offences "taken into consideration". This type of confession was briefly discussed in Chapter 2 in relation to allegations concerning the Kent Police.

How commonly are confessions retracted? This may vary considerably internationally or even within the same country. Inbau, Reid and Buckley (1986) go as far as to suggest that most guilty suspects subsequently retract their confessions. They state:

> "Most confessed criminal offenders will subsequently deny their guilt and allege that they either did not confess or else were forced or induced to do so by physical abuse, threats or promise of leniency. Occasionally, the defendant in a criminal case will even go so far as to say that he was compelled to sign a written confession without reading it or having had it read to him, or that he was forced to place his signature on a blank sheet of paper and all that appears above it was inserted later" (p. 176).

As discussed in Chapter 3, Inbau, Reid and Buckley do not consider the possibility that anybody who retracts a previously made confession could possibly be innocent. They work on the misguided assumption that their recommended tactics and techniques *never* induce an innocent person to falsely confess. There are sufficient numbers of proven cases of innocent persons retracting false confessions to demonstrate that this belief of Inbau, Reid and Buckley is unfounded. What their statement does highlight is the fact that criminal suspects very commonly retract their previously made confessions to the police and give various excuses for having done so. Inbau, Reid and Buckley are wrong to assume that *all* such retractions involve guilty people claiming to be innocent.

The process of denial may continue to operate after people have been convicted. In a recent study, Kennedy and Grubin (1991) found that convicted sex offenders who pleaded guilty to their offence at the time of their trial begin to deny their offences once they are in prison. As we saw in Chapter 2, this process of denial may serve some important psychological functions.

There is indication from the outcome in Crown Court trials that defendants commonly dispute their confession, particularly in a large city like London. For example, in the study by Baldwin and McConville (1980), which was quoted in some detail in Chapter 4, about 10% of the defendants assessed in Birmingham and 24% of those in the London sample pleaded "not guilty" at their trial after having provided the police with a written confession. Taking into account both verbal and written confessions, over 25% of those who pleaded "not guilty" at their trial in the two cities had verbal and written confessions recorded against them. Not surprisingly, verbal confessions were much more frequently disputed at the trial than written confessions. Kalven and Zeisel (1966), in an American study, found that about 20% of confessions are disputed when cases go to court.

Although not pleading guilty cannot be directly equated with a retraction of the confession, these results support the argument that a sizeable proportion of defendants in criminal trials retract their previously made confessions. There may be significant differences between cities and countries in the extent to which defendants do this. The implications of the differences in the figures between London and Birmingham are not discussed by Baldwin and McConville.

THE INNOCENT PLEADING GUILTY

It would be expected that suspects who falsely confess would retract their confessions before their cases went to trial. However, there is evidence that some defendants in criminal trials may plead guilty to offences they did not commit (Dell, 1971; Bottoms and McClean, 1976). How often this happens is not known, but the results from Dell's (1971) important survey of female prisoners in Holloway Prison indicates that "inconsistent pleading" was a major problem in the lower courts in the early 1970s.

Dell (1971) found that of 527 women tried at Magistrates' Courts, 106 (20%) had claimed to the researchers that they were innocent of the offence with which they were charged. Of these 106 women, 56 (53%) pleaded guilty in court. Dell refers to these women as "inconsistent pleaders". She compared them with a control group of 47 women who claimed to be innocent and pleaded not guilty. The inconsistent pleaders were found to be younger than the other women, but both groups had similar social and medical backgrounds. Four further differences between the two groups emerged:

1. Inconsistent pleaders were more commonly charged with offences related to public disorder, such as soliciting and drunkenness, than the control group.
2. They were less commonly legally represented at court.
3. Inconsistent pleaders were less likely than the controls to be remanded in custody prior to their trial.
4. A large number of the inconsistent pleaders had no previous convictions.

What reasons did the inconsistent pleaders give for their inconsistency? According to Dell, the most common reasons given by the women were

1. Police pressure and persuasion;
2. They saw no point in denying the allegation as it would be just their word against that of the police;
3. They wanted to avoid being remanded in custody;
4. They thought they might get a heavier sentence if they pleaded "not guilty".

Dell concluded that inconsistent pleading stems from a number of factors, which include lack of legal advice and police persuasion. She suggests that one way of reducing inconsistent pleading is to ensure that every accused person is allowed to speak to a solicitor before entering a plea. This is what seems to happen in the Crown Court, where inconsistent pleading was not found to be a problem.

A study by Bottoms and McClean (1976) also indicated that some defendants may plead guilty to offences of which they are innocent for some instrumental gain (e.g. the probability of a lower sentence). The young and socially disadvantaged were most likely to plead guilty. Eighteen per cent of defendants were suspected of having pleaded guilty to an offence of which they were innocent. Bottoms and McClean recommended that the court should carefully examine guilty pleas before accepting them.

There have, of course, been many changes within the British judicial system since the Dell and Bottoms and McClean studies. Perhaps most importantly, legal representation in the Magistrates' Court is now commonplace and more detainees are being interviewed in the presence of a solicitor. However, this does not mean that some defendants do not still plead guilty in the Magistrates' Court to offences they have not committed. In fact, solicitors may advise their clients to plead guilty to certain offences where they are likely to be found guilty in any case, irrespective of their guilt or innocence, as a guilty plea typically results in a less severe sentence. Furthermore, some innocent defendants may plead guilty to charges as a way of avoiding being remanded in custody or having their case delayed.

Finally, on a related theme, plea-bargaining, a procedure which is more common and formalized in the United States of America than it is in England, encourages defendants to plead guilty to offences in exchange for a lesser penalty (Bordens and Bassett, 1985).

THE CAUSES OF FALSE CONFESSIONS

What are the principal causes of false confession? According to Munsterberg (1908), who was the first psychologist to write on the topic, a false confession can be elicited when emotional shock distorts people's memory during interrogation. Munsterberg viewed a false confession very much as a normal phenomenon which was triggered by unusual circumstances.

Undoubtedly, there are a number of different causes, or indeed different combinations of factors, which depend upon the individual case. However, Kennedy (1986) considers that "over-zealousness" on the part of the police officer is the single most common cause. The process involves the police having some circumstantial piece of evidence connecting a person to the alleged crime. Being highly motivated to obtain results, the police:

"... allow their suspicions to harden into certainty. Believing they are serving the best interests of justice, they then:

(a) Try to browbeat the suspect into a confession.
(b) Pressurize witnesses to say what they want them to say.
(c) Suppress or ignore the evidence of other witnesses whose evidence is favourable to the accused.
(d) "Lose" documents such as timesheets that support the accused's alibi."

Kennedy's observation summarizes well the kind of police procedural factors that can lead to wrongful conviction. These are consistent with the results from the descriptive studies discussed above with regard to miscarriages of justice.

Kennedy gives an excellent illustration of how the above process led to the wrongful conviction and subsequent imprisonment of Noel Fellows. Fellows was a former policeman who was working as a taxi-driver when he was arrested in 1970 for the murder of a 67-year-old debt-collector. Unfortunately for Fellows, his mother-in-law's name had been discovered in the dead man's collection book and a witness alleged that he had seen the victim get into a taxi on the day of his murder.

With these two flimsy pieces of evidence the police became convinced that Fellows was the murderer. He was subjected to intensive police interrogation for about 6 hours, during which he made no self-incriminating admissions. The police then "persuaded" witnesses that Fellows had a grudge against the victim, whom Fellows had never met. The police then suppressed evidence which was favourable to Fellows and the taxi firm's records, which showed where Fellows was working at the time of the alleged murder, went "missing". As a result, it was not possible to corroborate Fellows' alibi.

Fellows was subsequently convicted of manslaughter and received a 7-year prison sentence. He was released on parole after serving 4 years in prison for a crime he never committed. Several years later the real murderer was apprehended and in July 1985 Fellows' conviction was quashed by the Court of Appeal

What Kennedy's elegant framework does not broach are the kinds of psychological factors that can make some individuals susceptible to making a false confession. Although Fellows never confessed to the murder of the debt-collector, extracts from his book (Fellows, 1986) give an important illustration of the type of interrogation techniques and psychological factors that can result in a false confession in vulnerable individuals.

"By this time, the adrenalin was flowing and I could feel the sensation of fear creeping upon me. *What on earth is happening?* I thought to myself. *They wouldn't invent things like this*" (p. 15).

"The fear grew as Mounsey started to say things like, 'We know you've done it, lad, Why don't you get it off your chest? We know you didn't really mean to kill him.' As I continued to plead my innocence, he became more determined. He started shouting and banging his fist upon the table. By this time fear had totally engulfed me and I just broke down. I could not control my emotions. As I tried to fight the tears back, they just kept on flowing. Deep shock set in and I was inwardly fighting to get words out of my mouth" (p. 15)

"Six hours of intense questioning and still they didn't believe a word I said. All I repeated throughout that time was that I had never met the man and that I had absolutely nothing to do with the offence. By now signs of tiredness and frustration appeared in both their faces and voices. The tension mounted and they became more irate. We had gone full circle and were back to the more aggressive style of injecting fear by shouting accusations and desk-banging with clenched fists. This approach certainly worked to raise the level of fear within me, but if you are innocent, how can you confess to something you haven't done?" (p. 18).

Undoubtedly, there are a number of different psychological reasons why people confess to crimes they have not committed. Based on observations of anecdotal cases reported in the literature, and psychological theories of attitude change, Kassin and Wrightsman (1985) suggest three psychologically distinct types of false confession. These they call the "voluntary", the "coerced-compliant" and the "coerced-internalized" types respectively. Kassin and Wrightsman discuss these types as if they are mutually exclusive. As will be discussed below, I will argue that in some cases there may be a certain overlap between two or more of these psychological types.

Voluntary False Confessions

Voluntary false confessions are offered by individuals without any external pressure from the police. Commonly these individuals go voluntarily to the police station and inform the police that they have committed the crime in question. They may have read about the crime in a newspaper or seen it reported on television. Alternatively, no crime may have been committed and the individual may be deliberately misleading the police, or believe mistakenly that he or she has committed a crime.

Kassin and Wrightsman give three reasons why people voluntarily give a false confession. They indicate that the most important reason could be a "morbid desire for notoriety" (p. 76). That is, the individual has a pathological need to become infamous, even if it means having to face the prospect of punishment, including imprisonment. Kassin and Wrightsman use the fact that over 200 people confessed falsely to the famous Lindbergh kidnapping as a good example of voluntary false confessions being the result of desire for notoriety.

The second reason for voluntary false confession, according to Kassin and Wrightsman, is the person's "unconscious need to expiate guilt over previous transgressions via self-punishment" (p. 77). In my view, the guilt over previous transgressions can relate to some imagined act as well as a real one. Furthermore, there is no reason to believe that the "guilt" has invariably to be linked to some previous identifiable transgression. In fact, the feeling of guilt may be generalized, rather than caused by specific transgression. For example,

Gudjonsson and Roberts (1983) found, in their study of "secondary psychopaths", that the subjects' poor self-concept and high trait anxiety were reflected in a constant feeling of guilt, regardless of whether or not they were reporting a dishonest act. In contrast, normal subjects only rated themselves as feeling guilty after they had violated some specific norms of behaviour. One implication of the findings is that some individuals have a high level of generalized guilt, which is not related to a specific transgression, and this may influence a range of their behaviours, including their need to volunteer a false confession.

The third main reason why people may give a voluntary false confession occurs when people are unable to distinguish between facts and fantasy. In other words, they are unable to differentiate between real events (i.e. events actually experienced) and events which originate in their thinking, imagination or planning. It was argued in Chapter 5 that such a breakdown in "reality monitoring" (Johnson and Raye, 1981) is normally associated with major psychiatric illness, such as schizophrenia, but it may be found in a mild form in normal everyday behaviour (Cohen, Eysenck and Levoi, 1986).

Another important reason why people may volunteer a false confession is in order to assist or protect the real culprit. This may be a common reason in minor cases, but in rare instances it may also be found in major criminal cases, such as homicide.

There is some evidence that confessing to crimes in order to protect somebody else (e.g. a friend) may be common among juvenile delinquents. For example, Richardson (1991) found that, out of 60 residents in a specialized forensic unit for juveniles, 14 (23%) claimed to have made a false confession to the police (they had nothing to gain by saying so at the time of the study); all said the reason had been to protect a friend or a relative from possible prosecution.

It is not known how often voluntary false confessions occur or how easily they are recognized by police officers.

Coerced-compliant False Confessions

The coerced-compliant type of false confession results from the pressures of coerciveness of the interrogation process. The suspect does not confess voluntarily, but comes to give in to the demands and pressures of the interrogators for some immediate instrumental gain. Kassin and Wrightsman (1985) define compliance, in the context of this type of false confession:

> ". . . as an overt, public acquiescence to a social influence attempt in order to achieve some immediate instrumental gain" (p. 77).

The perceived instrumental gain may include the following:

1. Being allowed to go home after confessing;
2. Bringing the interview to an end;

3. A means of coping with the demand characteristics, including the perceived pressure, of the situation;
4. Avoidance of being locked up in police custody.

The suspect's perceived immediate instrumental gain of confessing has to do with an escape from a stressful or an intolerable situation. The suspect may be vaguely or fully aware of the potential consequences of making the self-incriminating confession, but the perceived immediate gains outweigh the perceived and uncertain long-term consequences. In addition, making a false self-incriminating admission or confession is perceived as more desirable in the short term than the perceived "punishment" of continued silence or denial.

Suspects may naively believe that somehow the truth will come out later, or that their solicitor will be able to rectify their false confession.

Cocerced-internalized False Confessions

Coerced-internalized false confessions occur when suspects come to believe during police interviewing that they have committed the crime they are accused of, even though they have no actual memory of having committed the crime. Gudjonsson and MacKeith (1982) argue that this kind of false confession results from a "memory distrust syndrome", where the suspect distrusts his own memory and begins to rely on external sources of information. This syndrome is associated with two kinds of distinct conditions.

The first kind is where the suspect has no memory of the alleged offence, even if he or she committed it. This, as we saw in Chapter 5, may be due to amnesia or alcohol-induced memory problems. In cases where suspects did not commit the crime they are accused of, they may have no clear memory of not having done so. In other words, these people have no clear recollection of what they were doing at the time the alleged offence was committed and come to believe that they must have committed the offence.

The second type of memory distrust syndrome relates to suspects who, at the beginning of the police interview, have clear recollection of not having committed the alleged offence, but because of subtle manipulative influences by the interrogator they gradually begin to distrust their own recollections and beliefs. Ofshe (1989) conceptualizes this type of coerced-internalized false confession as analogous to "thought reform". That is, coercive and manipulative interrogation tactics and techniques induce in suspects "sufficient self-doubt and confusion to cause them to adjust their perceptions of reality" (pp. 4–5).

THEORETICAL IMPLICATIONS OF THE DIFFERENT TYPES OF FALSE CONFESSION

Several conclusions can be drawn about the nature and implications of voluntary false confessions. First, voluntary confessions which are given because of "morbid desire for notoriety" are probably best construed as a pathological attempt to enhance self-esteem. The basic assumption here is that these individuals are experiencing marked feelings of inadequacy and have a strong need for recognition, even if it means being identified and labelled as a "criminal" and being punished for something they did not do.

People who confess in order to aid or protect the real criminal are undoubtedly the least psychologically disturbed of all the voluntary confessors. The motive, in general, is unlikely to arise from mental illness or pathological feelings of inadequacy. Rather the person makes a decision, which indeed may be a quite rational decision, to volunteer a confession so that somebody else is spared the potential penal consequences of the crime committed (e.g. in the case of juveniles the younger ones may falsely confess to protect older ones from prosecution). This type of false confession does not always have to be given voluntarily. It can arise out of police interrogation where the person is a suspect in the case, but he or she realizes that, unless a confession is made, the real offender, who may be somebody close to them, is likely to be apprehended. Being faced with two undesirable alternatives, the person chooses to make a false, self-incriminating confession rather than chance the apprehension of the real offender.

A false confession which is given in an attempt to relieve guilt, whether generalized or concerned with some specific previous transgression, would be most likely to be associated with depressive symptoms or illness. However, a very small proportion of all depressed people appear to actually volunteer a confession to the police concerning a crime they have not committed. Probably important mediating variables, which will be illustrated by case reports in Chapter 11, are related to the depressed person's personality.

False voluntary confessions which arise because the person is unable to distinguish between fantasy and reality are most likely to arise in cases of mental illness, such as schizophrenia. Here the people's perceptions of reality are distorted and their thought processes are adversely affected. These people's false confessions result from a false belief, without there necessarily being a strong feeling of guilt attached to the perceived criminal act.

Kassin and Wrightsman (1985) highlight two potentially important implications concerning differences between coerced-compliant and coerced-internalized false confessions. The first refers to the timing of the suspect's subsequent retraction of the confession. The other relates to the type of interrogation techniques that are most likely to elicit compliant and internalized false confessions.

Coerced-compliant false confessors are likely to retract or withdraw their false confession as soon as the immediate pressures are over (e.g. when seen by a solicitor or a relative after being charged). Coerced-internalized false confessors, on the other hand, will only retract after they themselves have become convinced, or suspect, that they are innocent of the crime they are accused of. How long this takes depends on the individual case (Ofshe, 1989, 1991b). In one case reported by Ofshe (1991b), it took months before the defendant realized that he had not committed the crime of which he was accused. The critical issue is to what extent, if at all, the suspect's original memory for events becomes permanently distorted as the result of coercive and manipulative police interviewing.

Kassin and Wrightsman (1985) state that what is most concerning about coerced-internalized false confessions

". . . is that the suspect's memory of his or her own actions may be altered, making its original contents potentially irretrievable" (p. 78).

If the internalized false confessor's memory is potentially permanently altered during police interrogation, as Kassin and Wrightsman argue, then the implications are very serious. That is, innocent people potentially remain permanently convinced that they have committed a crime of which in fact they are innocent. Gudjonsson and Lebegue (1989) provide some evidence that the original memory may not necessarily be as permanently distorted, as Kassin and Wrightsman suggest.

Ofshe (1989) also reports cases in which suspects were induced to make coerced-internalized false confessions which were repudiated as soon as the social environment that supported them was disturbed. The limited empirical evidence that is available suggests that coerced false confessions are believed when they are made but, like other externally generated perceptions (e.g. the production of thought reform), are highly unstable (Ofshe, 1991a).

Kassin and Wrightsman discuss two separate processes whereby coerced-internalized false confessions can occur. One type of process involves "a trance-like state of heightened suggestibility", similar to that found in hypnosis (Foster, 1969), whereas the other proposed process results from changes in "self-perception" and relates to the classic work of Bem (1966) and Lepper (1982).

The precise factors that determine whether or not a false confession is going to become internalized are not fully understood. One powerful determining factor is probably the type of interrogation techniques utilized by the police.

Kassin and Wrightsman argue, on the basis of "self-perception" theory (Lepper, 1982), that coerced-compliant false confessions are most likely to occur when "powerful and highly salient techniques of social control" are utilized, whereas "internalization is best achieved through more subtle, less coercive methods" (p. 77). Similar arguments have been put forward by Bem (1967) in relation to false confession.

Ofshe (1989) attempted to explore the process whereby people come to falsely believe, as the result of interrogation, that they have committed a serious crime for which they have no memory. He looked closely at four cases of coerced-internalized false confessors and stated:

"The four people whose interrogations are commented on here are victims of the unconscious use of the sorts of interrogation tactics commonly practised throughout the United States. All four displayed substantial belief change and, for varying periods of time, became convinced that they had committed the crimes of which they were accused. They each came to believe in their guilt and acted on this belief by confessing. They confessed despite having no memory of the crime that they had supposedly committed" (p. 3).

Ofshe argues that the primary mechanism consists of inducing sufficient self-doubt and confusion in the suspects' minds to permit the alteration in their perceptions of reality. This involves the interrogator successfully convincing the suspects that:

1. There is incontrovertible evidence that they committed the crime they are accused of, even though they have no recollection of it;
2. There is a good and valid reason why they have no memory of having committed the crime.

The types of interrogation techniques and tactics that appear to increase the likelihood of coerced-internalized false confessions (Ofshe, 1989) are as follows:

1. The interrogator repeatedly states, with great confidence, his belief in the suspect's guilt.
2. The suspect is isolated from people who undermine or contradict the interrogator's premise of the suspect's guilt. In addition, information that contradicts the interrogator's premise is concealed from the suspect.
3. Typically there is lengthy interrogation and considerable emotional intensity.
4. The interrogator repeatedly claims that there is incontrovertible scientific proof of the suspect's guilt.
5. The suspect is repeatedly reminded about his or her previous memory problems or blackouts, when these exist. When these do not exist the interrogator argues for the existence of a mental disorder that would explain the lack of memory for the crime (e.g. multiple personality, dissociation, etc.). These ploys tend to undermine the confidence that suspects have in their ability to accurately recall that they had not committed the alleged crime.
6. The interrogator demands that the suspect accepts his premises and explanations of the alleged crime.
7. The interrogator attempts to induce fear in the suspect's mind about the potential consequences of repeated denials. Ofshe maintains that tactics of interrogation in which American interrogators are trained will render them able to produce the result without being aware that they are generating false confession.

Not all of the above tactics and techniques are likely to be evident in every case of coerced-internalized false confession, but they are the type of factors that facilitate the process. What seems to happen is that these tactics and techniques make the suspect lose confidence in his memory, he becomes very confused about what is happening, and as a result is unable critically and rationally to evaluate the predicament he finds himself in.

The four individuals that comprise Ofshe's small study of coerced-internalized false confessors had all been assessed psychologically. None of them were considered mentally ill. Three common personality factors were evident, although not particularly extreme:

1. Good trust of people in authority;
2. Lack of self-confidence;
3. Heightened suggestibility.

Ofshe argues that these personality characteristics made the false confessors vulnerable to the influence of manipulative forms of interrogation. In his view, these vulnerabilities "probably contributed most significantly to the speed with which the process of thought reform could be carried out" (p. 14). The implication is that suspects who are not in any significant way psychologically vulnerable at the beginning of the interrogation can make coerced-internalized confessions, provided they are interrogated for extensive periods of time and the "relevant" techniques and tactics are used by interrogators.

Ofshe (personal communication) believes that coerced-internalized false confessions are typically characterized by tentative expressions, such as "I guess I must have", and "I think I did this next".

CONCLUSIONS

The literature on false confession has been reviewed and discussed within the context of miscarriages of justice. False confessions, which most commonly result from psychological coercion during police interrogation, are known to be the cause of wrongful conviction in a sizeable proportion of all cases where miscarriages of justice have occurred. The English Criminal Justice System, unlike that in Scotland and the United States of America, requires no corroboration with regard to confession evidence (Pattenden, 1991). In other words, in England defendants can be convicted on confession evidence alone, even in the most serious of cases, such as those involving terrorism and murder.

Once a confession has been obtained by the police, the likelihood of a conviction is greatly enhanced. When a miscarriage of justice is alleged or suspected to have occurred, there are certain "appeal" procedures which are supposed to operate as a "safety net". There are at least three problems with these procedures as far as false confession cases are concerned:

1. The Court of Appeal confines itself to questions of law and "new evidence" and does not specifically deal with questions related to guilt or innocence;
2. The "new evidence" that is required to satisfy the Court of Appeal that wrongful conviction has occurred is in the great majority of cases very hard or impossible to come by. Such evidence is generally discovered because of the hard, and commonly unpaid, work of some dedicated individuals, who believe in the defendant's innocence and fight, sometimes for many years and against all odds, in order for justice to be done;
3. Studies into miscarriages of justice indicate that the judiciary itself is very bad at discovering, admitting to, and doing something about, the errors which they make.

There are three distinct types of false confession, which are referred to as "voluntary", "coerced-compliant", and "coerced-internalized". Each type has a distinctive set of antecedents, conditions and psychological consequences. Much of the early knowledge about the psychology of "coerced" false confessions came from research into attitude change within the field of social psychology. Of particular importance is the extensive work that has been carried out into coercive persuasion among communist interrogators. This has provided valuable empirical findings which have resulted in extensive theoretical formulations and developments. What is now needed is a more detailed study of individual cases where people falsely confessed to serious crime of which they are subsequently proven innocent. Of particular importance would be a careful analysis of the language structure used by false confessors during interrogation, which may be linguistically distinguishable from genuine confessions.

CHAPTER 11

The Psychology of False Confession: Case Examples

In this Chapter the different psychological types of false confession are discussed by giving case examples for each type. Some of the cases provided were assessed in detail by my interviewing the people concerned. Other cases have been obtained from colleagues or from literature reviews. The cases chosen for inclusion undoubtedly only represent the tip of the iceberg of cases where a false confession has occurred. The cases of the Guildford Four and the Birmingham Six will be discussed separately in Chapter 12 in view of their special significance. I have also assessed many other cases, some of which will be alluded to in Chapter 14, where it is possible that the alleged offenders were innocent and wrongly convicted. For every proven case of false confession, there are likely to be many more which for various reasons remain unproven or are unreported.

Some sceptical readers may believe that not all the cases presented in this Chapter have been proven innocent. This is a perfectly reasonable position to take. The reality is that 100% proof for a defendant's innocence, in cases of retracted confession, is very rare and one is often dealing with cases where some "new evidence" throws serious doubts on the defendant's guilt. It seems that many people believe that innocent individuals would never confess to a serious crime during police interrogation, when it is so blatantly against their self-interest. The implicit assumption is that people always act in a self-serving way. In reality this is often not the case. For example, when placed under pressure, many individuals are more likely to serve their immediate self-interests than their long-term ones, even though the former may be to their eventual detriment. The sad fact is that some people who are not obviously mentally ill or handicapped do confess falsely to serious crimes and are consequently wrongfully convicted. Greater awareness of this is an important step forward in achieving justice. Scepticism about retracted confessions is very often justified, but when it is taken to the extreme, as is sometimes the case, then our system of justice is seriously undermined. The opposite position is equally undesirable. Accepting uncritically all those in prison who persistently insist that they are innocent would bring the criminal justice system to a halt.

SOME NOTORIOUS BRITISH CASES

There are a number of well-publicized British cases of false confession. One of the earliest cases reported dates back to the year 1660 (Ayling, 1984). The case involves the confession of John Perry to the murder of William Harrison. During extensive interrogation by the Justice of the Peace, Perry implicated himself, his brother and mother. All three were publicly executed on the basis of Perry's confession. There was some circumstantial evidence to link Perry with Harrison's disappearance, in that Perry had failed to return home after being sent out to look for his master (Harrison). Two years after the execution of the Perrys, the alleged murder victim reappeared, very much alive. He had been kidnapped and held as a slave in Turkey.

Perry's case resulted in legal re-evaluation of uncorroborated confessions in England, although a "corroboration requirement was never universally accepted and was not applied to prosecutions other than murder" (Ayling, 1984, p. 1126).

In more modern times there have been four highly publicized alleged false confession cases that all resulted in a public inquiry. These are the Timothy Evans case (Kennedy, 1988), the Confait case (Price and Caplan, 1977); the Cyprus Spy Trial (Calcutt, 1986) and the Guildford Four case (Kee, 1989; McKee and Franey, 1988). The Guildford Four case is most recent, and in view of its complexity and significance it will be discussed with the case of the Birmingham Six in Chapter 12. The Timothy Evans and Confait cases will be discussed briefly, prior to illustrations of the "voluntary", "coerced-compliant", and "coerced-internalized" types.

Case 1: Timothy Evans

On 30th November 1949, Timothy Evans, who was 25 years of age at the time, walked into Merthyr Police Station in South Wales and voluntarily confessed to having disposed of his wife's body down a drain outside his home at 10 Rillington Place, North London. He made two statements to the police in Wales. The first statement consisted of his telling the police that his wife was pregnant and had died after he had given her some abortion pills that he had obtained from a stranger in a cafe in East Anglia. The Welsh police telephoned the Notting Hill police in North London about Evans's statement. They went around to 10 Rillington Place, inspected the drain and found no body there. Being confronted with this, and the fact that it took three policemen to lift the manhole cover, Evans was interviewed again and made a further statement. He then implicated his landlord, John Christie, who had allegedly performed an abortion on his wife and told Evans that she had died as a result of medical complications. Evans said that Christie had told him that he had disposed of the body in one of the drains. Evans told the police that, after his wife's death, Christie had arranged for their baby daughter Geraldine to be looked after by a couple in East Anglia. Unknown to Evans was the fact that Christie had strangled to death both his wife and his baby daughter about 3 weeks earlier.

After a subsequent search at 10 Rillington Place, the police found the bodies of Evans's wife and daughter in a wash-house. Evans was brought to London and interrogated. He made two detailed statements on the 2nd and 3rd December and in both he confessed to the murder of his wife and daughter. After his appearance in a Magistrates' Court Evans was remanded in custody and taken to Brixton Prison, South London, where on admission he confessed again to the Principal Medical Officer. The following day, during a visit by his mother, Evans retracted his confession after his mother asked him why he had committed the murders.

"I didn't do it, Mum. Christie done it. Ask him to come and see me. He's the only one who can help me now" (Kennedy, 1988, p. 141).

Unfortunately, for Evans, Christie and his wife became prosecution witnesses at Evans's trial and gave evidence against him.

Evans's case opened at the Central Criminal Court on 11th January 1950. Evans's defence was that it was Christie and not himself who had murdered his wife and daughter. The defence relied on Evans's second statement in Wales as being reliable. The complicating factor was that at the time it was not known or suspected that Christie's abortion story was a lie enabling Christie to possess Mrs Evans and subsequently explain her death to Evans. In other words, Evans's second statement did not provide the real insight into why Christie would have had the motive to murder Mrs Evans. There was medical evidence that Mrs Evans had been sexually penetrated, probably after her death, but this evidence, which provided an important insight into the possibility of third-party involvement (e.g. Christie), was not used by the defence at Evans's trial. Furthermore, a forensic examination of the spermatazoa found in Mrs Evans's vagina, which was never analysed, could possibly have cleared Evans. It seems that, whereas Christie was remarkably lucky not to be implicated in the murders, Evans had no evidence in his favour at all.

Evans was found guilty by the jury of murdering his daughter (the jury were not asked by the judge to reach a verdict on Mrs Evans's death). He was sentenced to death and executed on 9th March 1950. He had persisted in maintaining his innocence to the end. Subsequent events were to show that Christie was indeed a murderer, as Evans had claimed. Three or 4 years prior to the murders of Evans's wife and daughter, he had murdered two women whom he had lured to his home. Both had been murdered by strangulation. In December 1952, Christie murdered his wife by strangulation.

Three more women were to die before Christie was finally apprehended at the end of March 1953. Christie confessed to killing seven women, including Mrs Evans. He denied having murdered Evans's daughter. Kennedy gives two reasons why it might have been in Christie's interest to deny the child's murder; first, the fact that it meant he had been responsible for sending an innocent man, Evans, to his death, and second, unlike the other killings, which Christie tried to justify, he could see no possible justification for killing a baby. Christie was tried at the Central Criminal Court, convicted and sentenced to death. He was hanged on 15th July 1953.

Kennedy provides a very convincing case for Evans's innocence and gives five main reasons for his wrongful conviction:

1. Evans did not report his wife's death to the police immediately after discovering her body when he returned home from work;
2. The police blindly believed in Evans's guilt, in spite of evidence from workmen that cast serious doubts on the validity of Evans's confession. In fact, the police suppressed this important evidence from the defence lawyers and an important time-sheet curiously went missing whilst in the possession of the police;
3. The defence lawyers appear to have believed in Evans's guilt and failed to appreciate and obtain evidence pointing to Evans's innocence;
4. The biased and inadequate summing-up by the judge at Evans's trial;
5. The incriminating evidence of Christie against Evans. Whereas Christie appears to have been a man of good intellect, and a former Special Constable, Evans was of low intelligence (he was said to have an IQ of no more than 75) and had a reputation as a pathological liar. It is easy to see how the jury believed Christie and not Evans.

Kennedy has made an interesting analysis of Evans's confession, which focuses on the circumstances in which they were obtained and on Evans's vulnerabilities. First, he points to the discrepancy between the police and Evans in the timing of the two statements made. The Notting Hill police officers alleged that the confession was voluntary and spontaneous and without any prompting or prior questioning. Evans claimed that he was kept up and questioned for hours into the night until he confessed. Second, some of the vocabulary and phraseology seems to have been more consistent with that of police officers, rather than of Evans who was uneducated and illiterate. Svartvik (1968) analysed some of the linguistic features of Evans's statements and concluded that the linguistic discrepancies observed supported Evans's standpoint.

According to Kennedy, Evans was under considerable stress when he confessed to the police, much of which was self-induced. Following his wife's death he became increasingly upset and concerned about what had happened, which resulted in his going to the police station in Wales. Once arrested he was kept in custody (which largely consisted of solitary confinement) for over

2 days before being handed over to the London police. He had not been informed about what was happening, except that he knew that his wife's body had not been found in the drain as expected. This resulted in uncertainty and confusion. Once he arrived at Notting Hill Police Station he was shown his wife's and daughter's clothing, in addition to the ligature that was used to murder his daughter. He began to feel very guilty about not having done more to prevent their deaths, which Kennedy considers to have been an important contributory factor to his confession. The realization that his daughter had also been murdered must have been an enormous shock to him.

It is not clear from Kennedy's detailed account of the case whether Evans ever came to believe that he might have done the killings himself (i.e. a coerced-internalized false confession). Kennedy argues that Evans went through a "period of conversion" (p. 140) and hints that he may temporarily have come to believe in his confession. However, the evidence that Evans's confession had become internalized is extremely weak and speculative. Kennedy's inferences about the nature of Evans's confession appear to have been heavily influenced by Sargant's (1957) book *Battle for the Mind*, which deals with interrogations among the Chinese communists discussed in Chapter 10. Kennedy appears to have been unaware of the subtle distinction between the coerced and compliant type of false confession. My view is that it is more likely that Evans's confession was of the coerced-compliant type, but nobody will ever know as no detailed statement was ever taken from Evans about his beliefs at the time of the interrogation.

Irving and McKenzie (1989) have recently made an interesting analysis of the Evans case by attempting to see to what extent improved legislation in England (Police and Criminal Evidence Act—PACE—1984) would hypothetically have made a difference in preventing a miscarriage of justice, had it been in existence at the time. The conclusion is that the new legislation might have given Evans more legal protection than that available at the time, but even so there is no guarantee that he would not have been convicted.

There were two official inquiries into the case of Timothy Evans, following Christie's confession about Mrs Evans's murder. The first inquiry, conducted in 1953 by Mr J. Scott Henderson, QC, came to the conclusion that no miscarriage of justice had taken place. That is, the case against Evans was seen as overwhelming, he was considered responsible for both his wife's and daughter's deaths, and Christie's confession about having murdered Mrs Evans was rejected. Not surprisingly, in view of the Inquiry's ill-founded conclusions, it was severely criticized in the House of Commons (Kennedy, 1988). The second inquiry into the case was conducted in 1965-1966 by Sir Daniel Brabin, a High Court Judge (Brabin, 1966). Evans was again considered guilty, but with a difference. Brabin thought that Evans probably had not killed his daughter (for which he was hanged), but thought he had murdered his wife (for which crime he was never tried).

On 18th October 1966, 16 years after his execution, Evans was granted a free pardon by the Queen, on the recommendation of the then Home

Secretary, Mr Roy Jenkins. Evans's innocence had at last been officially recognized.

Case 2: The Confait Case

In the early hours of 22nd April 1972, firemen and police attended a fire at 27 Doggett Road, South London. The body of a 26-year-old man, Maxwell Confait, was discovered. According to the pathologist who attended the scene, death was caused by strangulation with a ligature. Two days later, three youths, Colin Lattimore, Ronald Leighton and Ahmet Salih, were arrested following some fires. The three boys were detained from about 5.30 p.m. and within 2½ hours they made verbal confessions regarding Confait's murder. By 11 p.m. that same evening all three boys had signed confession statements in the presence of their parents. No solicitors or third parties were present during the critical interviews. The three boys subsequently retracted their confessions but were nevertheless convicted.

Lattimore was 18 years of age at the time of his arrest. He was mentally handicapped (IQ=66) and illiterate. Leighton, aged 15, was of borderline intelligence (IQ=75) and near-illiterate. Salih, of Turkish Cypriot background, was the youngest of the three boys. He was only 14 at the time of his arrest and appears to have been of normal intelligence, although it is worth pointing out that no intelligence testing appears to have been carried out in his case. He spoke English as a second language.

On 24th November 1972, Lattimore was found guilty of manslaughter on the grounds of diminished responsibility, Leighton was found guilty of murder, and all three boys were found guilty of arson at Confait's home.

There was a Court of Appeal hearing in October 1975 where the convictions of the three boys were quashed on the basis that they were "unsafe and unsatisfactory". The boys were freed after having spent 3 years in prison. There was a subsequent Inquiry, conducted by Sir Henry Fisher (1977). The Fisher Report found that there had been three breaches of the existing legislation, which was the Judges' Rules and Administrative Directions. These were that:

1. Two of the boys (Lattimore and Leighton) had been interviewed without their parents being present;
2. None of the boys had been informed of their rights to a solicitor and their entitlement to communicate with any other person; and
3. The police questioning of Lattimore was leading. The police were at the time aware of Lattimore's mental handicap, but chose to ignore it.

However, in spite of the Report's criticisms of the police, it concluded, erroneously as it turned out, that the confessions of the three boys could not have been made unless at least one of the boys had been involved in the murder of Confait. The main basis for this conclusion was that the boys seemed to know so much about the murder. This, according to Fisher, indicated that they had to have been involved in Confait's murder. Fisher did not consider the other possibility, that the police had unwittingly communicated details about the murder to the boys. Two years after the Fisher Report was published, all three boys were exonerated after two other people confessed to the murder and provided information that showed the three boys to be innocent.

As in the Evans case, Irving and McKenzie (1989) have placed the information available on the Confait case into the hypothetical context of PACE. Would the interrogation and confessions of the three young men have been different if PACE had been in operation at the time? Irving and McKenzie attempted to answer this question by reviewing the case under five headings: "the arrest", "the duration of detention", "the record of custody", "interrogation tactics and records", and "the presence of third parties and the questions of vulnerability". Their conclusion is that there would have been no important differences with regard to the arrest and detention. However, a detailed recording of what went on during custody and interrogation would have been required under the new legislation. In fact PACE, and its accompanying Codes of Practice, require a detailed "Custody Record" to be kept for every detainee and this would have made it easier to establish in retrospect what the circumstances of the interrogations and confessions were.

Two further safeguards would have been important if PACE had been available in 1972. First, a senior interrogator stated in the presence of a junior officer, during the critical phase of the interrogation, that the boys would be allowed to go home after the interviews were over. Irving and McKenzie believe that this kind of an inducement would constitute a breach under PACE. Second, and possibly most important, it is more likely under the current legislation that the boys would have been allowed access to a solicitor and a third party at the beginning of their interrogation. Whether or not the three boys would have confessed in spite of these added safeguards is impossible to predict, but they might have reduced the likelihood of the subsequent miscarriage of justice that resulted from their confessions. However, Thomas (1987) argues that the irregularities that occurred in the interrogation of the three youths might still occur under the PACE Codes of Practice.

VOLUNTARY FALSE CONFESSIONS

Three case illustrations are given below about voluntary false confessions. These case illustrations are not intended to provide examples of all possible types of voluntary false confessions. Rather they highlight important differences in the nature of false confessions between three clinical conditions—schizophrenia, depression and personality disorder. The case presented with regard to personality disorder (Case 5) is psychologically the most complicated one, because the false confessions made seemed to comprise three overlapping features, loss of reality testing, an element of depression, and a need for notoriety.

It was mentioned in the last Chapter that schizophrenic patients have been known to confess falsely to a crime as a consequence of their mental state, which involves a loss of reality testing, and hence their inability to distinguish between reality and their own distorted thought processes. Another type of voluntary false confession comes from the nosological group of those suffering from psychotic depression. Professor Lionel Haward (personal communication) argues that false confessions made by schizophrenic and depressed people originate from very different processes of psychopathology, which lead to the following hypotheses:

1. Schizophrenic patients have their false confessions evoked by external contemporary events, while those of depressed patients are internally determined and emerge spontaneously;
2. The false confession of the depressed patient is precipitated by deep-seated and longstanding feelings of guilt. The guilt is generated by past events and experiences and is projected onto some external event which becomes the focus for the patient's guilt;
3. The paranoid persecutions of the depressed patient differ from those of the paranoid schizophrenic by being accusatorial, i.e. the delusions of the depressed patient interpret the imagined persecution as stemming from the patient's past behaviour towards the persecutors. The locus of guilt is thus kept firmly within the patient and normally prevents any aggression from being directed outwards against others. This may explain why depressed patients commonly attempt suicide (i.e. self-directed aggression), whereas the paranoid schizophrenic patient is more outwardly aggressive.

Professor Haward has provided me with two cases to illustrate these salient differences between the false confession of the schizophrenic and depressed patients.

Case 3: Miss S

Miss S, a middle-aged spinster, had been diagnosed as suffering from paranoid schizophrenia. One day she was admitted to hospital following a number of disturbances of the peace in which the patient accused neighbours of conspiring against her. Her disturbed behaviour subsided under heavy sedation, and she was allowed out of the hospital grounds, but she continued to maintain the delusion that others were trying to harm her. Following publicity about a local murder, she confessed to a uniformed constable that she was the person responsible for the murder. After being taken to the police station and interviewed she was returned to the hospital, where the medical officer on duty provided an irrefutable alibi and an explanation of her behaviour. Paranoid schizophrenics not uncommonly assault innocent victims in what they believe is self-defence, under the delusion that the person concerned is a threat to their well-being. In the present case, the patient was not only confused from heavy medication, but also had impaired reality testing, a characteristic of psychosis. In the context of constant ward conversation about the murder, and her own thoughts of doing so to protect herself, it was not difficult for the wish to be replaced by the deed in her thinking.

Case 4: Mrs H

Mrs H was a 38-year-old woman who suffered from severe depression following the birth of her only child 2 years previously. She failed to improve despite a variety of treatments in three different hospitals, and suffered so intensely from delusions of persecution that psychosurgery was recommended by her doctor. Mrs H made false confessions to the police on two separate occasions. In both instances she did so in the expressed belief that if she confessed her misdeeds and was publicly punished, the imagined persecution would cease. Since the onset of her psychiatric illness she had believed that she was wanted by the police, and sometimes took the most extreme steps to avoid arrest. For example, on one occasion her husband returned home one evening to find her and their 2-year-old child concealed in a cupboard under the kitchen sink. They had crouched there all day without food after a police siren had been heard in the vicinity during the morning rush hour.

Following this episode, and in an attempt to convince his wife that she was not wanted by the police, Mr H took her to the police station by arrangement, where a sympathetic and patient police inspector spent some hours demonstrating her absence from the lists and photographs of various wanted persons. The police inspector also introduced Mrs H to colleagues who assured her that the police had nothing against her and gave her a guided tour of the police station. She remained unconvinced, but was reassured by their manner. However, Mrs H returned to the police station later during the week and confessed to an imaginary offence. A statement was taken. The police officer judged her to be mentally disordered by her behaviour and the nature of the statement given. He pretended to take her statement seriously and told her that she was "being let off this time". Mrs H gained a few hours of transitory relief by her confession, but her delusions returned within days and she returned to the police station and was interviewed by another police officer. He appeared to have less insight into her condition than the previous officer and it was several hours before Mrs H's psychiatric problems were realized.

There is little doubt that this pattern of confession would have continued had Mrs H not been threatened with a Hospital Order should her behaviour continue. Mrs H had suffered a puritanical upbringing by elderly, rigid and repressive parents, such that the slightest peccadillo resulted in excessive guilt. It is the sheer intensity of the guilt experienced, which can readily lead to suicide, that provides both the motive and the drive to confess by the psychotically depressed patient.

Case 5: Mr M

This case involves false confessions by a man (Mr M) in his mid-thirties who confessed to having committed several unsolved murders between 1979 and 1985. He first confessed to a murder to the police in 1979, but he was not charged as the police had reason to believe that he was not the murderer. Mr M was subsequently arrested in 1986 for a suspected sexual offence and before long he had confessed voluntarily to eight publicized murders. The reason he gave for the confessions was that he felt guilty about what he had done and wanted the killings to stop. Mr M was finally only charged with two of the eight murders as the evidence did not support his involvement in the others. There was no forensic evidence to link Mr M with the two murders he was charged with, but in his confessions he provided the police with some information which was to a certain extent suggestive of his guilt (i.e. he gave information which was not public knowledge).

A major problem with all the confessions was the fact that, even though Mr M claimed to feel very guilty about the murders he had committed, he appeared to have no clear recollection of having actually carried them out. In many instances the information Mr M provided about the killings was factually wrong. The police worked on the assumption that Mr M suffered from amnesia and they questioned him with this in mind. It was clear to the police that Mr M could not have committed all the murders he confessed to. For example, in the case of one of the murders he was actually in hospital at the time and very far away.

Whilst on remand for two of the murders, Mr M confessed to further murders he could not possibly have done. One case involved claiming responsibility for a brutal murder someone else had committed for a financial reward. The real murderer, whom he met whilst in prison on remand, is alleged to have provided Mr M with intimate details about the murder which were not public knowledge, and offered him a large sum of money for confessing to it so that he himself would be freed. The police confronted Mr M with the confession when they realized that he could not possibly have committed the murder.

It was clear that Mr M did not confess to murders at random. Nor did he feel responsible for all murders he read about in the newspapers or saw on television. There was at least one murder that he was questioned about by the police to which he did not confess. The common characteristic about the murders to which Mr M confessed was the general location where they had occurred. The critical factor seemed to be whether Mr M himself had ever been to the general region where the murder had taken place. If he had been to that part of the country at some point in his life then this became a salient trigger for a chain of thoughts that gradually hardened into the belief that he was responsible for the murder.

I interviewed Mr M prior to his trial in 1987, where he was found unfit to plead, and again in 1990 when the case was taken up by the courts again. I gave evidence twice at Mr M's trial about his personality and readiness to confess to murders. One part of my evidence involved describing how I had subtly implanted in Mr M's mind a completely fictitious murder, to which he subsequently confessed. I interviewed Mr M twice in prison after his conviction for the two murders, where I gained further insight into his apparent compulsion to confess and the gratification he gained from it.

Mr M had a disturbed and turbulent childhood. He reported his family life as having been very unhappy, he truanted a great deal from school, and soon he had a long list of criminal convictions. The offences for which he was convicted dated back to the age of 14 years. These included burglaries, road traffic violations, acts of violence and sexual offences. Mr M performed poorly at school and was transferred to a special school. He appears to have been sexually disinhibited from early adolescence (i.e. there were frequent reports of indecent exposure) and continued to expose himself to women until his latest arrest. He had been drinking excessively since adolescence and there were several reported instances of suicide attempts as an adult. He appeared to have had some history in childhood of falsely confessing to the police. On one occasion his mother intervened, as Mr M had been with her at the time of the alleged offence. Mr M reported having falsely confessed in childhood for the excitement of it and in order to raise his status in the eyes of his peers.

In various psychiatric reports Mr M was consistently diagnosed as "severely personality disordered". This diagnosis was consistent with the psychological findings which were obtained from extensive testing, conducted in 1987 by myself and repeated in 1990. Mr M proved to be of borderline intelligence (IQ=76), and reported a severe degree of depressive symptomatology. He showed marked symptoms of anxiety and intrusive thoughts about the various murders he reported having committed. Mr M proved to be highly suggestible on the GSS 1 and GSS 2. The results from the various tests administered in 1990 were entirely consistent with the 1987 results, except that Mr M's free recall on the GSS narrative was considerably better in 1990 than it had been in 1987. This was strikingly so for the GSS 1 story, and was undoubtedly related to one important experimental manipulation which was incorporated into the 1990 assessment. That is, I added one sentence to the end of the GSS 1 narrative. The story describes a woman, "Anna Thompson", being robbed whilst being on holiday in Spain. The added sentence read, "A few months later the woman was sexually assaulted and stabbed to death whilst visiting a friend in South-west London". The reason for adding this sentence to the story, which was presented to Mr M as a memory task, was to see if Mr M's tendency to confess to murders could be produced by experimental means about a completely fictitious murder. The big question was, would Mr M take the bait?

I presented the GSS 1 story to Mr M as a memory task, as I also did for the GSS 2 story which was also administered during the same session, but unlike the GSS 1 it contained no added sentence to the standardized narrative. As both stories had previously been administered to Mr M 3 years previously, I asked him if he had ever heard of either story before. He said he did not think so. After reading out both the stories I made no further mention of the sentence added. I knew that within a few days Mr M was to be seen by a psychiatrist. I telephoned the psychiatrist and told him about what I had done and requested that he would ask Mr M what he knew about the murder of "Anna Thompson". In the meantime Mr M had time to let the idea of "Anna Thompson's" murder ferment in his mind.

A few days later the psychiatrist visited Mr M and carried out his own forensic assessment, during which time he casually asked about the murder of "Anna Thompson". Mr M quickly took the cue and gave a detailed account of her murder, which included considerable confabulation in addition to accurate material contained in the story. According to the psychiatrist, Mr M's reaction to the story was quite remarkable. He seemed to genuinely believe that he was involved in the murder and remained completely unaware of its origin. The fictitious story seemed to have become a reality and subsequently came to feature in Mr M's mind similarly to the other murders he had confessed to.

About 2 months after the interview with the psychiatrist, and whilst Mr M was waiting to be transferred to a Maximum Security Hospital after being convicted for two murders, I interviewed him again and asked him to tell me about all the murders he "felt" he had committed. Among the many murders there was the murder of "Anna Thompson". His recollection of the GSS 1 story was excellent and there had been hardly any deterioration in his memory from the initial free recall over 2 months previously. In contrast, Mr M claimed to have no recollection whatsoever of the GSS 2 story which had been administered at the same time. The most likely explanation is that the added sentence about "Mrs Thompson's" murder had focused Mr M's mind on the content of the story and helped with its consolidation and retrieval. Of course, there had been a certain amount of rehearsal as Mr M repeatedly went through the "murder" in his mind.

On the basis of Mr M's own statements to the police, he was a very dangerous serial killer. His confessions were problematic because of their incompleteness, apparent unreliability and lack of supportive evidence. In his own evidence to the jury at his trial, Mr M said he felt as if he had committed the murders, but had no actual memory of having done so. The general impression Mr M gave was that, even if he was not responsible for the two murders for which he was being tried, he was well capable of brutal murder and might do so at a future date. The jury learned that Mr M had a long history of fantasizing about murders, which he commonly incorporated into his sexual fantasies. The jury must have been left with the general impression that Mr M was a very dangerous man and needed long-term

confinement. It therefore came as no surprise to me that they found him guilty
of the two murders he was charged with.

In spite of the fact that Mr M was convicted of two murders, it is clear that
he also made a number of confessions that were false. Indeed, he appears
to have had a long history of falsely confessing to crimes. Although the reason
for confessing to each crime may have varied, there appeared to be three main
reasons for his confessions, which were generally elicited without external
pressure:

1. Mr M told me that he found confessing to gruesome murders very exciting.
    He reported thoroughly enjoying the notoriety and the attention he
    received from the police. The more horrific the murder, the more exciting
    he found it. Mr M described feeling very important when he featured
    significantly in a murder investigation. In other words, it appears to have
    markedly enhanced his self-esteem.
2. Mr M reported a long history of masturbating to the thought of murdering
    people. He found the idea of murdering people very exciting and it
    stimulated him sexually. He reported on occasions having fantasized that
    it was he who had committed the murders reported by the media. He told
    me that he had noticed a gradual decrease over the years in his desire
    to masturbate to violent themes. I asked him why he thought this was
    the case. He said he had noticed it in the context of his sex drive being
    reduced as he became older. Although Mr M reported being sexually
    excited by the fantasies of murder, he said it also made him feel very bad
    and he tried "to push the thoughts away". With time the thoughts
    appeared to become more consolidated within his mind, which he reported
    finding most distressing. The way Mr M described the thoughts indicated
    that they may have had an intrusive component to them. Having
    interviewed Mr M on many occasions about his fantasies and about the
    murders he "felt" he had committed, I was in no doubt that he was very
    distressed by them and wanted to talk about them. Confessing to the
    murders may therefore have given him a sense of temporary relief. His
    distress apeared to be at least partly due to the fact that he was having
    increasingly little control over the intrusive thoughts and had serious
    problems distinguishing factual material from fantasy.
3. Some psychiatrists involved in the case argued that Mr M's false
    confessions originated from his inability to distinguish between facts and
    fantasies. In other words, his severe personality disorder interfered with
    his reality monitoring, without there being any evidence of clear psychotic
    illness. His faulty reality monitoring seemed mostly related to difficulties
    in distinguishing between what he had experienced or done and what he
    had fantasized about. In addition, for some reason Mr M seemed
    remarkably unable to identify the source of any knowledge concerning
    the murders. For example, he could not easily differentiate between events
    he had read or been told about and those he had actually experienced.

Even the GSS 1 narrative he reported as a real-life event he had been personally involved in.

The three reasons given for Mr M's tendency to make false confessions can all be construed as having arisen from his severely disordered personality. The confessions fulfilled some important psychological needs, such as enhanced self-esteem, sexual gratification and emotional relief. It was argued by the prosecution at Mr M's trial that he may have been falsely confessing to crimes in order to confuse the issues and "water down" the impact of his true confessions. This may of course have been the case, and there was evidence that Mr M was capable of major manipulative behaviour for instrumental gains. I discussed this possibility with Mr M in detail after his conviction. My impression is that he was not falsely confessing to crime as a way of influencing the outcome of his trial. Most importantly, perhaps, Mr M did have a history of falsely confessing to crimes prior to his arrest in 1986.

COERCED-COMPLIANT FALSE CONFESSIONS

Case 6: Mr F

In 1987 two frail and elderly women were found battered to death in their home. The police thought that the murderer had entered the house through an unlocked rear door in the early hours of the morning. The women had been sexually assaulted either before or after their deaths.

A few days after the murder a 17-year-old neighbour (Mr F) was arrested and interrogated about the murders. Apparently a statement he had previously given to the police during a routine door-to-door enquiry about his movements on the night of the murder was inconsistent with statements given by two of his neighbours.

Mr F was arrested early on a Saturday morning and was kept in custody for about 3½ hours before his first formal interview commenced. The interviews lasted for nearly 14 hours with various breaks in between. The interview was contemporaneously recorded in accordance with PACE. Five police officers questioned him at different times, including a senior detective who, after questioning him about his sexual habits and alleged failure with girls, eventually elicited a confession to the murders and sexual assault. This confession later proved to be false.

At the beginning of the first interview the police officers repeatedly challenged Mr F's claim that he had been nowhere near the scene of the murders and continually accused him of being a liar. The police claimed that they had witnesses (two of Mr F's neighbours) who had seen Mr F near the scene of the murders around the material time. Many of the questions asked were leading and accusatory. After a while Mr F began to show signs of distress, including sobbing, shaking and crying. He gradually began to give in to the interrogators, at first admitting that he had been out at the material time and then that he had been near the victims' house. After being asked about his sexual habits and alleged failure with girls, Mr F was asked the following:

> "Now listen to me. You were in the back entry late last night, early morning, and were having a wank, is that right?"

Answer:

> "Yes."

Mr F then went on to say how angry and frustrated he had been at the time, which had previously been suggested to him by the interrogators as a motive for the murders. This was followed by detailed confession to the murders, sexual assault on the women, and theft of money from their house.

The following day Mr F was interviewed again by the police, but this time in the presence of a solicitor. Early on in the interview Mr F attempted to retract the admissions he had made the previous day concerning the murders and his presence in the victims' house, explaining that he had falsely confessed because of persistent pressure by the interrogators. Mr F was then again subjected to persistent pressure by the same senior detective to confess again:

> "I've been fair with you . . ."

> "I want you to tell me now properly, with some of the remorse that you showed last night, what went on . . . It's not going to be easy but do it . . . Come on . . . Do it."

> "Look at me . . . Some of the things that you told me would only be known by a person who was at the house that night."

> "I've taken the trouble and interest in discussing your problems that you obviously have, and even listening about your pornographic magazines . . ."

> "I know that you've not had much success with girls . . . I know how frustrated you get. I know that you were reading that pornographic magazine on Saturday night . . . I know that in that magazine there were explicit sexual acts shown."

After some more questions about the explicit nature of the pornographic magazine and Mr F's alleged sexual frustration, he again made a full and detailed confession. Mr F subsequently made further incriminating admissions to prison staff and to another inmate whilst at the beginning of his remand. A few days after his original confession, Mr F was interviewed in prison by the senior detective, in the presence of a different solicitor, concerning the self-incriminating admissions to the prison staff and inmate. Mr F admitted having made the admissions but stated:

"The truth is that I have lied all the way along and I have never hurt or touched them" (meaning the two murder victims).

The senior detective became impatient and commented:

"I do not propose to ask you any more questions because I am of the firm opinion that you are lying and wasting valuable police time in this enquiry".

From that time onwards Mr F persistently claimed to be innocent of the murders and the related offences. Undoubtedly, he would have been convicted if the real murderer had not been apprehended whilst Mr F was on remand waiting trial for the two murders he had not committed.

Whilst on remand Mr F had been assessed by two psychiatrists and a psychologist. The two psychiatrists failed to identify his specific vulnerabilities. The psychologist, who had been instructed by the defence, identified two related vulnerabilities on psychological tests, in spite of Mr F being of average intelligence: proneness to anxiety, as measured by the Eysenck Personality Questionnaire (Eysenck and Eysenck, 1975); and an abnormal tendency to give in to interrogative pressure, as measured by the Gudjonsson Suggestibility Scale (Gudjonsson, 1984a). The psychologist concluded, on the basis of his findings, that Mr F "would be very likely to shift his evidence during interrogation if any pressure was exerted."

Together with a psychiatrist colleague, Dr James MacKeith, I assessed Mr F on two occasions after he had been acquitted and released from prison and studied all the documents available to Mr F's solicitor (Gudjonsson and MacKeith, 1990). Mr F's parents were also interviewed and gave valuable information about how he had changed following his release from 11 months in custody. According to the parents, Mr F was no longer the unassertive and timid young man he had been prior to his arrest. His prison experience seemed to have hardened him, his self-confidence had markedly improved after his acquittal, and he had learned to resist pressure rather than give in to it. These changes in Mr F's personality were clearly evident on psychological tests (Gudjonsson and MacKeith, 1990), and were causing his parents some concern because he had become more difficult to live with.

The above case fulfils the criteria of coerced-compliant false confession. Mr F never came to believe that he had murdered the two women, but falsely confessed to escape from the persistent and lengthy pressure placed upon him by the interrogating officers. It appeared to be particularly important that Mr F's self-esteem had been manipulated by playing on his feelings of sexual inadequacy and alleged failures with girls. It is evident that the police officers strongly believed that Mr F had committed the murders and tried very hard to obtain a confession from him. They mistakenly believed that he had knowledge that only the real murderer would possess, knowledge which Mr F alleged originated from newspaper articles and from the police. (Similarly mistaken belief by the police is well illustrated by Kellam, 1980, in a case involving an alleged sexual offence.)

Mr F's vulnerabilities when placed under pressure were again highlighted at the beginning of his remand, when he made false self-incriminating admissions in prison in order to escape from pressure. On the face of it, these further self-incriminating admissions appeared to support Mr F's guilt concerning the two murders.

Mr F claimed that during the police interviews he never thought about the potential long-term consequences of his confession, believing naively that his alibi witnesses, especially his parents, would prove his innocence. Sadly, he had placed too much hope in the ability of his parents to prove his innocence, a fact that he realized only too late.

Case 7: Mr P

Mr P was a 21-year-old man with a history of mental handicap. He had gone to a police station to report the theft of a cheque belonging to him. While at the police station the detective asked him questions about an attempted robbery which had taken place the week before. The reasons for the police officer's suspiciousness related to the fact that the young man had gone to the police station on a bicycle (the alleged assailant had been riding a bicycle) and he fitted the victim's description in that he looked untidy. Mr P was cautioned and interviewed by the detective constable. No other persons were present during the interview. The interview, which was allegedly contemporaneously recorded, lasted for nearly 1½ hours, during which time Mr P made damaging admissions. Five days later he was interviewed in the presence of his mother. Mr P had told his mother that he had not committed the offence and the mother forwarded this comment to the police officer prior to the interview. The officer told her that her son had definitely done it and interviewed him in her presence. During the 20-minute interview that followed, Mr P reiterated his admissions from the previous interview. Even though the victim in the case had clearly stated that she would recognize the man who tried to rob her, there was no identification parade. The case was referred to me before the Crown Court hearing. At court I asked the detective why there had been no identification parade. He said that in view of the confession it had not been considered necessary.

I conducted a pre-trial assessment on Mr P and found him to have a mild mental handicap (IQ 66). His comprehension and reasoning were particularly limited. He obtained abnormally high suggestibility scores on the GSS 1 and GSS 2, the Total Suggestibility scores being 17 and 16 on the two tests, respectively (i.e. above the 95th percentile rank for normal subjects). I assessed Mr P's understanding of his legal rights. He claimed to understand the police caution, but when I asked him to describe to me what it meant, he was unable to do so. Mr P claimed to be innocent of the robbery. The interview record showed few leading questions and he claimed to have falsely confessed because the detective "kept going on and on" and he feared being locked up. Mr P appeared to have confessed quite readily after his initial denials. The two interviews, on the basis of the contemporaneous record, were not obviously coercive, although the detective had been somewhat persistent in his questioning.

The case went to the Crown Court and I was requested to attend to give evidence on Mr P's psychological vulnerabilities. While waiting outside the court room for the case to commence, the victim took a good look at her alleged assailant. She immediately notified the prosecution that the defendant was definitely not the man who had attacked her. The woman gave a detailed written statement to that effect and the charges against the defendant were dropped. A few minutes later I came across the detective questioning Mr P outside the court room. The conversation went as follows: "How come you knew so much about the offence? Did the person who did it tell you about it?" He answered, "Yes." I stopped the questioning being taken any further and took Mr P to one side. I asked him what the police officer had been asking him. He said, "Something about the person who did it." I said, "Do you know who robbed the woman?" He replied, "No." I asked, "Why did you tell the police officer you did know?" He replied, "I wanted to help." Clearly, Mr P had not learned from his previous mistakes.

The lesson to be learned from this case is that after obtaining a confession the police relied on it far too much. From the start the detective was certain that he had the assailant and he did not consider other possibilities. In other words, he approached the case with a closed mind after his suspicions were initially aroused. Most importantly, the police unwisely did not consider it necessary to conduct an identification parade, even though the victim had taken a good look at her assailant and claimed that she would definitely recognize him again. Had they taken this logical step, it would undoubtedly have saved both the victim and the defendant unnecessary distress, not to mention the costs involved.

COERCED-INTERNALIZED FALSE CONFESSIONS

Case 8: Mr R

Whilst serving as a police detective with the Reykjavik Criminal Investigation Police before becoming a clinical psychologist, I interviewed a man in his late twenties in connection with an alleged theft of a purse from a woman with whom he had been drinking the previous evening. The suspect (Mr R) had met the woman at a discotheque and had later gone to the woman's flat, where they continued drinking. The following morning, and shortly after the man had gone, the woman found that her purse, which contained some money, was missing. She reported the alleged theft of her purse to the police. Her drinking partner from the previous evening became the immediate suspect, because the woman had noticed the purse whilst the man was in the flat and nobody else had entered the flat from the time she had last seen the purse and until she had discovered it was missing.

Mr R was asked to attend the police station for questioning and was presented with the allegation. He had several previous convictions for minor theft and alcohol-related offences. He explained that he could not remember much about the previous evening, but had some recollection about having gone to the woman's flat after the discotheque closed. He said he had no recollection of having actually taken the purse but, as he frequently had memory blackouts after heavy drinking, he thought it was quite likely. When confronted with the woman's allegation that the purse had disappeared whilst he was in her flat, he said, "I do not remember doing it, but I must have done it." He signed a statement to that effect.

A few days later the woman telephoned the police and said that she had found her purse; it appeared to have fallen behind her settee where the couple had sat whilst drinking.

This case is a good example of the way in which the circumstances of a particular alleged offence can be the critical factor that elicits the false confession rather than the interrogation techniques utilized. The man was not interrogated, but was presented with the woman's allegation, which was sufficient because of his general distrust of his memory and his belief in the woman's honest reporting of the theft. What none of us knew at the time was that no crime had been committed in the first place.

Case 9: Peter Reilly

The most publicized case of internalized false confession is that of Peter Reilly, who has been the subject of two books (Barthel, 1976; Connery, 1977). In 1973, Reilly was an easy-going and well-liked 18-year-old youth. He lived in Canaan, Connecticut, with his 51-year-old mother. At 8 p.m. on 28th September he went to a Methodist Church for a Youth Centre meeting. He returned home around 9.50 p.m. to discover his mother's mutilated body. She had been brutally murdered minutes before Reilly arrived home. He immediately called for an ambulance and was clearly in a distressed state. Within hours he became the prime suspect for the murder and after intensive interrogation he made a self-incriminating confession, which resulted in his arrest and conviction for manslaughter.

Connery (1977) states:

"Suddenly an orphan, and still in his teens, with no close ties to relatives, Peter was subjected to four great shocks in a day's time: the murder of his mother, the realization that he was suspected of being the murderer, his own amazed agreement that he might be his mother's killer, and his arrest. He was put behind bars and there he remained for 143 days before going to trial" (p. 21).

As the police investigation commenced Reilly remained voluntarily in police custody for several hours. He was eager to help the police to apprehend the murderer and, according to police sources, was fully cooperative. There was insufficient evidence to arrest him and he declined to have a lawyer present during the subsequent interrogation. Three years later he explained why he had not exercised his right to a lawyer:

"Because I hadn't done anything wrong, and this is America, and that's the way I thought it was" (Connery, 1977, p. 42).

Reilly's interrogation commenced at about 6.30 a.m., nearly 9 hours after he had found his mother dead. It was tape-recorded. His interrogator noted that Reilly appeared very relaxed, well poised, and exhibited no emotion. For the next 2 hours Reilly gave a general description of his movements on the day of the murder and his discovery of the body. He was asked questions about his mother's sex life and whether he had ever had a sexual relationship with her. Reilly was later to say that these personal questions upset him a great deal.

After a 4-hour break Reilly was asked to take a polygraph test. He agreed, because:

"I was sure of my innocence. I just wanted to get all the police garbage out of the way so I could get some rest and be with my friends" (Connery, 1977, p. 57).

Prior to the polygraph examination, the examiner told Reilly about the effectiveness of the instrument:

"The polygraph reads your brain for me."

"Does it actually read my brain?" Reilly asked.

"Oh, definitely, definitely. And if you've told me the truth this is what your brain is going to tell me."

After the polygraph examination Reilly was told that he had a deceptive outcome. This was followed by more than 6 hours of interrogation, during which time Reilly was subtly persuaded that he had murdered his mother, even though he had no recollection of having done so.

Following the polygraph examination, Reilly still insisted that he did not kill his mother. The interrogator, who was also the polygraph examiner, presented Reilly with different scenarios ("theme development") of what he thought might have happened on the night of the murder. His basic premise seemed to be that Reilly had mental problems and as a result he could not remember killing his mother. The "theme development" (see Chapter 3) included such statements as:

"What happened here was a mercy thing."

"Something happened between you and your mother last night and one thing led to another and some way you accidentally hurt her seriously."

"Your mother flew off the handle and went for you or something and you had to protect yourself" (Connery, 1977, pp. 65-67).

Reilly's confidence in his memory began to weaken:

"Now there is doubt in my mind. Maybe I did do it" (Connery, 1977, p. 66).

Reilly vacillated for a while, saying "I believe I did it", then expressing doubts that he did do it. He then stated:

"The polygraph thing didn't come out right. It looked like I'd done it."

The interrogator asked:

"Well, what's it look like now?"

Reilly answered:

"It really looks like I did it."

The interrogator asked:

"You did it?"

Reilly replied:

"Yes."

The interrogation continued with different themes and scenarios being presented to Reilly to assist with his recollections about specific details. Reilly eventually gave a confession statement, declaring himself as his mother's killer. The confession was written down by a police friend of his. In it he stated, among other things:

> "I remember slashing once at my mother's throat with a straight razor I used for model airplanes. This was the living room table. I also remember jumping on my mother's legs."

Reilly also stated that he thought he might have raped his mother, but this was discounted by the interrogator as there had been no physical evidence of rape.

Reilly three times told the police officer who was writing out the confession to make sure that he mentioned in the statement the fact that he was not really sure of what he was saying. The officer promised to do so, but did not keep his promise. The officer was subsequently to allege that Reilly had made a verbal admission (i.e. "I killed her") immediately prior to his written confession statement. There was no record of this having been said from the tape-recording of the interview, although the officer insisted in court that it had been said and tape-recorded. There were some differences between what the officer had written down in the confession statement and what Reilly was trying to say.

What is evident from Reilly's interrogation, which was tape-recorded, is that he was never completely sure that he had murdered his mother. He clearly came to doubt his own recollection, largely, it seems, because of the persistence of the interrogators that the polygraph is infallible and that he had a temporary mental block about what had really happened on the night of the murder. Reilly seems to have become very confused by the polygraph results and by the interrogators' repeated and suggestive questioning, which made him very unsure about his own memory of events on the evening of the murder.

There was some evidence that he was generally very trusting of police officers and respected them. Indeed, had expressed an interest in becoming a police officer himself and had police officers as friends.

Before the trial there was a pre-trial hearing concerning the admissibility of Reilly's confession. As the confession was the only significant evidence against Reilly, it was important for the defence to have the judge rule it inadmissible. The defence argued that the confession was caused by psychological coercion and was therefore not voluntary. Conversely, the prosecution argued that the interrogation had been conducted properly and that Reilly's confession was voluntary. The judge decided in favour of the State:

> "There may have been some repetitive, suggestive questioning, or the planting of ideas, by members of the State Police, but not enough to deprive the defendant of due process" (Connery, 1977, p. 133).

The case went to trial and the prosecution argued that the evidence against Reilly was "overwhelming". In reality, the only evidence against Reilly, except for some circumstantial evidence, was his self-incriminating confession. No forensic evidence was ever found to link him with the murder, and the prosecution tried hard to explain how Reilly could have changed his blood-stained clothes after the murder in order to avoid detection. It was emphasized by the prosecuting counsel that Reilly had been informed of his legal rights four times. Furthermore, Reilly was "an intelligent, articulate, calm and alert individual" and his alleged off-the-record comment "I killed her" surely indicated his guilt (Connery, 1977, p. 248). Reilly repeated his confession to two police officers after the interrogation was terminated, which was used by the prosecution to further indicate his guilt.

Reilly testified at the trial. According to Connery (1977), he made a poor witness and came across as vague, defensive and evasive. The main problem seemed to be that his recollection of what had been said and done during the lengthy interrogation was poor, and this left the jury and the judge with an unfavourable impression about his honesty and willingness to tell the truth.

The jury found Reilly guilty of manslaughter in the first degree. He was sentenced in May 1974 to imprisonment "for a term of not less than 6 nor more than 16 years" (p. 267).

No psychological or psychiatric opinions were offered at the trial. Psychological testing had been arranged while the trial was in progress, but as the evidence was not entirely favourable it was not offered in evidence. On the Wechsler Adult Intelligence Test (WAIS) Reilly obtained a Full Scale IQ of 115, which placed his intellectual functioning in the "bright normal" range. The psychologist argued that Reilly had poor self-esteem and was easily influenced by others. However, the psychological report seems to have included speculative comments suggesting that in spite of Reilly's compliance, he seemed crafty or cunning, and exhibited "profound mistrust and vigilance" (Connery, 1977, p. 240).

After the trial Reilly was still claiming to be innocent of his mother's murder. Five new people came to his rescue and they were, according to Connery (1977), instrumental in providing new evidence to prove his innocence. These were a lawyer, an eminent playwright, a private detective, a psychiatrist and a forensic pathologist.

The psychiatrist, who testified at a new trial hearing in 1976, found that Reilly had:

> "None of the personality attributes, none of the measurements, that you would expect of a person who would develop amnesia; two, that he was able to give an account of every time segment; and three, when he was given the chance to lie, he didn't lie. So I came to the conclusion that he didn't have amnesia and that he was telling the truth" (Connery, 1977, p. 293).

The question the psychiatrist was trying to answer related to the possibility that Reilly might have suffered from amnesia after allegedly murdering his mother.

In evidence, the psychiatrist considered that Reilly had, in 1973, uncritically accepted the police officers' unfounded premises because of confusion, poorly integrated identity, and long-standing respect for police officers. Reilly's vagueness and uncertainties during the interrogation were considered to be the result of a confusional state, induced by the demand characteristics of the interrogative situation, rather than due to psychogenic amnesia.

Prior to the re-trial it was discovered that the prosecuting counsel had suppressed "seven statements and seventeen pieces of evidence that the defense was entitled to" (Connery, 1977, p. 314). The most important statements were discovered after the death of the original prosecuting counsel in the case. The new State Attorney handed the statements over to the defense counsel, statements which his predecessor had clearly deliberately suppressed because they contradicted his mistaken and obsessive belief that Reilly was guilty of his mother's murder. The statements were those of two witnesses who had seen Reilly drive in the direction of his home at 21.40 on the night of the murder. Reilly could therefore not have been at his home until 21.45

at the earliest, which gave him insufficient time to have committed the murder and changed his clothing. The outcome was that the State had no alternative but to drop its case against Reilly. The persistent fight for proving Reilly's innocence had paid off. He was at long last a free man.

Case 10: Sergeant E

Sergeant E was a 27-year-old Serviceman with the American Air Force, stationed in England (see Gudjonsson and Lebegue, 1989, for a detailed account of the case). He was charged with murdering his best friend on their last evening out together before his friend returned to America. At around midnight on a clear winter's night, the two friends had gone for a walk along some cliffs after having consumed a quantity of alcoholic drinks. Shortly afterwards Sergeant E telephoned the local police and told them that his friend had had an "accident". He explained that he had asked his friend to lie by his side at the cliff edge to look at the sea and the moon, but his friend suddenly fell over the cliff, which resulted in his death. The friend's alcohol level at the time of his death was 212 mg/100 ml. Sergeant E was similarly intoxicated, having consumed about seven pints of beer over the 5 hours prior to his friend's death.

According to the British police, the friend's death was accidental. The case was handed over to the American Office of Special Investigation (OSI) and Sergeant E was required to take a polygraph test in order to clear himself of any suspicion concerning his friend's death. Unfortunately for Sergeant E, he "failed" the polygraph test (i.e. the test produced a deceptive outcome) and three further tests were administered on other occasions, all of which he "failed". In conjunction with the polygraph tests, Sergeant E was interrogated extensively by OSI special agents for a total of 24 hours over 3 days. Towards the end of the lengthy interrogation Sergeant E signed a self-incriminating confession, implicating himself in the death of his friend. In fact, he had become persuaded by the agents that he had murdered his friend, even though he had no memory of having done so. As a consequence of the confession, Sergeant E was charged with his premeditated murder.

Sergeant E's confession resulted from extensive interrogation by the special agents, who employed the "scenario technique" described in Chapter 3. The special agents testified at the military hearing that they had 100% faith in the outcome of the polygraph and had tried to persuade Sergeant E that he had to have been involved in his friend's death as the polygraph "never lies". They admitted having deliberately played on Sergeant E's feelings of guilt and distress about what had happened to his friend, in an attempt to obtain a confession from him. Most importantly, as Sergeant E began to become confused by the questioning, the agents presented him with different scenarios about what they thought had happened and refused to allow him to talk about his own account of an accidental fall. They repeatedly suggested a scenario in which Sergeant E struggled with his friend, and eventually Sergeant E accepted that the agents' scenario could be correct, but he claimed to have no recollection of it having happened that way.

Sergeant E was assessed psychologically by me, and I testified at the military hearing (Gudjonsson and Lebegue, 1989) as to the unreliability of his confession. Sergeant E was of low average intelligence. On psychological testing he proved to be a compliant and a suggestible individual, who was emotionally labile and prone to strong feelings of guilt. He stated that he had trusted the special agents and tried hard to cooperate with them. He was puzzled at his failure in the polygraph tests, believing what the special agents had told him about the 100% accuracy of the polygraph. He said he had at the time of the interrogation felt very guilty about his friend's death, which he believed he should have been able to prevent. As the special agents repeatedly told him, with marked confidence, that he must have caused his friend's death (after all the polygraph "never lies"), he became confused and began to distrust his own memory of what had happened. Although he accepted the special agents' scenario of having pushed his friend over the cliff, this scenario appears to have coexisted with his pre-existing "true" memories, rather than permanently contaminating or distorting them.

Within a couple of days of signing the incriminating confession, Sergeant E became fully convinced that his initial account of what had happened on the cliff was correct and that the agents' scenario was not what had happened. This appears to have coincided with Sergeant E's confusional state resolving when the pressure of the interrogation was over, and he had time to think logically through what had really happened on the night of the tragedy. After becoming completely convinced of his innocence, Sergeant E was faced with the difficult task of proving his innocence before a court martial.

There was never any evidence to link Sergeant E with his friend's death, except for his confession, which the defence successfully argued had been obtained by psychological coercion. The case was heard by a military judge who dismissed the case after the prosecutor for the Government announced, on the eleventh day of the trial, that he would not continue to proceed with the case. Sergeant E was a free man and resigned from the US Air Force.

CONCLUSIONS

In this Chapter case examples have been provided to illustrate some of the critical components of the different psychological types of false confession that were discussed in Chapter 10. The cases demonstrate the importance of having a good conceptual framework for understanding the processes and mechanisms of false confession. The different types of false confession should not be viewed as exclusive categories, because there may be an overlap between the different groups. For example, suspects may be partly persuaded by the police that they were involved in the alleged crime, but nevertheless confess mainly for instrumental gain (i.e. in spite of partly believing the police's account of events, they confess in order to escape from an intolerable situation).

There appear to be different critical factors operating in several of the cases reviewed. Specific vulnerabilities, such as low intelligence, mental illness, recent bereavement, proneness to anxiety, high suggestibility, strong tendency to comply with people in authority, and language problems, may all contribute in varying degree to the way the accused copes with his or her predicament. However, the cases discussed clearly illustrate that false confessions are not confined to the mentally handicapped or the mentally ill. The view that apparently normal individuals would never seriously incriminate themselves when interrogated by the police is totally wrong, and this should be recognized by the judiciary.

It is clear from the cases discussed that innocent suspects do sometimes give information to the police that, on the face of it, seems to have originated from the accused, whereas the information was probably unwittingly communicated to them by the police in the first place. Such apparently "guilty knowledge", which often makes the confession look credible, is then used to substantiate the validity of the confession given. The lesson to be learned is that, unless the information obtained was unknown to the police, or actually results in the discovery of evidence to corroborate it (e.g. a body or murder weapon), then great caution should be exercised in the inferences that can be drawn from it about the accused's guilt. Police officers will undoubtedly find it difficult to believe that they could inadvertently communicate salient information to suspects in this way. They may gain some comfort from the fact that the possibility of unconscious transmission of evidence, even by qualified psychologists, alerted the British Society of Experimental and Clinical Hypnosis to recommend that psychologists called in by the police to hypnotize witnesses should be kept ignorant of all details of the crime, in order not to transmit such knowledge unwittingly during hypnotic interrogation.

CHAPTER 12

The Guildford Four and the Birmingham Six

G. H. Gudjonsson and J. A. C. MacKeith

The cases of the Guildford Four and the Birmingham Six have been described in newspapers as the worst miscarriages of justice in England this century. The two cases date back to 1975 when 10 individuals, nine Irish men and one English woman, were convicted and sentenced to life imprisonment for terrorist offences. Eight of the 10 individuals had made self-incriminating statements during custodial interrogation, which were subsequently retracted. All claimed to be innocent of the charges brought against them, and more than a decade later their convictions were eventually quashed by the Court of Appeal. In this Chapter we describe the background and circumstances to these cases, as well as some of the results of our own involvement in the medical, psychiatric and psychological assessment of the people concerned.

THE GUILDFORD FOUR

On 5th October 1974, members of the Irish Republican Army (IRA) planted bombs in two public houses in Guildford, Surrey; the Horse and Groom and the Seven Stars. No warning was given. The bomb in the Horse and Groom exploded at about 8.50 p.m. Five people were killed instantaneously and a further 57 were injured. At 9.25 p.m. there was a massive explosion at the Seven Stars. Fortunately, it had been evacuated by all the customers following the explosion in the Horse and Groom. Some injuries were caused to the landlord and his bar staff, who had failed to find the bomb during a search of the premises. The explosion caused public outrage and some 150 detectives were drafted into Guildford to work on the case.

At 10.17 p.m. on 7th November 1974, almost 5 weeks after the Guildford explosions, an IRA bomb exploded at the King's Arms in Woolwich, South London. Unlike the two time-bombs in Guildford, this bomb exploded after being thrown into the public house from outside. Two people died and a further 27 were injured. The Woolwich bomb was the sixth during that same autumn in mainland Britain and resulted in growing pressure on the police to apprehend the IRA Active Service Unit responsible (McKee and Franey, 1988).

On 28th November 1974, Paul Hill, a young Irishman, was arrested in Southampton. He was taken to Guildford Police Station and interviewed. Within 24 hours he had made a written confession about his involvement in the Guildford bombings and had implicated his friend, Gerry Conlon. Mr Conlon was arrested in Belfast on 30th November and brought to Guildford for questioning. He confessed within 2 days and implicated a number of people, including Paddy Armstrong and Carole Richardson. Armstrong and Richardson were arrested on 3rd December 1974, and within 48 hours they had also made serious self-incriminating admissions. A large number of other people were arrested in connection with the Guildford bombing case. Eight people were initially charged with the bombings. Of these, only four made confessions; Hill, Conlon, Armstrong and Richardson. All four had been denied any access to a solicitor for several days through the newly introduced Prevention of Terrorism Act. The charges against the remaining four defendants were dropped prior to the trial of the Guildford Four in September 1975.

On 16th September 1975, the trial of the Guildford Four opened at the Central Criminal Court. All four were charged with the Guildford bombings; Hill and Armstrong were in addition charged with the Woolwich bombing. The prosecution argued that Hill, Conlon and Armstrong were all members of the IRA, but no evidence was ever produced to support this claim. Miss Richardson was Armstrong's 17-year-old English girlfriend. There was no identification or forensic evidence ever produced to link them with the bombings. The prosecution relied almost exclusively on the confession statements that the four had made during the interrogation. There was highly circumstantial evidence produced at the trial in the case of Armstrong, which consisted of a Smith's pocket-watch found in a flat where Armstrong had previously stayed for a fortnight and a testimony from a fellow squatter of Armstrong's (McKee and Franey, 1988).

The defence of the Four consisted of challenging the admissibility and reliability of the confession statements, and alibi witnesses were produced to show that the defendants had all been elsewhere at the time of the bombings. The Four maintained that the confessions were not obtained voluntarily and were the result of pressure and coercion. The police completely denied impropriety of any kind. During the trial it was revealed that there were over 140 inconsistencies and inaccuracies between the statements of the four defendants. For example, Richardson said that she had been responsible for bombing both of the Guildford public houses. The police's own time plans showed that the persons who bombed the Horse and Groom could not have planted the bomb in the Seven Stars. Richardson also claimed to have thrown a bomb, which was incompatible with the prosecution case. The prosecution argued that the inconsistencies and inaccuracies in the statements were deliberate counter-interrogation ploys, the object being to confuse the police. It was a far-fetched speculation. The truth was that the inconsistencies and inaccuracies were caused by the lack of knowledge the defendants had about the bombings, because they were in no way involved.

The alibi evidence produced by the defendants was very mixed. Conlon's alibi was that he was in a hostel at Quex Road, London, on 5th October 1974. He named people who he said could give evidence about his whereabouts on that day. The prosecution were in possession of one statement which amounted to verification of his alibi, but failed to disclose it to the defence. Conlon was not implicated in relation to the Woolwich bombing and therefore only had to provide an alibi for the 5th October 1974.

Armstrong had an alibi that he was in a "squat" on that night, during which time people were arrested by the police outside the squat. Witnesses testified to having observed that event, but no evidence was provided by the police to confirm that such an incident had taken place on 5th October 1974. Armstrong also had an alibi for 7th November 1974, the night of the Woolwich bombing. That alibi was not seriously challenged in court because his confession to the police had only described his going on a reconnaissance trip on an unspecified date prior to the bombing. That made him a party to the bombing as a principal in the second degree, which was sufficient to attract a conviction.

Hill gave alibi evidence for both the Guildford and Woolwich bombings. In relation to the 5th October 1974, his alibi was that he was in Southampton with his girlfriend, Gina Clark. That alibi was discredited when Hill withdrew it in the presence of Gina Clark at the time he was being interrogated by the police, but it was subsequently reasserted by him at the trial. His alibi for the 7th November 1974 was that, at the time of the Woolwich bombing, he was visiting his aunt and uncle. There was an independent witness to his visit, whom Hill had forgotten about. For some unknown reason, although present at the Old Bailey, she was not required to give evidence at the trial.

Richardson did not need to give any alibi for 7th November 1974. Her alibi evidence concerning 5th October 1974 was by far the most compelling, because it was clearly established that between 7.30 and 8.30 on the evening of 5th October she was at the South Bank Polytechnic attending a "Jack the Lad" concert. Indeed, there was a photograph available of her posing with the band. Stretching the crucial times to their limits, the prosecution maintained that Miss Richardson could have travelled from South West London to Guildford, which was almost 40 miles away, and planted the bomb there before returning to South London about 50 minutes later. A police driver, who ignored the speed limit, claimed to have made the journey in about 45 minutes. This was used by the prosecution to argue that Richardson might have had just enough time to have been to Guildford.

The all-male jury took 27 hours to reach their unanimous verdict of "Guilty" on all charges. All four were sentenced to life imprisonment, with the following recommendations for the minimum sentence served: not less than 30 years for Conlon; not less than 35 years for Armstrong; and Hill was never to be released. Because of her young age no minimum recommendation was made for Richardson.

At the end of October 1975, the Guildford Four began to serve their life sentences, and they were to remain in prison until 19th October 1989, when their convictions were quashed by the Court of Appeal. They were free at last, after spending more than 15 years in prison for crimes they did not commit.

The fight for the release of the Guildford Four had begun soon after their conviction in 1975. Their eventual release was due to the combined efforts of many individuals. However, the four defendants would probably still be in prison had it not been for Alastair Logan, who from the beginning believed in their innocence and worked almost continuously on the case, unpaid, for over a decade. He was originally Paddy Armstrong's solicitor and for a while represented all four defendants. Later, Hill and Conlon were to be represented by other solicitors. The two have told their own stories (Hill and Bennett, 1990; Conlon, 1990).

Following the so-called "Balcombe Street Siege" in December 1975, where four IRA terrorists were arrested, two of them admitted to the police that they had carried out the Woolwich bombings and stated that Hill and Armstrong had nothing to do with it. The Director of Public Prosecutions was soon informed about this revelation, but the solicitors of Hill and Armstrong were not informed and no official action was taken (McKee and Franey, 1988). The four defendants of the Balcombe Street Active Service Unit were tried at the Central Criminal Court in January 1977, but refused to plead on the basis that they had not been charged with the Guildford and Woolwich bombings, for which they claimed responsibility in addition to the other charges.

Before their conviction, Alastair Logan interviewed the four Balcombe Street defendants and another convicted terrorist, and obtained testimony from four of them stating that they had carried out the Woolwich bombing. Two of them admitted to both the Guildford and Woolwich bombings. Furthermore, they stated that, to their knowledge, the four young people convicted of the bombings were totally innocent. This new evidence was presented at the appeal hearing of the Guildford Four in October 1977. The appeal failed and the convictions were upheld.

In 1987 a delegation led by Cardinal Hume was pressing the Home Secretary to look at the case again, with particular reference to some new evidence concerning Carole Richardson's mental state at the time of her confession in 1974. The delegation was supported by two former Home Secretaries and two distinguished law lords. On 16th January 1989, the Home Secretary announced in the House of Commons that the case of the Guildford Four was to be referred back to the Court of Appeal. The reasons given were related to new alibi evidence for two of the Guildford Four and questions over the mental state of Carole Richardson at the time of her interrogation in

December 1974 (Ford and Tendler, 1989). A date for the Court of Appeal hearing was subsequently set for January 1990. That date was brought forward to 19th October 1989.

The Avon and Somerset Police, who were appointed by the Home Secretary in 1987 to look at the confessions of the Guildford Four, discovered from the archives at the Surrey Police Headquarters that crucial evidence concerning the confessions of Hill and Armstrong had been fabricated. The Director of Public Prosecutions responded by requesting that the convictions of the Four be quashed by the Court of Appeal. Lord Chief Justice Lane and his two co-judges had no alternative but to concede that the police officers "had lied" at the trial of the Guildford Four. The convictions of the Four were accordingly quashed.

Medical and Psychological Evidence

Except for the dubious circumstantial evidence in the case of Paddy Armstrong, the only evidence against the Guildford Four was their confessions. Alastair Logan soon realized that the reliability of the confessions had to be challenged. This led to employing experts, such as psychologists and psychiatrists. The first expert to become involved was Dr Tooley, a consultant psychiatrist at the London Hospital in London.

On 8th October 1975, after a day in court, Armstrong was given a barbiturate-aided interview by Dr Tooley. The intention was not to enhance Armstrong's recollection about events in 1974; the drug was used on the assumption that Armstrong would be more likely to tell the truth whilst under the influence of the drug. The information obtained confirmed Armstrong's previous accounts of the police interviews and his state of mind at the time.

The assumption that Armstrong could not have lied whilst under the influence of the drug, had he so wished, was ill-founded in view of the poor validity of barbiturate-aided interviews as a "truth drug" (see Chapter 8 for a detailed discussion on this point).

On 1st October 1977, Armstrong was interviewed in Wakefield Prison by Lionel Haward, a Professor in Clinical Psychology at the University of Surrey, Guildford. Professor Haward induced in Armstrong a light hypnotic trance and interviewed him about his involvement in the Guildford and Woolwich bombings. The purpose of the hypnosis-aided interview was similar to that of Dr Tooley. Haward asked Armstrong in detail about his experience and knowledge of firearms. Haward had previously been a firearm instructor in the Royal Air Force (RAF) and concluded that Armstrong had no experience of firearms and that he was an unlikely IRA candidate. Furthermore, Haward concluded from Armstrong's answers during the hypnosis that he had falsely confessed because of immense anxiety and fear of the police.

Before the appeal of the Guildford Four in 1977, Alastair Logan asked Barrie Irving, a social psychologist who had provided evidence at the inquiry into the Maxwell Confait case, to comment on Armstrong's confession statements. He did not examine Armstrong but carefully examined the relevant documents in the case. Irving highlighted a number of concerns about Armstrong's confession, which related to his poor physical and mental state at the time of the interrogation, and concluded that Armstrong's confession should not have been accepted without corroboration.

What was the "new" medical evidence that resulted in the Home Secretary reopening the case in January 1988? This related to the mental state of Carole Richardson in December 1974 and questions over medication she was said to have received from a police surgeon who had been called to examine her prior to her confession. We had examined Miss Richardson in April 1986 at Styal Prison at the request of the Prison Medical Service. A medical officer was very concerned about her welfare. He believed her to be innocent of the terrorist offences of which she was convicted and wanted an independent assessment conducted. The issue of false confession was relevant to his concern about appropriate psychiatric treatment of Richardson.

During our first interview with Richardson (there were to be further meetings) we spent about 5 hours with her. Miss Richardson's demeanour was impressive. She looked pleased to see us when we arrived, although she was not expecting us. During the next 5 hours she appeared to try hard to answer our questions. We kept firing difficult questions at her but all her answers were spontaneous and seemed unguarded. Her vulnerable qualities were also evident. She proved to be articulate and intelligent. Although psychiatrically well at the time of our interview, she was very vulnerable to interrogative pressure and this was clearly evident on psychological testing. Further testing repeatedly demonstrated her tendency to avoid conflict and confrontation when faced with pressure. Our concern was also about Richardson's mental state whilst in police custody in 1974, which included her state of withdrawal from illicit barbiturates, on which she was dependent at that time. We expressed great concern about the reliability of Richardson's confession in our reports to the Prison Medical Service.

However, in spite of the firm conclusions we had reached in our reports, the Home Secretary made no mention of them in his address to Parliament in January 1987, when he decided to remit the case of the Birmingham Six back to the Court of Appeal but refused to do the same for the Guildford Four. There was some strong media coverage about our findings and in August 1987 we submitted fresh reports directly to the Home Office with the permission of Mr Logan, by whom we were then instructed. Our revised reports were partly the basis on which the Home Secretary decided to reopen the case. An important development was that a social worker colleague of ours, Don Steuart-Pownall, had been able to trace the whereabouts of the police surgeon, Dr Makos, who had examined Miss Richardson in police custody in December 1974. One of us (MacKeith) interviewed Dr Makos abroad in August 1987, when he stated that he had injected Richardson with pethidine shortly before her first confession to him on 4th December. Several months later, when interviewed by the police for the second time, the doctor withdrew his revelation to Dr MacKeith, which had been repeated to the police during their first interview with him. In fact, whether or not the police surgeon had administered pethidine to Richardson, which she incidentally had no recollection of, may actually have been of no great significance. Even if he had not done so, she would have been suffering from barbiturate withdrawal at the time of her confession.

In fact, Richardson had been abusing various drugs for several months preceding her arrest on 3rd December 1974. On the day of her arrest she had been taking Tuinal barbiturate tablets, which were obtained about 2 days prior to her arrest. She reported to us that taking drugs alleviated thoughts and feelings which made her unhappy. She had made attempts to come off drugs but had experienced a period of tremulousness, depression, physical weakness and restlessness.

Richardson's Confession

Miss Richardson was arrested at about 7.00 p.m. on 3rd December 1974. She claimed to have taken about 20 Tuinal capsules that day. Her interrogation began the following day; the time at which it commenced is disputed. The police were questioning her about her whereabouts on 5th October (the time of the Guildford bombing) and during the day she appears to have become increasingly distressed. A police surgeon, Dr Makos, was called in to examine Richardson at about 8.15 p.m. In his company, and in the presence of a woman police constable, Richardson is alleged to have admitted to having planted the bomb in Guildford with Armstrong. Richardson has no recollection of having made the admission to Dr Makos, and indeed disputes having done so.

Miss Richardson was to make a total of four statements to the police. Three were in her own handwriting. The four statements were dated 4th, 5th, 6th, and 9th December 1974. Richardson alleges that after her arrest she was preoccupied about getting out of the police station, because for days she was not allowed to notify anybody of her arrest and found the police pressure very difficult to cope with. She says she confessed falsely mainly out of fear. Various matters were suggested to her by the police, and some of the statements were dictated by the police, whereas others she knowingly invented to satisfy the police. Part of the problem was that the intense questioning by the police made her confused and she began to doubt her own recollections (e.g. where she had been on the day of the Guildford bombing). She was not allowed to see a solicitor until 11th December, when she told him that she was innocent of the crimes she was accused of. On 12th December Richardson was interviewed at Guildford Police Station by two detectives from the Bomb Squad at New Scotland Yard. She again admitted involvement in the Guildford bombings, although the interview appears not to have been in any way coercive. However, from Richardson's point of view, she did not want the police to reinterrogate her and went along with what she had told the police in her last statement.

Possibly the most psychologically interesting part of Richardson's reaction to the intense police interrogation relates to the extent to which she eventually began to believe that perhaps she had planted the bomb in Guildford without having any recollection of having done so. According to her own account, she initially confessed as a way of escaping from an intolerable situation. The police pressure was unbearable and she went along with the police interrogators, knowing that she had nothing to do with the explosions, or indeed with the IRA. After realizing that she was not going to be released, all she wanted was to be left alone. This Miss Richardson believes is the main reason for her false confession, in conjunction with the fear she had of the police. It was not so much the interrogators' questions that bothered her, but their attitude and apparent confidence about her involvement. After being allegedly hit by a policewoman, she realized that the police were in full control of the situation and that there was no point in resisting. At this point her confession was of the *coerced-compliant* type. That is, she knew she had nothing to do with the bombings but went along with the interrogators as a way of easing the pressure.

After several days in police custody, Richardson began to believe that perhaps she had been involved in the Guildford bombing and was blocking it out from her memory. In other words, her alleged involvement in the Guildford bombings had become *internalized*. A decisive factor appears to have been the police officers' confidence in her involvement and the fact that she could not recall precisely where she had been on 5th October 1974. By this time she had become very confused; the "memory distrust syndrome" had begun to set in. After having spent about 2 days in Brixton Prison on remand, she felt the pressure easing off and she began to gain complete confidence in her own recollection of events, particularly with regard to her innocence.

More Recent Developments

It was alleged in a *Panorama* programme in 1990 that at the trial of the Guildford Four in 1975 and at the appeal in 1977 the prosecution withheld from the defence crucial forensic and alibi evidence, which might very well have altered the outcome of the trial had it been known to the jury. The "suppressed" forensic evidence linked the bombs that exploded in Guildford and Woolwich to several other bombs, which had exploded both before and after the Guildford and Woolwich bombs. It strongly indicated that all the bombs, 32 in total, had a "common source of supply, information and expertise". Furthermore, it pointed to the operation of a single IRA unit operating on the mainland of Britain. Some of the members of this unit were known to the police and had been identified through fingerprints which had been discovered on bombs that had failed to explode. These had no known associations with the Guildford Four. The remaining unidentified fingerprints were not those of the Guildford Four, neither were they ever questioned about the other bombings.

The other "new" evidence allegedly suppressed by the prosecution relates to Gerry Conlon's alibi. He has always maintained that at the time of the Guildford bombings he was in a Roman Catholic hostel in Kilburn, London, which is over 30 miles away from Guildford. At his trial it was argued by the prosecution that Conlon's alibi totally lacked corroboration. In fact, according to the recent *Panorama* programme, two independent witnesses had corroborated his statements to the police, but crucial evidence from one witness was withheld from the defence by the prosecution.

At present, all the evidence in the Guildford Four case is being reviewed by the Judicial Inquiry set up by Sir John May. The purpose of the inquiry is to study the circumstances surrounding the convictions of the Guildford Four, including how the confessions came to be made. Price (1989) argues that if similar previous inquiries are anything to go by, then the outcome will do nothing to exonerate the innocent Guildford Four. He states:

> "Over the past three decades there have been several similar inquiries into the behaviour of the police and the legal system: Brabin on Evans, Fisher on Confait and Calcutt on the Cyprus ex-servicemen. None did anything to exonerate the innocent victims concerned, and one expressly purported to reconvict them. All displayed an astounding naivety about the psychology of admissions made in police custody" (p. 18).

Time will tell about the outcome of Sir John May's Inquiry into the Guildford Four case. The early indication is that the inquiry is being conducted seriously, conscientiously and thoroughly. The advantage over previous Judicial Inquiries is that the psychological understanding about the phenomenon of false confession has advanced considerably in recent years. This greatly widens the knowledge base upon which Sir John May and his team can draw before forming their conclusions.

THE BIRMINGHAM SIX

On 21st November 1974, two public houses in Birmingham were bombed by the IRA. Twenty-one people were killed. Later that same night four Irishmen (Gerry Hunter, Richard McIlkenny, William Power and John Walker) were stopped for questioning as they were boarding a ferry to Ireland. They were asked to accompany the police to Morecambe Police Station for forensic tests. They happened to mention that one of their friends (Patrick Hill) had been travelling with them. Hill, who had already boarded the ferry, was arrested. The five men were subjected to a Greiss test by Dr Frank Skuse, a Home Office scientist. The method, named after the chemist who discovered it, was at the time thought to be a foolproof way of detecting nitroglycerine, which is a substance commonly found on people's hands if they have been handling explosives. Nitroglycerine was allegedly found on the hands of two of the six men (Power and Hill). Dr Skuse told the police that he was 99% sure that two of the men had recently handled commercial explosives (Mullin, 1989). As the five men were travelling together, they were all subjected to extreme pressure during the interrogations that were to follow (Mullin, 1989). The first to confess was Power. He signed a six-page confession, implicating himself and five of his friends in the Birmingham bombings. The fifth man, Hugh Callaghan, who was not travelling with the others at the time of their arrest, was arrested the following night at his home. Like McIlkenny, Power, and Walker, Callaghan was to sign a confession to the Birmingham bombings. Two of the men (Hill and Hunter) did not write or sign any self-incriminating statements, but the police allege that they made some verbal admissions which both have always strongly denied that they ever made.

The six men were charged with the largest number of murders in British history and in June 1975 they were tried in Lancaster. The trial lasted 45 days. The evidence against the six men consisted of Dr Skuse's forensic evidence and the written confessions of four of the men. There was also circumstantial evidence about associations with known IRA people. The admissibility of the confessions was disputed by the defence on the basis that they had been beaten out of the defendants. The judge allowed the confessions to go before the jury. All six defendants were convicted. As the judge, Mr Justice Bridge, sentenced them to life imprisonment, he stated:

> "You stand convicted on each of twenty-one counts, on the clearest and most overwhelming evidence I have ever heard, of the crime of murder" (Mullin, 1989, p. 206).

As recent evidence indicates, the Birmingham Six were wrongly convicted in 1975, in spite of the judge's strong words about "overwhelming evidence". In the United Kingdom during the late 1980s new evidence was gathered and public feeling about the defendants' innocence grew. Various people argued for their innocence, including Christopher Mullin, a Member of Parliament. Sixteen years were to pass before the Appeal Court eventually quashed the convictions of the six men.

On 28th October 1985, *World in Action*, a Granada Television programme, presented evidence that seriously challenged, if not completely demolished, the validity of Dr Skuse's forensic science findings. The programme had commissioned two scientists to carry out a series of Greiss tests on a number of common substances, including nitrocellulose. The results showed that there are a number of common substances that will give a positive reaction on a Greiss test, including those that can be obtained from being in contact with playing cards. The five men who were tested for nitroglycerine had been playing cards shortly before their arrest, which could explain why two of them apparently had traces of nitroglycerine on their hands. In other words, the positive Greiss test reaction on the hands of two of the men could quite easily have been due to an innocent contamination.

Mullin (1989) claims to have traced and interviewed three of the men who are responsible for the Birmingham bombings. According to Mullin, they made it clear to him that none of the Birmingham Six were ever members of the Birmingham IRA, neither had they been involved in any way in the bombings for which they were convicted. The information that these people gave of the Birmingham bombings suggested an apparent insightful knowledge about the explosions and supported the claims of innocence of the six men convicted. In 1990, Granada Television's *World in Action* programme named four men who were alleged to be the real bombers.

In October 1986, an ex-policeman, Tom Clarke, contacted Chris Mullin and told him that in 1974 he had been on night duty at Queen's Road Police Station during the two nights that the Birmingham Six were held there. Clarke (Mullin, 1989) gave an account of ill-treatment of the men during their period in custody, which included a dog handler encouraging a dog to bark throughout the night in an attempt to keep the six suspects awake.

In the autumn of 1987 the case of the Birmingham Six went to the Court of Appeal. The defence argued on two fronts: First, that the forensic evidence presented by Dr Skuse at the original trial was no longer valid; second, that the written confessions of the four men were unreliable and involuntary. Evidence to support this claim was given by Tom Clarke, the ex-police officer, and other witnesses. In January 1988, Lord Lane dismissed their appeal against conviction and stated:

"The longer this hearing has gone on, the more convinced this court has become that the verdict of the trial was correct".

On Thursday 14th March 1991, the Birmingham Six finally won their freedom. In March 1990 the Home Secretary had ordered a new inquiry into the case after representations from the men's solicitors in which the forensic police evidence was challenged. Following the Inquiry of Sir John May into the wrongful conviction in the Maguire case (May, 1990), which was closely linked to the Guildford Four case, the credibility of the forensic science techniques used in the Birmingham Six case to test for traces of explosives was totally demolished. In August 1990, the Home Secretary referred the case back to the Court of Appeal after the police inquiry had, quite independently, found discrepancies in the police interview record of one of the men. It seemed, as in the Guildford Four case, that the police had fabricated documentary evidence against the six men. The Director of Public Prosecutions could no longer rely on either the forensic or the police evidence that convicted the six men in 1975. The Court of Appeal heard the case at the beginning of 1991 and quashed the convictions of the six men.

The Psychological Findings

Considering that two of the six defendants did not make a written confession during the intensive interrogation in 1974, whereas four did, it is interesting

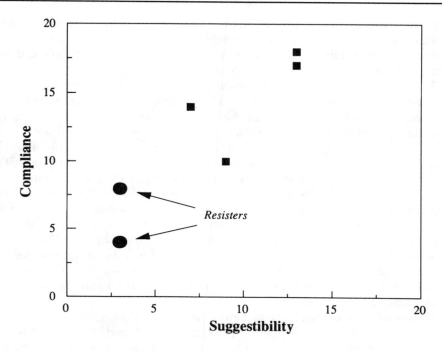

Figure 12.1. The suggestibility and compliance scores of the Birmingham Six defendants

to look at their personality in terms of suggestibility and compliance. Thirteen years after their interrogation we had the opportunity in 1987 of assessing them, which included assessing their cognitive and personality functioning. The Gudjonsson Suggestibility Scales and the Gudjonsson Compliance Scale were administered to the six defendants whilst they were serving their sentence in prison. The GSS 1 and GCS scores are given in Figure 12.1. It is clear from the graph that there is a great variability in the suggestibility and compliance scores among the six defendants. Two were very high on both measures and two scored very low. The remaining two defendants' scores fall in between the two pairs. In fact, their scores fall in the average range. It is of interest to note that the two defendants who scored the lowest on the scales were the two defendants who did not confess. Hill's scores were particularly low.

The importance of the psychological findings is that they highlight immense variation in the suggestibility and compliance scores of the six prisoners, which appears to reflect whether or not they had made written confessions in 1974. The implications are that their relative suggestibility and compliance have remained stable for over 13 years, and that their personality at the time influenced how they responded to the police interrogation in 1974. Of course, nobody knows exactly what suggestibility and compliance scores they would have obtained had they been tested prior to their arrest in 1974. We had some behavioural ratings of compliance completed by relatives of the six men with regard to their behaviour prior to their arrest. The findings corresponded very well with the men's self-report compliance scores.

The present analysis involves placing the men's psychological test scores retrospectively in the context of their behaviour in 1974. That is obviously different to being able to predict behaviour prospectively. One problem is the possibility that the behaviour itself (i.e. confessing) somehow influences how people subsequently perform on the psychological tests. This may be problematic, especially in the case of compliance as measured by the GCS, because it is a self-report inventory. Having previously given in to interrogative pressure (e.g. by confessing) this may itself alter suspects' own perceptions of themselves. The change in their perception of themselves could then affect how they fill in the self-report scale. This is much less likely to be a problem on the Suggestibility Scales, because these measure how people respond *behaviourally* to a simulated interrogation, and do not rely on self-report. However, this does not exclude the remote possibility that the shock of having confessed itself influences how suspects respond behaviourally to interrogation in the future.

The respective personality characteristics of the Birmingham Six were not considered relevant to the legal arguments in the Court of Appeal, because the emphasis was on the physical coerciveness of the police tactics used and on the unreliability of the forensic science evidence. The individual strengths and weaknesses of the six men are of interest because they possibly explain why four of the men confessed whilst two did not.

CONCLUSIONS

Many people would argue that the cases of the Guildford Four and the Birmingham Six represent the worst cases of miscarriage of justice in Britain this century. In the former case four defendants spent over 14 years in prison before having their convictions quashed by the Court of Appeal in October 1989. Almost 2½ years later the Birmingham Six had their convictions quashed, having spent about 16 years in prison.

There are certain similarities and differences between the cases of the Guildford Four and the Birmingham Six. Both cases arose out of the devastating IRA bombing campaign in mainland Britain in 1974. The police were under immense public pressure to apprehend the culprits and bring them to justice. Emergency laws were laid down in Parliament to deal with increased threats from terrorist activities, which allowed the police to detain people suspected of terrorist activities for extended periods without being charged. In both cases the police are alleged to have coerced the defendants to confess by subjecting them to psychological and physical pressure. Many years later, the police were discovered to have fabricated evidence concerning some of the defendants' interview records. Evidence favourable to the defence is alleged to have been suppressed by the prosecution when the cases went to court and at their appeal hearings.

All the Guildford Four made written self-incriminating confessions, which they subsequently retracted and alleged were made under duress. Four of the Birmingham Six made written confessions, two did not. All of the Birmingham Six allege that they were extensively physically threatened and assaulted during their custodial interrogation in 1974; the Guildford Four have also made allegations of physical threats and assaults, but of lesser severity than those reported by the Birmingham Six.

Whereas the Guildford Four were convicted on the basis of uncorroborated confessions, there was forensic science evidence presented against two of the Birmingham Six, evidence which has subsequently been totally discredited.

In this Chapter we have presented psychological data on one of the Guildford Four (Richardson) and on all of the Birmingham Six. The most striking psychological finding regarding the Birmingham Six is the difference in personality scores between the two defendants who did not confess and the four who did. Thirteen years after their interrogations, the two defendants who did not make written confessions scored exceptionally low on tests of suggestibility and compliance. We have argued that this may explain why they were able to resist extensive and coercive interrogations in 1974, whilst the remaining four, who were subjected to similarly intense questioning, confessed.

All of the 8 defendants who made written self-incriminating confessions made confessions that are of the *coerced-compliant* type. However, there is some evidence provided from one of the Guildford Four (Richardson) that "saying may become believing" as Bem (1966) would describe it. That is, a *coerced-compliant* type of false confession may turn into a *coerced-internalized* type, given the right circumstances. The reason for this seems to be that after confessing for instrumental gain, the persistent questioning continues and the accused becomes increasingly confused and puzzled by the interrogators' apparent confidence in the accused's guilt. In Richardson's case, she had difficulty in recalling what she had been doing on the day of the Guildford bombing and kept asking for her diary, which had been left behind in the squat where she lived. It was only after the pressure of the police questioning ceased that she says she became totally convinced of her innocence. Conlon (1990) describes a similar, but less striking, example of having temporarily begun to doubt his innocence during the intense police interrogation.

CHAPTER 13

Legal Aspects
of Disputed Confessions

When assessing a case of retracted or disputed confession, the clinical psychologist needs to be familiar with the relevant law and practice. The reason is twofold. First, without some basic understanding of the relevant legal issues, the assessment may not cover the crucial areas of concern. For example, in many countries certain safeguards are provided for mentally ill and handicapped persons and, without knowing what these are, the expert witness may fail to assess the relevant disabilities or psychological vulnerabilities. Second, the expert witnesses' findings have to be placed in the context of the relevant legal issues. For example, what is the relevance of the psychological findings for the court's evaluation of psychological "coercion", "voluntariness", "oppression" and "reliability"? Of central importance is an understanding of the "exclusionary rules" and suspects' legal rights during custodial interrogation.

In this Chapter, the background is given to the basic legal issues that are relevant to the psychological and psychiatric assessment of disputed confessions in England and the United States of America. A particularly detailed account is given about mental handicap and the special protection to which such persons are entitled under English legal provisions.

THE ENGLISH LAW ON CONFESSIONS

In English Law, defendants can be convicted on the basis of uncorroborated confessions (Mitchell and Richardson, 1985, p. 1093; Zuckerman, 1989), and in practice they often are. In Scottish Law, on the other hand, there must be some evidence from an independent source that can corroborate or substantiate the confession (McEwan, 1991).

The central legal issues regarding confessions in England are the "confession" and "exclusion" issues (Mirfield, 1985). The "confession" issue deals with claims by the defence that the alleged confession was never made in the first place. This is particularly likely with verbal admissions which have not been written down and signed. The "exclusion" issue is the one more commonly raised in court. Here the defendant admits to having made the confession that is alleged by the prosecution, but claims that it was made under coercion and duress, or by hope of some advantage (e.g. being free to go home). In other words, the confession is said to have been made under such circumstances as to make it either involuntary or unreliable, or both.

The legal significance of confession evidence in England and Wales is regulated by the Police and Criminal Evidence Act (PACE) 1984 (Home Office, 1985a), which began to be implemented in January 1986. The Act is supplemented by four Codes of Practice, referred to as Codes A, B, C and D (Home Office, 1985b, 1991). Prior to the new Act the law was guided by the Judges' Rules and Home Office Administrative Directions (Home Office, 1978), which had been originally issued in 1912 and revised in 1918 and 1964 (Morris, 1980). The Judges' Rules stated that the fundamental condition for the determination of admissibility is that the self-incriminating statement:

> "... shall have been voluntary, in the sense that it has not been obtained from him by fear of prejudice or hope of advantage, exercised or held out by a person in authority, or by oppression."

Administrative Directions supplemented the Judges' Rules and specified the conditions under which a suspect was to be questioned. One of the conditions most relevant to psychology was that police officers should apply special care when interviewing people with a mental handicap. Breaches of the Judges' Rules and Administrative Directions by police officers could result in judges rendering the confession inadmissible either because it was not considered voluntary or had been the product of oppressive questioning. However, the legal safeguards contained in the Judges' Rules and Administrative Directions were in fact commonly ignored without the confession being rendered inadmissible at the defendant's trial (Irving, 1990).

The Judges' Rules came under serious criticism (Softley, 1980) and, following the Fisher Report into the Confait case (Fisher, 1977), the Royal Commission on Criminal Procedure was set up in 1978 to evaluate the process of pre-trial criminal procedure in England and Wales. The Royal Commission published a number of Research Studies reports (e.g. Baldwin and McConville, 1980; Barnes and Webster, 1980; Irving, 1980; Irving and Hilgendorf, 1980; Morris, 1980; Softley, 1980), where various recommendations were made about changes in custodial interrogation legislation. Many of the recommendations were incorporated into PACE and its Codes of Practice. The new legislation superseded the provisions in the Judges' Rules as well as introducing new material and safeguards.

The recommendations of the Royal Commission were significantly influenced by the empirical data gathered by researchers, much of which was psychological in nature (Irving, 1990). Therefore, psychological thinking and the empirical data presented to the Royal Commission influenced, to a certain extent, the development of PACE and its Codes of Practice.

The new Act (PACE) attempts to provide a working definition for the word "confession". It is construed in Section 82(1) as including:

"... any statement wholly or partly adverse to the person who made it, whether made to a person in authority or not and whether made in words or otherwise" (Home Office, 1985a, p. 75).

As far as the admissibility of confessions is concerned, there are two broad tests, both of which are contained in Section 76(2) of the Act. These are:

"If, in any proceedings where the prosecution proposes to give in evidence a confession made by an accused person, it is represented to the court that the confession was or may have been obtained:

(a) by oppression of the person who made it; or
(b) in consequence of anything said or done which was likely, in the circumstances existing at the time, to render unreliable any confession which might be made by him in consequence thereof;

the court shall not allow the confession to be given in evidence against him except in so far as the prosecution proves to the court beyond reasonable doubt that the confession (notwithstanding that it may be true) was obtained as aforesaid" (Home Office, 1985a, p. 73).

The recent case of *R. v. Cox* (1990, Crim. L. R. 276) demonstrates that the crucial question with regard to Section 76, is whether the confession was made in consequence of anything done likely to render it unreliable, not whether it is true. Cox had an IQ of 58 and was abnormally suggestible, but he was nevertheless interviewed by the police in the absence of an "appropriate adult", which was a breach of the Codes of Practice (Code C: 13.1). His appeal against conviction was successful, because the trial judge had wrongly focused on the likely truthfulness of the confession, rather than its reliability.

The concept of "voluntariness", which was used in the Judges' Rules, has been replaced by the concept of "reliability". This means that confessions are excluded when it can be shown that they were obtained by such means or in conditions which are likely to render them *unreliable*. The concept of "oppression" is retained in the new Act and

"... includes torture, inhuman or degrading treatment, and the use of threat of violence (whether or not amounting to torture)" (Home Office, 1985a, p. 73).

Besides Section 76(2), two further Sections are relevant to possible exclusion of confession evidence. These are Sections 78(1) and 82(3), respectively. The former deals with the "exclusion of unfair evidence", whilst the latter leaves some room for exclusion, for whatever reason, at the judge's discretion. Section 78(1) states:

"In any proceedings the court may refuse to allow evidence on which the prosecution proposes to rely to be given if it appears to the court that, having regard to all the circumstances, including the circumstances in which the evidence was obtained, the admission of the evidence would have such an adverse effect on the fairness of the proceedings, that the court ought not to admit it" (Home Office, 1985a, p. 73).

Section 82(3) states:

"Nothing in this Part of this Act shall prejudice any power of a court to exclude evidence (whether by preventing questions from being put or otherwise) at its discretion" (Home Office, 1985a, p. 76).

Birch (1989) describes the three legal "tests" as comprising three "hurdles", where each hurdle needs to be completed before the next one can be attempted. The first hurdle relates to Section 76. Here the burden of proof lies with the prosecution. That is, they have to show that the confession was not obtained by oppression or in a manner that is likely to render it unreliable.

The second hurdle relates to Section 78. Here the burden of proof is not made explicit in the Act, but it is commonly believed that it rests with the defence. This means that the defence has to present evidence to indicate that all the circumstances of the case are such that it would be unfair if the proceedings were to use the confession. Here it is the fairness of the proceedings that is crucial, rather than any arguments about police impropriety, although impropriety can also be relevant to the legal arguments (Feldman, 1990).

The final hurdle, if the other two have failed, lies with Section 82. The full discretionary powers of the judge to exclude evidence under this Section are not made clear in the Act, but they cover the exclusion of evidence when the prejudicial effect outweighs its probative value. According to Birch (1989):

"In the context of confessions this would mean evidence the reliability of which is more apparent than real, for example the confession of an unusually suggestible defendant" (p. 97).

The two most important Sections with regard to confession evidence are undoubtedly Sections 76 and 78 (Birch, 1989; McEwan, 1991). There are a number of differences between these two Sections, one of which, as already stated, relates to where the onus of the burden of proof lies. Perhaps the most fundamental difference, however, relates to discretionary powers. That is, Section 76 involves "proof of facts", whereas Section 78 involves "the exercise of judgement by the court" (Birch, 1989, p. 96). Another difference is the emphasis in Section 76 on police behaviour and the reluctance of judges to include under this provision unreliability due solely to internal factors (e.g. drug withdrawal, disturbed mental state). There is generally the need to establish some kind of impropriety with regard to Section 76; that is, it would be unlikely to succeed in cases of ordinary and proper police questioning. However, there are some notable exceptions. For example, in the case of *Harvey* (1988, Crim. L.R. 241), Section 76(2)(b) was successfully invoked for a mentally disordered woman of low intelligence who confessed, allegedly in order to protect her lover from prosecution after hearing him confessing to murder. In a more recent case (*R. v. Moss*, Court of Appeal, March 9, 1990), the Court of Appeal held that the confession of a man of borderline IQ should not have gone before the jury. The crucial confession was elicited after the man had been in custody for several days and was interviewed without a solicitor being present. He was convicted of an indecent assault exclusively on the basis of his confession and was sentenced to 5 years' imprisonment. His conviction was successfully appealed against on the basis of Sections 76 and 78.

Section 78 may be violated with or without any impropriety on the part of the police. The kinds of impropriety that may lead to invoking Section 78 include deliberate deceit and deception, such as lying to the suspect that his fingerprints were found at the scene of the crime (e.g. *Mason*, 1987, 3 All E.R. 481), or denying a suspect access to a solicitor on inadequate grounds (e.g. *Alladice*, 188, Crim. L.R. 608). The case of *Goldenberg* (1989, Crim. L.R. 678) is commonly used to indicate that a confession resulting from a disturbed mental state without proof of impropriety by the police may not be excluded under Section 76 (b). This case involved a heroin addict who claimed to have confessed as a result of drug withdrawal symptoms, and the Court of Appeal held that Section 76 (b) requires the unreliability to be the consequence of something *said* or *done*, and by someone other than the suspect. The implication is that self-induced or inherent factors that undermine reliability have to be dealt with under Sections 78 or 82.

McEwan (1991) argues that PACE is simply not designed to deal with the problem of self-induced unreliability. She recommends greater judicial acceptance of psychological evidence (e.g. personality characteristics that make people susceptible to unreliable testimony without mental illness or mental handicap).

Emphasis on the characteristics of the individual when interpreting psychological coercion is recognized by some judges. For example, in the judgement of *R. v. Priestley* (1966, 50, Cr. App. R. 183) it was stated:

> "What may be oppressive as regards a child, an invalid or an old man, or somebody inexperienced in the ways of the world, may turn out not to be oppressive when one finds that the accused is of tough character and an experienced man of the world" (quoted in Bevan and Lidstone, 1985, p. 299).

The Mentally Ill or Handicapped

Section 77(1) of the Act deals with confessions obtained from persons with a mental handicap. It states that in such cases the court shall warn the jury:

> ". . . that there is a special need for caution before convicting the accused in reliance on the confession".

The warning is contingent upon:

(a) "The case against the accused depends wholly or substantially on a confession by him; and
(b) The court is satisfied:
    (i) That he is mentally handicapped; and
    (ii) That the confession was not made in the presence of an independent person."

Section 77 (3) of the Act defines a person with "mental handicap" as one who "is in a state of arrested or incomplete development of mind which includes significant impairment of intelligence and social functioning" (p. 73). PACE gives greater protection to persons with a mental handicap than the Judges' Rules, apparently as a result of the adverse publicity following from the Confait case (Bevan and Lidstone, 1985). No mention is made in PACE about a similar protection for the mentally ill, but this is covered in the accompanying Codes of Practice, where it falls under the heading of "mental disorder" (Home Office, 1991). There have been some changes made to the original Codes of Practice, which came into force on 1st April 1991 (Home Office, 1991). These are described in detail by a document produced by the Metropolitan Police (1991).

The Codes of Practice (Code C) have important provisions for the detention and interviewing of "special groups", such as foreigners who do not speak much English, juveniles, deaf people and persons who are mentally ill or handicapped (Home Office, 1991). Where communicating in English is a problem, an interpreter must be called to assist. The relevant legal provision for other "special groups" includes:

"A juvenile or a person who is mentally disordered or handicapped, whether suspected or not, must not be interviewed or asked to provide or sign a written statement in the absence of the appropriate adult unless" (p. 60). . . "delay will involve an immediate risk of harm to persons or serious loss of or damage to property" (p. 74).

The reasoning for the special protection of the mentally ill or handicapped relates to their being considered disadvantaged during police interviewing (i.e. they are considered to be "vulnerable persons"). More specifically, they may:

". . . without knowing or wishing to do so, be particularly prone in certain circumstances to provide information which is unreliable, misleading or self-incriminating" (p. 79).

Considering the potential vulnerabilities of mentally handicapped persons from a broader perspective than is specifically indicated in PACE and the Codes of Practice, one can list a number of ways in which they may be disadvantaged or psychologically vulnerable during custodial interrogation. Some of these are as follows.

1. The Question of Identification

A proper definition of mental handicap for legal and clinical purposes needs to take into consideration the suspect's social functioning as well as any intellectual deficits. The former relate to the ability of the person to look after his or her practical needs (i.e. caring for themselves) and take responsibility. This is more difficult to assess objectively than intellectual skills.

There is empirical evidence from American studies that the majority of mentally handicapped defendants do not receive a pre-trial evaluation of their handicap (Brown, Courtless and Silber, 1970; McAfee and Gural, 1988). This means that only those with the most severe handicap will be identified (Allen, 1966; Denkowski and Denkowski, 1985). Those who are only mildly mentally handicapped are least likely to be identified, especially if their social functioning seems relatively satisfactory. At one extreme one may have an autistic individual, whose social functioning is always severely impaired, but whose intellectual functioning may be relatively unimpaired. The police would probably identify the handicap because of the social deficits and the necessary safeguards provided in law would be invoked. At the other extreme, which is undoubtedly much more common, the police interview an individual who is significantly impaired intellectually but whose social functioning seems adequate and masks the true intellectual deficits. Of course, there may also be those cases where both intellectual and social deficits are present, but the police nevertheless fail to identify or take appropriate action.

In my experience of several hundred court cases, the police often fail to identify mental handicap and interview the suspect without an "appropriate adult" and a solicitor being present. When the case goes to court, a later pre-trial assessment may reveal the handicap and the self-incriminating confession is thus likely to be ruled inadmissible by the judge. Therefore, the failure of the police to identify mental handicap may prevent the suspect from exercising his or her full rights during custodial interrogation. If the handicap is still not identified when the case goes to court, then a miscarriage of justice may result. In other words, the mental handicap of the defendant, which may have significant bearing on the reliability of the confession and the fairness of the proceedings, cannot be taken into consideration by the judge and jury unless it has been correctly identified. Therefore, identification of the handicap during the early part of the police investigation may be crucial for both the defendant and the police.

Possibly, the most common reason for the failure of police officers to identify mental handicap prior to or during custodial interrogation is that many mildly mentally handicapped adults function quite well socially (Richardson, 1978). This can disguise their more subtle disabilities. Another problem is that many police officers appear unaware of how to identify suspects with a mild mental handicap, and why they may be vulnerable to giving unreliable information during interrogation (Williamson, 1990). Even when police officers are presented with unequivocal information about specific vulnerabilities (e.g.

previous medical history), many fail to identify the suspect as being "at risk" (Pearse, 1991). The younger officers were much poorer at identification than the older officers, which indicates that maturity and experience are important for appreciating vulnerabilities.

It is very important to realize that it is not just the police who commonly fail to identify mild mental handicap. I have come across numerous cases where prison medical officers and psychiatrists have grossly overestimated the intellectual functioning of defendants; an error which could have resulted in miscarriages of justice. *Clinical impressions by mental health professionals about the defendant's intellectual strengths and weaknesses are often misleading.* In one case, a prison medical officer described a defendant in court as being of "average intelligence". It was only during the cross-examination of the doctor, at my instigation, that it transpired that his conclusion was based on a clinical impression from a very brief (5–10 minute) interview and certainly not on actual testing. I had tested the defendant and found him to have a Full Scale IQ of 69!

There is some recent evidence (Clare and Gudjonsson, 1991a) that the majority of persons with a mild mental handicap do not realize that they should inform the police of their handicap if detained at a police station. Furthermore, 30% of the subjects in the study stated that they would not tell the police about their mental handicap, because they regarded the information as private and personal. This means that many persons with a mental handicap may deliberately try to cover up their deficits, including reading disability, which may inadvertently mislead the police.

Another problem with the identification of mental handicap is that professional views on what should be the upper limit with regard to IQ vary immensely. Denkowski and Denkowski (1985) report that the cut-off scores for legal purposes range from 60 to 78. In the WAIS-R manual a score below 70 is considered to define mental handicap. The cut-off point of 70 is quite arbitrary and was chosen on an historical rather than scientific basis. In fact, an IQ of 75, which represents the bottom 5% of the adult population, would be more in line with scientific thinking about a significant impairment and abnormality. An IQ of 70 represents the bottom 2% of the general population and it is the figure that the Lord Chief Justice adopted in the case of *Masih* (1986, Crim. L.R. 395). He considered an IQ of 69 or below as a definition of mental handicap. The problems with this rigid legal definition are that no account is taken of social functioning and the "standard error of measurement" of any given intelligence test. In certain cases, an assessment of social functioning is undoubtedly relevant to the deliberations of the judge and jury.

The "standard error of measurement" (SEM) of a given test has an important legal significance (Matarazzo, 1990), because it indicates the actual band of error around the obtained IQ score. This band of error is associated with variations in scores when people are tested on different occasions due to inherent unreliability of the test itself. Therefore, a score obtained from a single test administration, for example, an IQ of 69, is not a "true" score as a certain margin of error would be expected due to the imperfection of the test. By a "true" score we mean the average IQ score obtained from several administrations of the test. Therefore, if the person was tested on several separate occasions, several months apart and with practice effect controlled for, the IQ scores could easily vary by a few points. The SEM of the WAIS-R Full Scale IQ is 2.53 (Wechsler, 1981), which means that the chances are about two out of three that the score obtained (e.g. IQ of 69) lies ithin 2.53 points of the "true" score (i.e. approximately IQs 66–72). Doubling the SEM, which is a much more stringent test of probability, means that the chances are 19 out of 20 (i.e. 95% probability) that the "true" score lies within 5.06 IQ points of the score obtained during any one administration (i.e. IQs of approximately 64–75).

Legally, there appears to be a certain mystique associated with the scientific concept of IQ. The SEM indicates that the IQ obtained during any given administration is not fixed; certain allowances must therefore be made for inherent weaknesses in any given test. Another factor which is often not appreciated by the courts is that IQ tests measure certain verbal and non-verbal skills rather than some "fixed" overall abilities. The precise IQ score obtained depends on the specific skills measured at a given time and the nature of the test used. The test most commonly used is the Wechsler Adult Intelligence Scale (WAIS-R, Wechsler, 1981). Some of the individual subtests used may have greater relevance to legal issues in a given case than others. For example, in cases of retracted confession it is, in my experience, often assumed by the courts that verbal skills (e.g. vocabulary, comprehension and reasoning) are more indicative of how able the accused was in handling police questioning than non-verbal intellectual skills. This is probably generally true, although I would hesitate to suggest that non-verbal skills are unimportant. In fact, one of the non-verbal subtests of WAIS-R, Picture Arrangement, appears to measure social awareness and participation (Schill, Kahn and Meuhelman, 1968), which could be relevant to the identification of "mental impairment". I have noticed that many of the defendants who superficially appear strikingly good in their social functioning, even when their verbal abilities are significantly impaired, score relatively high on the Picture Arrangement subtest. This is interesting because it is the subtest that has the highest correlation with interrogative suggestibility (Gudjonsson, 1990c).

2. Detainees' Understanding of their Legal Rights

Persons who are detained at a police station have four basic rights, which need not be exercised immediately:

1. They have the right to remain silent, which is a part of the police caution. The caution must be given before the suspect is asked any questions about the alleged offence. It is stated in the following terms:

"You do not have to say anything unless you wish to do so, but what you
say may be given in evidence" (Home Office, 1991, p. 57).

2. They have the right to consult a solicitor.
3. They have the right to have somebody informed of their arrest and
   detention.
4. They have the right to consult a copy of the Codes of Practice and to obtain
   a copy of the Custody Record. After advising detainees about these rights,
   the Custody Officer gives them a leaflet explaining their rights.

Recent research (Gudjonsson, 1990e, 1991b; Clare and Gudjonsson,
1991a) proves that the leaflet was so complicated to read and understand
that the great majority of detainees would not understand it fully.
Persons with a mental handicap are particularly disadvantaged in that
they would understand very little of the leaflet. In fact, the majority of them
do not fully understand the right to silence (Clare and Gudjonsson, 1991a).
Their limited intellectual functioning is highly relevant here, but so is their
tendency to claim to have understood the caution when they did not. Here
acquiescence is particularly relevant (Gudjonsson, 1990c). My standard
practice when interviewing defendants of low intellectual ability is to read
out the caution and ask if they understand it. Most say they understand it,
but when I ask them to explain it, it is clear that many have no idea of what
it means. Standard police practice in England is that officers read out the
caution and say "Do you understand?" When persons of low intellectual
ability say "Yes" it is not a reliable indication of their understanding of the
caution.

Clare and Gudjonsson (1991a) found that even after having their rights read
out to them from the Notice to Detained Persons, many persons with a mild
mental handicap have problems with retaining information. The most likely
explanation is that the information contained in the document is so
complicated that persons with a mild mental handicap fail to encode it. These
problems are undoubtedly exacerbated when the material to be encoded, like
the Notice to Detained Persons, is difficult to comprehend (Gudjonsson, 1991b).

Beaumont (1987) describes two defendants whose inability to understand
the police caution, accompanied by an incidental breach of the Code of Practice
in relation to having an "appropriate adult" present during the police
interviews, resulted in successful submission with regard to Section 76 (b).
I have been involved in several similar cases where mentally handicapped
individuals were interviewed without an "appropriate adult" or a solicitor
present. Sometimes it could be clearly demonstrated that they did not
understand the police caution. In such cases, when no corroborative evidence
is available, it is common for the prosecution to withdraw the charges or for
the judge to rule the confession inadmissible.

The special protection afforded to juveniles, and the mentally ill and
handicapped during custodial interrogation, relates to their mandatory access

to an "appropriate adult". The person chosen to fulfil this role may be a defendant's relative or guardian, or

> "... someone who has experience of dealing with mentally disordered or mentally handicapped persons but is not a police officer or employed by the police" (Home Office, 1991, p. 38).

This role is usually fulfilled by social workers and only occasionally by psychologists and psychiatrists. The requirement for an "appropriate adult" is that without such a provision these vulnerable individuals could make confessions which are inherently unreliable.

According to the Codes of Practice, the "appropriate adult" should be informed by the police that he or she is not acting simply as an observer:

> "The purposes of his presence are, first, to advise the person being questioned and to observe whether or not the interview is being conducted properly and fairly, and secondly, to facilitate communication with the person being interviewed" (Home Office, 1991, p. 60).

It is very important that those who act as an "appropriate adult" are fully aware of their responsibilities. The effectiveness of "appropriate adults" as a social support system is unknown.

My recommendation to psychologists is that, when assessing defendants of borderline intelligence or mental handicap in disputed confession cases, the subjects' understanding of the police caution and other legal rights at the time of the police interview needs to be assessed. This is particularly the case if no solicitor or "appropriate adult" was present during the police interview.

Given that many people of low intellectual ability may have little knowledge about their legal rights, it is also the case in my experience that they may be at a disadvantage in the sense that even if they understand their rights, they are often less able to assert and implement them. For example, they might be easily persuaded by the police that they have no need to consult a solicitor.

3. *The Question of Suggestibility*

It is commonly argued that the mentally handicapped are more suggestible than normal people (Brandon and Davies, 1973; Woolgrove, 1976; Tully, 1980; Craft, 1984). There is substantial empirical evidence to support this view (Tully and Cahill, 1984; Clare and Gudjonsson, 1991b), but it is worth remembering that the relationship between suggestibility and intelligence is mediated by a number of factors, including previous interrogative experiences and convictions (Sharrock and Gudjonsson, 1991). However, I have assessed many persons with a mental handicap who were far from being suggestible or compliant. Therefore, one cannot assume that these persons are necessarily unduly suggestible, even though their condition increases the likelihood that they are. Conversely, there are many people of good intellectual ability who prove to be abnormally suggestible on testing. In other words, *suggestibility needs to be assessed directly rather than assumed on the basis of IQ scores*. Furthermore, when drawing inferences about an individual case, *possible situational sources of suggestibility must not be overlooked*.

Persons with a mental handicap are often considered to be prone to making false confessions because of their heightened suggestibility and eagerness to please people in authority (Brandon and Davies, 1973; Craft, 1984). Their understanding of questions and their ability to express themselves verbally in an interview situation is limited (Keane, 1972; Sigelman and Werder, 1975). A particular danger with regard to interviewing is to rely unduly on simple yes-no questions, because persons with a mental handicap are likely to answer such questions in the affirmative irrespective of content (Sigelman et al., 1980, 1981, 1982). Dent (1986) suggests, on the basis of her empirical study, that the optimal interview technique for completeness and accuracy with children who have mental handicap is one that uses general rather than specific questions. In contrast, normal children give the most reliable account when asked to give free recall without using general or specific questions (Dent and Stephenson, 1979). It seems that when interviewing persons with a mental handicap, exclusive reliance on free recall results in incomplete accounts. Therefore, a certain amount of prompting is required in order to build on the sparse details given in their initial free recall. However, because of the likelihood of high suggestibility and acquiescence, interviewers should avoid asking specific questions. Broad and general questions of a non-leading nature give the best results (e.g. "What happened next?" rather than "What did you do next?").

4. The Question of Immediate Consequences

The social context of police interrogation requires a complicated decision-making process (Irving and Hilgendorf, 1980). It would be expected that suspects of low intellectual abilities would be disadvantaged because their decision-making would be principally directed towards immediate gratification (e.g. terminating the police questioning, being free to go home) rather than careful appreciation of the long-term consequences (e.g. prosecution and possibly conviction) of their actions (e.g. Menninger, 1986). This could in certain circumstances result in their confessing to crimes they had not committed.

We do not know the number of persons with mental handicap who are so disadvantaged during interrogation that they make a false confession. There is evidence that persons with mental handicap tend to confess particularly readily during custodial interrogation (Brown, Courtless and Silber, 1970). However, little is known about the characteristics that make mentally handicapped persons likely to confess falsely during custodial interrogation, as opposed to making a true confession. They would be expected, generally speaking, to have fewer intellectual and social resources to cope with the demand characteristics of the interrogation and confinement. However, the factors that make persons with a mental handicap likely to confess falsely vary from case to case. We have to look at the combination of factors rather than any one acting in isolation. What is required is to identify specific vulnerabilities that are potentially relevant and evaluate these in the context of the total circumstances of the case. Just because a defendant is mentally handicapped, it does not necessarily mean that he or she is prone to making false confessions or erroneous statements during interrogation. Each case must be assessed and considered on its own unique merits.

The Assessment of Social Functioning

The importance of social functioning in the definition of PACE is not clear. There have been several trials in England where the argument has been put forward by counsel that the sentence "includes significant impairment of intelligence and social functioning" does not mean that *both* intelligence and social functioning necessarily need to be significantly impaired. From the point of view of the Mental Health Act definition, *both* would be required to define a mental handicap (British Psychological Society, 1991). A similar requirement is recommended by the American Association on Mental Deficiency (Matarazzo, 1972).

There are scales available for measuring social functioning, such as the Vineland Social Maturity Scale (Doll, 1965) and the Adaptive Behavior Scale (American Association of Mental Deficiency, 1974; Atkinson, 1990). These developmental scales, which are usually completed by people who know the person with a mental handicap very well, focus on evaluating the ability of the mentally handicapped to cope with practical and social demands. There are at least five problems with using these scales to define mental handicap in cases of alleged false confession:

1. Since independent informants are required (e.g. parents, teachers, carers) they are commonly much more time-consuming and problematic to administer than a standard intelligence test;
2. The subjects tested often have considerable life experience, not taken into consideration by the test, which makes interpretations of their scores difficult;
3. The correlations between tests of intelligence and tests of social functioning are often low (Sparrow, Balla, and Cicchetti, 1984);
4. The results from these scales are more subjective than the scores from intelligence tests;
5. It is not clear how well these relate to the legal issues. Their significance in disputed or retracted confession cases is less clear than that of IQ.

The fact that social functioning is difficult to measure and evaluate meaningfully does not mean that no attempt should be made to evaluate social functioning. However, I should like to illustrate anecdotally the kind of problems that may arise in court with regard to the measurement of social functioning.

Case 1: Mr B

Mr B was a 43-year-old man who was charged with assisting in the disposal of a body following a murder. He had been interviewed by the police without a solicitor or an "appropriate adult" present. During two interviews, he made serious self-incriminating confessions. The defence solicitor referred the case to me for an assessment of his intellectual functioning and suggestibility. The defendant had attended a "special school" for backward children and stayed there until aged 16, and in view of his history the question of mental handicap was raised. During my assessment Mr B obtained a Verbal IQ of 66 and a Performance IQ of 76. His Full Scale IQ was 69. I did not formally assess Mr B's social functioning, because it would have required, in my view, speaking to people who knew him well, as well as possibly visiting his home. This had not been requested or authorized by the solicitors who referred him. In addition, I was very much aware of the practical difficulties involved in carrying out such an assessment, because the only person who knew Mr B well was his wife, who was herself mentally handicapped. However, Mr B's general appearance and behaviour had all the hallmarks of limited social functioning and I did comment in my report that I thought his mental handicap was easily recognizable, even on brief acquaintance.

In spite of his intellectual limitations he understood the police caution and was not abnormally suggestible on the GSS 2. He did have previous convictions and appeared reasonably familiar with police procedures. Because of Mr B's low intelligence, the defence argued that there should have been an "appropriate adult" present during the police interviews. If this argument could have been substantiated then the police would have been in breach of the Codes of Practice. The defence were going to cite the cases of *R. v. Everett* (1988, Crim. L. R. 826) and *R. v. Lamount* (1989, Crim. L. R. 813) to support their arguments for exclusion of Mr B's confession under Sections 76 (2) (b) and 78.

The prosecution obtained a report from their own expert. He read my report and assessed Mr B's intellectual and social functioning. He rightly pointed out that I had not formally assessed the defendant's social functioning. I was sent a copy of the prosecution expert's report. His conclusion, based on his own assessment, was that Mr B had no significant impairment in social functioning. We both turned up in court and were prepared to give our evidence. The prosecution psychologist was carrying several textbooks on mental handicap under his arm in support of his arguments that the defendant could not be classified as mentally handicapped. We were in for a long and tiring day, or so I thought. Unexpected events were to prove otherwise.

My approach to this case was to present the IQ scores and state that we did not know about Mr B's social functioning, although I was prepared to say that his general appearance and behaviour during my assessment of him did not suggest these to be of a high level. I considered the conclusion of the prosecution psychologist about the defendant's satisfactory social functioning to be fundamentally flawed. The reason was that he had unwisely administered the Vineland Adaptive Behavior Scale to the defendant himself, rather than having independent informants complete it. Even if Mr B understood all the questions contained in the scale, he may well have exaggerated his claims of various skills in order to impress the psychologist. Apparently, the prosecution psychologist thought differently, which was to prove an embarrassing experience for him. Neither he nor I knew that when Mr B was arrested at his home the police were so concerned about the poor hygiene of his home (e.g. they took several photographs which showed dog faeces on the floor in the various rooms, including the kitchen) that they called in the Social Services and Mr B's children were taken into care. The photographs were placed in front of the prosecution psychologist and he was asked what it told him about Mr B's social functioning. He retracted his evidence of the defendant's satisfactory social functioning. After that the prosecution fully accepted that Mr B was mentally handicapped within the meaning of PACE and offered no evidence. The case was dismissed by the judge.

This case has important lessons for both the police and psychologists.

1. If the police had identified Mr B as a person with a mental handicap, which they should have done in view of the state of his house, his history of having attended a "special school" and his general appearance, they might well have won the case, provided they had given him the legal protection to which he was entitled under PACE and the Codes of Practice. Not taking the right steps to ensure that an "appropriate adult" is called in a case like this may have serious consequences for the police.
2. Crucial evidence of Mr B's poor social functioning was available of which neither the prosecution nor the defence psychologists were made aware.

The Voire Dire

In order to decide on the question of admissibility the judge conducts "a trial within a trial" which is known as the *voire dire*. The purpose of the *voire dire* is:

"... to enable the judge to determine an issue of fact, namely whether the alleged confession was, or may have been, obtained by oppression or in circumstances making it likely to be unreliable" (Rowe, 1986, p. 226).

The *voire dire* is heard in the absence of the jury in accordance with the exclusionary rules, which are designed for the protection of the defendant. The jury are asked to withdraw while the questions of law are being discussed by the legal advocates. After both sides have made their submissions and the judge has made his ruling, the jury is invited back. If the confession evidence is made admissible, then the jury is allowed to hear it. If the judge rules it inadmissible, the jury will hear nothing of it, in which case the trial may proceed on the basis of other evidence, or the prosecution decides to "offer no evidence". In a case where the only evidence against the defendant is his or her confession, the inadmissibility of that evidence means that the prosecution case collapses.

How much time is spent on challenging the reliability or accuracy of police interrogation evidence? According to Barnes and Webster (1980), about 5% of the Crown Court's trial time is taken up with this kind of a dispute. Similar findings have been reported by Vennard (1984). In both studies infrequent use was made of the *voire dire*. Vennard found that *voire dire* took place in only 7% of contested Crown Court cases, whereas Barnes and Webster reported a figure of 11%. Overall, in only about 13% of contested cases in the Crown Court and 6% in the Magistrates' Courts are the issues of statement unreliability raised, during either the *voire dire* or the trial proper (Vennard, 1984).

How effective is the *voire dire* for excluding confession evidence? In the great majority of cases the submission to exclude confession evidence fails. According to Vennard's (1984) findings, only about 15% of *voire dire* cases in the Crown Courts succeed.

The Admissibility of Expert Evidence

The question of admissibility can arise with regard to any evidence, including expert testimony. When lawyers seek to introduce the expert opinion or findings of psychologists, then the judge has to decide on the admissibility of the evidence. Submissions and legal arguments by the defence and prosecution are heard by the judge in the absence of the jury. The fundamental criteria for the admissibility of expert testimony were stated by Lord Justice Lawton in the case of *R. v. Turner* (1975, 60 Cr. App. R. 80, C.A.). These are:

> "An expert's opinion is admissible to furnish the court with scientific information which is likely to be outside the experience and knowledge of a judge or jury" (Mitchell and Richardson, 1985, p. 476).

According to the *Turner* principle, it is not admissible for experts, whether psychiatrists or psychologists, to give evidence about how an ordinary person is likely to react to stressful situations. Neither can experts give evidence about matters directly related to the likely veracity of witnesses or defendants. This means that English law has a rather restrictive approach to the admissibility of evidence from expert witnesses (Fitzgerald, 1987).

Accordingly, psychologists are not allowed to give evidence on such matters as eyewitness testimony, unlike their counterparts in America (Davies, 1983). Their evidence, like that of psychiatrists, has to deal with the presence of mental abnormality. When this involves mental illness or mental handicap the evidence is readily admissible.

Problems can arise when dealing with diagnosis of "personality disorder" rather than mental illness or mental handicap. For example, in the case of *R. v. Mackinney and Pinfold* (1981, 72 Cr. App. R. 78) a social psychologist was not allowed to talk about the likely unreliability of the testimony of a "psychopathic" prosecution "supergrass" whom he had observed in court but never formally interviewed. The decision to exclude the psychologist's evidence was upheld by the Court of Appeal. It was decided that:

> "Whether or not a witness in a criminal trial is capable of giving reliable evidence is a question of fact for the jury" (Mitchell and Richardson, 1985, p. 420).

Another important case which is relevant to the admissibility of expert testimony concerning the reliability of testimony, is that of *Toohey v. Commissioner of Metropolitan Police* (1965, A.C. 595, H.L.). Here the Court of Appeal held that the trial judge had been wrong in not admitting the evidence of a police surgeon to the effect that soon after alleging an assault, a prosecution witness had been in such a state of hysteria, which had been exacerbated by alcohol, that anything he said at the time was likely to be unreliable.

Broadly speaking, the expert evidence is allowed when there is evidence of mental illness or mental handicap. According to the judgement in the case of *Masih* (1986, Crim. L. R. 395), an IQ of 69 or below is required for a defendant to be formally classified as mentally handicapped, and here the expert evidence would be admissible, whenever it was considered relevant. In the *Masih* case the defendant's IQ was 72, which falls at the lower end of the "borderline range" (i.e. bottom 3% of the population). Lord Lane's view was that expert testimony in a borderline case will not as a rule be necessary and should therefore be excluded.

However, in spite of Lord Lane's ruling in *Masih* there have subsequently been many examples of judges allowing psychologists' evidence when the defendant's IQ was above 70. Beaumont (1987) gives two examples. I have personally given evidence in a large number of cases in Britain where the defendants' IQ was in the borderline range or above. About 20% of defendants referred to me for a psychological assessment in cases of retracted confession have IQs below 70, and a further third have IQs that fall in the borderline range (i.e. 70-79). My personal experience is that judges are generally reluctant to exclude psychological evidence when it seems relevant, even though within the rigid guidance from the Appeal Court the evidence should perhaps be made inadmissible. There are in practice some notable exceptions.

In one case, heard at the Central Criminal Court, a defendant's IQ was 70, which is one point above the "magic" figure of 69. The judge read my report and listened to legal submissions. He disallowed my evidence as the IQ was 70 and not 69 or below. However, during his summing up the judge referred to some of my findings without specifically stating that he did so. The first I learned about it was when the results of my assessment were mentioned on the radio. In the view of the barrister involved in the case, "The judge gave your evidence for you." There have been other similar cases where judges have disallowed the psychological evidence, but have themselves come to the same conclusion as that expressed in the expert's report.

The evidence of a significant impairment in intellectual functioning is routinely accepted, but problems sometimes arise when dealing with abnormal personality traits, such as suggestibility and compliance. Here no clear guidelines are available for judges, but my experience is that in the majority of such cases the psychological findings are allowed, even when there is no significant accompanying intellectual impairment.

The reverse proposition is never put forward by the prosecution; that is, the argument that a person of superior intellect and abnormally low suggestibility is less susceptible than the average person to pressure, manipulation or coercion. Such evidence would not be admissible in English courts. Similarly, even if it can be shown that the suspect fully understood his legal rights unaided, a failure to read him his rights prior to custodial interrogation would normally, but not inevitably, be considered a breach. For example, in *Alladice* (1988, Crim. L.R. 608) a suspect had been arrested so often that it was assumed that he knew his rights already; therefore the refusal to have access to a solicitor was not a sufficiently serious breach to demand exclusion, as he did not need the advice.

Of course, the prosecution can use certain positive characteristics to support their case during rebuttal (i.e. when cross-examining the defence experts). For example, there are cases where defendants have been shown to suffer from a mental handicap, which makes the expert evidence admissible, but personality testing showed them to be exceptionally resistant to interrogative pressure. The defence would place emphasis on the low IQ with regard to the defendant's disputed confession, but the prosecution may use the personality findings (e.g. low suggestibility) to argue that in spite of low intellectual abilities the defendant is reasonably able to stand up to interrogation. Two cases illustrate this point (see below). The third case shows that even if there is no evidence of deliberate police malpractice or internal vulnerabilities, the confession may still be excluded simply on the basis of the words used by the police.

Case 2: Mr F

Mr F was a 27-year-old man who was charged with armed robbery. He had several previous convictions for similar offences. The psychological assessment revealed that Mr F was of borderline intelligence (Full Scale IQ of 74), but he did not prove to be unduly suggestible or compliant on testing. A copy of my report was given to the prosecution before I gave my evidence at the Central Criminal Court during a *voire dire*. The judge stated in court that he would allow my evidence during this part of the proceedings but he might not if the confession went before the jury. During my evidence the defence concentrated on Mr F's borderline IQ and how that could have made him disadvantaged during the interrogation. In rebuttal, the prosecution noticed the reference in my report to the modest suggestibility and compliance scores and used it to support their argument that Mr F was well able to cope with the interrogation that resulted in his confession. The judge allowed the confession to go before the jury. Mr F was convicted and sentenced to prison.

Case 3: Mr G

Mr G was a 25-year-old man with a mental handicap. He had been charged with murdering an elderly lady in her own home, which he had broken into. He had been assessed by a psychiatrist and a psychologist for the defence. Mr G had been interviewed for 45 minutes in the presence of a solicitor and an "appropriate adult". During the interview Mr G made a confession to the murder and to having set fire to the room in which the woman had been murdered. Mr G subsequently retracted his confession, claiming that he had been frightened of the police and that they had put pressure on him to confess. Mr G's solicitors had succeeded, during a previous trial of arson, in having his confession excluded on the basis of his mental handicap. The police had then interviewed him without an "appropriate adult".

Subsequently, following his arrest on suspicion of the murder, the police had interviewed him conscientiously and had ensured that both a solicitor and an "appropriate adult" were present. Nevertheless, at Mr G's trial the defence sought to have the confession excluded. I had assessed Mr G on behalf of the prosecution. I found him to have an IQ of 60, which was identical to that found when he had been previously tested by the defence psychologist. However, Mr G obtained low scores on the GSS 1 and GSS 2, on which he had been tested on two separate occasions. I concluded that Mr G was a person with a mental handicap, but in spite of this I found no evidence to indicate that he was unusually suggestible and vulnerable to interpersonal pressure. Indeed, considering his mental handicap, he seemed overall less suggestible than most persons with a mental handicap whom I had tested in similar circumstances.

During Mr G's trial I gave evidence twice in rebuttal to the defence experts, first during the *voire dire* and again in front of the jury. On both occasions I was asked to comment on the tests I had used and on the interviewing technique used by the police. The defence had assumed Mr G was suggestible and susceptible to erroneous evidence because of his mental handicap. My evidence showed that in spite of the mental handicap he appeared well able to cope with interrogative pressure. Furthermore, in my view, Mr G had been carefully interviewed by the police with the minimum number of leading questions.

The judge, at Maidstone Crown Court, allowed Mr G's confession to go before the jury who convicted him of manslaughter on the grounds of diminished responsibility.

Case 4: Mr S

Confession evidence can be excluded on the basis of police misconduct or because of the idiosyncratic vulnerability (e.g. low IQ, high suggestibility), or a combination of both. Even when no misconduct has taken place, the inadvertent use of the wrong words or phrases by the police may be sufficient to have the confession excluded. The following case illustrates the point.

Mr S was a 37-year-old man of average intelligence. He was charged with gross indecency concerning his teenage daughter. I assessed the man psychologically, but there were no specific vulnerabilities that were likely to assist the defence. However, the contemporaneous record of the police interview revealed a conversation which supported inadmissibility according to Section 76 (2) (b). The relevant record was as follows:

Q. "Did you touch her private parts whilst she was in bed?"
A. "As a deliberate movement, no."
Q. "Did you take her into your bedroom whilst your wife was out working during the evening?"
A. "I did not take her into the bedroom."
Q. "Tell me what happened."
A. "You are asking me to say something I don't want to."
Q. "You've got to, let's clear the air and get it over and done with."
A. "It just disgusts me."

(The suspect then went on to describe in great detail what is alleged to have happened.)

The judge in this case, in Lewes Crown Court, ruled the confession inadmissible, because of the words used by the police officer. From the police point of view the remark may have been quite innocent and spontaneous, but it had serious consequences with regard to the exclusion of a detailed self-incriminating confession from being heard by the jury. Mr S was acquitted by the jury after it heard the evidence of the daughter.

THE AMERICAN LAW ON CONFESSIONS

There are many similarities between the English and American law on confessions, as well as salient procedural differences. Both legal systems place great emphasis on the fact that the confession must be made voluntarily; that is, it must have been given freely and knowingly. The tests used to judge voluntariness have become more sophisticated over the years and take into consideration the proper implementation of the suspect's legal rights, the absence of psychological or physical coercion and the mental state of the suspect during the custodial interrogation. Any infringements of the voluntary nature of the confession may result in it being excluded from being given in evidence. Therefore, confession evidence is neither automatically accepted or rejected. Admissibility is judged on an individual basis by considering all the surrounding circumstances and especially the voluntariness of the confession. In general, there has been a trend towards greater emphasis on fair procedure and considerations of the accused's legal rights, as well as attempts to deter police misconduct. This is the situation both in England and in America. Broadly speaking, the purpose of an "Exclusionary Rule" is to disallow evidence that is considered to have been obtained illegally, or when it is thought to be in some way unfair to allow it. Unlike English law, the majority of American courts require confessions to be corroborated by evidence from an independent source. However, there have been some exceptions to this rule and it is often not implemented satisfactorily by the courts (Ayling, 1984).

Ayling argues that there are three potential problems with the corroboration rule as it is currently practised in the United States of America, which makes it insufficient to protect the reliability of confessions:

1. The police can, deliberately or unwittingly, suggest corroborating evidence to suspects which subsequently becomes incorporated into the confession as if it had originated from the suspects;
2. The corroboration rule does not protect those who overstate their involvement in an alleged crime;
3. Juries and judges are not able to evaluate independent evidence once they have heard the suspect's confession.

American trial procedures differ from State to State, but court decisions in each State will ultimately fall under the jurisdiction of the Supreme Court of the United States. Therefore, each State is obliged to follow judgements and recommendations made by the Supreme Court.

According to Stuntz (1989), the American "exclusionary rule" was born in 1914, when *Weeks v. United States* (232 U.S. 383) was decided. Here the Supreme Court held that evidence obtained in violation of the Fourth Amendment was inadmissible in federal criminal trials. However, the exclusionary rule did not apply to State cases, which were by far the most frequent. In 1949, in *Wolf v. Colorado* (338 U.S. 25, 1949) the Supreme Court held that the States as well as federal bodies were bound by the Fourth Amendment, but the rule was limited in that breaches of constitutional restrictions by the police did not have to be enforced by the courts. A more important development took place in 1961, when the case of *Mapp v. Ohio* (367 U.S. 643, 1961) was decided (Stuntz, 1989). Here it was made mandatory, with certain exceptions (e.g. during "hot pursuit"), for police officers to obtain a search warrant before entering a private property. When this requirement is violated, any evidence that results from the search is automatically excluded.

Undoubtedly, the most important development in American law with regard to interrogations relates to the case of *Miranda v. Arizona*, which was decided in 1966 (384 U.S. 436, 1966). The purpose of this additional constraint on confession admissibility was to ensure that *all* criminal suspects in police custody would be warned against self-incrimination, and made aware of their constitutional right to remain silent and to have access to a lawyer before and during custodial interrogation. These rights have to be actively *waived* by the accused before interrogation can commence. Suspects who have waived these rights can change their mind at any time after the warning. Violations of the *Miranda* requirements make any subsequent confessions inadmissible as evidence, even though they were otherwise given voluntarily.

It is important to realize that the *Miranda* warning is only relevant to *custodial interrogation*, that is, the warning only needs to be given to suspects who have been arrested and are therefore technically in police custody. Interrogating somebody who is not under arrest does not require a *Miranda* warning (*Beckwith v. United States*, 425 U.S. 341, 1976). In the *Miranda* decision the Supreme Court was very critical of police trickery techniques which were capable of overbearing the suspect's will. For example, the "Mutt and Jeff" technique, described in Chapter 6, was condemned as it involved trickery. Other deceptions include lies by the police that they have physical or witness evidence that implicates the accused in the crime.

According to Stuntz (1989), the Supreme Court attempted to achieve two distinct objectives by its decision in *Miranda*. These were to deter police misconduct and to correct certain injustices which had resulted from police deception. Thus, the police were obliged to inform suspects that they could at any time halt the interrogation, and also request a lawyer if they so wished. The aim of this requirement was to reduce the risk of physical and emotional abuse of suspects by police officers. If the police were using blatantly coercive techniques, suspects might react by invoking their right to terminate the questioning. Any statement obtained after the suspect requested the ending of questioning would be inadmissible.

The second objective of the Supreme Court with regard to the *Miranda* warning was broader. Here police trickery and deception was construed as depriving suspects of the opportunity of making informed and rational decisions about their right not to incriminate themselves. However, in recent years there have been certain changes in the way the Supreme Court deals with proven police trickery and deception (Stuntz, 1989). The trend is to limit the *Miranda* decision to cases where there has been police coercion, whilst police trickery which deprives suspects of the opportunity of making an informed and rational choice regarding self-incrimination has been allowed by the courts. In addition, violation of the *Miranda* warning is acceptable under certain circumstances, for example, when public safety is at stake (*New York v. Quarles*, 467 U.S. 649, 1984).

Before a self-incriminating statement can be used against a defendant, the prosecution must prove its voluntariness by a "preponderance" of the evidence (*Lego v. Twomey*, 404 U.S. 477, 1972). The legal test is whether, considering the totality of the circumstances, the police obtained the confession by coercion or improper inducement so that the accused's will was overborne (*Schneckloth v. Bustamonte*, 412 U.S. 218, 1973).

The type of factors that are relevant to the determination of voluntariness are numerous. They include:

1. Characteristics of the accused (e.g. age, mental illness and handicap, physical illness or injury, intoxication);
2. The conditions of detention (e.g. failure to give advice of legal rights, lack of access to a solicitor, length of detention prior to interrogation, periods held incommunicado);
3. The nature of the interrogation (e.g. threats, psychological or physical abuse, repeated and prolonged questioning, inducements, promises).

CONCLUSIONS

Under English and American law the courts are confronted with certain practical problems with regard to assessing the probative weight of confessions (Zuckerman, 1989). These relate to the fact that police interrogations are conducted without outside supervision, so that police officers would be motivated to suppress evidence of impropriety, whilst suspects who regret making a confession would have a motive to fabricate allegations of police malpractice.

It is a fundamental assumption in both English and American law that the greatest reliance can be placed on a confession that is given freely and voluntarily. As a matter of law, confessions deemed to be involuntary are excluded. Confession evidence can be excluded on the basis of police misconduct or because of some idiosyncratic vulnerability (e.g. youth, low IQ, high suggestibility), or indeed, the combination of both. Even when no deliberate police misconduct has taken place, the use of the wrong words or phrases during the interrogation may be sufficient to have the confession excluded. The introduction of the *Miranda* principle in American law and the Police and Criminal Evidence Act 1984 (PACE) in England and Wales have had an impact in deterring police misconduct and in protecting the legal rights of suspects. However, two problems persist. First, American police officers, unlike their English colleagues, are allowed to use deliberate trickery and deception as a technique for obtaining confessions. Second, both the American and English legal provisions only apply to *custodial interrogation*. They provide insufficient protection for suspects who are questioned whilst not under arrest (e.g. they may initially be interviewed informally and "softened up" prior to the formal interrogation).

The English courts are much more restrictive than the American courts about the admissibility of expert witnesses' testimony. Even courts that follow the same leading English cases for admissibility (i.e. *R. v. Turner* and *Toohey v. Metropolitan Police Commissioner*) differ widely in allowing psychiatric and psychological evidence (Pattenden, 1986). The main differences and conflicts relate to two issues:

1. The extent to which psychological and psychiatric evidence can be given about normal individuals (i.e. those who are not mentally ill or mentally handicapped);
2. The admissibility of evidence that relates to opinions concerning the veracity of witnesses' and defendants' statements. Evidence about veracity is generally considered to lie within the prerogative of the judge and jury and is invariably excluded (Gudjonsson, 1983b).

Strictly speaking, expert psychiatric or psychological testimony is only admissible in the English courts when it deals with some mental abnormality, particularly in relation to mental illness and mental handicap. However, in spite of the restrictive approach of the Court of Appeal to expert testimony, trial judges often seem reluctant to exclude psychological evidence when it is relevant to the legal issues, even when there is no evidence of mental illness or mental handicap. Of particular importance is evidence that relates to certain personality traits (e.g. suggestibility and compliance). Such evidence is often relevant to the legal issues in cases of retracted confessions. English judges are more reluctant to admit this kind of evidence than evidence of low intellectual abilities, but they are increasingly recognizing its importance and are often allowing it, during the *voire dire* and the trial proper. Once the psychological findings have been allowed in evidence it may help the judge to decide on issues related to confession admissibility, or if presented in front of the jury it may help them to deliberate on the weight and reliability of the confession.

POSTSCRIPT

Following the recent Court of Appeal judgement in the case of Engin Raghip (*Regina v. Raghip*; Law Report, *The Independent*, Friday 6th December 1991, p. 19), the guidance to trial judges about the admissibility of psychological evidence has altered drastically. Firstly, the criteria for admissibility have been broadened, and they now include less reliance on arbitrary cut-off IQ points and recognition of the importance of suggestibility and compliance. Secondly, an important distinction was drawn between psychological and psychiatric evidence. Thirdly, the judgement made it clear that trial judges and jurors may be greatly assisted by a comprehensive psychological evaluation in cases of disputed confession.

CHAPTER 14

Disputed Confessions: the Psychological Assessment

Until the early 1980s clinicians had no satisfactory conceptualized framework for the assessment of disputed confession cases. To illustrate the point, a psychiatrist (Coid, 1981), in his assessment of a retracted confession case, devised six criteria for assessing suggestibility:

1. That the defendant can be made to change his story as a result of persuasion;
2. That the defendant could be made to believe false information that would be obvious to most people of normal intelligence;
3. That the defendant is unable to understand the implications of his or her predicament;
4. That the defendant is unable to understand the words and concepts used in the incriminating statement;
5. That the defendant has a tendency to confabulate or exhibits pseudologia fantastica (i.e. pathological lying);
6. That the defendant is unable to understand the concept of truth.

Coid applied his "suggestibility criteria" to a homicide case where the major evidence against the defendant was his confession. The defendant proved not to be suggestible according to the six criteria.

Coid's "suggestibility criteria" were poorly conceptualized and crudely "estimated" on the basis of a clinical judgement. No psychological instruments were used to measure the six "criteria". Like his colleagues at the time, Coid was faced with the lack of standardized assessment procedures and techniques. Extensive developments in recent years have markedly improved the knowledge and techniques available to clinicians who are preparing court reports in cases of disputed confession. A detailed conceptual framework for the assessment of such cases is provided by Gudjonsson and MacKeith (1988). In this Chapter I shall build upon our earlier work in this field and expand it considerably. Detailed case illustrations will provide further insight into the variety of assessment techniques and procedures that are available.

THE PSYCHOLOGICAL ASSESSMENT

Psychologists are increasingly being referred cases directly from solicitors (Gudjonsson, 1985, 1990f). Their contribution to the assessment of cases involving disputed or retracted confessions is probably growing faster than most other areas (Fitzgerald, 1987). There appear to be three principal reasons for this increased demand.

First, there is growing awareness among the legal profession that psychologists have a unique contribution to make. The assessment of disputed confessions was originally provided by psychiatrists. My impression in the early 1980s was that these cases were only occasionally referred to either psychiatrists or psychologists, and when they were, the question of mental illness or mental handicap was typically raised. In recent years it has become evident that in the majority of these cases the critical questions are psychological rather than psychiatric. Psychologists now have greater knowledge and techniques available for the assessment of disputed confession cases.

Second, there appears to be increased legal acceptance of the psychologist's evidence. In 1985 I was commissioned by the British Psychological Society to study the involvement of psychologists as expert witnesses in the British courts (Gudjonsson, 1985). The results indicated that the demand for psychological services was on the increase and the majority of psychologists involved stated that the courts were favourable towards accepting their evidence.

Third, recent legal provisions have focused on regulating the behaviour of police officers during custodial interrogation and on improving the rights of detainees. The focus is now more on identifying inherent psychological vulnerabilities that may have a bearing on the legal issues.

Basic Requirements for Assessment

What are the most critical aspects of the assessment of retracted confessions? There are three basic prerequisites for a complete assessment, which are equally true whether the case is being referred by the defence or by the prosecution.

First, the psychologist must be properly instructed by the lawyers who refer the case. This includes receiving clear instructions about the issues to be addressed in the expert's report. Referral letters are often vague and a telephone conversation with the lawyer concerned may be necessary before the assessment can be undertaken. Often solicitors do not specify the legal issues to be addressed in the report. They may ask for "intelligence and suggestibility to be assessed", which are straightforward instructions. However, during the assessment the psychologist may discover other relevant factors that need to be assessed, such as alcohol and drug abuse or specific anxiety problems. The broadest type of assessment, which is the common instruction in American cases but not in England, involves assessing voluntariness, psychological coercion, and reliability or self-incriminating admissions. The assessment of cases in England is often more restricted because the courts are reluctant to allow psychologists to comment on the ultimate question of reliability. Generally speaking, they have to limit their comments on the results of their assessment (e.g. low intelligence, literacy problems, suggestibility). However, in court psychologists are sometimes asked questions about their observations on the relevant police interviews.

Second, the psychologist must have access to all relevant documents and papers in the case, which include witnesses' statements, records of police interviews, the Custody Record, the defendant's statements to his solicitors ("Proof of Evidence" and comments on the prosecution papers), medical reports, previous psychological reports, and school reports. These should be carefully studied before the defendant is interviewed and the psychologist should make a note of the questions that need to be asked of the defendant with regard to these. If interviews have been tape-recorded, and soon all police interviews in England will be tape-recorded (Home Office, 1988), then these must be listened to before interviewing the defendant. Even when interviews have been transcribed the tapes should always be listened to. *Psychologists should never rely on transcribed records when tape-recordings of the interviews are available.* I have on several occasions come across important errors or omissions in the transcription of tapes which were critical to the case. In addition, listening to interview tapes may give important further information about the way the interview was conducted and how the defendant coped during it. Informants may need to be interviewed for further information or as a way of corroborating information provided by the defendant.

Psychologists should be aware that they may not be presented by the referral agent with all the evidence in the case, because of the adversarial nature of the proceedings (Haward, 1991). This could be important when psychologists are attempting to interpret their findings within the broader context of the case.

Third, the psychologist should be familiar with the literature on false and retracted confessions. He or she should know about the basic assessment tools, including the validation data for the tests used. Furthermore, the psychologist needs to be able to relate the findings of the assessment to the particular circumstances of the case. This is the most difficult part of the assessment and requires considerable experience.

The Types of Factors to be Assessed

The psychological assessment, when dealing with issues relevant to voluntariness and reliability of self-incriminating statements, may require an evaluatation of four groups of factors, which can be labelled as:

1. Characteristics of the Defendant;
2. The Circumstances of the Arrest and Custody;
3. Mental and Physical State During Custody;
4. Interrogative Factors.

It is important to briefly discuss each of these in turn.

1. Characteristics of the Defendant

There are a number of characteristics associated with the defendant that can make him or her specially vulnerable to erroneous testimony during interrogation. These fall into three groups:

(a) Physical characteristics, such as age, gender and race. It is generally accepted that the very young and very old are least able to cope with the demands of police interrogation. The importance of gender and race are not known;

(b) Lack of life experience and unfamiliarity with police procedures and interrogation may place some defendants at a disadvantage;

(c) The psychological characteristics of the defendant. This includes his or her cognitive skills (e.g. intelligence, reading ability, memory capacity), personality (e.g. suggestibility, compliance, assertiveness, self-esteem, tendency to confabulate, anxiety proneness), specific anxiety problems (e.g. claustrophobia, extreme fear of police dogs), and mental illness (e.g. depressive illness, psychosis).

A mental state examination should give an indication of any current mental problems that the defendant has, which serves as an important baseline for inferences to be drawn about his or her mental state whilst in police custody.

Psychologists should be aware that even when mental illness, mental handicap or abnormal personality traits (e.g. suggestibility, compliance) are present, this does not necessarily mean that the defendant falsely confessed, even when this is alleged to be the case. The specific abnormalities and vulnerabilities detected may very well be relevant to the possible unreliability and involuntariness of the self-incriminating confession, but they should not be viewed in isolation from the surrounding circumstances of the case.

2. The Circumstances of the Arrest and Custody

The circumstances surrounding each case and their importance to the accused vary immensely. A person who is woken up in the early hours of the morning by armed police officers breaking into his home is likely to be in a different frame of mind than the one who goes to the police station as a witness and subsequently becomes a suspect. The more sudden and violent the arrest, the more likely the person is to be in a state of shock when taken to the police station for questioning. The timing of the interrogation may also be important. For example, interrogation late at night, when the accused would normally be asleep, places them at their lowest level of resistance and resilience.

Suspects who are accused of murdering someone close to them, such as a spouse, an offspring or a close friend, are often specially vulnerable during interrogation. This is irrespective of their guilt or innocence and relates to the fact that loss of a close one results in grief and bereavement (Parkes, 1986; Curle, 1989; Bluglass, 1990).

3.   Mental and Physical State During Custody

The mental and physical state of the accused whilst in police custody can affect the reliability of any statement, self-incriminating or otherwise, that he or she makes to the police. The work of Irving and his colleagues at Brighton Police Station illustrates that many suspects are not in a normal physical or mental state whilst being interviewed by the police. This may be caused by the stress associated with their arrest and confinement, or by factors associated with alcohol intoxication and drug abuse.

Physical illness and disease are also important factors that may need to be assessed. When we are physically ill we are more vulnerable when having to cope with a stressful situation, such as interrogation. In cases of heart disease and diabetes, fear of not being able to obtain medication or medical care may be additional stressors that make people focus excessively on the short-term or immediate consequences of their behaviour (e.g. making a self-incriminating statement) at the expense of the long-term consequences (e.g. being prosecuted, convicted and sentenced).

A reconstruction of the suspect's mental and physical state whilst in police custody needs to be carried out. If there are medical or psychiatric issues to be considered, then the psychologist should recommend to the solicitor that the case be referred to an appropriate medical person for a further report. In my experience, almost all cases involving alleged false confession involve psychological issues that are best addressed by psychologists. In some cases medical and psychiatric issues need to be considered as well. I have worked jointly on many cases with psychiatrists and often our individual contributions have complemented one another very well indeed.

Three sources of information are potentially useful for the reconstruction of the defendant's mental state at the time of the police interrogation. First, the Custody Record needs to be scrutinized for information, such as visits by relatives or a police surgeon. Refusal to accept food or inability to consume it may be noted in the Custody Record. In addition, note should be made of recorded sleep disturbance, which may include police officers going into the suspect's cell late at night or general sleeplessness. The less the suspect has been able to sleep, whether due to interruptions or sleeplessness, the less rested he or she is likely to be when subsequently interrogated.

The second source of information is the accused. A detailed interview will give an insight into his or her mental and physical state at the time of confinement and interrogation. The reporting of various mental symptoms, including lack of appetite, disturbed sleep, nightmares, severe anxiety, a disturbed mood, specific phobic symptoms and hallucinations, may be important in terms of evaluating the reliability of self-incriminating admissions. Physical pain or discomfort may be similarly important.

I have come across two cases where the stress of confinement resulted in apparent hallucinations. In both cases the accused felt that the doors, the walls or the ceiling in the cell were moving in on them. In one of the cases, the accused reported the cell door moving like rubber and this caused him great distress.

The third source of potential information is people who visit the accused at the police station before or after interrogation. Relatives, friends or doctors, just to mention a few potential informants, are often able to give useful information about the likely physical and mental state of the accused. The role of police surgeons is particularly important, although they do not have psychiatric training and would generally not be in a position to carry out a detailed mental state examination on the accused. Wood and Guly (1991) have recently drawn our attention to the potential dangers of failing to scrutinize the reliability of unsubstantiated confessions among mentally disordered patients.

On occasions, police officers may provide an important insight into the mental and physical state of the accused. For example, in one case a police officer reported that the accused had physically collapsed and fainted on the way to an interview room, after being told that he was suspected of being involved in his mother's death. This corroborated the account the accused gave me about the distress he experienced at the accusation that he had murdered his mother. His distress was further augmented during subsequent interrogations, when he was repeatedly accused by the interrogators of having neglected and badly treated his mother whilst she was alive. Following the accusations the son admitted to having suffocated his mother to death. At his trial the judge refused to allow the confession statements in evidence and accused the two police officers concerned of having bullied a murder confession out of him.

Any information obtained from the accused must, whenever possible, be supported or corroborated by other evidence, because it is essentially self-serving. Irrespective of whether people are guilty or innocent of the crime of which they are accused, they may deliberately lie or misrepresent the facts as a way of improving their chances of acquittal. Sometimes the information they give is contradicted by the other evidence in the case. For example, in one murder case the accused told me that the police officers had gone to his cell on several occasions to question him in between formal interviews. This was one of the reasons he gave for having falsely confessed. There was no evidence from the Custody Record to support this claim that the police officers had gone to his cell to question him. During his evidence in court the accused conceded that he had lied to me about it. Not surprisingly, in view of the detrimental effects on the defence when defendants are shown during their testimony to have lied (Shaffer, 1985; Bedau and Radelet, 1987), the accused in that case was convicted of the murder.

4. Interrogative Factors

Interrogative factors cover a range of verbal and non-verbal communication associated with the interrogation itself. Video-recording of the interrogation provides the most informative account of what was said and done and the manner in which the interrogation was conducted. Tape-recordings, which are nowadays the most common way of recording interrogations conducted in English police stations, give less overall information, but they are a formidable improvement on note-taking methods. Not only is the recording more accurate than note-taking, but often certain attitudes and signs of distress are evident. Interrogators' bias and style of questioning may be observed as well as the techniques utilized. When leading questions have been asked by the interrogators and persuasive manipulation and pressure used, then these have to be related to the accused's personality and mental state, as well as to the circumstances of the situation. Occasionally police officers are found to play on suspects' weaknesses, which in vulnerable suspects can result in a false confession. The manipulation of feelings of guilt, particularly in suspects who are accused of murdering loved ones, can markedly increase the likelihood of an unreliable statement.

The Court Report and Oral Evidence

The amount of work involved in the assessment of the defendant and the preparation of a court report vary immensely. Generally, there is an absolute minimum of 2 hours of testing and interviewing. Often it takes considerably longer. Ideally, the defendant should be assessed on more than one occasion, but this may not be possible or practical. With the introduction of tape-recorded police interviews, time must be allocated to listen to those. In my own experience, cases generally take between 5 and 10 hours of clinical time.

It is not uncommon in practice to find that the psychological assessment consists of both favourable and unfavourable findings. For example, a defendant may prove to have poor intellectual abilities, but score low on tests of suggestibility which imply that he or she may be able to cope reasonably well with interrogation in spite of limited cognitive abilities. Similarly, although the test findings are favourable, he or she may be caught lying during the interview with the psychologist. In one case the defendant of borderline intelligence had told his girlfriend and his solicitor that he had obtained five "A" levels. He told me the same lie, but when challenged about it he admitted that he had lied as he had wanted everybody, including the jury, to think that he was "clever". Since he had made some serious self-incriminating admissions to attempted murder it was an advantage for the defence to be able to demonstrate that he was of low intelligence, as indeed he was. Another defendant lied to everybody about his age and other matters. I spotted the lie when I was confirming his age from school reports. The case was written up by Sharrock and Cresswell (1989) in an attempt to explore the relationship between pathological lying and suggestibility.

If the psychological findings are not favourable, then the defendant's solicitors have three choices. They can keep the report from the prosecution, they can instruct another psychologist for a report in the hope that it will be more favourable, or they can ask the psychologist to delete the unfavourable findings from the report. With regard to the last option, there have been some instances where solicitors have asked my colleagues or me to delete the unfavourable findings from the report. This I refuse to do, and no psychologist should ever be tempted to comply with the solicitors' wishes to alter the report in such a way that it could mislead the court. In one major criminal case, the solicitors had my report retyped, with the unfavourable findings deleted from it, returned it to me by a courier and asked me to sign it! I refused and the report was used in full in court. Generally speaking, the only time a psychologist should ever alter the report is when something in the report is worded in such a way as to be potentially misleading or ambiguous. The report could then be clarified or expanded. Otherwise the psychologist runs the risk of misleading the court.

It is important that the psychologist's findings are presented clearly and succinctly. The conclusions drawn should be substantiated and made relevant to the issues addressed. When the findings are presented clearly, and are relevant to the legal issues, then the report may be accepted by the respective legal advocates without the psychologist having to give oral evidence. This is a common occurrence; in only about one-fifth of retracted confession cases does the psychologist have to give oral evidence in court, sometimes during both the *voire dire* and the trial proper. When giving evidence the psychologist can be asked probing and challenging questions by the various legal advocates. He or she should be fully prepared. *It must not be assumed that the psychologist will only be asked questions about his or her report.* Psychologists can be asked any question that arises out of their assessment, including going in detail through police interview records. Often the psychological findings are accepted, but having to place them within the context of the totality of the case during one's evidence in court can be a difficult task. Having carefully considered the wider implications of the psychological findings before giving oral evidence often helps.

THE TOTTENHAM RIOT TRIALS

On 6th October 1985, there was a major public disturbance on the Broadwater Farm Estate, Tottenham, North London. Several buildings and vehicles were damaged or destroyed by fire. Most tragically, a police officer, Keith Blakelock, was descended upon by a mob of between 30 and 50 people and brutally murdered (Burnham Report, 1987). Several other police officers were injured. The riot was precipitated by the death, from a heart attack, of Mrs Cynthia Jarrett, after police officers had entered her home in order to search it for stolen property following her son's arrest (Broadwater Farm Inquiry, 1986). About 100 people, mainly youngsters, gathered outside Tottenham Police Station to protest about Mrs Jarrett's death. The protest turned into a full-blown riot.

In the aftermath of the riot many houses on the estate were raided by the police and many arrests were made. The police investigation was hampered by the fact that there was no forensic or other tangible evidence to assist in the murder inquiry concerning PC Blakelock, and the police began to rely on statements that were obtained from witnesses and suspects, many of whom were youths of limited education. There appears to have been a general feeling of antipathy towards the police and cooperation was not readily forthcoming from the people on the estate. This made the job of the police very difficult and the evidence that they were able to gather consisted almost invariably of uncorroborated confessions.

By May 1986, 359 people had been arrested in connection with the disturbance (Broadwater Farm Inquiry, 1986). Another 10 people appear to have been arrested subsequently, bringing the total figure up to 369. Seventy-one per cent were black and 25% were white. Eighteen per cent were juveniles (i.e. 17 or younger). Most detainees were denied access to a solicitor or their family, or waived their rights to a solicitor. Those detained were held "incommunicado" and their families were not informed of where they were (Broadwater Farm Inquiry, 1986). One hundred and sixty-seven people (45%) were charged with offences arising out of the disturbance (Broadwater Farm Area Housing Committee, 1988). Of the 167 charged, 71 (43%) were charged with affray, riot, petrol bomb offences or murder. The remaining people were charged with such offences as looting, trespassing, burglary and handling stolen goods. Only three of the 71 defendants had a solicitor present at the time they made admissions.

According to the report produced by the Broadwater Farm Area Housing Committee (1988), out of the 71 most serious cases, 28% pleaded guilty. Of 49 defendants who pleaded not guilty (i.e. contested trials), 45% were convicted. Self-incriminating admission or confession were the *only* prosecution evidence presented in court in 76% of the disputed cases. In the remaining cases some additional evidence was produced, such as witnesses and photographs. Therefore, one of the most striking features of the Tottenham Riot trials was the reliance of the prosecution on confession evidence without any supportive evidence. The additional evidence produced by the prosecution was often very weak and appears to have had no significant effect upon the conviction rate.

As the police investigation into the riot was seriously hampered by lack of forensic or other tangible evidence, many arrests appear to have been made as a way of obtaining information and/or confession. According to the police evidence in court (Broadwater Farm Area Housing Committee, 1988), every person arrested was a potential suspect to the murder of PC Blakelock and this, defence counsels argued in court, was used as a deliberate ploy by the police to enhance cooperation and compliance. It is not difficult to see how a potential murder charge could have softened up some suspects to the extent that they confessed to less serious crimes and implicated other people.

Certainly, any possible threat, whether explicit or implicit, of being charged with the murder of PC Blakelock is likely to have influenced the behaviour of many suspects during questioning. What we do not and never will know, is how many of the cases involved false confession. In the majority of cases (55%) the jury believed it was unsafe to convict on the evidence presented to the court. It is also of interest to note that in every case involving affray, the judge refused a submission for a *voire dire* on the basis that it was for the jury to decide upon the weight of the confession evidence.

Psychological Evidence

At least 15 of the 71 defendants who faced the most serious charges arising from the Tottenham Riot were assessed psychologically. I personally assessed eight cases for pre-trial defence court reports. I know of a further seven cases that were assessed by two other psychologists. One of the cases involved Engin Raghip, in whose case I was to become involved after his conviction for murder. His case is discussed in detail later in this Chapter.

In two further cases mental illness had been diagnosed by psychiatrists. In all the eight cases that I assessed, the defendants alleged that they had been coerced into making a confession, believing that the interrogation would continue until they had confessed to something. According to the defendants' accounts, the confessions were all of the coerced-compliant type.

Out of the eight cases that I assessed, I gave oral evidence in four at the Central Criminal Court in front of the jury. All four were charged with affray and were acquitted by a jury. Of the remaining cases, where I did not give oral evidence, three out of the four were convicted. The outcome of the eight cases is significantly related to whether or not I testified in court (Fisher Exact Probability Test, $p < 0.05$). This is, of course, an indirect way of evaluating the impact of the psychological evidence before the jury, because in any one case there are a number of factors that determine the outcome, including the defendant's own testimony and any corroborating evidence that is available to support the prosecution or defence case.

In the cases where I testified, of what did the psychological evidence consist? The answer is that it varied in all four cases, but in all instances it was concerned with potentially challenging the reliability of the confession that the defendants had made during the police interrogation. It did not focus on the more technical issues, such as the defendants' understanding of their legal rights (e.g. understanding of the police caution or the right to a solicitor).

The Full Scale IQs of the four defendants, as measured by the WAIS-R, were 65, 76, 78 and 93. Therefore, only one was functioning intellectually in the mental handicap range. Two were borderline. The defendant with the lowest IQ was the one who proved least suggestible and compliant on testing. The critical evidence in court was his low intellectual ability and this is what the defence focused on. The jury returned a not guilty verdict after 4 hours of deliberation. At the other extreme, the brightest defendant was most suggestible and compliant on testing. The prosecution objected to the admissibility of the psychological evidence because of the defendant's average intellectual functioning, but the judge nevertheless allowed it in evidence. The cross-examination of my evidence was most taxing in this case and lasted over 3 hours. Most of the cross-examination was spent on my going over the record of the police interviews. The defendant was acquitted by the jury in a matter of a few minutes. The remaining two cases, where the defendants were of borderline intellectual abilities, focused on their relatively low IQ and limited reading ability. In addition, high acquiescence and difficulties in understanding simple questions were focused on in one case; in the other it was the difficulty in coping with interrogative pressure (high Shift on GSS 1 and GSS 2) that I was asked about in greatest detail.

The Murder Charges

Six defendants were charged with murder. Three were under the age of 17, that is they were juveniles as far as the English judicial system is concerned. The charges against them with respect to murder were dismissed by the judge at their trial in January 1987. One of them had not confessed to the murder during interrogation; he was the only one of the six to be interviewed in the presence of a solicitor and his father. The evidence against him was that of a witness who admitted in court, during a *voire dire*, that he had lied to the police. As a result the prosecution withdrew the charge of murder and the judge directed the jury to find the defendant not guilty of murder. In the case of the second juvenile, the judge ruled during the trial that the behaviour of police during the interviews had been oppressive and the confession was unreliable. The jury were directed to find him not guilty. The third juvenile had his confession ruled inadmissible by the judge after a clinical psychologist (Olive Tunstall) found that he had not understood the police caution (Beaumont, 1987, 1988). The judge directed the jury, who had heard the expert evidence, to find the defendant not guilty. This defendant had been previously assessed by another psychologist for a pre-trial report. The psychologist did not trust the validity of his IQ findings, and the defence instructed Olive Tunstall, an experienced and very able psychologist, for a second opinion. She carried out a detailed assessment and interpreted her findings within the context of the relevant legal issues, which demolished the prosecution case in court.

The remaining three defendants, Winston Silcott, Mark Braithwaite and Engin Raghip, were tried and convicted of murder, riot and affray. Raghip's defence solicitors had instructed a psychologist for a pre-trial report but, as he did not feel he could trust the validity and reliability of his findings, his report was not used in court.

At the murder trial, the case against Silcott was the weakest because he made no written or signed confession during the five interviews with the police in October 1985, which were conducted over a period of 2 days. Furthermore, there was no evidence against him except for some alleged self-incriminating remarks, which he disputed were ever made. Nevertheless, Silcott was convicted and sentenced to life imprisonment, with the recommendation by the judge that he serve a minimum of 30 years.

Of the three, Braithwaite was the last one to be arrested. He was interviewed seven times and made some self-incriminating admissions, which he subsequently retracted. He admitted having hit a police officer twice with a bar, but did not think it was Blakelock. He was convicted because his admitted attack on a police officer, which the prosecution alleged was Blakelock, was seen as a joint or a common enterprise with a group of others, even if the blows given by Braithwaite did not kill the officer. Braithwaite was sentenced to life imprisonment with a recommendation that he serve a minimum of 8 years.

The Case of Engin Raghip

Engin Raghip was one of the three people convicted of the murder of Keith Blakelock. He was sentenced to life imprisonment and, like Braithwaite, was given a recommended minimum of 8 years to serve. He was arrested at his home at about 7.20 in the morning of the 24th October 1985, and over the next 5 days he was interrogated on 10 separate occasions, which lasted a total of over 14 hours. On the third day of his detention Raghip was charged with affray and taken to a Magistrates' Court. He was remanded in custody for further interrogation, but the Magistrates recommended that he should be only interviewed further in the presence of a solicitor. This recommendation was not followed by the police and Raghip subsequently made incriminating admissions concerning the murder. The case against Raghip on the murder charge rested entirely on contested evidence, which consisted of his admitting during interrogation that he had at the time of Blakelock's murder wanted to get close to the police officer so that he could hit him with a broom handle. He denied having any intention of killing the police officer. In spite of Raghip never confessing to actually hitting the police officer, he was convicted on the basis that the mob of which Raghip was part had a common purpose (i.e. to kill Blakelock).

Raghip was 19 years of age at the time of his arrest. His parents, who were Turkish, had come to England in 1955. Raghip was born and brought up in England. He had serious learning difficulties as a child, and remains illiterate.

He was recommended for a special school but did not bother to attend regularly. At Raghip's trial in January 1987, two expert reports were available. One was a psychiatric report, in which Raghip was described as being probably of average intelligence but dyslexic. The other report consisted of psychological testing, relating to Raghip's intelligence, reading ability and suggestibility. Raghip obtained a Full Scale IQ of 73 on the WAIS-R and had a reading age of 6 years and 3 months. He completed the GSS 1 and his scores were described as average. Neither the psychiatric or psychological reports were used at Raghip's original trial, presumably because they were not entirely favourable to the defence. The psychologist appears to have played down the importance of Raghip's low IQ scores and expressed doubts about the validity of the scores. This appears to have been due to Raghip's average score on two of the Performance subtests. The psychologist concluded that Raghip suffered from limited educational experience rather than a true intellectual deficit.

After the trial and before an appeal was heard in December 1988, a different firm of solicitors represented Raghip. They referred the case to me because of my experience in assessing retracted confession cases. They requested an objective assessment of the reliability of Raghip's confession. I visited Raghip twice in Wormwood Scrubs Prison and carried out a detailed psychological assessment, which consisted of interviewing him in detail, in addition to testing his intelligence, reading ability, suggestibility, acquiescence, compliance, trait and state anxiety and self-esteem. I also interviewed Raghip's common-law wife, who was very helpful and insightful about her husband.

Whilst in prison Raghip had been tested on the WAIS-R by a prison psychologist. He obtained a Full Scale IQ of 74. The pattern of the scores was very similar to those obtained when Raghip was tested by the pre-trial defence psychologist 8 months earlier.

The main results from my assessment were as follows: Raghip obtained a Verbal IQ of 73 and a Performance IQ of 77. His performance on one of the subtests (Picture Arrangement) fell in the 63rd percentile rank. The pattern of the subtest scores was remarkably similar to those found by the pre-trial and prison psychologists. He was also found to be illiterate. With regard to suggestibility, some interesting findings emerged on the GSS 1 and GSS 2, which were administered 11 days apart. On both tests Raghip scored low on Yield 1, but abnormally high on Yield 2 and Shift. In other words, his level or suggestibility was quite normal until he was placed under pressure, which was administered in the form of negative feedback. It was his inability to cope with interrogative pressure that was most striking. This pattern was consistent with a high (17) compliance score on the GCS. Raghip reported high trait and state anxiety, and in terms of self-esteem he rated himself as very timid and submissive.

There were three broad aspects to Raghip's case which I discussed in my report in relation to his retracted confession. First, there were the psychological findings, which highlighted some of his limitations and weaknesses. These included his borderline intellectual abilities, his marked literacy problems, his high level of anxiety and his marked responses to interrogative pressure.

Second, there were the circumstances of Raghip's arrest, interrogation and continued custody. Raghip was arrested by the police because a "garrulous and silly friend" (his solicitor's phrase) mentioned his name whilst being interviewed by the police, after claiming to the *Daily Mirror* that he had seen PC Blakelock's murder. No other person mentioned Raghip's name, but he was nevertheless brought in for questioning. The intensity and duration of Raghip's interrogation, during which he was interviewed without a solicitor or an "appropriate adult" present, was undoubtedly very taxing. Indeed, on the third day, when Raghip was taken to the Magistrates' Court he spoke briefly to a solicitor and told him that he could not cope with further interrogation.

The solicitor has subsequently stated publicly that he found Raghip distressed and disorientated and did not think he was fit to be interviewed on the charge of murder. However, Raghip was to be further interviewed, during which he was to make an admission which in English law amounted to an admission of murder.

Third, there was the question of Raghip's mental state at the time of the police interviews. For a few days prior to his arrest Raghip had been drinking heavily and smoking cannabis. He had not been sleeping well for several days, neither was he eating properly. Shortly before his arrest Raghip's common-law wife had left him, following an argument, and took with her their young baby. Raghip appeared to have been very upset about this. During Raghip's detention he complained of feeling ill and a police surgeon was called twice to examine him. The doctor found Raghip to have mild fever and enlarged neck glands. Raghip told the doctor that he was vomiting after meals. Therefore, at the time of his interrogation, Raghip was not physically or mentally well. These factors may well have exacerbated his existing vulnerabilities, such as his low IQ, high anxiety and difficulties in coping with interrogative pressure.

Armed with the findings of my report, Raghip's solicitors asked for Leave to Appeal against his conviction. The case was heard in the Court of Appeal on 12th and 13th December 1988. The applications of Silcott and Braithwaite were heard at the same time. All three applications failed. At the hearing Lord Lane discussed my evidence in the context of the pre-trial defence reports which were never used at the trial. The fact that the pre-trial psychologist had doubted the validity of his own findings was raised by Lord Lane. The psychologist's conclusion was:

> "Unfortunately the very wide range of scaled scores, from 3 to 10 scale score points, taken in context of Mr Raghip's personal and educational history, compels me to question the validity and reliability of the IQ figures obtained".

This in conjunction with the psychiatrist's opinion that Raghip was probably of average intelligence, but dyslexic, did not help Raghip's application for appeal.

The Appeal Court judges considered Raghip's IQ results in the context of the judgement in *Masih*. As Raghip's IQ was above the "magic" cut-off point of 69 the psychological evidence was not considered admissible. Furthermore, Lord Lane stated in his summing up:

> "The jury had ample opportunity to gauge the degree of intelligence and susceptibility of Raghip when he gave evidence."

Another area of contention was the suggestibility scores of Raghip. The pre-trial psychologist had found Raghip's suggestibility to be average. When I tested him on two separate occasions, he was abnormally suggestible when placed under interrogative pressure. This raised a nagging question, "What accounts for such marked discrepancies between the assessments?" There was no indication in the pre-trial psychologist's report to indicate why this apparently suggestive young man, a characteristic which had been noted clinically by the psychiatrist who assessed him, scored so low on the GSS 1. As the psychologist had made no reference to the mental state of Raghip at the time of the assessment, I contacted the psychologist and asked him to tell me about it. The psychologist replied, "He appeared angry and suspicious."

Unfortunately, the psychologist had failed to mention this important observation in his report. Had he done so it would have been easy to explain the low suggestibility scores obtained, when placed in the context of existing work in this area (Gudjonsson, 1989d). There is no doubt that anger and suspiciousness reduces the person's ordinary susceptibility to suggestions.

In 1986 I was faced with an almost identical case concerning another Tottenham Riot defendant. He was very suspicious of me during the assessment, and proved non-suggestible on testing. Having recognized the importance of such a negative mood on behaviour, I gave him another appointment for the following week. His suspiciousness of me had gone by then and on this occasion he proved highly receptive to interrogative pressure, in an almost identical way to Raghip.

Following the dismissal of the application to appeal, Raghip's solicitor sent a copy of my report to the pre-trial psychologist for his comments. He subsequently made a public statement on a television programme about the case. He was asked on the programme what he would be able to say if he was giving evidence in the case today. He replied:

> "With the advantage of repeat intelligence testing, and with the suggestibility test done under a much more cooperative situation, one would now be in a position to say, one, that he was very suggestible, and secondly, that he is of very low intelligence".

In July 1990, the pre-trial psychologist wrote a report to confirm his current views on the Raghip case. The Home Secretary responded to the pre-trial psychologist's comments on my findings by referring the case back to the Court of Appeal (Tendler, 1990).

What does Raghip's case teach us about the clinical assessment of retracted confession cases? There are two important lessons to be learned. Firstly, we cannot rely on clinical impressions of intellectual functioning. As was illustrated in Chapter 13, often such impressions are wrong. In all fairness to the psychiatrist involved, he did identify Raghip's reading problems and his poor vocabulary, and considered him susceptible to suggestion. And most importantly, he did recommend that Raghip be tested by a psychologist. A problem arose when the psychologist who assessed him did not believe that the IQ results obtained were reliable or valid.

The second lesson to be learned is that when we doubt the validity of our test results then we must, whenever possible, assess the defendant further so that erroneous inferences cannot be drawn from the assessment. For example, if faking is suspected with regard to cognitive functioning, then tests can be administered to substantiate or disprove this possibility (Gudjonsson and Shackleton, 1986). If the mental state of the defendant is such that it compromises the possible validity of the test results, then this should be made clear in the report. Further testing may be required once the defendant's mental state has improved.

THE BEREAVED AMERICAN SERVICEMAN

During the past decade I have assessed a number of defendants who were charged with the murder of their own child. These cases are invariably difficult to assess, because the normal process of bereavement associated with the loss of the child is compounded by the mode of death, which is often sudden, and the parents' realization that they are implicated. In many of the cases that I have assessed, the people concerned were at the time of the child's death under a great deal of stress and simply could not cope any more. They may, on impulse, have hit the child or suffocated it as an immediate way of stopping it crying. The major legal problem is often the question of intent. To illustrate some of the issues concerned in the assessment of these cases I will give a brief description of the assessment and trial of a serviceman with the American Air Force, who was stationed in West Germany. The court martial in the case was conducted under the law of the United States of America.

Mr C was 25 years of age at the time of the tragic death of his 4-month-old daughter. Just after 1 o'clock on a winter afternoon, Mr C telephoned the fire department at the barracks where he was stationed and asked for assistance. He explained that his daughter had stopped breathing. The conversation was tape-recorded and Mr C sounded very distressed and distraught. Soon the fire department arrived, but in the meantime Mr C attempted to revive his daughter by cardiopulmonary resuscitation (CPR). As they arrived, Mr C was described by the fire chief as "hysterical" and kept shouting, "Lord, please don't let my baby die". All attempts to revive the baby failed and she was transported to hospital, where she was pronounced dead.

Later that same day Mr C was interviewed by Office of Special Investigations (OSI) agents, first as a witness and later as a suspect. There were no outward signs on the baby of foul play, but Mr C had been interviewed by one of the agents before in connection with suspected physical abuse to his other two children, with which he was never charged. Most importantly, according to the agents, they had medical evidence from radiographs that the dead baby had broken ribs and collarbone. It seemed that the baby might have died from compression on the chest. The agents apparently formed the view that Mr C had intentionally murdered the baby, and interviewed him accordingly. According to the agents, he was initially reluctant to talk, but they soon gained his trust and he told them that he had placed a pillow over the bassinet to muffle the baby's crying. The agents did not believe Mr C's story and he was interviewed again, after a short break. They confronted him with what they thought had happened and told him that the autopsy would prove that he had been deceitful about his daughter's death. They presented him with scenarios of what they thought had happened. Before long Mr C admitted that he had squeezed his baby's chest to quieten her and at the time thought it could kill her. He signed a statement to that effect.

Mr C was interviewed again by the agents 2 days later. By this time the autopsy had been completed and the agents presented Mr C with what they thought had happened. Mr C was that same evening to sign a statement admitting that he had wanted his daughter to die as he squeezed her chest. His confession was sufficient for him to be charged with his daughter's murder. Mr C was to be tried by a Court Martial.

The case was referred to me by Mr C's defence counsel. I interviewed the defendant and gave him a number of psychological tests in order to assess his intellectual abilities and personality. Mr C obtained a Full Scale IQ of 92 on the WAIS-R. In spite of his average intellectual abilities, he proved to be abnormally suggestible (GSS 2: Yield 1=5; Yield 2=12; Shift=15) and compliant (GCS=20) on testing. He also scored abnormally high on tests for trait and state anxiety, which was corroborated by my clinical interview with him and by people who knew him. Independent informants described Mr C's high level of compliance.

I attended Mr C's trial at a US Air Force base in Germany and gave evidence. The critical legal issue was whether Mr C's confession statements were the product of psychological coercion, and therefore were involuntary. I sat in court and listened to other witnesses giving evidence, including the two OSI agents.

It was evident from the OSI chief interrogator's testimony in court that he had suspected Mr C of murder and believed that "he did not have the will-power to come out with it . . . so we played on his emotions". He stated that he had deliberately placed Mr C under stress, after having built up trust and sympathy, in order to overcome his resistance and "make him feel more culpable". The interrogation techniques used were similar to those recommended by Inbau, Reid and Buckley (1986). These consisted of subtle psychological manipulation (e.g. getting Mr C to admit initially that it had been an accident and then building on it; playing on his guilt concerning physical injuries that had been discoverd on all three children; telling him to "be a man and own up to it"). The agent finally stated, "I go in with the premise that the person committed the offence. He has to prove to me that he is innocent."

Mr C told me, and in his testimony in court said, that the agents had played on his religious feelings, but this was denied by the agents. He had had a very strict and religious upbringing (his father was a minister) and claimed to have felt very distressed and guilty about his daughter's death. There was an independent confirmation of his apparent distress from a psychiatrist who examined Mr C on the day between the two OSI interviews. He found Mr C to be "acutely depressed . . . bereaved . . . dissociating . . . confused by it all." The doctor considered Mr C very vulnerable at the time and "easily manipulated."

I stated in evidence that I could not categorically say that the two statements Mr C made to the OSI agents were in their entirety unreliable, but there were certain factors that pointed to unreliability. These were:

1. Mr C did possess certain personality characteristics that would have made him vulnerable to psychological manipulation and pressure (e.g. suggestibility, compliance, emotional lability).
2. Mr C was apparently in a state of bereavement and acute depression after his daughter's death. He told me that he felt very guilty about her death because he had been minding her at the time of her death and blamed himself for her death. He said that he had felt exasperated that his attempts to comfort her had not stopped her continual crying. He had had serious problems with sleep over a period of several weeks preceding the OSI agents' interviews, and his daughter's continual crying had made this worse. He claimed to have felt very upset about not having been able to speak to his wife privately after their daughter's death. At the time of the agents' interviews he claimed to have been distraught and in a state of emotional shock. He told me that he had pressed his daughter's chest to stop her crying but had not considered that this would kill her. Although many of Mr C's self-reported comments were potentially self-serving, I believed it to be unwise to reject them out of hand. In fact, some of Mr C's claims were corroborated (e.g. his sleep problems, the stress he had been under at the time of his daughter's death, the apparent shock at his daughter's death).
3. Mr C had been psychologically manipulated by the OSI agents, who had interviewed him whilst he was in a very vulnerable emotional state. In

particular, manipulating his feelings of guilt as a means of increasing his legal culpability was, I believed, a recipe for a potentially unreliable self-incriminating confession. Mr C's extremely high level of suggestibility and compliance on psychological testing were also, in my view, relevant to considering the possible "psychological coerciveness" of the OSI interviews and the way he is likely to have reacted to the pressures that he was placed under by the agents.

On the basis of the testimony of one of the agents in court, their stated wish of wanting to overcome his will-power by playing on his emotions appeared to be close to an infringement of the voluntariness of the defendant's statements. The critical point was that the agent's belief that Mr C had intended to kill his daughter was unfounded. It was an assumption that may or may not have been true. Nobody knows for sure what Mr C's intentions were at the time of his daughter's death, except perhaps Mr C himself.

My own view, which was presented in evidence, was that parts of Mr C's self-incriminating statements were probably true (e.g. that he had squeezed her chest to stop her crying, which he claimed to have done successfully before), but I believed it was unsafe to rely on the reference in the second statement to his having had deliberate intentions of killing her. My reasoning was that the agents had manipulated Mr C's guilt in order to make him feel more culpable for his actions. At the time Mr C was undoubtedly feeling very guilt-ridden about his daughter's death as a result of a normal bereavement reaction, which had been compounded by the circumstances of her death. He was in such a vulnerable state that it would, in my view, have been relatively easy to have him take greater blame for his daughter's death than was just.

Mr C was convicted of the 9th lowest degree of culpability out of 10, which was "aggravated assault". This means that he was thought likely to have inflicted grievous bodily harm to his daughter by squeezing her torso. Most importantly for Mr C, he was acquitted of all the most serious charges, which means that the members (jury) found his confession with regard to intent and asphyxiation unreliable and unsafe.

THE MAN ON DEATH ROW

On 5th February 1979, Barbara Kline and her 15-year-old daughter, Michelle, were murdered in their apartment in Norfolk, Virginia. Barbara Kline had been stabbed to death, whereas her daughter had been strangled and apparently raped. The two women had been sharing the apartment with a 21-year-old man, Joe Giarratano. The first police learned about Giarratano as a potential suspect was when he walked up to a police officer at a Greyhound bus station in Jacksonville, Florida, at 3.20 a.m. on 6th February, and said, "I killed two people in Norfolk, Virginia, and I want to give myself up."

Giarratano's original confession to the Jacksonville police alleged that he had killed Barbara Kline in an argument over money. Michelle was then killed to remove her as a witness. Here there was no mention of a sexual assault. This appears to have been a spontaneous account and no knowledge about the crime could possibly have been communicated to Giarratano by the Jacksonville officers as they had no details of the crime before the confession statements were made. Two days later Giarratano gave a totally different account to Norfolk detectives. He now claimed to have raped Michelle before murdering her, and then killed her mother to cover up the crime. This account was consistent with what the Norfolk detectives had told Giarratano, prior to interviewing him, about their knowledge of the murders. Whilst in a State Psychiatric Hospital for a pre-trial examination Giarratano reverted back into the original version. At his trial, the second version was accepted as it seemed to correspond better with the medical examiner's report and the police assumptions about the murders. Everybody at the trial, including Giarratano, accepted that he had murdered the two women and the reliability of the Norfolk confession was never disputed, in spite of the fact that it was in several respects inconsistent with the physical and crime scene evidence.

Giarratano's trial only lasted half a day. Nobody, including the defence, appeared to have looked long and hard at the serious flaws in the evidence that was to send Giarratano to Death Row. Apart from the confessions, the remaining evidence against him was mostly circumstantial. No tangible evidence has ever emerged that clearly indicates that Giarratano committed the two murders.

There is considerable evidence that Giarratano genuinely believed that he had been responsible for the women's death, even though he never appears to have had any clear recollection of having committed the crime. He claims to have woken up in the apartment where he lived with the two women and found them murdered. He *assumed* he had committed the murders and felt very guilty about what he thought he had done. As a result, he desperately wanted to die. This is evident from his suicide attempts whilst on remand and after being convicted, and from his expressed wish to be executed by the State for his deeds (Giarratano refused to accept plea-bargaining to save his life and declined appeals after being convicted).

In 1983 Giarratano began to be seen in prison by a paralegal, Marie Deans, who was giving support and legal advice to prisoners on Death Row. For the first time in his life he was able to talk about his horrific childhood. Marie Deans discovered that Giarratano had no recollection of having killed the two women, but he still assumed that he had done so. With her extensive help over several years Giarratano began to question his own involvement in their death. He no longer wanted to die and began to fight for his life. By 1990 all appeals had been exhausted and Giarratano's time was running out.

In February and March 1990, Dr MacKeith and I spent several days in Virginia working on the case, which included speaking to several independent informants, including one of the police officers from Jacksonville who had interviewed Giarratano before he made the most damaging confession to the Norfolk detectives. We watched two video-recorded interviews with a psychiatrist who had interviewed him at length in 1979 and 1989. We interviewed Giarratano for 12 hours at the Mecklenburg Correctional Facility. The main purpose of our assessment was to evaluate the likely reliability of the self-incriminating admissions made by Giarratano to the police on the 6th and 8th February 1979. There were both psychological and psychiatric aspects to the case, as in the case of Carole Richardson, which meant that Dr MacKeith and I could fruitfully utilize our complementary approaches and expertise. Of particular medical importance were the effects of extensive drug and alcohol abuse on Giarratano's mental state, as well as probable depressive symptoms, whilst he was interrogated by the police in February 1979. Giarratano's psychological strengths and weaknesses were assessed and these were interpreted with reference to the likely reliability of his confessions. The purpose of our assessment was not to attempt to establish whether Giarratano had committed the crimes of which he was convicted. All we were attempting to address was the reliability of his confessions, irrespective of whether or not he had killed the two women.

The aims of our interview with Giarratano were two-fold: first, to interview him about the circumstances of the confessions, his background and substance abuse, his relationship with the two victims, and his mental state in 1979 and afterwards; second, to assess his present mental state and personality, which included Giarratano completing a number of psychological tests. The psychological tests which I administered fell into four groups according to their purpose:

1. Tests designed to give a general profile of Giarratano's personality;
2. Tests which focused on his current mental state, including possible anxiety, depressive, psychotic and phobic symptoms;
3. Tests directly relevant to how Giarratano handled questioning and interrogative pressure;
4. Rating scales of how Giarratano perceived himself and the police officers who interviewed him in 1979.

No intellectual assessment was conducted, as this had been carried out in 1986 by an American neuropsychologist. At that time, Giarratano was found to be of average intellectual ability, but a detailed neuropsychological assessment revealed certain significant deficits in mental processing which were thought to reflect the residual effects of alcohol and drug abuse, and head injuries sustained in fights and falls prior to his arrest.

What were the main findings from the current psychological assessment? They were as follows. There had been a very marked change in Giarratano's emotional and mental functioning since 1979. He now came across as an assertive and articulate man. He was able to talk freely and openly about his feelings and thoughts. He showed none of the retarded and expressionless verbal and non-verbal responses that he did in 1979, which were strikingly evident from a video-recorded interview with a psychiatrist. His self-esteem appeared to have improved very markedly and there was no evidence of depressive symptoms.

In spite of Giarratano's improvement since 1979, which seemed to be related to regular meetings with Marie Deans since 1983 and abstinence from drugs and alcohol, he was still left with a *marked* residual deficit in his memory processing, which related to a strong tendency to confabulate. This was noted on the free recall part of the GSS 1 and GSS 2. This deficit was subtle and possibly not immediately apparent without specific testing, although it is worth pointing out that a prosecution psychiatrist had made a reference to Giarratano's confabulation tendency at his trial in 1979. However, because everybody assumed Giarratano's confession to the Norfolk detectives was reliable, the importance of his vulnerability was not recognized.

Giarratano's clearest vulnerability when I tested him related to his *abnormal* tendency to fill gaps in his memory with confabulated material, that is, imaginary experiences that he believed to be true. Even for material that he had reasonable memory about, he confabulated. In my view, this was a problem which related to how Giarratano had in the past learned to cope with gaps in his memory. It was not possible to say whether or not his tendency to confabulate resulted from his extensive substance abuse, but if it existed before that then the substance abuse is likely to have exacerbated the condition very markedly. Abstinence from substance abuse over a period of several years is likely to have made him less prone to confabulation, even though he was still left with very substantial vulnerability, of which he and his lawyers appeared totally unaware.

A related problem to the confabulation was Giarratano's tendency to incorporate post-event information into his memory recollection. In particular, being asked specific questions, which he said helped him focus his mind and improve his memory, markedly distorted his subsequent recollection, without his apparently being aware of it. On the surface, Giarratano appeared quite resistant to suggestions. However, his resistance to suggestions was superficial and he was far more suggestible than was immediately apparent. His susceptibility to suggestions was probably mediated by his marked inability to detect discrepancies between what he observed and what was suggested to him.

Did the findings of confabulation and suggestibility have any bearing on the likely reliability or unreliability of the self-incriminating confessions Giarratano made to the police in 1979? There was no doubt in my mind that Giarratano's confabulation and suggestibility tendencies seriously challenged the reliability of the confessions he made to the police in 1979. As far as I was concerned, the question of unreliability centred around Giarratano's impaired memory and specific vulnerabilities at the time of the police interviews. In 1979 his tendency to confabulate and his level of suggestibility were undoubtedly much more marked than they are at present because of his extensive substance abuse, distressed mental state, and apparently very low self-esteem.

It was evident that some time before the first police interview at about 3 a.m. on Tuesday 6th February 1979, Giarratano had some knowledge about the two murders. He certainly knew that the two women had been murdered. How he obtained that basic information was not known. He told us that he woke up in the flat and discovered the two women murdered, but claimed to have no recollection of having actually committed the murders. One had to be cautious about even the "memory" of having seen the bodies of the two women in the flat, which seemed very clear and definite in his mind, because the specific details he remembered in 1979 did not entirely fit in with all the known facts. A major problem was that Giarratano had seen the police video of the scene and the photographs and, bearing in mind his tendency to incorporate post-event information into his recollection, I did not think it was safe to rely on what he believed he observed at the time. As far as the police interviews were concerned, the statement to the Norfolk detectives on 8th February 1979 was particularly worrying, because by that time Giarratano had been asked many questions by the police and may have been presented with different scenarios that seemed to fit the known facts at the time.

My final conclusion was that, in view of Giarratano's idiosyncratic vulnerabilities and the circumstances of the confessions, I considered it unsafe to rely on the self-incriminating confessions he had made to the police on 6th and 8th February 1979. Dr MacKeith, looking at the reliability of the confessions from a psychiatric perspective, came to a similar conclusion. We submitted to the defence attorneys our reports, which were made available to the Governor of Virginia.

The day for Giarratano's execution was set for Friday 22nd February 1991. His lawyers petitioned the Governor of Virginia, Lawrence Douglas Wilder, for a conditional pardon. All other appeal procedures had failed and the execution had been ordered by His Honour Thomas R. McNamara, Judge of the Circuit Court of the City of Norfolk. Two days before Giarratano's execution Governor Wilder, in view of the circumstances of the case and the "new" evidence presented by the defence, invoked his clemency powers and commuted the death sentence to life imprisonment, and made Giarratano eligible for parole after he had served a minimum of 25 years in prison. The Governor left the possibility of a re-trial at the discretion of the Attorney General of Virginia, who has issued a public statement that she does not intend to initiate further legal proceedings. Giarratano's life has been spared. His lawyers will no doubt continue to fight for a re-trial so that all the new evidence in the case, including the psychological and psychiatric evidence, can be considered by a jury.

CONCLUSIONS

This chapter provides a conceptual framework for psychologists who are instructed to conduct an assessment on the reliability of testimony. There are a number of different areas that may need to be covered, depending on the individual case. Each case needs to be assessed on its own merit, because there are invariably different problems and issues that need to be considered. Some cases are very complicated and require extensive interviewing and testing. The psychologist should whenever possible carry out a comprehensive assessment so that any vulnerabilities or potentials that could be relevant to the case are identified. The psychological findings may need to be interpreted in court within the total circumstances of the case. The most difficult cases are typically those where the psychologist is asked to testify as to the reliability of the self-incriminating statements, because this involves a careful consideration of *all* the surrounding circumstances of the case.

The knowledge base for the psychological assessment of disputed confessions is growing. Assessment procedures and tests have been developed and these form an important part of the psychologist's armoury. However, it is simplistic to think that any one test or procedure will provide all the answers to an individual case. Human behaviour is complex and often a careful consideration of all the available material is required before firm conclusions can be drawn about the reliability of the self-incriminating statements.

Psychological tests, like those which measure intellectual skills and interrogative suggestibility, often provide important information about the strengths and vulnerabilities of particular individuals, but these have to be interpreted in conjunction with the other material available in the case. Considerable advances have been made in recent years regarding the psychological aspects of disputed confessions, but we still have a great deal more to learn.

POSTSCRIPT

The cases of the Tottenham Three (Silcott, Braithwaite and Raghip) were heard in the Court of Appeal in London between 25th and 27th November 1991. The convictions of the three swere quashed. Silcott's conviction was quashed because his interview record had been interfered with by the police. As a result, there was a contamination effect on the cases of Braithwaite and Raghip. There was evidence heard from three psychologists in the case of Raghip. I was the first to testify. The psychologist who made the pre-trial assessment of Raghip, testified next, saying that he fully accepted my findings. He stated that he had changed his opinion about his pre-trial findings after reading my report. Mrs Olive Tunstall testified last. She presented important background information about Raghip, which corroborated the psychological findings.

CHAPTER 15

Summary and Conclusions

I have discussed in detail the theoretical and empirical aspects of police interrogations and confessions, and have highlighted specific points throughout the book by giving extensive case illustrations. I agree with Davies (1991) that it is only by creatively integrating theory and practice that interviewing can move closer to a science than to an art. We are still a long way from a full "creative synthesis" of theory and practice, but important advances have been made in recent years, many of which are discussed in detail in this book.

Interviewing is one of several fact-finding methods that the police have at their disposal when investigating crime. It is primarily concerned with the gathering of accurate and complete information. The most important task of the interviewer is to maximize *relevant* and *valid* (reliable) pieces of information.

There are a number of factors that may *inhibit* the flow of information during interviewing. Often, these relate either to the *unwillingness* or the *inability* of the subject to provide the information sought. Communication can be maximized by utilizing certain *facilitators*, which function to motivate the subject to cooperate optimally with the interview.

A certain bias is inherent in most police interviews, in that police officers enter the interview with certain assumptions, expectations and hypotheses about the event they are investigating. This bias generally does not cause many problems when the police officers' premises are well founded, and indeed may facilitate the interview process by making it more focused on the essential issues. Problems arise, however, when police officers approach the interview situation with unfounded or erroneous premises. Interviewers should try to minimize bias as far as they can. They should also be aware of the possible misleading effects of bias, and take the appropriate steps to verify the information they obtain.

There are several different approaches to police interrogation. At one extreme, which is highlighted in the detailed police manual of Inbau, Reid and Buckley (1986), the ability of the interrogator to "read" deceptive signs and apply subtle psychological manipulation and trickery is seen as an essential part of the tactics and techniques used. At the other extreme,

Shepherd (1991a) argues that resistance can be overcome by skilful interviewing without the need for persuasive questioning.

The tactics and techniques recommended by Inbau and his colleagues are apparently highly effective in overcoming resistance and eliciting confessions. In my view, some of the tactics recommended in order to obtain a confession (e.g. police officers lying to suspects that they themselves have committed similar offences) are totally unethical. Furthermore, the statement by the authors of these techniques that they never result in a false confession is naive. What we do not know is how often such techniques result in a false confession and other types of erroneous testimony. This is particularly unfortunate and devastating in those parts of the world where the death penalty is operated. Tragically, on occasions victims assumed to have been killed have turned up very much alive after defendants have been executed for their murder.

Shepherd's "social skills" approach to interviewing is an appealing one on humanitarian grounds, but I remain unconvinced that we can, in effective outcome terms, entirely do without persuasive questioning. I believe that effective police interrogation can never be completely free of persuasion. The real issues are the extent and nature of the persuasion used, and the circumstances under which persuasion should or should not be applied.

Why do suspects confess when it is often so clearly against their self-interest? There are a number of different theoretical models of confession. Five such models have been discussed in this book. There is considerable overlap between some of the models, although each model makes somewhat different assumptions about why suspects confess during interrogation. Two recent studies (Gudjonsson and Petursson, 1991a; Moston, Stephenson and Williamson, 1990) have tested scientifically some of the hypotheses generated by these models. The findings indicate that suspects confess due to a combination of factors, rather than to one factor alone. However, there are three broad reasons why suspects confess to crimes they have committed. All three factors appear to be relevant, in varying degrees, to most suspects. First, and far the most important, suspects are most likely to confess when they *perceive* the evidence against them as being strong. In other words, denials are seen as futile by the suspects. Second, many suspects appear to feel remorse about the crime they have committed and have the need to talk about it and give their account of what happened. Third, external pressure (e.g. the stress of confinement and police persuasiveness) is important in some cases in eliciting a confession, because there are often powerful forces present that inhibit or prevent offenders from confessing.

The predominant reason why suspects confess appears markedly to influence their feelings about having made a confession. Those who confess because of strong evidence against them, and who have an internal desire to confess, are subsequently most contented about their confession. Confessions that result from coercive police interrogation techniques leave many suspects resentful, even many years afterwards, and undoubtedly increase the likelihood that the confession is going to be retracted, even when it is true.

The frequency with which suspects confess to crimes in England has fallen in recent years from over 60% to between 40 and 50%. This appears to have followed the implementation of the Police and Criminal Evidence Act (PACE), which came into force in January 1986. The reasons for this decrease seem to be associated with the increased use of solicitors by detainees, and changes in custodial interrogation and confinement procedures. The presence of solicitors during interrogation is most likely to discourage suspects from confessing where the evidence against them is weak. The influence upon the reliability of testimony of having an "appropriate adult" present during the interview of vulnerable persons (e.g. children, the mentally disordered, the mentally handicapped) is unknown. The effect of routine tape-recording on the frequency and quality of confessions is uncertain at present and requires careful research in the future.

How important are confessions in solving crimes? The answer to this question depends upon the strength of the alternative evidence against suspects. Where the alternative evidence is strong a confession may add little or nothing to the prosecution case, although in some cases it does provide important additional information about motive and intent. It seems from the available studies that confession evidence may be crucial or important in about 20% of criminal cases. Once a suspect has confessed, even where there is little or no corroborative evidence, the chances of a conviction are very substantial.

Special care needs to be exercised by police officers when they interview "special groups", such as children, the mentally ill and persons with a mental handicap. People in these groups are potentially vulnerable, in that under certain circumstances they may give information which is misleading and unreliable. Young children and persons with a mental handicap sometimes have difficulties because they are, in general, less able than adults to retrieve factual information from memory. Their spontaneous accounts are often incomplete and interviewers practically always have to go well beyond the sparse detail given in their free narrative account. This means asking either general or specific questions, which may interfere with their memory. One reason for the potential interference with their memory relates to their heightened susceptibility to incorporate post-event information.

There are certain differences between the vulnerabilities of children and persons with a mental handicap which need to be clarified, as they have important legal and psychological implications.

Undoubtedly, the most important difference between these two "special groups" relates to the ease with which their vulnerabilities can be *identified* and *understood*. Children, especially the younger ones, are readily identified by their physical appearance and their age is generally easy to ascertain. In other words, the interviewer is immediately aware that he or she is dealing with a child or a young person. In contrast, the great majority of persons with a mild mental handicap, at least, cannot readily be identified as such by the police. As a consequence, when interviewed as suspects, they are not provided with the legal protection to which they are entitled. Their main legal protection in England relates to their entitlement to have an "appropriate adult" present during the police interviews. The finding that the "appropriate adult" is present extremely infrequently during investigative interviews (Williamson, 1990) supports the view that persons with a mental handicap, and other vulnerable individuals, are not being readily identified by the police.

If suspects are identified subsequent to the police interview as suffering from a mental handicap, then any confession that they made to the police interviewer may be ruled inadmissible by the judge at the trial. It is therefore in the interests of the police, as well as the suspect, that an effort is made to identify vulnerable suspects and provide them with their legal entitlement.

Why are the police apparently not identifying persons with a mild mental handicap? There are a number of reasons for this, which include:

1. Some persons with a mental handicap appear superficially to have satisfactory social functioning, which disguises their vulnerabilities;
2. Persons with a mental handicap see their vulnerabilities as being private and personal. As a consequence, many would not inform the police of their limitations and they may even deliberately attempt to hide them;
3. Many police officers do not seem knowledgeable about the "signs" that should alert them to the possibility that they are interviewing a person with a mental handicap;
4. Even when police officers are aware of certain background information that should alert them to persons' vulnerabilities (e.g. hospital admissions, "special" schooling) they may fail to appreciate the importance of that information.

Police officers are not the only people who fail to identify persons with a mental handicap. Indeed, clinical impressions of people's intellectual functioning are often wrong. For example, a doctor's mental state examination, without psychological testing, often fails to reveal important intellectual deficits. This means that qualified and experienced doctors are sometimes ineffective themselves in identifying a significant intellectual impairment. The reason is that intellectual deficits are often not immediately obvious on superficial examination.

Other differences between children and persons with a mental handicap relate to their memory functioning and susceptibility to suggestions. Children of about 12 years or older seem able to provide as much free recall information as adults, and they do not appear to be any more suggestible than adults *unless their answers are subjected to interrogative pressure.* Such pressure may be in the form of "negative feedback" (i.e. the answers they give to the interviewer are criticized, or simply the same questions are repeated). This indicates that young persons are generally able to resist yielding to leading questions as well as adults, but it is their tendency to "shift" their answers when subjected to pressure by people in authority that makes them particularly vulnerable to giving unreliable information during interrogation.

The vulnerabilities of persons with a mild mental handicap are in some respects similar to those of children between the ages of 8 and 10 years of age. Both groups have limited memory retrieval capacity and tend to yield readily to leading questions, especially when they involve peripheral details.

Persons with a mental handicap appear to have special problems in relation to acquiescence (i.e. the tendency to answer questions in the affirmative, irrespective of content), which seems to relate to the fact that they have learned to give affirmative answers to questions even if they do not understand them. This is perhaps one way in which they have learned to cover up their limitations. There is no evidence that this happens in the case of children.

In spite of their obvious limitations, both children, even as young as 3 years of age, and persons with a mental handicap can give reliable descriptions and accounts of events when interviewed carefully. The same holds true for people suffering from mental illness. The effects of mental illness on the reliability of people's testimony are much more varied and unpredictable than is found in mental handicap, because mental illness has such idiosyncratic effects on cognitive and emotional processes.

Memory is an active and constructive process, which is commonly described in terms of three distinct phases: *acquisition, retention* and *retrieval.* These phases are highly susceptible to interference and distortion. I have reviewed in detail three techniques for *enhancing* or *eliciting* memory during interviewing. These are, "investigative hypnosis", the "cognitive interview" and "drug-aided interviews". Of the three, the "cognitive interview" has the widest application and appears to interfere least with the memory process. It is particularly valuable in that the techniques it comprises can be easily taught to police officers. The other two techniques have certain diagnostic and special applications which complement the "cognitive interview".

There are a number of psychological tests and techniques available for *evaluating* the reliability of testimony. These were reviewed in detail in Chapter 9. These include:

1. The polygraph, which is concerned with the psychophysiological detection of deception;
2. Statement Reality Analysis, which is a semi-objective technique for evaluating the truthfulness of witness statements, particularly those of children who are alleged to have been sexually abused;
3. Stylometry, which is a psycholinguistic technique for evaluating the authenticity of written documents.

Each technique potentially makes a unique contribution to the assessment of an individual case. The greatest overlap is between the use of the polygraph and Statement Reality Analysis.

These three techniques complement clinical tools and procedures for evaluating the reliability of testimony, where the main objective is to identify salient and relevant psychological vulnerabilites that may have a bearing on the legal issues in the individual case (e.g. intellectual deficits, heightened suggestibility and compliance, anxiety proneness, a tendency to confabulate, depression, bereavement, dementia, literacy problems and language difficulties).

In Chapter 14, the clinical assessment of retracted confession cases was discussed in detail. This is a highly specialized area of forensic psychology and often requires considerable intuition, skill and experience. I have argued that in recent years the conceptual framework for assessing such cases, and the development of psychological tests for assessing individual vulnerabilities, have advanced immensely. One important development has been the construction and standardization of scales for assessing *interrogative suggestibility*. This is a special type of suggestibility which has direct application to police interviewing (Gudjonsson, 1991e). The scales developed measure objectively how an individual copes with leading questions and interrogative pressure.

One of the most difficult questions with regard to such concepts as "suggestibility" and "compliance" relates to the extent to which one can generalize from test scores to trait concepts. It is clear from the evidence reviewed in this book that both suggestibility and compliance can be markedly influenced by situational determinants, such as state anxiety and mood (e.g. anger and suspiciousness generally make people less receptive to suggestions and less compliant, whereas anxiety increases suggestibility and compliance). Furthermore, the police interview is a *dynamic* rather than a static process (Gudjonsson and Clark, 1986).

However, in spite of potentially important situational determinants, suggestibility and compliance have certain trait-like characteristics and can be reliably measured, at least in adults. There is no doubt that some individuals are generally more suggestible and compliant than others in a wide range of situations. In general, test scores do give an indication of how an individual is likely to react to a given situation when asked leading questions and subjected to interrogative pressure. This makes test scores potentially valuable in the assessment of forensic cases, although it is simplistic to think that any one test or procedure can provide all the answers to an individual case. Each case must be considered individually. Human behaviour is highly complex and often a careful consideration of all the available material is required before conclusions can be drawn about the reliability of self-incriminating admissions or confessions. Just because a person tends to be abnormally suggestible or compliant on testing does not mean that he or she is unable to give reliable testimony. Individual vulnerabilities, whatever they are, need to be considered within the totality of the circumstances surrounding the case. Conversely, persons who are generally resistant to suggestions and stable emotionally can, under certain circumstances, give misleading and unreliable testimony, including giving a false confession.

How often do false confessions occur during custodial interrogation? The answer is that there is no way of telling. It is unlikely that there is a large number of people who are totally innocent of a serious crime to which they have confessed. However, I have presented evidence in this book to demonstrate that false confessions do sometimes occur in major criminal cases. This can even happen *among suspects who are not mentally ill or handicapped*. In addition, there is some evidence to suggest that adolescents, below the age of criminal responsibility, may under certain circumstances readily confess to crimes that they have not committed in order to protect a friend or a relative from facing criminal prosecution.

Research into "show" trials and public confessions in Stalin's Russia, and the "coercive persuasion" of American Military personnel and Western civilians by Chinese communists, demonstrate how readily even stable and intelligent persons confess falsely under *psychological pressure*, given the right circumstances.

There are also those suspects who overstate their involvement in the crime they are accused of as a result of interrogative pressure. Such cases are likely to be much more common than suspects confessing falsely to crimes of which they are totally innocent.

Why should people make self-incriminating admissions or confessions that are false? Kassin and Wrightsman (1985) suggested three psychologically distinct types of false confession, which they called *voluntary, coerced-compliant* and *coerced-internalized* types, respectively. Each type has a distinctive set of antecedent conditions and psychological consequences.

Early knowledge about the psychology of *coerced-compliant* and *coerced-internalized* false confessions came from research into attitude change within the field of social psychology. Particularly important was the work that was carried out into coercive persuasion among communist interrogators. It provided valuable empirical findings which have resulted in extensive theoretical formulations and developments. I have discussed these developments in detail in the context of subsequent work. Case illustrations of actual criminal cases, many of whom I have assessed myself, are given in the book to highlight the psychological mechanisms involved in each type.

Some important findings in relation to the psychological types of false confession have emerged. First, a *coerced-compliant* type of false confession may occasionally turn into a *coerced-internalized* type, given the right circumstances, or vice versa. For example, after confessing for instrumental gain (e.g. to relieve police pressure), the accused may become increasingly confused and puzzled by the interrogators' apparent confidence in his or her guilt and come to believe temporarily in the confession. This is theoretically consistent with Bem's (1966) view that, under certain circumstances, "saying becomes believing" (i.e. confessing and repeating the confession may make some vulnerable individuals come to believe in the confession).

Second, the subtle manipulative interrogation techniques recommended in American police manuals appear to be particularly likely to result in a *coerced-internalized* type of false confession, whereas the more blatant techniques used by some interrogators (e.g. as alleged in the case of the Birmingham Six) are likely to be associated with the *coerced-compliant* type.

It is evident from some of the cases discussed in this book that innocent suspects do sometimes give information to the police that, on the face of it, seems to have originated from the accused, whereas the information was probably unwittingly communicated to them by the police in the first place. Such apparently "guilty knowledge", which often makes the confession look credible, is then used to substantiate the validity of the confession. The lesson to be learned is that unless the information obtained was unknown to the police, or unless it is supported by corroborative evidence (e.g. the discovery of a body or murder weapon), then great caution should be exercised in the inferences that can be drawn about the accused's guilt.

I have provided the reader with a framework of the relevant English and American law concerning disputed confession cases. English law is much more restrictive than American law with regard to the admissibility of expert testimony. Strictly applied to guidance from the Court of Appeal, expert testimony should only be allowed in England when the defendant possesses some discrete mental abnormality (e.g. mental illness, mental handicap). However, in my experience of the English Criminal Courts, many judges use their discretion and allow psychological evidence without the defendant having been diagnosed as mentally ill or having a mental handicap. Abnormal personality traits, such as extreme suggestibility or compliance, or neurotic/emotional problems, in addition to the psychological effects of situational determinants and certain interrogation techniques, are often relevant to the evaluation of the likely reliability of self-incriminating statements. Such psychological evaluations should be more freely admitted in evidence.

From a psychologist's point of view, a common problem with expert testimony in English courts is the tendency of judges to view psychological evidence in definite and discrete terms: either the person is suggestible or he is not; a person with an IQ of below the "magic" point of 70 is "mentally handicapped" whereas a person with an IQ of 70 or above is not. What is needed is greater flexibility by judges about the admissibility of psychological evidence and less emphasis on arbitrary cut-off points on test scores. The practice of stating confidence limits when presenting IQ scores, as recommended by the British Psychological Society (1991), is an important procedure which could be incorporated into court reports.

The introduction in 1966 of the *Miranda* principle in American law and the Police and the Criminal Evidence Act 1984 (PACE) in England and Wales have had an impact in deterring police misconduct and in protecting the legal rights of suspects. However, the legal rights provided only apply to custodial interrogation. *There appears to be insufficient protection for suspects who are questioned whilst not under arrest* (e.g. off-the-record comments). Greater protection for persons interrogated whilst not under arrest is urgently needed.

What can be done to reduce the likelihood of false confessions in the future? Major improvements have followed the implementation of PACE, which has provided some important safeguards against false confession. These include: fewer repeated interrogations, fewer interrogations conducted at night, the supervisory role of the custody officer, the use of the custody record, greater access to solicitors, the mandatory use of the "appropriate adult" in certain cases, and improved monitoring of the interview record (i.e. contemporaneous note-taking, and especially tape-recording of interviews).

There is major scope for further *improvements* in five important areas:

1. Police officers commonly fail to identify vulnerable persons (e.g. persons with a mental handicap or mental disorder) prior to and during interrogation. There is scope for improved methods in identification and interviewing techniques (see below);
2. PACE has by no means eliminated the risk of false confession. Further legal improvements (e.g. a corroboration requirement) or guidelines are needed to reduce the likelihood of false confessions occurring;
3. There are still inadequate methods available for discovering false confessions when they do occur. There is an immense scope for improvement here in both legal and psychological areas;
4. Even when a high probability of unreliable confession evidence has been demonstrated after conviction, the legal system is often slow and reluctant to act;
5. Police officers and judges are generally very sceptical about alleged false confessions. Greater awareness about the nature and risk of false confessions, and the circumstances under which they are most likely to occur, is an important step forward.

There is immense scope for *improved police training* in relation to interrogation and confessions. Such training should include:

1. Greater understanding and awareness of the nature and psychological effects of the tactics and techniques used. Police officers often use specific techniques without knowing why they use them. Greater awareness of what they are doing and why is an important step forward;
2. Police officers need to be carefully trained to identify individuals who are vulnerable to giving misleading and unreliable information. Such training should include explanations of *why* and *how* such persons are likely to be vulnerable. There should also be greater liaison between the police and forensic medical examiners. The latter should themselves receive training in the identification of psychological vulnerabilities;
3. Greater awareness by police officers of the type of psychological vulnerabilities, situational determinants, and interrogation techniques that may produce unreliable testimony is important if we are to minimize the risk of false confession in the future;

4. Improved training in interviewing and interrogation techniques is needed. There should be specialized training in the interviewing of certain special groups, such as children, the mentally ill, persons with a mental handicap and persons who may have been sexually abused;
5. The effectiveness of police training *must* be objectively evaluated.

At the beginning of this chapter, I implied that it was desirable for police interviewing to move closer to science than art. Some readers may very well ask, why a science rather than an art? Indeed, what is wrong with interviewing remaining as an art and what is so special about science? After all, in the past, many police interrogators have been very successful at obtaining confessions. Every police officer has heard of a "macho star performer" who had a reputation for being able to obtain a confession from even the most resistant suspect!

The problem with interviewing as an art is that it undermines professionalism and objectivity. A successful police force cannot rely on the intrinsic quality of individual "star performers". Indeed, good practice and professionalism are not advanced by a few "star performers". What is required is an interaction between theory and practice, with emphasis on awareness, objectivity, hypothesis testing, training, quality control evaluation and research. The objective should be that *every* police officer views these qualities as being within his or her reach, subject to training. Knowledge about skilful interviewing and appropriate training must not be confined to a few educated senior officers.

What are the general implications of the content of the book? The main message is that there have been major recent advances in psychological theory and research relevant to investigative interviewing and confessions. These advances should improve the professionalism of the police service as a whole, provide psychologists with new and innovative assessment techniques, and offer important insights for the judiciary about how to improve safeguards against false confessions. There is immense scope for further work in this exciting and important area of human endeavour. This book should point the way.

Bibliography

Abel, G. G., Becker, J. V., Cunningham-Rathner, J., Rouleau, J., Kaplan, M. and Reich, J. (1984). *The Treatment of Child Molesters*. Available from SBC-TM, 722 West 168th Street, Box 17, New York, NY 10032.

Abramson, L. Y., Seligman, M. E. P. and Teasdale, J. D. (1978). Learned helplessness in humans: critique and reformulations. *J. Abn. Psychol.* **87**, 49-74.

Allen, R. C. (1966). Toward an exceptional offender's court. *Mental Retardation*, **4**, 3-7.

Alper, A., Buckhout, R., Chern, S., Harwood, R. and Slomovits, M. (1976). Eyewitness identification: accuracy of individual vs. composite recollection of a crime. *Bull. Psychonom. Soc.*, **8**, 147-149.

Amador, M. (1989). Field tests of the cognitive interview: enhancing the recollection of actual victims and witnesses. *J. Appl. Psychol.*, **74**, 722-727.

American Association of Mental Deficiency (1974). *Adaptive Behavior Scale: Manual*. American Association of Mental Deficiency: Washington, D. C.

Anderson, R. C. and Pichert, J. W. (1978). Recall of previously unrecallable information following a shift in perspective. *J. Verbal Learning Verbal Behav.*, **17**, 1-12.

Arens, R. and Meadow, A. (1957). Psycholinguistics and the confession dilemma. *Columbia Law Review*, **56**, 19-46.

Arntzen, F. (1982). Die Situation der Forensischen Aussagepsychologie in der Bundesrepublik Deutschland. *In Reconstructing the Past: The Role of Psychologists in Criminal Trials* (Ed. A. Trankell), P. A. Norstedt & Soners forlag, pp. 107-119.

Arons, H. (1967). *Hypnosis in Criminal Investigation*. Charles C. Thomas: Springfield, IL.

Asch, S. E. (1951). Effects of group pressure upon the modification and distortion of judgments. In: *Groups, Leadership, and Men* (Ed. H. Guetzkow). Carnegie Press: Pittsburgh, PA.

Asch, S. E. (1952). *Social Psychology*, Prentice Hall: New York.

Asch, S. E., Block, H. and Hertzman, M. (1938). Studies in the principles of judgements and attitudes: two basic principles of judgement. *J. Psychol.*, **5**, 219-251.

Atkinson, L. (1990). Intellectual and adaptive functioning: some tables for interpreting the Vineland in combination with intelligence tests. *Amer. J. Mental Retard.*, **95**, 198-203.

Aveling, F. and Hargreaves, H. (1921). Suggestibility with and without prestige in children. *Br. J. Psychol.*, **11**, 53-75.

Ayling, C. J. (1984). Corroborating confessions: an empirical analysis of legal safeguards against false confessions. *Wisconsin Law Review*, **4**, 1121-1204.

Baernstein, L. N. (1929). *An Experimental Study of the Effects on Waking Suggestibility of Small Doses of Scopolamine Hydrobromide*. Dissertation, University of Wisconsin.

Bailey, R. W. and Dolezel, L. (1968). *An Annotated Bibliography of Statistical Stylistics*. The University of Michigan: Ann Arbor.

Baldwin, J. (1990). Police interviews on tape. *New Law J.*, May, 662-663.

Baldwin, J. and McConville, M. (1980). *Confessions in Crown Court Trials.* Royal Commission on Criminal Procedure, Research Study No. 5. HMSO: London.

Bandura, A., Ross, D. and Ross, S. A. (1963). A comparative test of the status envy, social power, and secondary reinforcement theories of identificatory learning. *J. Abn. Soc. Psychol.*, **67**, 527-534.

Barber, T. X. and Calverley, D. S. (1964). "Hypnotic-like" suggestibility in children and adults. *J. Abn. Soc. Psychol.* **66**, 589-597.

Barnes, J. A. and Webster, N. (1980). *Police Interrogation: Tape Recording.* Royal Commission on Criminal Procedure, Research Study No. 8. HMSO: London.

Barthel, J. (1976). *A Death in Canaan.* Thomas Congdon Books: New York.

Bartlett, F. C. (1932). *Remembering: A Study in Experimental and Social Psychology.* Cambridge University Press: Cambridge.

Baxter, J. S. (1990). The suggestibility of child witnesses: a review. *Applied Cognitive Psychology*, **3**, 393-407.

Beaumont, M. (1987). Confession, cautions, experts and the sub-normal after *R. v. Silcott and others. New Law J.*, **August 28**, 807-814.

Beaumont, M. (1988). Psychiatric evidence: over-rationalising the abnormal. *Crim. Law Rev.*, 290-294.

Beck, F. and Godin, W. (1951). *Russian Purge and the Extraction of Confession.* Hurst & Blackett Ltd: London.

Bedau, H. A. and Radelet, M. L. (1987). Miscarriages of justice in potentially capital cases. *Stanford Law Rev.*, **40**, 21-179.

Beins, B. C. and Porter, J. W. (1989). A ratio scale measurement of conformity. *Ed. Psychol. Measure.*, **49**, 75-80.

Belmont, J. M. and Butterfield, E. C. (1971). Learning strategies as determinants of memory deficiencies. *Cogn. Psychol.*, **2**, 411-420.

Bem, D. J. (1966). Inducing belief in false confessions. *J. Pers. Soc. Psychol.*, **3**, 707-710.

Bem, D. J. (1967). When saying is believing. *Psychol. Today*, **1**, 21-25.

Berggren, E. (1975). *The Psychology of Confessions.* E. J. Brill: Leiden.

Bernheim, H. (1888). *Hypnosis and Suggestion in Psychotherapy.* Reprinted by University Books, New York, 1964.

Bernheim, H. (1910). *Hypnotisme et Suggestion.* Doin et Fils: Paris.

Bertrand, A. (1823). *Traité due Somnambulisme.* Dentu: Paris.

Bevan, V. and Lidstone, K. (1985). *A Guide to the Police and Criminal Evidence Act 1984.* Butterworths: London.

Bickman, L. (1974). Social roles and uniforms; clothes make the person. *Psychology Today*, **April**, 49-51.

Billings, A. G. and Moos, R. H. (1981). The role of coping responses and social measures in attenuating to stress of life events. *J. Behav. Med.*, **4**, 139-157.

Binet, A. (1900). *La Suggestibilité.* Doin & Fils:Paris.

Binet, A. (1905). La Science du temoignage. *Année Psychologique*, **11**, 128-136.

Biondo, J. and MacDonald, A. P. (1971). Internal-external locus of control and response to influence attempt. *J. Pers.*, **39**, 407-419.

Birch, D. (1989). The pace hots up: confessions and confusions under the 1984 Act. *Crim. Law Rev.*, 95-116.

Bleckwenn, W. J. (1930a). Production of sleep and rest in psychotic cases. *Arch. Neurol. Psychiat.*, **24**, 365-372.

Bleckwenn, W. J. (1930b). Narcosis as therapy in neuropsychiatric conditions. *J. Amer. Med. Assoc.*, **95**, 1168-1171.

Bluglass, K. (1990) Bereavement and loss. In:*Principles and Practice of Forensic Psychiatry* (Eds. R. Bluglass and P. Bowden). Churchill Livingstone: London, pp. 587-596.

Borchard, E. M. (1932). *Convicting the Innocent: Sixty-five Actual Errors of Criminal Justice.* Doubleday: Golden City.

Bordens, K. S. and Bassett, J. (1985). The plea-bargaining process from the defendant's perspective: a field investigation. *Basic Appl. Soc. Psychol.*, **6**, 93-110.

Bottomley, K., Coleman, C., Dixon, D., Gill, M. and Wall, D. (1991) The detention of suspects in police custody. *Br. J. Criminol.*, **31**, 347-364.

Bottoms, A. E. and McClean, J. D. (1976). *Defendants in the Criminal Process.* Routledge and Kegan Paul: London.

Bower, G. H. (1981). Mood and Memory. *Amer. Psychol.*, **36**, 129-148.

Bower, G. H., Gilligan, S. C. and Monteiro, K. P. (1981). Selectivity of learning caused by affective states. *J. Exper. Psychol. Gen.*, **110**, 451-472.

Brabin, D. (1966). *The Case of Timothy John Evans. Report of an Inquiry by the Hon. Mr. Justice Brabin.* HMSO: London.

Bradford J. and Smith, S. M. (1979). Amnesia and homicide: the Padola case and a study of thirty cases. *Bull. Amer. Acad. Psychiat. Law*, **7**, 219-231.

Bradley, B. P. and Baddeley, A. D. (1990). Emotional factors in forgetting. *Psychol. Med.*, **20**, 351-355.

Bradley, M. T. and Janisse, M. P. (1981). Extraversion and the detection of deception. *Pers. Indiv. Diffs.*, **2**, 99-103.

Braid, J. (1846). *The Powers of the Mind over the Body.* John Churchill: London.

Brandon, R. and Davies, C. (1973). *Wrongful Imprisonment.* George Allen & Unwin: London.

Brehm, J. W. (1966). *A Theory of Psychological Reactance.* Academic Press: New York.

Brehm, S. S. and Brehm, J. W. (1981). *Psychological Reactance: A Theory of Freedom and Control.* Academic Press: New York.

Bridge, J. W. (1914). An experimental study of decision types and their mental correlates. *Psychol. Monogr.*, **17** (1).

British Psychological Society (1991). Mental Impairment and Severe Mental Impairment. *The Psychologist*, 4 373-376.

Broadwater Farm Area Housing Committee (1988). *The Operation of the Criminal Justice System as Applied to the Broadwater Farm Investigation.* London Borough of Haringey, Broadwater Farm Area Housing Committee: London.

Broadwater Farm Inquiry (1986). *Report of the Independent Inquiry into Disturbance of October 1985 at the Broadwater Farm Estate, Tottenham. Chaired by Lord Gifford, QC.* Karia Press: London.

Bronks, I. G. (1987). Amnesia: Organic and Psychogenic. *Br. J. Psychiat.*, **151**, 414-415.

Brown, B. S., Courtless, T. F. and Silber, D. E. (1970). Fantasy and Force: a study of the dynamics of the mentally retarded offender. *J. Crim. Law Criminol. Police Sci.*, **61**, 71-77.

Brown, B. S. and Courtless, T.S. (1971). *The Mentally Retarded Offender.* National Institute of Mental Health, Center for Studies of Crime and Delinquency: Rockville, MD.

Brown, D. (1989). *Detention at the Police Station under the Police and Criminal Evidence Act 1984.* Home Office Research Study No. 104. HMSO: London.

Brown R. and Kulik, J. (1977). Flashbulb memories. *Cognition*, **5**, 73-99.

Bruce, V. and Young, A. (1986). Understanding face recognition. *Br. J. Psychiat.*, **77**, 305-327.

Bryan, W. J. (1962). *Legal Aspects of Hypnosis.* Charles C. Thomas: Springfield, IL.

Buckhout, R. (1974). Eyewitness testimony. *Sci. Amer.*, **231**, 23-31.

Burke, D. M. and Light, L. L. (1981). Memory and ageing: the role of retrieval processes. *Psychol. Bull.*, **90**, 513-546.

Burnham Report (1987). *Report of Findings of International Jurists in Respect of Broadwater Farm Trials.* Broadwater Farm Defence Campaign: London.

Burtt, H.E. (1948). *Applied Psychology*. Prentice-Hall: New York.

Calcutt, D. (1986). *Report by David Calcutt Q.C. on his Inquiry into the Investigations Carried out by the Service Police in Cyprus in February and March 1984*. HMSO: London.

Carlsmith, J. M. and Gross, A. E. (1969). Some effects of guilt on compliance. *J. Pers. Soc. Psychol.*, **11**, 232-239.

Cattell, J. M. (1895). Measurements of the accuracy of recollection. *Science*, **2**, 761-766.

Ceci, S. J., Ross, D. F. and Toglia, M. P. (1987). Age differences in suggestibility: narrowing the uncertainties. In: *Children's Eyewitness Memory* (Eds. S. J. Ceci, M. P. Toglia and D. F. Ross). Springer-Verlag: New York, pp. 79-91.

Chesshyre, R. (1990). *The Force Inside the Police*. Pan: London.

Christianson, S. A. and Loftus, E. F. (1991). Remembering emotional events: the fate of detailed information. *Cogn. Emot.*, **5**, 81-108.

Clare, I. and Gudjonsson, G. H. (1991a). *Recall and Understanding of the Caution and Rights in Police Detention Among Persons of Average Intellectual Ability and Persons with a Mental Handicap*. Issues in Criminological and Legal Psychology, British Psychological Society: Leicester, in press.

Clare, I. and Gudjonsson, G. H. (1991b). Suggestibility, acquiescence and confabulation among persons with a mild mental handicap (in preparation).

Clifford, B. R. (1979). The relevance of psychological investigation to legal issues in testimony and identification. *Crim. Law Rev.*, 153-163.

Clifford, B. R. (1983). Memory for voices: the feasibility and quality of earwitness evidence. In S. M. A. Lloyd-Bostock and B. R. Clifford (Eds), *Evaluating Witness Evidence*. Wiley: Chichester, pp.189-218.

Clifford, B. R. and Hollin, C. R. (1981). Effects of the type of incident and the number of perpetrators on eyewitness memory. *J. Appl. Psychol.*, **66**, 364-370.

Clifford, B. R. and Richards, V. J. (1977). Comparison of recall of policemen and civilians under conditions of long and short durations of exposure. *Percept. Mot. Skills*, **45**, 503-512.

Clifford, B. R. and Scott, J. (1978). Individual and situational factors in eyewitness testimony. *J. Appl. Psychol.*, **63**, 352-359.

Coffin, T. E. (1941). Some conditions of suggestion and suggestibility: a study of certain attitudinal and situational factors influencing the process of suggestion. *Psychol. Monogr.*, **53**, 1-121.

Cohen, G., Eysenck, M. W. and Levoi, M. E. (1986). *Memory: A Cognitive Approach*. Open University Press: Milton Keynes.

Cohen, R. L. and Harnick, M. A. (1980). The susceptibility of child witnesses to suggestion. *Law Human Behav.*, **4**, 201-210.

Coid, J. (1981). Suggestibility, low intelligence and a confession to crime. *Br. J. Psychiat.*, **139**, 436-438.

Comish, S. E. (1987). Recognition of facial stimuli following an intervening task involving the Identi-Kit. *J. Appl. Psychol.*, **72**, 488-491.

Conlon, G. (1990). *Proved Innocent. The Story of Gerry Conlon of the Guildford Four*. Hamish Hamilton: London.

Connery, D. S. (1977). *Guilty until Proven Innocent*. G. P. Putnam's Sons: New York; Longman Canada Ltd: Toronto.

Coons, P. M. (1988). Misuse of forensic hypnosis: a hypnotically elicited false confession with the apparent creation of multiple personality. *Int. J. Clin. Exp. Hypnosis*, **36**, 1-11.

Coopersmith, S. (1967). *The Antecedents of Self-esteem*. Freeman: San Francisco, CA.

Cowdry, Q. and Oakley, R. (1990). Electro-static test puts evidence in doubt. Birmingham Six cases go to second appeal. *The Times*, **August 30**, 1.

Craft, M. (1984). Low intelligence, mental handicap and criminality. In: *Mentally Abnormal Offenders* (Eds. M. Craft and A. Craft). Baillière Tindall: London, pp. 177-185.

Cronbach, L. J. (1946). Response sets and test validity. *Educ. Psychol. Meas.*, **6**, 475-494.

Crowder, R. G. (1976). *Principles of Learning and Memory*. Erlbaum: Hillsdale, NJ.

Crowne, D. P. and Marlowe, D. (1960). A new scale of social desirability independent of psychopathology. *J. Consult. Psychol.*, **24**, 349-354.

Crutchfield, R. S. (1955). Conformity and character. *Amer. Psychol.*, **10**, 191-198.

Cunningham, C. (1973). Interrogation. *Medico-legal J.*, **41**, 49-62.

Curle, C. E. (1989). An Investigation of Reaction to Having Killed amongst Male Homicide Patients Resident in a Maximum Security Hospital. Unpublished PhD thesis: University of London.

Danto, B. L. (1979). The use of brevital sodium in police investigation. *Police Chief*, **46**, 53-55.

Davies, G. M. (1983). The legal importance of psychological research in eyewitness testimony: British and American experiences. *J. Foren. Sci. Soc.*, **24**, 165-175.

Davies, G. M. (1986). Context effects in episodic memory: a review. *Cahiers de Psychologie Cognitive*, **6**, 157-174.

Davies, G. (1991). Research on children's testimony: implications for interviewing practice. In: *Clinical Approaches to Sex Offenders and their Victims* (Eds. C. R. Hollin and K. Howells). Wiley: Chichester, pp. 93-115.

Davies, G. and Brown, L. (1978). Recall and organisation in five-year-old children. *Br. J. Psychol.*, **69**, 343-349.

Davies, G., Flin, R. and Baxter, J. (1986). The child witness. *Howard J.*, **25**, 81-99.

Davies, G. M., Shepherd, J. W. and Ellis, H.D. (1979). Effects of interpolated mugshot exposure on accuracy of eyewitness identification. *J. Appl. Psychol.*, **64**, 232-237.

Davies, G. M., Tarrant, A. and Flin, R. (1989). Close encounters of the witness kind: children's memory for a simulated health inspection. *Br. J. Psychol.*, **80**, 415-429.

Deeley, P. (1971). *Beyond Breaking Point: A Study of the Techniques of Interrogation*. Arthur Barker: London.

Deffenbacher, K. A. (1983). The influence of arousal on reliability of testimony. In: *Evaluating Witness Evidence: Recent Psychological Research and New Perspectives* (Eds. S. M. A. Lloyd-Bostock and B. R. Clifford). Wiley: Chichester.

Dell, S. (1971). *Silent in Court*. Occasional Papers on Social Administration, Number 42, The Social Administration Trust: London (ISBN 07135 15767).

Denkowski, G. C. and Denkowski, K. M. (1985). The mentally retarded offender in the state prison system: identification, prevalence, adjustment and rehabilitation. *Crim. Justice Behav.*, **12**, 55-70.

Dent, H. R. (1986). An experimental study of the effectiveness of different techniques of questioning mentally handicapped witnesses. *Br. J. Clin. Psychol.*, **25**, 13-17.

Dent, H. R. and Stephenson, G. M. (1979). An experimental study of the effectiveness of different techniques of questioning child witnesses. *Br. J. Clin. Psychol.*, **18**, 41-51.

Dession, G. H., Freedman, L. Z., Donnelly, R. C. and Redlich, F. C. (1953). Drug-induced revelation and criminal investigation. *Yale Law.*, **62**, 315-347.

Diamond, B. L. (1980). Inherent problems in the use of pretrial hypnosis as a prospective witness. *Calif. Law Rev.*, **68**, 313-349.

Dodd, D. H. and Bradshaw, J. M. (1980). Leading questions and memory: pragmatic constraints. *J. Verbal Learning Verbal Behav.*, **19**, 695-704.

Doll, E. A. (1965). *Vineland Social Maturity Scale: Manual of Directions*. American Guidance Service: Minneapolis.

Dombrose, L. A. and Slobin, M. S. (1958). The IES Test. *Percept. Motor Skills*, **8**, 347-389.

Dristas, W. J. and Hamilton, V. L. (1977). Evidence about evidence: effect of presupposition, items salience, stress, and perceived set on accident recall. Unpublished manuscript, University of Michigan.

Driver, E. D. (1968). Confessions and the social psychology of coercion. *Harvard Law Rev.*, **82**, 42-61.

Dundee, J. W. (1990). Fantasies during sedation with intravenous midazolam or diazepam. *Medico-legal J.*, **58**, 29-34.

Dyer, C. (1990). Suspects' leaflet may be reworded. *The Guardian*, **November 30**, 7.

Dysken, M. W., Chang, S. S., Casper, R. C. and Davis, J. M. (1979). Barbiturate-facilitated interviewing. *Biol. Psychiat.*, **14**, 421-432.

Eagly, A. H. (1978). Sex differences in influenceability. *Psychol. Bull.*, **85**, 86-116.

Easterbrook, J. A. (1959). The effect of emotion on cue utilization and the organization of behavior. *Psychol. Bull.*, **66**, 183-201.

Eisenberg, G. H. (1978). The Relationship of Locus of Control to Social Influence. A Test of Reactance Theory. Unpublished Master's Thesis, University of South Florida.

Ekman, P. (1985). *Telling Lies.* Norton: New York and London.

Elaad, E. and Kleiner, M. (1990). Effects of polygraph chart interpreter experience on psychophysiological detection of deception. *Police Sci. Admin.*, **17**, 115-123.

Ellis, H. D. (1984). Practical aspects of face memory. In: *Eyewitness Testimony: Psychological Perspectives* (Eds. G. L. Wells and E. F. Loftus). Cambridge University Press: Cambridge, pp. 2-37.

Ellis, H. D. (1988). The Tichborne claimant: person identification following very long intervals. *Appl. Cogn. Psychol.*, **2**, 257-264.

Ellis, H. D., Davies, G. M. and Shepherd, J. W. (1977). Experimental studies of face recognition. *Nat. J. Crim. Def.*, **3**, 219-234.

Eugenio, P., Buckhout, R., Kostes, S. and Ellison, K. W. (1982). Hyperamnesia in the eyewitness to a crime. *Bull. Psychonom. Soc.*, **19**, 83-86.

Evans, F. J. (1967). Suggestibility in the normal waking state. *Psychol. Bull.*, **67**, 114-129.

Evans, F. J. (1989). The independence of suggestibility, placebo response, and hypnotizability. In: *Suggestion and Suggestibility. Theory and Research* (Eds. V. A. Gheorghiv, P. Netter, H. J. Eysenck and R. Rosenthal). Springer-Verlag: London, pp. 145-154.

Everitt, B. (1974). *Cluster Analysis.* Heinemann Educational Books: London.

Eysenck, H. J. (1943). Suggestibility and hysteria. *J. Neurol. Psychiat.*, **6**, 22-31.

Eysenck, H. J. (1947). *Dimensions of Personality.*Routledge & Kegan Paul: London.

Eysenck, H. J. and Eysenck, S. B. G. (1975). *Manual of the Eysenck Personality Questionnaire.* Hodder and Stoughton: London.

Eysenck, H. J. and Furneaux, W. D. (1945). Primary and secondary suggestibility: an experimental and statistical study. *J. Exp. Psychol.*, **35**, 485-503.

Eysenck, H. J. and Gudjonsson, G. H. (1989). *The Causes and Cures of Criminality.* Plenum Press: New York and London.

Eysenck,. H. J. and Rees, W. L. (1945). States of heightened suggestibility: narcosia. *J. Ment. Sci.*, **91**, 301-310.

Eysenck, S. B. G. and Eysenck, H. J. (1978). Impulsiveness and venturesomeness: their position in a dimensional system of personality description. *Psychol. Rep.*, **43**, 1247-1255.

Eysenck, S. B. G. and Haraldsson, E. (1983). National differences in personality: Iceland and England. *Psychol. Rep.* **53**, 999-1003.

Farber, I. E., Harlow, H. F. and West, L. J. (1957). Brainwashing, conditioning and DDD. *Sociometry*, **20**, 271-285.

Farr, J. N. and Jenkins, J. J. (1949). Tables for use with the Flesch Reliability Formulas. *J. Appl. Psychol.*, **33**, 275-278.

Feldman, D. (1990). Regulating treatment of suspects in police stations: judicial interpretations of detention provisions in the Police and Criminal Evidence Act 1984. *Crim. Law Rev.*, 452-471.

Fellows, B. J. (1986). The concept of trance. In: *What is Hypnosis? Current Theories and Research.* Open University Press: Milton Keynes, pp. 37-58.

Fellows, N. (1986). *Killing Time.* Lion Publishing Company: Oxford.

Festinger, L. (1953). An analysis of compliant behavior. In: *Group Relations of the Crossroads* (Eds. M. Sherif and M. O. Wilson). Harper: New York, pp. 232-256.

Festinger, L. (1954). A theory of social comparison processes. *Human Relations, 1,* 117-140.

Festinger, L. (1957). *A Theory of Cognitive Dissonance.* Row, Peterson: Evanston, IL.

Firth, A. (1975). Interrogation. *Police Rev., 4324,* 1507.

Fisher, H. (1977). *Report of an Inquiry by the Hon. Sir Henry Fisher Into the Circumstances Leading to the Trial of Three Persons on Charges Arising out of the Death of Maxwell Confait and the Fire at 27 Doggett Road, London, SE6.* HMSO: London.

Fisher, R. P., Geiselman, R. E. and Amador, M. (1989). Field test of the cognitive interview: enhancing the recollection of actual victims and witnesses of crime. *J. Appl. Psychol., 74,* 722-727.

Fisher, R. P., Geiselman, R. E. and Raymond, D. S. (1987). Critical analysis of police interview techniques. *J. Police Sci. Admin., 15,* 177-185.

Fitzgerald, E. (1987). Psychologists and the law of evidence: admissibility and confidentiality. In: *Psychological Evidence in Court* (Eds. G. Gudjonsson and J. Drinkwater). Issues in Criminological and Legal Psychology, No.11. British Psychological Society: Leicester, pp. 39-48.

Flesch, R. (1946). *The Art of Plain Talk.* Harper & Brothers: New York.

Flesch, R. (1948). A new readability yardstick. *J. Appl. Psychol., 32,* 221-233.

Flexser, A. and Tulving, E. (1978). Retrieval independence in recognition and recall. *Psychol. Rev., 85,* 153-171.

Ford, R. and Tendler, S. (1989). Guildford pub bomb four get fresh hearing. *The Times,* **January 17,** 1.

Foster, H. H. (1969). Confessions and the station house syndrome. *De Paul Law Rev., 18,* 683-701.

Fraisse, P. (1984). Perception and estimation of time. *Ann. Rev. Psychol., 35,* 1-36.

Frank, J. (1957). *Not Guilty,* Doubleday: New York.

Fraser, K. A. (1988). Bereavement in those who have killed. *Med. Sci. Law, 28,* 127-130.

Freedman, J. L. and Fraser, S. C. (1966). Compliance without pressure: the foot-in-the-door technique. *J. Pers. Soc. Psychol., 4,* 195-202.

Freedman, J. L., Wallington, S. A. and Bless, E. (1967). Compliance without pressure: the effect of guilt. *J. Pers. Soc. Psychol.,7,* 117-124.

Freedman, L. Z. (1967). "Truth" drugs. *Sci. Amer.,* **January,** 3-8.

Freud, S. (1940). An outline of psychoanalysis. In: J. Strachey (Ed.). *Standard Edition of the Complete Psychological Work of Sigmund Freud,* Vol. 23. London: Hogarth.

Gardner, D. S. (1933). The perception of memory of witnesses. *Cornell Law Q., 8,* 391-409.

Geiselman, R. E. and Fisher, R. P. (1985). Interviewing victims and witnesses of crime. *Nat. Inst. Justice Res. Brief* (NCJ-99061).

Geiselman, R. E. and Fisher, R. P. (1989). The cognitive interview technique for victims and witness of crime. In: *Psychological Methods in Criminal Investigation and Evidence* (Ed. D. C. Raskin). Springer: New York, pp. 191-215.

Geiselman, R. E., Fisher, R. P., Mackinnon, D. P. and Holland, H. L. (1985). Eyewitness memory enhancing in the police interview: cognitive retrieval mnemonics versus hypnosis. *J. Appl. Psychol., 70,* 401-412.

Geiselman, R. E., Fisher, R. P., Mackinnon, D. P. and Holland, H. L. (1986). Enhancement of eyewitness memory with the cognitive interview. *Amer. J. Psychol., 99,* 385-401.

Geiselman, R. E., Fisher, R. P., Firstenberg, I., Hutton, L. A., Sullivan, S., Avetissian, I. and Prosk, A. (1984). Enhancement of eyewitness memory: an empirical evaluation of the cognitive interview. *J. Police Sci. Admin.*, **12**, 74-80.

Gerson, M. J. and Victoroff, V. M. (1949). Experimental investigation into the validity of confessions obtained under sodium amytal narcosis. *J. Clin. Psychopathol.*, **9**, 359-375.

Gheorghiu, V. A. (1972). On suggestion and suggestibility. *Scientia*, **16**, 811-860.

Gheorghiu, V. A. (1989a). The difficulty in explaining suggestion: some conceivable solutions. In: *Suggestion and Suggestibility: Theory and Research* (Eds. V. A. Gheorghiu, P. Netter, H. J. Eysenck and R. Rosenthal). Springer-Verlag: London, pp. 99-112.

Gheorghiu, V. A. (1989b). The development of research on suggestibility: Critical considerations. In: *Suggestion and Suggestibility: Theory and Research* (Eds. V. A. Gheorghiu, P. Netter, H. J. Eysenck and R. Rosenthal). Springer-Verlag: London, pp. 3-55.

Gibb, F., Tendler, S. and Webster, P. (1989). Three bomb case police suspended. Judge to lead inquiry after Guildford four are cleared. *The Times*, **October 20**, 1.

Gibson, H. B. (1962). An Investigation of Personality Variables Associated with Susceptibility to Hypnosis. PhD thesis, University of London.

Gibson, H. B. and Heap, M. (1991). *Hypnosis in Therapy*. Lawrence Erlbaum Associates: Hove, East Sussex.

Gieson, M. and Rollinson, M. A. (1980). Guilty knowledge versus innocent association: effects of trait anxiety and stimulus context on skin conductance. *J. Res. Pers.*, **14**, 1-11.

Gill, P., Jeffreys, A. J. and Werrett, D. J. (1985). Forensic application of DNA "Fingerprints". *Nature*, **318**, 577-579.

Gill, P. and Werrett, D. J. (1987). Exclusion of a man charged with murder by DNA fingerprinting. *Foren. Sci. Int.*, **35**, 145-148.

Gill, P., Lygo, J. E., Fowler, S. J. and Werrett, D. J. (1987). An evaluation of DNA "fingerprinting" for forensic purposes. *Electrophoresis*, **8**, 38-44.

Glaus, R. A. (1975). Suggestibility in young drug dependent and normal populations. *Br. J. Addict.*, **70**, 287-293.

Goffman, E. (1959). *The Presentation of Self in Everyday Life*. Doubleday Anchor Books: New York.

Goodman, G. S., Aman, C. and Hirschman, J. (1987). Child sexual and physical abuse: children's testimony. In: *Children's Eyewitness Memory* (Eds. S. J. Ceci, M. P. Toglia and D. F. Ross). Springer: New York, pp. 1-23.

Goodman, G. S. and Reed, R. S. (1986). Age differences in eyewitness testimony. *Law Hum. Behav.*, **10**, 317-332.

Goodwin, D. W., Crane, J. B. and Guze, S. B. (1969). Phenomenological aspects of the alcoholic "blackout". *Br. J. Psychiat.*, **115**, 1033-1038.

Gorden, R. (1975). *Interviewing: Strategy, Techniques and Tactics*. Dorsey: Homewood, Ill.

Gottschalk, L. A. (1961). The use of drugs in interrogation. In: *The Manipulation of Human Behavior* (Eds. A. D. Biderman and H. Zimmer). Wiley: Chichester, pp. 96-141.

Graef, R. (1990). *Talking Blues. The Police in their own Words*. Fontana: London.

Graf, R. G. (1971). Induced self-esteem as a determinant of behavior. *J. Soc. Psychol.*, **85**, 213-217.

Grant, A. (1987). Videotaping police questioning: a Canadian experiment. *Crim. Law Rep.*, 375-383.

Greene, E., Flynn, M. S. and Loftus, E. F. (1982). Inducing resistance to misleading information. *J. Verbal Learning Verbal Behav.*, **21**, 207-219.

Gregg, V. H. (1987). *Introduction to Human Memory*. Routledge & Kegan Paul: London.

Gregg, V. H. and Mingay, D. J. (1987). Influence of hypnosis on riskiness and discriminability in recognition memory of faces. *Br. J. Exper. Clin. Hypnosis*, 4, 65-76.

Griffin, G. R. (1980). Hypnosis: towards a logical approach in using hypnosis in law enforcement agencies. *J. Police Sci. Admin.*, 8, 385-389.

Griffiths, J. and Ayres, R. E. (1967). A postscript to the Miranda project: interrogation of draft protesters. *Yale Law J.*, 77, 300-319.

Grinker, P. and Spiegel, J. P. (1945). *War Neuroses*. Blakiston: Philadelphia.

Grisso, T. (1980). Juveniles' capacities to waive Miranda rights: an empirical analysis. *California Law Rev.*, 68, 1134-1166.

Grisso, T. (1986). *Evaluating Competencies. Forensic Assessments and Instruments*. Plenum Press: New York.

Gudjonsson, G. H. (1979a). Electrodermal responsivity in Icelandic criminals, clergymen and policemen. *Br. J. Soc. Clin. Psychol.*, 18, 351-353.

Gudjonsson, G. H. (1979b). The use of electrodermal responses in a case of amnesia (A case report). *Med. Sci. Law*, 19, 138-140.

Gudjonsson, G. H. (1982). Extraversion and the detecting of deception: Comments on the paper by Bradley and Janisse. *Pers. Individ. Diff.*, 3, 215-216.

Gudjonsson, G. H. (1983a). Suggestibility, intelligence, memory recall and personality: an experimental study. *Br. J. Psychiat.*, 142, 35-37.

Gudjonsson, G. H. (1983b). Lie detection: techniques and countermeasures. In: *Evaluating Witness Evidence* (Eds. S. M. A. Lloyd-Bostock and B. R. Clifford). Wiley: Chichester, pp. 137-153.

Gudjonsson, G. H. (1984a). A new scale of interrogative suggestibility. *Pers. Individ. Diff.*, 5, 303-314.

Gudjonsson, G. H. (1984b). Attribution of blame for criminal acts and its relationship with personality. *Pers. Individ. Diff.*, 5, 53-58.

Gudjonsson, G. H. (1984c). Interrogative suggestibility: comparison between "false confessors" and "deniers" in criminal trials. *Med. Sci. Law*, 24, 56-60.

Gudjonsson, G. H. (1984d). Interrogative suggestibility and perceptual motor performance. *Percept. Mot. Skills*, 58, 671-672.

Gudjonsson, G. H. (1985). Psychological evidence in court: results from the BPS survey. *Bull. Br. Psychol. Soc.*, 38, 327-330.

Gudjonsson, G. H. (1986). The relationship between interrogative suggestibility and acquiescence: empirical findings and theoretical implications. *Pers. Individ. Diff.*, 7, 195-199.

Gudjonsson, G. H. (1987a). Historical background to suggestibility: how interrogative suggestibility differs from other types of suggestibility. *Pers. Individ. Diff.*, 8, 347-355.

Gudjonsson, G. H. (1987b). A parallel form of the Gudjonsson Suggestibility Scale. *Br. J. Clin. Psychol.*, 26, 215-221.

Gudjonsson, G. H. (1987c). The relationship between memory and suggestibility. *Soc. Behav.*, 2, 29-33.

Gudjonsson, G. H. (1988a). Interrogative suggestibility: its relationship with assertiveness, social-evaluative anxiety, state anxiety and method of coping. *Br. J. Clin. Psychol.*, 27, 159-166.

Gudjonsson, G. H. (1988b). The relationship of intelligence and memory to interrogative suggestibility: the importance of range effects. *Br. J. Clin. Psychol.*, 27, 185-187.

Gudjonsson, G. H. (1988c). How to defeat the polygraph tests. In: *The Polygraph Test. Truth, Lies and Science.* (Ed. A. Gale). Sage: London, pp. 126-136.

Gudjonsson, G. H. (1989a) Compliance in an interrogation situation: a new scale. *Pers. Individ. Diff.*, 10, 535-540.

Gudjonsson, G. H. (1989b). The psychology of false confessions. *Medico-Legal J.*, 57, 93–110.

Gudjonsson, G. H. (1989c). Theoretical and empirical aspects of interrogative suggestibility. In: *Suggestion and Suggestibility* (Eds. V. A. Gheorghiu, P. Netter, H. J. Eysenck and R. Rosenthal). Springer-Verlag: London, pp. 135–143.

Gudjonsson, G. H. (1989d). The effects of suspiciousness and anger on suggestibility. *Med. Sci. Law*, 29, 229–232.

Gudjonsson, G. H. (1990a). The response alternatives of suggestible and non-suggestible individuals. *Pers. Individ. Diff.*, 11, 185–186.

Gudjonsson, G. H. (1990b). Self-deception and other-deception in forensic assessment. *Pers. Individ. Diff.*, 11, 219–225.

Gudjonsson, G. H. (1990c). The relationship of intellectual skills to suggestibility compliance and acquiescence. *Pers. Individ. Diff.*, 11, 227–231.

Gudjonsson, G. H. (1990d). One hundred alleged false confession cases: some normative data. *Br. J. Clin. Psychol.*, 29, 249–250.

Gudjonsson, G. H. (1990e). Understanding the notice to detained persons. *The Law Gazette*, 43, 28 November.

Gudjonsson, G. H. (1990f). The psychologist as an expert witness. In: *Principles and Practice of Forensic Psychiatry* (Eds. R. Bluglass and P. Bowden). Churchill Livingstone: London, pp. 167–169.

Gudjonsson, G. H. (1991a). The internal consistency and factor analysis of Yield and Shift-items on the Gudjonsson Suggestibility Scale (GSS 2). *Pers. Individ. Diff.* (in press).

Gudjonsson, G. H. (1991b). The "Notice to Detained Persons", PACE Codes, and Reading Ease. *J. Appl. Cogn. Psychol.*, 5, 89–95.

Gudjonsson, G. H. (1991c). Suggestibility and compliance among alleged false confessors and resisters in criminal trials. *Med. Sci. Law*, 31 147–151.

Gudjonsson, G. H. (1991d). The effects of intelligence and memory on group differences in suggestibility and compliance. *Pers. Individ. Diff*, 12, 503–505.

Gudjonsson, G. H. (1991e). The application of interrogative suggestibility to police interviewing. In: J. F. Schumaker (Ed.), *Human Suggestibility; Advances in Theory, Research and Application*. Routledge: New York, pp. 239–288.

Gudjonsson, G. H. and Adlam, K. R. C. (1983). Personality patterns of British Police officers. *Pers. Individ. Diff.*, 4, 507–512.

Gudjonsson, G. H. and Bownes, I. (1991). The reasons why suspects confess during custodial interrogation: data for Northern Ireland. *Med. Sci. Law* (in press).

Gudjonsson, G. H. and Clark, N. K. (1986). Suggestibility in police interrogation: a social psychological model. *Soc. Behav.*, 1, 83–104.

Gudjonsson, G. H. and Gunn, J. (1982). The competence and reliability of a witness in a criminal court. *Br. J. Psychiat.*, 141, 624–627.

Gudjonsson, G. H. and Haward, L. R. C. (1982). Case Report—hysterical amnesia as an alternative to suicide. *Med. Sci. Law*, 22, 68–72.

Gudjonsson, G. H. and Haward, L. R. C. (1983). Psychological analysis of confession statements. *J. Foren. Sci. Soc.*, 23, 113–120.

Gudjonsson, G. H. and Hilton, M. (1989). The effects of instructional manipulation on interrogative suggestibility. *Soc. Behav.*, 4, 189–193.

Gudjonsson, G. H. and Lebegue, B. (1989). Psychological and psychiatric aspects of a coerced-internalized false confession. *J. Foren. Sci. Soc.*, 29, 261–269;

Gudjonsson, G. H. and Lister, S. (1984). Interrogative suggestibility and its relationship with perceptions of self-concept and control. *J. Foren. Sci. Soc.*, 24, 99–110.

Gudjonsson, G. H. and MacKeith, J. A. C. (1982). False confessions, psychological effects of interrogation. A discussion paper. In: *Reconstructing the Past: The Role of Psychologists in Criminal Trials* (Ed. A. Trankell). Kluwer: Deventer, Holland, pp. 253–269.

Gudjonsson, G. H. and Mackeith, J. A. C. (1988). Retracted confessions: legal, psychological and psychiatric aspects. *Med. Sci. Law*, **28**, 187-194.

Gudjonsson, G. H. and Mackeith, J. A. C. (1990). A proven case of false confession: psychological aspects of the coerced-compliant type. *Med. Sci. Law*, **30**, 329-335.

Gudjonsson, G. H. and Petursson, H. (1982). Some criminological and psychiatric aspects of homicide in Iceland. *Med. Sci. Law*, **22**, 91-98.

Gudjonsson, G. H. and Petursson, H. (1991a). Custodial interrogation: why do suspects confess and how does it relate to their crime, attitude and personality? *Pers. Individ. Diff.*, **12**, 295-306.

Gudjonsson, G. H. and Petursson, H. (1991b). The attribution of blame and type of crime committed: transcultural validation. *J. Foren. Sci. Soc.*, **31**, 349-352.

Gudjonsson, G. H., Petursson, H., Skulasson, S. and Sigurdardottir, H. (1989). Psychiatric evidence: a study of psychological issues. *Acta Psychiatr. Scand.*, **80**, 165-169.

Gudjonsson, G. H. and Roberts, J. C. (1983). Guilt and self-concept in "secondary Psychopaths". *Pers. Individ. Diff.*, **4**, 141-146.

Gudjonsson, G. H. and Sartory, G. (1983). Blood-injury phobia: a "reasonable excuse" for failing to give a specimen in a case of suspected drunken driving. *J. Foren. Sci. Soc.*, **23**, 197-201.

Gudjonsson, G. H. and Shackleton, H. (1986). The pattern of scores on Raven's Matrices during "faking bad" and "non-faking" performance. *Br. J. Clin. Psychol.*, **25**, 35-41.

Gudjonsson, G. H. and Singh, K. K. (1984a). Interrogative suggestibility and delinquent boys: an empirical validation study. *Pers. Individ. Diff.*, **5**, 425-430.

Gudjonsson, G. H. and Singh, K. K. (1984b). The relationship between criminal conviction and interrogative suggestibility among delinquent boys. *J. Adolescence*, **7**, 29-34.

Gudjonsson, G. H. and Singh, K. K. (1988). Attribution of blame for criminal acts and its relationship with type of offence. *Med. Sci. Law*, **28**, 301-303.

Gudjonsson, G. H. and Singh, K. K. (1989). The revised Gudjonsson Blame Attribution Inventory. *Pers. Individ. Diff.*, **10**, 67-70.

Gudjonsson, G. H. and Taylor, P. (1985). Cognitive deficit in a case of retrograde amnesia. *Br. J. Psychiat.*, **147**, 715-718.

Haaga, D. A. F. (1989). Mood-state-dependent retention using identical or non-identical mood induction at learning and recall. *Br. J. Clin. Psychol.*, **28**, 75-83.

Hall, D. F., Loftus, E. F. and Tousignant, J. P. (1984). Postevent information and changes in recollection for a natural event. In: *Eyewitness Testimony*, G. L. Wells and E. F. Loftus (Eds). Cambridge: New York.

Hamlet, C. C., Axelrod, S. and Kuerschner, S. (1984). Eye contact as an antecedent to compliant behavior. *J. Appl. Behav. Anal.*, **17**, 553-557.

Hammersley, R. and Read, J. D. (1986). What is interrogation? Remembering a story and remembering false implications about the story. *Br. J. Psychol.*, **77**, 329-341.

Haney, C., Banks, C. and Zimbardo, P. (1973). Interpersonal dynamics in a simulated prison. *Int. J. Criminol. Penol.*, **1**, 69-97.

Hansdottir, I., Thorsteinsson, H. S., Kristinsdottir, H. and Ragnarsson, R. S. (1990). The effects of instructions and anxiety on interrogative suggestibility. *Pers. Individ. Diff.*, **11**, 85-87.

Haraldsson, E. (1985). Interrogative suggestibility and its relationship with personality, perceptual defensiveness and extraordinary beliefs. *Pers. Individ. Diff.*, **6**, 765-767.

Hardarson, R. (1985). Samband Daleidslu-og Yfirheyrslusefnaemis og Fylgni; Vid Persenuleika og Namsarangur, B. A. Thesis (No. 173) in Psychology, University of Iceland.

Haward, L. R. C. (1963). The reliability of corroborated police evidence in a case of "Flagrante Delicto". *J. Foren. Sci. Soc.*, **3**, 71-78.

Haward, L. R. C. (1974). Investigations of torture allegations by the forensic psychologist. *J. Foren. Sci. Soc.*, **14**, 299-310.

Haward, L. R. C. (1980). Hypnosis of rape victims. *Bull. Br. Soc. Exp. Clin. Hypnosis*, **1**, 11-13.

Haward, L. R. C. (1981). *Forensic Psychology*. London: Batsford.

Haward, L. R. C. (1988). Hypnosis in Forensic Practice. In: M. Heap (Ed.) *Hypnosis: Current Clinical, Experimental and Forensic Practices*. Croom Helm: London, pp. 357-368.

Haward, L. R. C. (1990). *A Dictionary of Forensic Psychology*. Barry Rose: Chichester.

Haward, L. and Ashworth, A. (1980). Some problems of evidence obtained by hypnosis. *Crim. Law Rev.*, **August**, 469-485.

Heap, M. (1988). The nature of hypnosis. In M. Heap (Ed.) *Hypnosis: Current Clinical, Experimental and Forensic Practices*. Croom Helm:London, pp. 3-11.

Heaton-Armstrong, A. (1987). Police officers' notebooks: recent developments. *Crim. Law Rev.*, 470-472.

Heckel, R. V., Brokaw, H. C., Salzberg, H. D. and Wiggins, S. L. (1962). Polygraphic variations in reactivity between delusional, non-delusional and control groups in a "Crime Situation". *J. Crim. Law Criminol. Police Sci.*, **53**, 380-383.

Henningsen, G. (1980). *The Witches Advocate*. Nevada: University of Nevada Press: Reno.

Hepworth, M. and Turner, B. S. (1980). *Confession. Studies in Deviance and Religion*. Routledge and Kegan Paul: London.

Herman, M. (1938). The use of intravenous sodium amytal in psychogenic amnesic states. *Psychiat. Q.*, **12**, 738-742.

Hersch, P. D. and Scheibe, K. E. (1967). Reliability of internal-external control as a personality dimension. *J. Consult. Psychol.*, **31**, 609-613.

Hertel, P. T., Cosden, M. and Johnson, P. J. (1980). Passage recall: schema change and cognitive flexibility. *J. Ed. Psychol.*, **72**, 133-140.

Heslin, R., Nguyen, T. D. and Nguyen, M. L. (1983). Meaning of touch: the case of touch from a stranger or same-sex person. *J. Non-verbal Behav.*, **7**, 147-157.

Hiland, D. N. and Dzieszkowski, P. A. (1984). Hypnosis in the investigation of aviation accidents. *Aviation Space Environ. Med.*, **December**, 1136-1142.

Hilgard, E. R. (1974). Toward a neo-dissociation theory: multiple cognitive controls in human functioning. *Perspect. Biol. Med.*, **17**, 301-316.

Hilgard, E. R. and Loftus, E. F. (1979). Effective interrogation of the eye-witness. *Int. J. Clin. Exper. Hypnosis*, **27**, 342-357.

Hilgendorf, E. L. and Irving, B. (1981). A decision-making model of confessions. In: *Psychology in Legal Contexts. Applications and Limitations*, M. A. Lloyd-Bostock (Ed.). Macmillan: London, pp. 67-84.

Hill, P. and Bennett, R. (1990). *Stolen Years. Before and After Guildford*. Doubleday: London.

Hinkle, L. E. (1961). The physiological state of the interrogation subject as it affects brain function. In:*The Manipulation of Human Behaviour* (Eds. A. D. Biderman and H. Zimmer). Wiley: New York, pp. 19-50.

Hinkle, L. E. and Wolff, H. G. (1956). Communist interrogation and indoctrination of "Enemies of the States". *A. M. A. Arch. Neurol. Psychiat.*, **76**, 115-174.

Holgerson, A. (1990). Fakta I Malet — Vittnespsykologins bidrag vid bedomning av sakfragan i enskilda rottsfall. University of Stockholm, Sweden.

Hollin, C. R. (1981). Nature of the witnessed incident and status of interviewer in variables influencing eyewitness recall. *Br. J. Soc. Psychol.*, **20**, 295-296.

Hollin, C. R. (1989). *Psychology and Crime. An Introduction to Criminological Psychology*. Routledge: London.

Hollin, C. R. and Clifford, B. R. (1983). Eyewitness testimony: the effects of discussion on recall accuracy and agreement. *J. Appl. Soc. Psychol.*, **13**, 234-244.

Home Office (1978). *Judges' Rules and Administrative Directions to the Police.* Police Circular No. 89/1978. Home Office: London.

Home Office (1985a). *Police and Criminal Evidence Act 1984.* HMSO: London.

Home office (1985b). *Police and Criminal Evidence Act 1984 (S.66) Codes of Practice.* HMSO: London.

Home Office (1988). *Police and Criminal Evidence Act 1984 (S.60(1)(A)). Code of Practice (E) on Tape Recording.* HMSO: London.

Home Office (1989). *Report of the Working Group on the Right to Silence.* HMSO: London.

Home Office (1991). *Police and Criminal Evidence Act 1984 (S.66). Codes of Practice.* (revised edn). HMSO: London.

Hornik, J. (1988). The effect of touch and gaze upon compliance and interest of interviewees. *J. Soc. Psychol.*, **127**, 681-683.

Horsley, J. S. (1936). Narco-analysis. *J. Mental Sci.*, **82**, 416-422.

Horsley, J. S. (1943). *Narco-Analysis. A New Technique in Short-cut Psychotherapy: A Comparison with other Methods: and Notes on the Barbiturates.* Oxford University Press: Oxford.

Horsnell, M. (1990). Forensic evidence made May enquiry outcome inevitable. *The Times*, **June 15**, 2.

House, R. E. (1931). The use of scopolamine in criminology. *Amer. J. Police Sci.*, **2**, 328-336.

Howard, M. N. (1991). The Neutral Experiment: a plausible threat to justice. *Crim. Law Rev.*, 98-110.

Howells, T. H. (1938). A study of ability to recognize faces. *J. Abn. Soc. Psychol.*, **123**, 173-174.

Huff, C. R., Rattner, A. and Sagarin, E. (1986). Guilty until proven innocent: wrongful conviction and public policy. *Crime and Delinquency*, **32**, 518-544.

Hull, C. (1933). *Hypnosis and Suggestibility.* Appleton-Century-Crofts: New York.

Hunter, E. (1951). *Brainwashing in Red China.* Vanguard Press: New York.

Hunter, E. (1956). *Brainwashing.* Farrar, Strauss, and Cudahy: New York.

Inbau, F. E. and Reid, J. E. (1962). *Criminal Interrogation and Confessions.* Williams and Wilkins: Baltimore.

Inbau, F. E., Reid, J. E. and Buckley, J.P. (1986). *Criminal Interrogation and Confessions*, Third Edition. Williams and Wilkins: Baltimore.

Inman, M. (1981). Police interrogation and confessions. In: *Psychology in Legal Contexts. Applications and Limitations* (Ed. M. A. Lloyd-Bostock). Macmillan: London, pp. 45-66.

Irving, B. (1980). *Police Interrogation. A Case Study of Current Practice.* Research Studies No. 2. HMSO: London.

Irving B. (1987). Interrogative suggestibility: a question of parsimony. *Soc. Behav.*, **2**, 19-28.

Irving, B. (1990). The codes of practice under the Police and Criminal Evidence Act 1984. In:*Principles and Practice of Forensic Psychiatry* (Eds. R. Bluglass and P. Bowden). Churchill Livingstone: London, pp. 151-159.

Irving, B. and Hilgendorf, L. (1980). *Police Interrogation: The Psychological Approach.* Research Studies No. 1. HMSO: London.

Irving, B. L. and McKenzie, I. K. (1989). *Police Interrogation: The Effects of the Police and Criminal Evidence Act.* The Police Foundation: London.

Janis, I. L. (1959). Decisional conflicts: a theoretical analysis. *J. Conflict Resolution*, **3**, 6-27.

Janis, I. L. (1971). *Stress and Frustration.* Harcourt Brace Jovanovich: New York.

Jayne, B. C. (1986). The psychological principles of criminal interrogation. An Appendix. In:*Criminal Interrogation and Confessions*, 3rd Edition (Eds. F. E. Inbau, J. E. Reid and J. P. Buckley). Williams and Wilkins: Baltimore, pp. 327-347.

Jeffreys, A. J., Wilson, V. and Thein, S. L. (1985a). Hypervariable "minisatellite" regions in human DNA. *Nature*, **314**, 67-73.

Jeffreys, A. F., Wilson, V. and Thein, S. L. (1985b). Individual-specific "fingerprints" of human DNA. *Nature*, **316**, 76-79.

Johnson, M. K. (1985). The origin of memories. In:*Advances in Cognitive Behavioural Research and Therapy* (Ed. P. C. Kendall). Academic Press, London.

Johnson, M. K. and Raye, C. L. (1981). Reality monitoring. *Psychol. Rev.*, **88**, 67-85.

Johnson, M. K. and Foley, M. A. (1984). Differentiating fact from fantasy: the reliability of children's memory. *J. Soc. Issues*, **40**, 33-50.

Johnston, W. A., Greenberg, S. N., Fisher, R. P. and Martin, D. W. (1970). Divided attention: a vehicle for monitoring memory processes. *J. Exp. Psychol.*, **83**, 164-171.

Jones, D. P. H. (1987). The evidence of a three-year-old child. *Crim. Law Rev.*, 677-681.

Jones, D. P. H. (1988). *Interviewing the Sexually Abused Child*. Gaskell: London.

Jones, D. P. H. and McGraw, J. M. (1987). Reliable and fictitious accounts of sexual abuse to children. *J. Interpers. Violence*, **2**, 27-45.

Jones, D. P. H. and McQuiston, M. G. (1988). *Interviewing the Sexually Abused Child*. Royal College of Psychiatrists. Alden Press: Oxford.

Kalven, H. and Zeisel, H. (1966). *The American Jury*. Little, Brown: Boston.

Karlin, R. A. (1983). Forensic hypnosis—two case reports. *Int. J. Clin. Exp. Hypnosis*, **31**, 227-234.

Kassin, S. M. and McNall, K. (1991). Police interrogations and confessions. *Law Human Behav.*, **15**, 233-351.

Kassin, S. M. and Wrightsman, L. S. (1985). Confession evidence. In:*The Psychology of Evidence and Trial Procedure* (Eds. S. M. Kassin and L. S. Wrightsman). Sage: London, pp. 67-94.

Keane, V. E. (1972). The incidence of speech and language problems in the mentally retarded. *Mental Retardation*, **10**, 3-8.

Kee, R. (1989). *Trial & Error. The True Events Surrounding the Convictions and Trials of the Guildford Four and the Maguire Seven*. Penguin: London.

Keeler, L. (1933). Scientific methods of criminal detection with the polygraph. *Kansas Bar Assoc.*, **2**, 22-31.

Kellam, A. M. P. (1980). A convincing false confession. *New Law J.*, **10**, 29-33.

Kelman, H. C. (1950). The effects of success and failure on "suggestibility" in the autokinetic situation. *J. Abn. Soc. Psychol.*, **46**, 267-285.

Kelman, H. C. (1958). Compliance, identification and internalization: three processes of opinion change. *J. Conflict Resolution*, **2**, 51-60.

Kelman, H. C. and Holland, C. I. (1953). "Reinstatement" of the communicator in delayed measurement of opinion change. *J. Abn. Soc. Psychol.*, **48**, 327-335.

Kennedy, H. G. and Grubin, D. H. (1991). Patterns of denial in sex offenders. *Psychol. Med.* (in press).

Kennedy, L. (1986). Foreword. In: *Killing Time* (Ed. N. Fellows). Lion: Oxford, pp. 6-8.

Kennedy, L. (1988). *10 Rillington Place*. Grafton: London.

Kiesler, C. A. and Kiesler, S. B. (1970). *Conformity*. Addison-Wesley: Reading, MA.

Kiesler, C. A. and Pallak, M. S. (1976). Arousal properties of dissonance manipulation. *Psychol. Bull.*, **83**, 1014-2026.

Kinsey, A. C., Pomeroy, W. B. and Martin, C. E. (1948). *Sexual Behavior in the Human Male*. Saunders: Philadelphia, PA.

Kirby, T. (1989). New powers urged on DNA fingerprinting. *The Independent*, **September 27**, 3.

Kirby, T. and Coulson, J. (1989). The force of corruption. *The Independent Magazine*, **October 14**, 24-30.

Kleinke, C. L. (1977). Compliance to requests made by gazing and touching experimenter in field settings. *J. Exp. Soc. Psychol.*, **13**, 218-232.

Kleinke, C. L. (1980). Interaction between gaze and legitimacy on requests on compliance in a field setting. *J. Non-verbal Behav.*, **5**, 3-12.

Kobasigawa, A. (1974). Utilization of retrieval cases by children in recall. *Child Dev.*, **45**, 127-134.

Konoske, P., Staple, S. and Graf, R. G. (1979). Compliant reactions to guilt: self-esteem or self-punishment. *J. Soc. Psychol.*, **108**, 207-211.

Kopelman, M. D. (1987). Anorexia: organic and psychogenic. *Br. J. Psychiat.*, **150**, 428-442.

Krech, D. and Crutchfield, R. S. (1948). *Theory and Problems of Social Psychology.* McGraw-Hill: New York.

Krech, D., Crutchfield, R. S. and Ballachey, E. L. (1962). *Individuals in Society.* McGraw-Hill: New York.

Kuehn, L. (1974). Looking down a gun barrel: person perception and violent crime. *Percept. Mot. Skills*, **39**, 1159-1164.

Lambert, C. and Rees, W. L. (1944). Intravenous barbiturates in the treatment of hysteria. *Br. Med. J.*, **2**, 70-73.

Langer, E. J. (1983). *The Psychology of Control.* Sage: London.

Larson, J. A. (1932). *Lying and Its Detection.* University of Chicago Press: Chicago.

Lassiter, G. D. and Irvine, A. A. (1986). Videotaped confessions: the impact of camera point of view on judgements of coercion. *J. Appl. Soc. Psychol.*, **16**, 268-276.

Laughery, K. R., Alexander, J. E. and Lane, A. B. (1971). Recognition of human faces: effects of target exposure time, target positions, pose position, and type of photograph. *J. Appl. Psychol.*, **55**, 477-483.

Laurence, J. R. and Perry, C. (1983). Hypnotically created memories among highly hypnotizable subjects. *Science*, **222**, 523-524.

Laurence, J. R. and Perry, C. (1988). *Hypnosis, Will and Memory: A Psycho-legal History.* Guilford: New York.

Lee, C. D. (1953). *The Instrumental Detection of Deception. The Lie Test.* Charles C. Thomas: Springfield, IL.

Leiken, L. S. (1970). Police interrogation in Colorado: the implementation of Miranda. *Denver Law J.*, **47**, 1-53.

Leippe, M. R., Wells, G. L. and Ostrom, T. M. (1978). Crime seriousness as a determinant of accuracy in eyewitness identification. *J. Appl. Psychol.*, **63**, 345-351.

Leites, N. and Bernaut, E. (1954). *Ritual of Liquidation.* Free Press: Glencoe, IL.

Lepper, M. R. (1982). Social control processes, attributions of motivation, and the internalizations of social values. In: *Social Cognition and Social Behavior: A Developmental Perspective* (Eds. E. T. Higgins, D. N. Ruble and W. W. Hartup). Jossey-Bass: San Francisco.

Levey, A. B. (1988). *Polygraphy. An Evaluative review.* HMSO: London.

Lewin, K. (1947). Frontiers in group dynamics: concepts, method and reality in social science. *Human Relations*, **1**, 5-42.

Ley, P. (1977). Psychological studies of doctor-patient communication. In: *Contributions to Medical Psychology* (Ed. S. Rachman). Pergamon Press: Oxford.

Lifton, R. J. (1956). "Thought Reform" of Western civilians in Chinese prisons. *Amer. J. Psychiat.*, **110**, 732-739.

Lifton, R. J. (1961). *Thought Reform and the Psychology of Totalism.* W. W. Norton: New York.

Lindermann, E. (1932). Psychological changes in normal and abnormal individuals under the influence of sodium amytal. *Amer. J. Psychiat.*, **88**, 1083-1091.

Lindsay, D. S. and Johnson, M. K. (1987). Reality monitoring and suggestibility: children's ability to discriminate among memories from different sources. In: *Children's Eyewitness Memory* (Eds. S. J. Ceci, M. P. Toglia and D. F. Ross). Springer-Verlag: New York, pp. 92-121.

Lipton, J. P. (1977). On the psychology of eyewitness testimony. *J. Appl. Psychol.*, **62**, 90-95.

Lisman, S. A. (1974). Alcoholic "blackouts": state dependent learning? *Arch. Gen. Psychiat.*, **30**, 46-53.

Loftus, E. (1979a). *Eyewitness Testimony.* Harvard University Press: London.

Loftus, E. F. (1979b). Reactions to blatantly contradictory information. *Memory Cognit.*, **7**, 368-374.

Loftus, E. F. (1980). "Did I really say that last night?" Alcohol, marijuana and memory. *Psychol. Today*, **92**, (March), 42-56.

Loftus, E. F. (1981). Metamorphosis: alterations in memory produced by mental bonding of new information to old. In: *Attention and Performance*, Vol. IX (Eds. J. Long and A. Baddeley). Erlbaum: Hillsdale, NJ, pp. 417-434.

Loftus, E. F. and Burns, T. E. (1982). Mental shock can produce retrograde amnesia. *Memory Cognit.*, **10**, 318-323.

Loftus, E. F., Greene, E. L. and Doyle, J. M. (1990). The psychology of eyewitness testimony. In: *Psychological Methods in Criminal Investigations and Evidence* (Ed. D. C. Raskin). Springer: New York, pp. 3-45.

Loftus, E. F. and Hoffman, H. G. (1989). Misinformations and memory: the creation of new memories. *J. Exp. Psychol. Gen.*, **118**, 100-104.

Loftus, E. F., Loftus, G. R. and Messo, J. (1987). Some facts about "weapon focus". *Law Human Behav.*, **11**, 55-62.

Loftus, E. F., Miller, D. G. and Burns, H. J. (1978). Semantic integration of verbal information into a visual memory. *J. Exp. Psychol.: Human Learning and Memory*, **4**, 19-31.

Loftus, E. F. and Palmer, J. C. (1974). Reconstruction of automobile destruction: an example of the interaction between language and memory. *J. Verbal Learning Verbal Behav.*, **13**, 585-589.

Loftus, E. F., Schooler, J. W., Boone, S. M. and Kline, D. (1987). Time went by so slowly: overestimation of event diagnosis by males and females. *Appl. Cogn. Psychol.*, **1**, 3-13.

Lohr, J. M., Nix, J., Dunbar, D. and Mosesso, L. (1984). The relationship of assertive behaviour in women and a validated measure of irrational beliefs. *Cogn. Ther. Res.*, **8**, 287-297.

Luce, R. D. (1967). Psychological studies of risky decision making. In: *Decision Making.* (Eds. W. Edwards and A. Tversky). Penguin: London, pp. 334-352.

Ludwig, A. O. (1944). Classical features and diagnosis of malingering in military personnel: the use of barbiturates as an aid to detection. *War Med.*, **5**, 378-382.

Lykken, D. T. (1959). The GSR in the detection of guilt. *J. Appl. Psychol.*, **44**, 258-262.

Lykken, D. T. (1981). *A Tremor in the Blood: Uses and Abuses of the Lie Detector.* McGraw-Hill: New York.

Lynch, B. E. and Bradford, J. M. V. (1980). Amnesia: its detection by psychophysiological measures. *Bull. Amer. Acad. Psychiat. Law*, **8**, 288-297.

Macdonald, J. and Michaud, D. (1987). *The Confession. Interrogation and Criminal Profiles for Police Officers.* Apache Press: Denver, CO.

Macnamara, D. E. J. (1969). Convicting the innocent. *Crime and Delinquency*, **15**, 57-61.

Malpass, R. S. and Devine, P. G. (1981). Guided memory in eyewitness identification. *J. Appl. Psychol.*, **66**, 343-350.

Marshall, J. (1966). *Law and Psychology in Conflict.* Bobbs-Merrill: New York.

Marshall, J., Marquis, K. H. and Oskamp, S. (1971). Effects of kind of question and atmosphere on accuracy and completeness of testimony. *Harvard Law Rev.*, **84**, 1620-1643.

Marston, W. M. (1917). Systolic blood pressure symptoms of deception. *J. Exp. Psychol.*, **2**, 117-163.

Matarazzo, J. D. (1972). *Measurement and Appraisal of Adult Intelligence.* Williams and Wilkins: Baltimore.

Matarazzo, J. D. (1990). Psychological assessment versus psychological testing. *Amer. Psychol.*, **45**, 999-1017.

Matza, D. (1967). *Becoming Deviant.* Prentice Hall: Englewood Cliffs, NJ.

May, J. (1990). *Interim Report on the Maguire Case.* HMSO: London.

McAfee, J. K. and Gural, M. (1988). Individuals with mental retardation and the criminal justice system: the view from States' Attorneys General. *Mental Retardation*, **26**, 5-12.

McCann, T. E. and Sheehan, P. W. (1987). The breaching of pseudomemory under hypnotic instruction: implications for original memory retrieval. *Br. J. Exp. Clin. Hypnosis*, **4**, 112-114.

McCauley, C. (1989). The nature of social influence in groupthink: compliance and internalization. *J. Pers. Soc. Psychol.*, **57**, 250-260.

McCloskey, M. and Zaragoza, M. (1985). Misleading postevent information and memory for events: arguments and evidence against memory impairment hypothesis. *J. Exp. Psychol. Gen.*, **114**, 1-16.

McCloskey, M., Wible, C. G. and Cohen, N. J. (1988). Is there a special flashback memory mechanism?. *J. Exp. Psychol. Gen.*, **117**, 171-181.

McConville, M. and Morrell, P. (1983). Recording the interrogations: have the police got it taped! *Crim. Law Rev.*, 158-183.

McDougall, W. (1908). *An Introduction to Social Psychology*, Methuen: London.

McEwan, J. (1991). *Evidence and the Adversarial Process: The Modern Law.* Basil Blackwell: Oxford (in press).

McGeoch, J. A. (1932). Forgetting and the law of disuse. *Psychol. Rev.*, **39**, 352-370.

McKee, G. and Franey, R. (1988). *Time Bomb.* Bloomsbury: London.

McKenzie, I. K. (1981). Sexual offences and the mentally retarded. Newsletter of the Division of Criminological and Legal Psychology. *Br. Psychol. Soc. Newsletter*, **11**, 6-10.

Meerloo, J. A. M. (1951). The crime of menticide. *Amer. J. Psychiat.*, **107**, 594-598.

Meerloo, J. A. M. (1954). Pavlovian strategy as a weapon in menticide. *Amer. J. Psychiat.*, **110**, 809-813.

Megargee, E. I. (1966). Undercontrolled and overcontrolled personality types in extreme antisocial aggression. *Psychol. Monogr.*, **80** (611).

Menninger, K. A. (1986). Mental retardation and criminal responsibility: some thoughts on the idiocy defence. *Int. J. Law Psychiat.*, **8**, 343-357.

Metropolitan Police (1991). *A Change of PACE. A Guide to the Changes to the Codes of Practice.* New Scotland Yard: London.

Mikulincer, M., Babkoff, H., Caspy, T. and Singh, H. (1989). The effects of 72 hours of sleep loss on psychological variables. *Br. J. Psychol.*, **80**, 145-162.

Milberg, S. and Clark, M. S. (1988). Moods and compliance. *Br. J. Soc. Psychol.*, **27**, 79-90.

Milgram, S. (1974). *Obedience to Authority.* Tavistock: London.

Miller, J. G. (1957). Brainwashing: present and future. *J. Soc. Issues*, **13**, 48-55.

Miller, R. (1990). Serious trouble. *The Sunday Times Magazine*, **July 15**, 24-32.

Mirfield, P. (1985). *Confessions.* Sweet & Maxwell: London.

Mitchell, B. (1983). Confessions and police interrogation of suspects. *Crim. Law Rev.*, **September**, 596-604.

Mitchell, S. and Richardson, P. J. (1985). *Archbold. Pleading, Evidence and Practice in Criminal Cases*, 42nd Edition, Sweet and Maxwell: London.

Moore, H. T. (1921). The comparative influence of majority and expert opinion. *Amer. J. Psychol.*, **32**, 16-21.

Moos, R. and Billings, A. G. (1982). Conceptualizing and measuring coping resources and processes. In: *Handbook of Stress: Theoretical and Clinical Aspects.* (Eds. L. Goldberger and S. Brenznite). Free Press: New York.

Morris, D. P. (1945). Intravenous barbiturates: an aid in the diagnosis and treatment of conversion hysteria and malingering. *Military Surgeon*, **96**, 509-513.

Morris, P. (1980). *Police Interrogations: Review of the Literature*. Royal Commissions on Criminal Procedure, Research Study 3. HMSO: London.

Morris, R. A. (1990). The admissibility of evidence derived from hypnosis and polygraphy. In: *Psychological Methods in Criminal Investigation and Evidence* (Ed. D. C. Raskin). Springer: New York, pp. 333-376.

Morton, A. Q. (1978). *Literary Detection*. Bowker: London.

Morton, A. Q. and Michaelson, S. (1990). *The Qsum Plot*. Internal Report, James Clerk Maxwell Building, The King's Buildings, Mayfield Road, Edinburgh, EH9 3JZ. (Ref. CSR-3-90).

Moston, S. (1987). The suggestibility of children in interview studies. *First Language*, **7**, 67-78.

Moston, S. (1990a). How children interpret and respond to questions: situation sources of suggestibility in eyewitness interviews. *Soc. Behav.*, **5**, 155-167.

Moston, S. (1990b). The ever-so-gentle art of police interrogation. Paper presented at the British Psychological Society Annual Conference, Swansea University, April 5th.

Moston, S. (Ed.) (1991). *Investigative Interviewing*, Vol. 1. Metropolitan Police/Association of Chief Police Officers: London.

Moston, S. and Engelberg, T. (1991). The effects of social support on children's testimony. *Appl. Cogn. Psychol.* (in press).

Moston, S., Stephenson, G. M. and Williamson, T. M. (1990). The effects of case characteristics on suspect behaviour. Paper presented at the British Psychological Society Annual Conference, Swansea University, April 5th.

Moston, S., Stephenson, G. M. and Williamson, T. M. (1992). The incidence, antecedents and consequences of the use of right to silence during police questioning. *Br. J. Criminol.*, **32**, 23-40.

Mottahedin, I. (1988). Investigative hypnosis in South East England. In: *Hypnosis. Current Clinical, Experimental and Forensic Practices* (Ed. M. Heap). Croom Helm: London, pp. 369-375.

Mullin, C. (1989). *Error of Judgement. The Truth About the Birmingham Bombers*. Poolbeg Press: Dublin.

Munsterberg, H. (1908). *On the Witness Stand*. Doubleday: Garden City, New York.

Naples, M. and Hackett, T. P. (1978). The amytal interview; history and current uses. *Psychosomatics*, **19**, 98-105.

Nelson, H. E. (1982). *National Adult Reading Test*. NFER: Windsor, Berks, UK.

Neubauer, D. W. (1974). Confessions in Prairie City: some causes and effects. *J. Crim. Law Criminol.*, **65**, 103-112.

Niblett, B. and Boreham, J. (1976). Cluster analysis in court. *Crim. Law Rev.*, 175-180.

Nogrady, H., McConkey, K. M. and Perry, C. W. (1985). Enhancing visual memory: trying hypnosis, trying imagination and trying again. *J. Abn. Psychol.*, **94**, 195-204.

O'Connell, B. A. (1960). Amnesia and homicide. *Br. J. Delinquency*, **10**, 262-276.

O'Connor, P. (1990). The Court of Appeal: re-trials and tribulations. *Crim. Law Rev.*, **September**, 615-628.

Office of Technology Assessment (1983). *Scientific Validity of Polygraph Testing: A Research Review and Evaluation*. Congress of the United States: Washington, D.C.

Ofshe, R. (1989). Coerced confessions: the logic of seemingly irrational action. *Cultic Studies J.*, **6**, 1-15.

Ofshe, R. (1991a). Coercive persuasion and attitude change. In: *The Encyclopedia of Sociology* (Eds. E. Borgatta and M. Borgalla). Macmillan: New York (in press).

Ofshe, R. (1991b). Inadvertent hypnosis during interrogation: false confession due to dissociative state; mis-identified multiple personality and the satanic cult hypothesis. *Int. J. Clin. Exp. Hypnosis* (in press).

Orne, M. T. (1961). The potential uses of hypnosis in interrogation. In: *In the Manipulation of Human Behavior* (Eds. A. D. Biderman and H. Zimmer). Wiley: Chichester, pp. 169-215.

Orne, M. T. (1975). Implications of laboratory research for the detection of deception. *Polygraph*, **2**, 169-199

Orne, M. T. (1979). The use and misuse of hypnosis in Court. *Int. J. Clin. Exp. Hypnosis*, **27**, 311-341.

Orne, M. T., Whitehouse, W. G., Dinges, D. F. and Orne, E. C. (1988). Reconstructing memory through hypnosis: forensic and clinical implications. In: *Hypnosis and Memory* (Ed. H. M. Pettinoti). Guilford Press: New York, pp. 21-63.

Orwell, G. (1951). *Animal Farm*. Penguin: Harmondsworth.

Osgood, C. E. (1960). Some effects of motivation on style of encoding. In: *Style in Language* (Ed. T. A. Sebeck). Harvard University Press: Cambridge, MA and New York, pp. 293-306.

Osgood, C. E., Suci, G. J. and Tannebaum, P. (1957). *The Measurement of Meaning*. University of Illinois Press: Urbana, IL.

Overton, D. A. (1964). State-dependent or "dissociated" learning procedure with pentobarbital. *J. Comp. Physiol. Psychol.*, **57**, 3-12.

Parkes, C. M. (1986). *Bereavement: Studies in Grief in Adult Life*, 2nd Edition. Tavistock: London.

Parwatikar, S. D., Holcomb, W. R. and Menninger, K. A. (1985). The detection of malingered amnesia in accused murders. *Bull. Amer. Acad. Psychiat. Law*, **13**, 97-103.

Patrick, M. and Howells, R. (1990). Barbiturate-assisted interviews with modern clinical practice (Editorial). *Psychol. Med.*, **20**, 763-765.

Pattenden, R. (1986). Conflicting approaches to psychiatric evidence in criminal trials: England, Canada and Australia. *Crim. Law Rev.*, 92-102.

Pattenden, R. (1991). Should confessions be corroborated? *Law Q. Rev.*, **107**, 317-339.

Paulhus, D. L. (1983). Two-component models of socially desirable responding. *J. Pers. Soc. Psychol.*, **46**, 598-609.

Pear, T. H. and Wyatt, S. (1914). The testimony of normal and mentally defective children. *Br. J. Psychol.*, **3**, 388-419.

Pearse, J. (1991). Police Interviewing. Who is at risk? BSc Thesis, London School of Economics, London.

Perry, J. C. and Jacobs, D. (1982). Overview: clinical applications of the amytal interview in psychiatric emergency settings. *Amer. J. Psychiat.*, **139**, 552-559.

Pettigrew, T. F. (1958). Personality and sociocultural factors in intergroup attitudes: a cross-national comparison. *Conflict Resolution*, **11**, 29-42.

Petursson, G. H. and Gudjonsson, G. H. (1981). Psychiatric aspects of homicide. *Acta Psychiat. Scand.*, **64**, 363-372.

Pezdek, K., Whestone, T., Reynolds, K., Askari, N. and Dougherty, T. (1989). Memory for real world scenes: the role of consistency with schema expectation. *J. Exp. Psychol. Learn. Memory Cognit.*, **15**, 587-595.

Piaget, J. (1972). *Judgment and Reasoning in the Child*. (M. Warden, trans.) Littlefield, Adams: Totawa, NJ (originally published in 1924).

Powell, G. E., Gudjonsson, G. H. and Mullen, P. (1983). Application of the guilty-knowledge technique in a case of pseudologia fantastica. *Pers. Individ. Diff.*, **4**, 141-146.

Power, D. J. (1977). Memory, identifications and crime. *Med. Sci. Law*, **17**, 132-139.

Powers, P. A., Andriks, J. L. and Loftus, E. F. (1979). Eyewitness account of females and males. *J. Appl. Psychol.*, **64**, 339-347.

Praiss, D. M. (1989). Constitutional protection of confessions made by mentally retarded defendants. *Am. J. Law Med.*, **14**, 431-465.

Pratt, R. T. C. (1977). Psychogenic loss of memory. In: *Amnesia. Clinical, Psychological and Medicolegal Aspects*, 2nd Edition (Eds. C. W. M. Whitty and O. L. Zangvill). Butterworth: London, pp. 224-244.

Price, C. (1989). Studies in whitewash. *New Statesmen & Society,* **17 November,** 18-20.

Price, C. and Caplan, J. (1977). *The Confait Confessions.* Marion Boyars: London.

Price, G. E. and Terhune, W. B. (1919). Feigned amnesia as a defence reaction. *J. Amer. Med. Assn.,* **72,** 565-567.

Prideaux, E. (1919). Suggestion and suggestibility. *Br. J. Psychol.,* **10,** 228-241.

Putman, W. H. (1979). Hypnosis and distortions in eyewitness memory. *Int. J. Clin. Exp. Hypnosis,* **27,** 437-448.

Radin, E. D. (1964). *The Innocents.* William Morrow: New York.

Raginsky, B. B. (1969). Hypnotic recall of an aircraft crash. *Int. J. Clin. Exp. Hypnosis,* **27,** 1-19.

Raskin, D. C. (1982). The scientific basis of polygraph techniques and their uses in the judicial process. In: *Reconstructing the Past. The Role of Psychologists in Criminal Trials* (Ed. A. Trankell). Kluwer: Deventer, Holland, pp. 317-371.

Raskin, D. C. (1986). The polygraph in 1986: scientific, professional, and legal issues surrounding applications and acceptance of polygraph evidence. *Utah Law Rev.,* **1986,** 29-74.

Raskin, D. C. (1990). Polygraph techniques for the detection of deception. In: *Psychological Methods in Criminal Investigation and Evidence* (Ed. D. C. Raskin). Springer: New York, pp. 247-296.

Raskin, D. C. and Yuille, J. C. (1989). Problems in evaluating interviews of children in sexual abuse cases. In: *Perspectives on Children's Testimony* (Eds. P. S. J. Ceci, D. F. Ross and M. P. Toglia). Springer-Verlag: London, pp. 184-207.

Rathus, S. A. (1973). A 30-item schedule for assessing assertive behavior. *Behav. Ther.,* **4,** 398-406.

Rattner, A. (1988). Convicted but innocent. Wrongful conviction and the criminal justice system. *Law Human Behav.,* **12,** 283-293.

Redlich, F. C., Ravitz, L. J. and Dession, G. H. (1951). Narcoanalysis and truth. *Amer. Psychiat.,* **107,** 586.

Register, P. A. and Kihlstrom, J. F. (1988). Hypnosis and interrogative suggestibility. *Pers. Individ. Diff.,* **9,** 549-558.

Reid, J. E. (1947). A revised questioning technique in lie-detection. *J. Crim. Law Criminol.,* **37,** 542-547.

Reid, J. and Inbau, F. E. (1977). *Truth and Deception. The Polygraph ("Lie-detector") Technique,* 2nd Edition. Williams and Wilkins: Baltimore.

Reik, T. (1959). *The Compulsion to Confess: on the Psychoanalysis of Crime and Punishment.* Farrar, Straus and Cudahy: New York.

Reiser, M. (1976). Hypnosis as a tool in criminal investigation. *The Police Chief,* **4,** 39-40.

Reiser, M. (1980). *Handbook of Investigative Hypnosis.* Lehi: Los Angeles.

Reiser, M. (1985). Some current issues in investigative hypnosis. *Int. J. Invest. Foren. Hypnosis,* **8,** 41-56.

Reiser, M. (1990). Investigative hypnosis. In: *Psychological Methods in Criminal Investigation and Evidence* (Ed. D. C. Raskin). Springer: New York, pp. 151-190.

Relinger, H. (1984). Hypnotic hyperamnesia: a critical review. *Amer. J. Clin. Hypnosis,* **26,** 212-225.

Richard, C. L., Spencer, J. and Spooner, F. (1980). The mentally retarded defendant-offender. *J. Special Ed.,* **14,** 113-119.

Richardson, G. (1991). A Study of Interrogative Suggestibility in an Adolescent Forensic Population. MSc Dissertation, University of Newcastle upon Tyne.

Richardson, S. A., Dohrenwend, B. S. and Klein, D. (1965). *Interviewing: Its Forms and Functions.* Basic Books: London.

Richardson, S. A. (1978). Careers of mentally retarded young persons; services, jobs and interpersonal relations. *Amer. J. Mental Defic.,* **82,** 349-358.

Roediger, H. L. and Thorpe, L. A. (1978). The role of recall time in producing hyperamnesia. *Memory Cognit.*, **6**, 296-305.

Rogers, M. L. (1990). Coping with alleged false molestation: examination and statement analysis procedure. *Issues in Child Abuse Accusation*, **2**, 57-68.

Rogge, O. J. (1975). *Why Men Confess*. Da Capo Press; New York.

Roth, D. L. and Ingram, R. E. (1985). Factors in the self-deception questionnaire: associations with depression. *J. Pers. Soc. Psychol.*, **48**, 243-251.

Rotter, J. B. (1966). Generalized experiences for internal versus external control of reinforcement. *Psychol. Monogr.*, **80** (609).

Rowe, P. (1986). The *voire dire* and the Jury. *Crim. Law Rev.*, 226-232.

Roy, D. F. (1991). Improving recall by eyewitness through the cognitive interview. *Psychologist*, 4, 398-400.

Royal, R. F. and Schutt, S. R. (1976). *The Gentle Art of Interviewing and Interrogation. A Professional Manual and Guide*. Prentice-Hall: Englewood Cliffs, NJ.

Ryckman, R., Rodda, W. and Sherman, M. (1972). Locus of control and expertise relevance as determinants of changes in opinion about student activities. *J. Soc. Psychol.*, **88**, 107-114.

Sackeim, H. A. (1983). Self-deception, self-esteem, and depression: the adaptive value of lying to oneself. In: J. Masling (Ed.), *Empirical Studies of Psychoanalytic Theories*. Erlbaum: London, pp. 101-157.

Sackeim, H. A. and Gur, R. C. (1979). Self-deception, other-deception and self-reported psychopathology. *J. Consult. Clin. Psychol.*, **47**, 213-215.

Salter, A. (1988). *Treating Child Sex Offenders and Victims. A Practical Guide*. Sage: London.

Sanders, A. and Bridges, L. (1989). The duty solicitor scheme: an unreliable safety net. *Law Soc. Gaz.*, **44**, **December 6**, 12-14.

Sanders, G. S. and Simmons, W. L. (1983). Use of hypnosis to enhance eyewitness accuracy: does it work? *J. Appl. Psychol.*, **68**, 70-77.

Santucci, P. S. and Winokur, G. (1955). Brainwashing as a factor in psychiatric illness. *AMA Arch. Neurol. Psychiat.*, **74**, 11-16.

Sarason, I. G. and Stroop, R. (1978). Test anxiety and the passage of time. *J. Consulting Clin. Psychol.*, **46**, 102-108.

Sargant, W. (1957). *Battle for the Mind. A Physiology of Conversion and Brain-Washing*. Heinemann: London.

Sargant, W. and Slater, E. (1940). Acute war neuroses. *Lancet*, **ii**, 1-2.

Sartory, G., Rachman, S. and Grey, S. J. (1977). An investigation of the relation between reported fear and heart-rate. *Behav. Res. Ther.*, **15**, 435-438.

Saywitz, K. J. (1987). Children's testimony: age-related patterns of memory errors. In: *Children's Eyewitness Memory* (Eds. S. J. Ceci, M. P. Toglia and D. F. Ross). Springer-Verlag: New York, pp. 36-52.

Schacter, D. L. (1986a). Amnesia and crime. How much do we know? *Amer. Psychol.*, **41**, 286-295.

Schacter, D. L. (1986b). Feelings-of-knowing ratings distinguish between genuine and simulated forgetting. *J. Exp. Psychol. Learn. Memory Cogn.*, **12**, 30-41.

Schaffer, D. S. (1985). The defendant's testimony. In: *The Psychology of Evidence and Trial Procedure* (Eds. S. M. Kassin and L. S. Wrightsman). Sage: London, pp. 124-149.

Schare, M. L., Lisman, S. A. and Spear, N. E. (1984). The effects of mood variation on state-dependent retentions. *Cogn. Ther. Res.*, **8**, 387-408.

Schein, E. H. (1956). The Chinese indoctrination program for prisoners of war. A study of attempted "brainwashing". *Psychiatry*, **19**, 149-172.

Schein, E. H., Schneier, I. and Barker, C. H. (1961). *Coercive Persuasion. A Socio-psychological Analysis of the "Brainwashing" of American Civilian Prisoners by the Chinese Communists*. W. W. Norton: New York.

Schill, T., Kahn, M. and Meuhleman, T. (1968). WAIS PA performance participation in extracurricular activities. *J. Clin. Psychol.*, **24**, 95-96.

Schooler, J. W. and Loftus, E. F. (1986). Individual differences and experimentation: complementary approaches to interrogative suggestibility. *Soc. Behav.*, **1**, 105-112.

Schooler, J. W., Gerhard, D. and Loftus, E. F. (1986). Qualities of the unreal. *J. Exper. Psychol. Learn. Memory Cogn.* **12**, 171-181.

Sealy, A. P. and McKew, A. (1981). The effects of confessions and retraction on simulated juries: a pilot study. In: *Psychology in Legal Contexts. Applications and Limitation* (Ed. M. A. Lloyd-Bostock). Macmillan: London, pp. 85-92.

Shaffer, D. R. (1985). The defendant's testimony. In: *The Psychology of Evidence and Trial Procedure*, S. M. Kassin and L. S. Wrightsman (Eds). Sage Publications: London, pp. 124-149.

Shallice, T. (1974). The Ulster depth interrogation techniques and their relation to sensory deprivation research. *Cognition*, **1**, 385-405.

Sharrock, R. (1988). Eyewitness testimony: some implications for clinical interviewing and forensic psychology. In: F. N. Watts (Ed.) *New Developments in Clinical Psychology*, Vol. 2. Wiley: Chichester, pp. 208-225.

Sharrock, R. and Cresswell, M. (1989). Pseudologia fantastica: a case study of a man charged with murder. *Med. Sci. Law*, **29**, 323-328.

Sharrock, R. and Gudjonsson, G. H. (1991). Intelligence, experience and interrogative suggestibility: a path analysis of alleged false-confession cases (in press).

Sheehan, P. W. and Tilden, J. (1983). Effects of suggestibility and hypnosis on accurate and distorted retrieval from memory. *J. Exp. Psychol. Learn. Memory Cogn.*, **9**, 283-293.

Shepherd, E. (1984). Values into practice; the implementation and implications of human awareness training. *Police J.*, **57**, 286-300.

Shepherd, E. (1986). Interviewing development: facing up to reality. *Police J.*, **59**, 35-44.

Shepherd, E. (1991a) Resistance in interviews: the contribution of police perceptions and behaviour. Paper presented at the Division of Criminological and Legal Psychology Conference, University of Kent at Canterbury, 3-5 January.

Shepherd, E. (1991b). Ethical Interviewing. *Policing*, **7**, 42-60.

Shepherd, E. and Kite, F. (1988). Training to interview. *Policing*, **4**, 264-280.

Shepherd, E. and Kite, F. (1989). Teach 'em to talk. *Policing*, **5**, 36-47.

Shepherd, J. W., Ellis, H. D. and Davies, G. M. (1982). *Identification Evidence. A Psychological Evaluation.* Aberdeen University Press: Aberdeen.

Sherif, M. (1936). *The Psychology of Social Norms.* Harper & Brothers: New York.

Sherr, A. (1986). *Client Interviewing for Lawyers.* Sweet and Maxwell, London.

Sidis, B. (1898). *The Psychology of Suggestion.* Appleton: New York.

Sigelman, C. K., Budd, E. C., Spanhel, C. L. and Schoenrock, C. J. (1981). When in doubt say yes: acquiescence in interviews with mentally retarded persons. *Mental Retardation*, **19**, 53-58.

Sigelman, C. K., Budd, E. C., Winer, J. L., Schoenrock, C. J. and Martin, P. W. (1982). Evaluating alternative techniques of questioning mentally retarded persons. *Amer. J. Mental Deficiency*, **86**, 511-518.

Sigelman, C. K., Schoenrock, C. J., Spanhel, C. L., Hromas, S. G., Winer, J. L., Budd, E. C. and Martin, P. W. (1980). Surveying mentally retarded persons: responsiveness and response validity in three samples. *Amer. J. Mental Deficiency*, **84**, 479-486.

Sigelman, C. K. and Werder, P. R. (1975). The communication skills of the mentally retarded: a new analysis. *J. Dev. Disabil.* **1**, 19-26.

Singh, K. K. and Gudjonsson, G. H. (1984). Interrogative suggestibility, delayed memory and self-concept. *Pers. Individ. Diff.*, **5**, 203-209.

Singh, K. K. and Gudjonsson, G. H. (1987). The internal consistency of the "shift" factor on the Gudjonsson Suggestibility Scale. *Pers. Individ. Diff.*, **8**, 265-266.

Singh, K. K. and Gudjonsson, G. H. (1991). Interrogative suggestibility among adolescent boys. The powerful influence of negative feedback. *J. Foren. Psychiatry* (in press).

Smith, K. and Gudjonsson, G. H. (1986). Investigation of the responses of "fakers" and "non-fakers" on the Gudjonsson Suggestibility Scale. *Med. Sci. Law*, **26**, 66–71.

Smith, M. (1983). Hypnotic memory enhancement of witness: does it work? *Psychol. Bull.*, **94**, 387–407.

Smith, M. W. A. (1989). Forensic stylometry: a theoretical basis for further developments of practical methods. *J. Foren. Sci. Soc.*, **29**, 15–33.

Smith, S. (1979). Remembering in and out of context. *Exp. Psychol. Hum. Learn. Memory*, **5**, 40–47.

Smith, V. L. and Ellsworth, P. C. (1987). The social psychology of eyewitness accuracy: misleading questions and communicator expertise. *J. Appl. Psychol.*, **72**, 294–300.

Softley, P. (1980). *Police Interrogation. An Observational Study in Four Police Stations.* Home Office Research Study, No. 61. HMSO: London.

Sommer, R. (1959). The new look on the witness stand. *Canad. Psychol.*, **8**, 94–99.

Sommer, R. (1969). *Personal Space.* Prentice-Hall: Englewood Cliffs, NJ.

Spanos, N. P. (1986). Hypnotic behavior: a social psychological interpretation of amnesia, analgesia and "trance logic". *Behav. Brain Sci.*, **9**, 449–502.

Spanos, N. P. and McLean, J. (1986). Hypnotically created pseudomemories; memory distortions or reporting bias? *Br. J. Exp. Clin. Hypnosis*, **3**, 155–159.

Spanos, N. P., Gwynn, M. I., Comer, S. L., Baitruweit, W. J. and de Groh, M. (1989). Are hypnotically induced pseudomemories resistant to cross-examination? *Law Human Behav.*, **13**, 271–289.

Sparrow S. S., Balla, D. A. and Cicchetti, D. V. (1984). *Vineland Adaptive Behavior Scales, Interview Edition, Expanded Form Manual.* American Guidance Service: Circle Pines, MN.

Spencer, J. R. and Flin, R. (1990). *The Evidence of Children. The Law and the Psychology.* Blackstone: London.

Spielberger, C. D. (1969). *The State-Trait Anxiety Inventory.* Consulting Psychologists Press: Palo Alto, CA.

Stalnaker, J. M. and Riddle, E. E. (1932). The effect of hypnosis on long-delayed recall. *J. Gen. Psychol.*, **6**, 429–440.

Steller, M. (1989). Recent developments in statement analysis. In: *Credibility Assessment* (Ed. J. C. Yuille). Kluwer: The Netherlands, pp. 135–154.

Steller, M. and Koehnken, G. (1990). Criteria-based statement analysis. In: *Psychological Methods in Criminal Investigation and Evidence* (Ed. D. C. Raskin). Springer: New York, pp. 217–246.

Stephenson, G. M. (1984). Accuracy and confidence in testimony: a critical review and some fresh evidence. In: *Psychology and Law* (Eds. D. J. Muller, D. E. Blackman and A. J. Chapman). Wiley: Chichester, pp. 229–248.

Stern, W. (1910). Abstracts of lectures on the psychology of testimony and on the study of individuality. *Amer. J. Psychol.*, **21**, 273–282.

Stern, W. (1938). *General Psychology: From the Personalistic Standpoint.* Macmillan: New York.

Stern, W. (1939). The psychology of testimony. *J. Abn. Soc. Psychol.*, **34**, 3–20.

Stier, D. H. and Hall, J. A. (1984). Gender differences in touch: an empirical and theoretical review. *J. Pers. Soc. Psychol.*, **47**, 440–459.

Stricker, L. J., Messick, S. and Jackson, D. N. (1967). Suspicion of deception: implication for conformity research. *J. Pers. Soc. Psychol.*, **5**, 379–389.

Stukat, K. G. (1958). *Suggestibility: A Factor and Experimental Analysis.* Almqvist & Wiksell: Stockholm.

Stumphauzer, J. S. (1986). *Helping Delinquents Change: A Treatment Manual of Social Learning Approaches.* Haworth Press: New York.

Stuntz, W. J. (1989). The American exclusionary rule and defendants' charging rights. *Crim. Law Rev.*, 117-128.

Svartvik, J. (1968). *The Evans Statements. A Case for Forensic Linguistics.* Almqvist & Wiksell: Gothenburg.

Tangney, J. P. (1990). Assessing individual differences in proneness to shame and guilt: development of self-conscious affect and attribution inventory. *J. Pers. Soc. Psychol.*, **59**, 102-111.

Tata, P. (1983). Some Effects of Stress and Feedback on Interrogative Suggestibility: An Experimental Study. MPhil Dissertation, University of London, London.

Tata, P. R. and Gudjonsson, G. H. (1990). The effects of mood and verbal feedback on interrogative suggestibility. *Pers. Indiv. Diff.*, **11**, 1079-1085.

Taylor, P. J. and Kopelman, M. D. (1984). Amnesia for criminal offences. *Psychol. Med.*, **14**, 581-588.

Temple, R. (1989). *Open to Suggestion. The Uses and Abuses of Hypnosis.* Aquarian Press: Wellingborough, England.

Tendler, S. (1990). Blakelock killing conviction referred back to Appeal Court. *The Times*, **December 5**, 24.

The Times (1990). Judge urges care on Marsh "confession". *The Times*, **7th November**, 3.

Thomas, T. (1987). The Confait confessions. *Policing*, **3**, 214-225.

Tilkin, L. (1949). The present status of narcosynthesis using sodium penthothal and sodium amytal. *Dis. Nerv. Syst.*, **10**, 215-218.

Timm, H. W. (1981). The effect of forensic hypnosis techniques on eyewitness recall and recognition. *J. Police Sci. Admin.*, **9**, 188-194.

Timm, H. W. (1983). The factors theoretically affecting the impact of forensic hypnosis techniques on eyewitness recall. *J. Police Sci. Admin.*, **11**, 442-450.

Totty, R. N., Hardcastle, R. A. and Pearson, J. (1987). Forensic linguistics: the determination of authorship from habits of style. *J. Foren. Sci. Soc.*, **27**, 13-28.

Tousignant, J. P., Hall, D. and Loftus, E. F. (1986). Discrepancy detection and vulnerability to misleading postevent information. *Memory Cogn.*, **14**, 329-338.

Trankell, A. (1958). Was Lars sexually assaulted? A study in the reliability of witnesses and of experts. *J. Abn. Soc. Psychol.*, **56**, 385-395.

Trankell, A. (1972). *Reliability of Evidence.* Beckmans: Stockholm.

Treisman, A. M. (1969). Strategies and models of selective attention. *Psychol. Rev.*, **76**, 282-299.

Tully, B. (1980). Interrogating mentally handicapped suspects. In: *Law and the Mentally Retarded Citizen.* Report of the Thirteenth Spring Conference of Mental Retardation, University of Exeter, 11-13 April. MENCAP: Somerset.

Tully, B. and Cahill, D. (1984). *Police Interviewing of Mentally Handicapped Persons: An Experimental Study.* The Police Foundation of Great Britain: London.

Tully, B. and Tam, K. O. (1987). Helping the Police with their enquiries: the development of special care questioning techniques. *Children & Society*, **3**, 187-197.

Tulving, E. (1974). Cue-dependent forgetting. *Amer. Sci.*, **62**, 74-82.

Tulving, E. (1983). *Elements of Episodic Memory.* Oxford University Press: Oxford.

Udolf, R. (1983). *Forensic Hypnosis. Psychological and Legal Aspects.* Lexington Books: Lexington, MA.

Underwager, R., Legrand, R., Bartz, C. S. and Wakefield, H. (1988). Interrogation as a learning process. In: *Accusations of Child Sexual Abuse* (Eds. H. Wakefield and R. Underwager). Charles C. Thomas: Springfield, IL, pp. 19-47.

Underwager, R. and Wakefield, H. (1990). *The Real World of Child Interrogations.* Charles C. Thomas: Springfield, IL.

Undeutsch, U. (1967). Beurteilung der Glaubhaftigkeit von Zeugenaussagen. In: *Handbuch der Psychologie* (Ed. V. Undeutsch). Verlag fur Psychologie: Gottingen, pp. 76-181.

Undeutsch, U. (1982). Statement Reality Analysis. In: *Reconstructing the Past. The Role of Psychologists in Criminal Trials* (Ed. A. Trankell). Kluwer: Deventer, pp. 27–56.

Undeutsch, U. (1989). The development of statement reality analysis. In: *Credibility Assessment* (Ed. J. C. Yuille). Kluwer: Deventer, pp. 101–119.

Vennard, J. (1984). Disputes within trials over the admissibility and accuracy of incriminating statements: some research evidence. *Crim. Law Rev.*, 15–24.

Vennard, J. (1985). The outcome of contested trials. In: *Managing Criminal Justice. A Collection of Papers* (Ed. D. Moxon). HMSO: London.

Vizard, E. (1991). Interviewing children suspected of being sexually abused. A Review of Theory and Practice. In: *Clinical Approaches to Sex Offenders and Their Victims* (Eds. C. R. Hollin and K. Howells). Wiley: Chichester, pp. 117–148.

Wade, N. (1972). Technology in Ulster: rubber bullets hit home, brainwashing backfires. *Science*, **176**, 1102–1105.

Wagstaff, G. F. (1981). *Hypnosis, Compliance and Belief.* Harvester Press: Brighton.

Wagstaff, G. F. (1982). Hypnosis and recognition of a face. *Percept. Mot. Skills*, **55**, 816–818.

Wagstaff, G. F. (1983). Hypnosis and the law: a critical review of some recent proposals. *Crim. Law Rev.*, **March**, 152–157.

Wagstaff, G. F. (1984). The enhancement of witness testimony by "hypnosis": a review and methodological critique of the experimental literature. *Br. J. Exp. Clin. Hypnosis*, **22**, 3–12.

Wagstaff, G. F. (1988). Current theoretical and experimental issues in hypnosis: Overview. In: *Hypnosis: Current Clinical, Experimental and Forensic Practices* (Ed. M. Heap). Croom Helm: London, pp. 25–39.

Waid, W. M. and Orne, M. T. (1980). Individual differences in electrodermal lability and the detection of information and deception. *J. Appl. Psychol.*, **65**, 1–8.

Waid, W. M., Wilson, S. K. and Orne, M. T. (1981). Cross-model physiological effects of electrodermal lability in the detection of deception. *J. Pers. Soc. Psychol.*, **40**, 1118–1125.

Wake, W. C. (1957). Sentence length distributions of Greek authors. *J. Roy. Statist. Soc.*, **120**, 331–346.

Wakefield, H. and Underwager, R. (1988). *Accusation of Child Sexual Abuse.* Charles C. Thomas: Springfield, IL.

Wald, M., Ayres, R., Hess, D. W., Schantz, M. and Whitebread, C. H. (1967). Interrogations in New Haven: the impacts of "Miranda". *Yale Law J.*, **76**, 1519–1648.

Walkley, J. (1987). *Police Interrogation. A Handbook for Investigators.* Police Review Publication: London.

Walsh, D. P. J. (1982). Arrest and interrogation: Northern Ireland 1981. *J. Law Soc.*, **9**, 37–62.

Wambaugh, J. (1989). *The Blooding.* Bantam Press: London.

Ware, J. W. (1978). Effects of acquiescent response set on patient satisfaction ratings. *Medical Care*, **16**, 327–336.

Warnick, D. H. and Sanders, G. S. (1980). The effects of group discussion on eyewitness accuracy. *J. Appl. Soc. Psychol.*, **10**, 249–259.

Watson, D. and Friend, R. (1969). Management and social evaluative anxiety. *J. Consult. Clin. Psychol.*, **33**, 448–457.

Waxman, D. (1986). The development of hypnosis as a psychotherapeutic force. In: *What is Hypnosis? Current Theories and Research.* Open University Press: Milton Keynes, pp. 13–36.

Wechsler, D. (1981). *WAIS-R Manual.* The Psychological Corporation. Harcourt Brace Jovanovich: New York.

Weigartner, H. and Faillace, L. A. (1971). Alcohol state-dependent learning in man. *J. Nerv. Ment. Dis.*, **153**, 395–406.

Weinstein, E. A., Kahn, R. L., Sugarman, L. A. and Malitz, S. (1954). Serial administration of the "amytal test" for brain disease. Its diagnostic and prognostic value. *Arch. Neurol. Psychiat.*, **71**, 217-226.

Weitzenhoffer, A. M. (1957). *General Techniques of Hypnoticism.* Grune & Stratton: New York.

Wells, G. and Murray, D. M. (1984). Eyewitness confidence. In: *Eyewitness Testimony: Psychological Perspectives* (Eds. G. L. Wells and E. F. Loftus). Cambridge University Press: Cambridge

Whitten, W. and Leonard, J. (1981). Directed search through autobiographical memory. *Mem. Cognit.*, **9**, 566-579.

Wicklund, R. A. and Brehm, J. W. (1968). Attitude change as a function of felt competence and threat to attitudinal freedom. *J. Exper. Soc. Psychol.*, **4**, 64-75.

Wiggins, J. S. (1973). *Personality and Prediction: Principles of Personality Assessment.* Addison-Wesley: London.

Williamson, T. M. (1990). Strategic Changes in Police Interrogation: An Examination of Police and Suspect Behaviour in the Metropolitan Police in Order to Determine the Effects of New Legislation, Technology and Organizational Policies. Unpublished PhD Thesis, University of Kent.

Willis, C. F., Macleod, J. and Naish, P. (1988). *The Tape-Recording of Police Interviews with Suspects: a Second Interim Report.* Home Office Research Study No. 97, HMSO: London.

Winkler, J. D., Kanouse, D. E. and Ware, J. E. (1982). Controlling for acquiescence response set in score development. *J. Appl. Psychol.*, **67**, 555-561.

Woffinden, B. (1989). *Miscarriages of Justice.* Coronet Books, Hodder and Stoughton: Great Britain.

Wood, P. J. W. and Guly, O. C. R. (1991). Unfit to plead to murder: three case reports. *Med. Sci. Law*, **31**, 55-60.

Woolgrove, K. (1976). *The Questioning of the Mentally Backward.* A report commissioned by the Religious Society of Friends: Warwickshire.

Yarmey, A. D. (1984). Accuracy and credibility of the elderly witness. *Canad. J. Ageing*, **3**, 79-90.

Yarmey, A. D. (1986). Verbal, visual and voice identification of a rape suspect under different levels of illumination. *J. Appl. Psychol.*, **71**, 363-370.

Yarmey, A. D. (1987). Streetproofing and bystanders' memory for a child abduction. In M. M. Gruneberg, P. E. Morris and R. N. Sykes (Eds), *Practical Aspects of Memory: Current Research and Issues*, Vol. 1. Wiley: New York.

Yarmey, A. D. (1990). *Understanding Police and Police Work.* New York University Press: New York.

Yerkes, P. M. and Dodson, J. D. (1908). The relation of strength of stimulus to rapidity of habit formation. *J. Comp. Neurol. Psychol.*, **18**, 459-482.

Young, H. F., Bentall, R. P., Slade, P. D. and Dewey, M. E. (1987). The role of brief instructions and suggestibility in the elicitation of auditory and visual hallucinations in normal and psychiatric subjects. *J. Nerv. Ment. Dis.*, **175**, 41-48.

Yuille, J. C. and Kim, C. K. (1987). A field study of the forensic use of hypnosis. *Canad. J. Behav. Sci.*, **19**, 418-429.

Yuille, J. C. and McEwan, N. H. (1985). Use of hypnosis as an aid to eyewitness testimony. *J. Appl. Psychol.*, **70**, 389-400.

Yuille, J. C. and Tollestrup, P. A. (1990). Some effects of alcohol on eyewitness memory. *J. Appl. Psychol.*, **75**, 268-273.

Yule, G. V. (1938). On sentence length as a statistical characteristic of style in prose, with applications to two cases of disputed authorship. *Biometrika*, **30**, 363-390.

Yule, G. V. (1944). *The Statistical Study of Literary Vocabulary.* Cambridge University Press: Cambridge.

Zander, M. (1972). Access to a solicitor in the police station. *Crim. Law Rev.*, 342-350.

Zander, M. (1979). The investigation of crime: a study of cases tried at the Old Bailey. *Crim. Law Rev.*, 203-219.

Zaragoza, M. S. (1987). Memory, suggestibility and eyewitness testimony in children and adults. In: *Children's Eyewitness Memory* (Eds. S. J. Ceci, M. P. Toglia and D. F. Ross) Springer-Verlag: New York, pp. 53-78.

Zaragoza, M. S. and Koshmider, J. W. (1989). Misled subjects may know more than their performance implies. *J. Exp. Psychol. Learn. Mem. Cogn.*, **15**, 246-255.

Zaragoza, M., McCloskey, M. and Jamis, M. (1987). Misleading postevent informations and recall of the original event: further evidence against the memory impairments hypothesis. *J. Exp. Psychol. Learn. Mem. Cogn.*, **13**, 36-44.

Zelig, M. and Beidleman, W. B. (1981). The investigative use of hypnosis: a word of caution. *J. Clin. Exp. Hypnosis*, **29** 401-412.

Zimbardo, P. G. (1967). The psychology of police confessions. *Psychol. Today*, **1**, 17-27.

Zuckerman, A. A. S. (1989). *The Principles of Criminal Evidence.* Clarendon Press: Oxford.

Zuckerman, M. and Lubin, B. (1965). *Manual for the Multiple Affect Adjective Checklist.* Palo Alto, California.

Index